THE RED ATLANTIS

IN THE SERIES

Culture and the Moving Image,

edited by Robert Sklar

TEMPLE UNIVERSITY PRESS
PHILADELPHIA

THE

RED

ATLANTIS

Communist

Culture in the

Absence of

Communism

J. HOBERMAN

Temple University Press, Philadelphia 19122
Copyright © 1998 by J. Hoberman
All rights reserved
Published 1998
Printed in the United States of America

Text design by Kate Nichols

∞ The paper used in this publication meets the requirements
of American National Standard for Information Sciences—Permanence of Paper
for Printed Library Materials. ANSI Z39.48-1984

Library of Congress Cataloging-in-Publication Data
Hoberman, J.
The Red Atlantis: communist culture in the absence of communism /
J. Hoberman.
     p.   cm. — (Culture and the moving image)
  Includes Bibliographical references (p.   ) and index.
  ISBN 1-56639-643-3 (cloth : alk. paper)
    1. Communism—History—20th century. 2. Communist aesthetics—
History—20th century.   I. Title. II. Series.
HX40H5673   1998
335.43′097—dc21   98-16178

For my mother Dorothy,
my father Solomon,
and my sister Jane

CONTENTS

ACKNOWLEDGMENTS

Virtually everything in *The Red Atlantis* was previously published in some (often quite different) form. The editors responsible for assigning and shaping those pieces include Jack Bankowski, Robin Cembalest, Ian Christie, Karen Durbin, Howard Feinstein, David Frankel, Harlan Jacobson, Richard Jameson, Lisa Kennedy, Scott Malcomson, M. Mark, Abby McGanny Nolan, Art Spiegelman, Gavin Smith, Richard Taylor, and Ellen Willis. My thanks to them, as well as to Janet Francendese and Bob Sklar for their help reshaping the material into a book. Many other people were generous with their time and ideas, among them Wanda Bershen, Yvette Biró, Paul Buhle, Danny Czitrom, Éva Forgács, Mel Gordon, Richard Greeman, Naum Kleiman, Edith Kramer, Adrienne Mancia, David Marc, Annámaria Róna, Slava Tsukerman, Katalin Vajda (Hungarofilm), Tony Vasconcellos, and the staff of the Czech Film Archives. Mary Corliss, Robin Holland, Jennifer Kotter, and particularly Sylvia Plachy supplied wonderful photographs. As always, the book took longer than expected to complete. My agent Georges Borchardt was never less than patient—as were my wife Shelley and daughters Mara and Anna.

THE RED ATLANTIS

INTRODUCTION

Missing . . .

The Berlin Wall

*Maybe after the ruins of Pompeii,
Herculaneum, and the Roman Forum, it
was the most purely beautiful remnant of an
urban condition.*

—Rem Koolhaus, "Field Trip" (1973)

Once upon a time, this Thing ("breathtaking," Dutch architect Rem Koolhaus wrote, "in its persistent doubleness") was the irreducible brute fact of our political universe.[1]

"Today, the Endangered Frontier of Freedom runs through divided Berlin," President John F. Kennedy had warned the American people one summer evening in the course of the most frightening telecast ever orchestrated by an American leader up to that point (Tuesday, July 25, 1961). "The Communists control over a billion people and they recognize that, if we shall falter, their success would be imminent."[2]

That success didn't frighten me then. A twelve-year-old at summer camp, I was far more fascinated by the Congo crisis—clipping articles from my counselor's *New York Times* on the conflict between Moise Tshombe, Joseph Mobutu, and the followers of the murdered Patrice Lumumba. Germany seemed the last war. As the still-new president explained, however, West Berlin was not just an "isolated outpost"

Written in late November 1989, an early version of this piece was published in the January 1990 issue of *Artforum*. At the time, the Wall's breaching felt comparable to the old Max Fleischer cartoon *Earth Control*, in which Koko the Clown flicks a cosmic switch and throws the universe out of whack: "The long-frozen European order has gone all trippy and biomorphic. . . . The same bottled-up forces and sudden vacuums that bid to fissure the Baltic and Balkan states will compel German fusion (whatever this reunification is called). All bets are off, all borders mutable."

but the great testing place of our "courage and will." Accordingly, Kennedy announced his intention to fortify the German city, call up America's reserve forces, and request additional funds for civil defense. That the last measure included a massive fallout-shelter program raised—as no previous president so openly had—the possibility of thermonuclear warfare. (This was a scenario that I, for one, accepted as inevitable and had mentally scheduled for the distant year 1964.)

Three weeks later, in the early hours of Sunday, August 13 (the day my father turned forty-eight, my age now), Berlin subway trains ceased running, families were evacuated from certain apartment buildings, and tanks massed at the Brandenburg Gate. Russian and East German soldiers used storm fences and barbed wire to seal off the city's western sectors, even our famous Checkpoint Charlie. Thursday, a solid construction began to rise behind the fence. Soviet leader Nikita Khrushchev, Mr. Potatohead as supreme ruler, blandly described this project as the restoration of "border control."[3]

The one hundred miles of concrete slabs and stamped metal fencing, ten to thirteen feet high, that contained a billion Communist automatons and girdled West Berlin for twenty-eight years was the Iron Curtain made material. Prime candidate for Armageddon's ground zero, the Berlin Wall became a shrine—the NATO Mecca to which each American president, from JFK through Ronald Reagan, was required to pilgrimage while still in office. Perverse monument, eighth wonder of the world, foundation of a vast, invisible temple, the Berlin Wall was the metaphysical separation between life and death, freedom and slavery, heaven and hell.

Visiting Berlin for the first time in February 1984, I was impressed by the abruptness with which the Wall heaved into view, the ruthlessness of its unpredictable course, the spell of desolation it cast—and its normality. Time stood still. Cold war Berlin was a monument to the void. The sealed-off S-Bahn platform beneath Potsdamerplatz was only the largest of East Berlin's fifteen so-called *Geisterbahnhöfe* (ghost stations). Entrances leveled, they appeared on no map, and yet their presence could be felt as a seismic rumble beneath the East Berlin pavement each time a West Berlin subway train followed its permitted route through a bit of the Communist city. (Then, in the dim subterranean light, attentive West German commuters might catch sight of phantom East German soldiers guarding empty platforms marked for no-longer extant streets.)[4]

Passing through customs in the S-Bahn, one might search in vain for the traces of the city's prewar Jewish neighborhood. East Germany was not among the countries, such as Hungary and Czechoslovakia, where surprising remnants of Jewish life were frozen by cold war. East Berlin, as Victor Serge wrote of an apartment in Stalin's Moscow, was "a place where someone was waiting to vanish." Between the smoothly modular slabs of the cylindrically topped outer rampart and the parallel inner barricade of barbed wire and bricked-up apartment houses, on either side of the tar road that linked the watchtowers, lay the sandy gravel Death Strip—a floodlit movie-set zone of concealed dangers.[5]

Guarantor of wartime intrigue in the midst of anxious peace, marking the most famously impenetrable border on planet Earth, the Wall signified serious espionage—less the world of James Bond than of John Le Carré's *The Spy Who Came in from the Cold*. The opening sequence of the grim 1964 movie made from the Le Carré novel is a gleaming nocturne in which a returning agent is gunned down in the no-man's-land between East Berlin and Checkpoint Charlie. The action ends (how many nights later?) with the Rosenberg couple of our dreams—Claire Bloom's naive, beautiful Communist and Richard Burton's cynical spy-who-loves-her—shot attempting to scramble west over the Wall.[6]

This was the cold war omphalos—a sacred stone at the center of the world, washed in the blood of 190 martyrs, watched over by angels (at least in the films of Wim Wenders), not to mention 285 elevated watchtowers, each a machine-gun nest manned day and night.

With his trim goatee and garden-gnome physique, East German leader Walter Ulbricht required only a beret, a corduroy sports jacket, sandals (worn with socks), and a cramped colonial garden apartment to suggest someone's goofy peacenik uncle in the Red Diaper precincts of 1960s Queens.

"No one intends to build a wall," the general secretary of the ruling German Socialist Unity Party had—jovially or testily?—assured the West German journalist who, three months before the "antifascist rampart" materialized, asked him how he proposed to halt rampant *Republikflucht*, the westward flow of refugees (soon to exceed five hundred a day) from his German Democratic Republic.[7] After all, the Wall was always implicit: A 1951 drawing by the Communist artist Kurt Poltiniak shows a pathetic American eagle breaking its beak on the sturdy red-brick edifice of Soviet-

German friendship. Once made manifest in the summer of 1961, the wall concept was further refined over the next fifteen years—expanding from line to zone to reach its final state as a double edifice that ebbed and flowed as it coursed through the city.

The Wall "swelled to assume its maximum identity wherever possible," Rem Koolhaus noted in an appreciation written to mark the structure's tenth anniversary. A particular symbiosis existed between East and West. The Wall, Koolhaus felt, seemed "most confrontational," "consciously symbolic," and "shameless" when facing those western neighborhoods that "bristled with pseudo-hypervitality." (Or was this a factor of the anticipatory excitement that quickened the Western tourist's pulse whenever and wherever the Wall materialized?)[8]

Not a veil to conceal the actual state of affairs but the bulwark supporting that social reality, the Wall embodied the cold war as coproduction—indeed, the spectacular coproduction that brought forth, among other stars, the man who closed the show, Ronald Reagan. General Dwight Eisenhower's World War II error of not driving through Germany to liberate the Nazi capital turned out, in retrospect, to have been brilliant strategy. Similarly, Nikita Khrushchev's plan to encircle the city's western sectors proved a fantastic blunder. Far closer to the Polish than to the West German border, West Berlin became the neon oasis of liberation.

The Wall saturated the landscape with ideology and reified the yearning for freedom. Truly, the antifascist rampart was a magical Möbius strip allowing Berliners on both sides to feel themselves on the outside looking in. Half fortress, half prison, surrounded by rubble and lit up like a Christmas tree, cold war Berlin was as stylized an urban environment as Venice or Manhattan—and what's more, conceptually so. This "vitrine for Western prosperity," as Paul Goldberger put it, produced a distinctive culture as well.[9]

The heavily underwritten Berlin Film Festival, which I covered for more than a dozen years, was established in 1951 to promote the celluloid wonders of the free world. Among the festival's unexpected side effects were the wide-screen, color East German socialist musicals that were forced into existence in the late 1950s by the proximity of so powerful a culture industry. Later, the festival became the launching pad for the subsidized dissident cinema of Eastern Europe. In Cannes, you had paparazzi and topless beaches; in Berlin, there were spies and the bleak 1950s monument to the atom in the concrete waste of the East's Alexanderplatz.

Wim Wenders's 1987 *Der Himmel Über Berlin* (The sky above Berlin), released in the United States under the less flavorsome title *Wings of Desire,* is the movie that best captured the city's stoic melancholy, its somnolence, its self-absorption, its leaden brutality—the deep sense of loneliness and desertion that was sometimes called *Mauerkrankheit* (wall sickness) or *Insul Gefühl* (island feeling). Intimations of a sad Paradise Lost: Wender's film is the story, in a sense, of an East German angel who renounces the "objective necessity of history" to become mortal in the West. Its title echoes Konrad Wolf's 1963 *Der Geteilte Himmel* (The divided sky), in which an East German student visits her disaffected lover in West Berlin. Their alienated surroundings make it clear that communication has been destroyed: He has changed; she recognizes the law of historical development and returns home to the German Democratic Republic.

Anticipating the loss of a loss, *Wings of Desire* is particularly attached to the weed-and-debris emptiness of the unnamed wasteland around Potsdamerplatz. A wound in the city, the relentless Wall here transversed the obliterated Third Reich command center, including the Chancellery, Gestapo headquarters, and the Ministry of Aviation, slicing across streets, sidewalks, trolley tracks, cemeteries, the remains of Hitler's bunker. The Wall incorporated entire buildings—the back of the Reichstag itself. Only a visiting architectural radical such as Koolhaus could dare admit that it was "heartbreakingly beautiful."[10]

Khrushchev's misguided conceptual bravado beggared the most audacious, relentlessly serial conceits of environmental artists such as Christo and Richard Serra. For gonzo urban planning the Wall surpassed even the most megalomaniacal visions of Robert Moses and Nelson Rockefeller. Did the Communists admire their creation? The Wall (whose construction was a magnificent subject for a never-painted Socialist Realist canvas) may not have made its way into East German art—although Harald Thiel's 1962 severely rectangular canvas *Fahneneid* (Swearing in) surely suggests it in showing a formation of blocky soldiers at rigid attention, swearing allegiance to the German Democratic Republic flag, as they are tightly hemmed in by the podium, the grandstand, a grimly mountainous construction site, and a no less impassive row of upright stalwart spectators.

But then, as suggested by the crude observation platforms and elaborate graffiti murals that it inspired (at least on its western face), the Wall was itself a work of art. It belongs with the never-built Palace of the

Soviets, the Jewish autonomous region of Birobidzhan, Franz Kafka's posthumous career as a dissident writer, the Second Reality of Socialist Realism, the Crime of the Century, and the wreckage of Communist fantasy itself, submerged now in History's secret depths.

"For Germans in the West," wrote West Berliner Peter Schneider, "the Wall [had been] a mirror that told them, day by day, who was the fairest one of all."[11]

The night of November 9, 1989, as East Germans smashed it, they (and we) passed through that looking glass. Taken from the east looking west, the splendid Agence France-Presse news photo, splayed four columns wide across the front page of the November 10 edition of the *New York Times*, showed an orderly mob surging past the broken edifice, its advance into the future accentuated by the hasty look one youth threw back.[12]

All that was solid melted into air. The disorientation was such during those first dizzy weeks that even the hard-nosed neoliberal editorialists of the *New Republic* openly expressed a perverse nostalgia for the vanished world: "In terms of sheer stability," the cold war "possessed an austere elegance unlikely to be matched by any subsequent arrangement of nations."[13]

President George Bush's formulation that the austerely elegant Wall was a "monument to the Failure of Communism" implied that it was equally a monument to the success of capitalism. Nearly three decades after Billy Wilder's *One, Two, Three*—shot in West Berlin during the hot summer of 1961—had parodied the equation of American democracy with Coca-Cola, rival Pepsi-Cola telecast a corporate Christmas card that set the breaching of the Wall to Handel's "Hallelujah" chorus while identifying Pepsi with the gift of freedom.[14] Within three days of the breach, an anonymous East Berlin woman told the *New York Times*, she thought the Wall should be knocked down and sold for souvenirs: "We can wrap them in plastic and send them to America. I've heard Americans will buy anything, and East Germany certainly needs the money."[15] It was a good joke; but the market developed far more rapidly than the East Germans, still living on sleepy socialist time, could have ever imagined. By Christmas 1989, Bloomingdale's in New York had unloaded close to $200,000 worth of the Wall—broken down into fifteen thousand gift-sized, sealed, and certified chunks, priced at $12.50 apiece. (Nearly a decade later, tiny Wall slivers were still being sold in Berlin, affixed to postcards.)

Once, Communist dignitaries had exchanged such holy artifacts as packets of sand gathered on the beach at the Bay of Pigs in Cuba and plastic-encased samples of soil from Lenin's birthplace. Now the Free World had its own political relic. Approaching the border that winter, one heard a distinctive and persistent tap-tap-tapping. Continuously mined for salable fragments, the once-mighty Wall resembled a moth-eaten scarf.

Well before (re)unification, the Brandenburg Gate—long impassible, a wall within the Wall—became the site of a spontaneous going-out-of-business sale, a massive flea market for Communist uniforms, medals, texts, and icons. Dusan Makavejev's *Gorilla Bathes at Noon*—an affably episodic travelogue of the no longer divided city, shot in 1991—ends with the actor who plays the last Russian soldier left in Berlin selling his character's uniform at this very souk.[16] The month the Wall fell, bringing down the curtain on the short twentieth century, a pair of West German aesthetes were already cataloging examples of endearingly clunky, soon-to-be-lost East German product design.

Fossils from "the Galapagos Islands of the Design World," these articles did not have to be packaged to sell, the curators wrote. "No one needed to charm the consumer with catchy radio jingles, or create flattering, meaningless design. The fact is that they were the only products of their kind on the market. They adorned the shop windows of the local state retail stores—unmistakable and self-assured. They were neither desirable nor sophisticated. They simply never had to be."[17] In a similar spirit, the official gifts and homemade trinkets—the Party Congress plates, memorial chunks of coal, hammer-and-sickle conversation pieces, rocket-motif desk sets, Five-Year-Plan paperweights, miniature brass tanks, proletariat figurines—the vast array of indescribable Communist curios bestowed on the leaders of the former East Germany, were exhibited and preserved in a special collection of the Deutsches Historisches Museum. But the Wall that vanished so suddenly and utterly had to be reconstructed for *The Promise,* directed by Margarethe von Trotta in 1994 from Peter Schneider's screenplay.[18]

The *New York Times* reported in late 1993 that as plans for Berlin's new business center proceeded, even the "ugly two-story border tower from which East German agents surveyed and controlled the tense Checkpoint Charlie crossing, a building that once stood at the very center of world politics, [was] now on the collector's market." If the truth be known, the watchtower was available free to whoever might pay the moving cost and create a future museum display.[19] According to Schneider, all of the Wall's five thousand guard dogs had been adopted. And yet, "whenever they accompany their new Western masters on walks near where the Wall once stood, they are suddenly deaf to every call and run their programmed beat without veering right or left." Though even native Berliners could no longer remember precisely where the Wall once stood, the Wall dogs were said to move with absolute confidence along the crazy zigzags of the old border.[20]

In the spirit of those deterritorialized dogs and their implanted ideological memory, this book—itself a collection of exhumed and annotated fossils—acknowledges the loss of that Communist utopia which, in fact, never existed.

CHAPTER 1

"I Saw Stalin

Once When I Was

a Child": Socialist

Realism, the

Last Ism

To the Great Russian People! M. I. Khmelko (1949). (Photo courtesy of Institute for Contemporary Art/P.S. 1 Museum)

SOCIALIST REALISM = SECOND REALITY

There is a specter haunting modern art. An accursed vanguard, the last of the great European "isms," the most totalizing and the most monstrous, that movement known as Socialist Realism might be construed as the guilty secret, the evil twin, the secret sharer of the very enterprise it proposed to liquidate.

Socialist Realism has been doubly repressed. For the society that spawned it, classical Socialist Realism was, as Professor Boris Groys—a Russian émigré living in Germany—wrote in *The Total Art of Stalinism,* ultimately and officially "no less taboo than the art of the avant-garde." Indeed, during the thirty-five years between the death of Stalin and the height of perestroika, the two tendencies might well have been

---

I can date my interest in Socialist Realism to October 1982 and the brilliant Komar and Melamid show, marking the sixty-fifth anniversary of the Bolshevik Revolution, at Ronald Feldman's gallery, a laugh-out-loud extrapolation of the Stalinist idiom into the "new morning" of Ronald Reagan's America. Until the early 1990s, however, it was difficult to find even reproductions of the paintings that informed their work, let alone any discussion of this mutant modernism. This survey has been greatly expanded from three pieces published during the ensuing boom: a review of Boris Groys's *The Total Art of Stalinism* and four other books on Socialist Realism in the *Voice Literary Supplement* (March 1993), an essay on the relationship between Socialist Realism and Sots Art published in *Artforum* (October 1993), and a review of the exhibit "Stalin's Choice" for the *Forward* (28 January 1994).

crated up and hidden together in Soviet museum basements. But since the collapse of Soviet communism, its once-holy relics have become collectible, not to mention camp—the stuff of music videos and nightclub design.[1]

The Berlin Wall crashed and Socialist Realism emerged. Like hoards from a newly opened pharaoh's tomb, troves of bizarre hieroglyphics and sacred artifacts were assembled in certain museum exhibitions of the early and mid-1990s. Here, blinking in the sunlight, were academic pictures of frozen *kolkhoz* fiestas; ecstatic steel-factory cathedrals, illuminated by shafts streaming through unseen windows; solemnly bombastic portraits of the Soviet leadership.[2]

Oxford University Museum of Modern Art curator David Elliott declared that Socialist Realist "products" were, "in their way, just as visionary as those of the avant-garde artists" who preceded them. Groys had already gone further: Stalin's dictum that writers were engineers of the human soul was anticipated by supremacist painter Kazimir Malevich's visionary notion of the state as a form of enforced aesthetic education—a machine designed to regulate the nervous systems of its citizens.[3] Never mind that Malevich returned to painterly representation by 1930; Socialist Realism consummated the vanguard project to transcend the museum and fuse art with life. It was Socialist Realism that bridged the gap between elite culture and the masses. Groys's radical position was also advanced by his fellow émigré academic Igor Golomstock: Socialist Realism first crushed the vanguard, then "usurped and tried to realize the avant-garde idea" of a new community and a new cultural totality—albeit in a perverted form that resurrected the moldering concepts of the nineteenth century.[4]

Like the masterpieces of the medieval church, Socialist Realism originals could not be purchased. They could only be contemplated, as they hung in factory Houses of Culture or state Palaces of Labor. Now, Socialist Realism has returned to the people—although, theoretically, it always belonged to them. In the May 1992 issue of *Artforum*, Vitaly Komar and Alexander Melamid (émigrés who "rewrote" Socialist Realism to make themselves its greatest exponents) posed the classic Russian question "What is to be done?" as applied to the monumental propaganda of the former Soviet Union. The pair offered their own witty suggestions—adding, for example, an ism to the occupant's name on the Lenin Mausoleum.[5]

Some Socialist Realist pieces have been sold abroad. But there is more than enough statuary left over to create a Leninland theme park, separated from the EuroDisney outside Paris by a facsimile Berlin Wall. As early as 1993 something like this had happened in Hungary, where fifty-eight monuments celebrating Karl Marx, Béla Kun, Ho Chi Minh, the Red Army, and generically heroic workers were relocated to an empty field on the outskirts of Budapest—the specter's graveyard.

Socialist Realism was by no means restricted to the Soviet Union. The Museum of Chinese Revolution on Tiananmen Square is filled with musty examples.

Just as Chinese Communism has lived on beyond the Russian model, so Chinese Socialist Realism outlasted the Soviet variant. Witness Dong Xiwen's suitably cosmic *Grand Ceremony of the Founding of the People's Republic of China* (1953), in which Chairman Mao addresses the charged void of a buttermilk sky over Tiananmen Square, or the madly stilted merriment of Zhan Jianzun's 1976 *Mao Zedong Investigating the Peasant's Movement in Hunan,* in which the chortling young revolutionary leader— surrounded by red banners, pitchforks, and grinning acolytes—suggests nothing so much as the ventriloquist's dummy for his own speech.

Nor is this most reviled and purposeful of art movements limited to the various denominations of real or no-longer-existing socialism. The Woman's National Republican Club in New York City, where I once interviewed Yevgeny Yevtushenko, has a major collection, with life-size statues of Ronald Reagan, a bust of George Bush, oil portraits of Mamie Eisenhower. The centerpiece of the Richard Nixon Library in Yorba Linda, California, is a sixty-square-foot canvas commemorating the then vice president's 1957 visit to an Austrian camp for Hungarian refugees: The heroic Nixon, somewhat incongruous in an inexpensive raincoat he might have borrowed from television's Lieutenant Columbo (benign symbol of America in Wim Wenders's *Wings of Desire*), pats a child's head and stares at the viewer while reaching out to another refugee—perhaps the painter himself—pointing fiercely back at the smoke that rises from his unhappy homeland.

Strictly speaking, however, true Socialist Realism existed in the Stalin era alone. It was forged in the fiery debates that began with the 1928 Central Committee Conference on Agitation and Propaganda (which mandated that literature, drama, and film be designed to reach the entire population, according to the requirements of the First Five-Year Plan) and culminated in the 1934 First Writers' Conference. As described and deconstructed by the Canadian sociologist (and Red Diaper baby) Régine Robin, the Writers' Conference consigned modernism to history's dustbin, engaging in a repetition that mistook itself for innovation and yet, even so, brought forth something new under the sun—namely, naturalized allegory, the representation of a purely ideological landscape.[6]

The essence of Socialist Realism is this combination of strict idealization and naive, almost goofy idealism. "Soviet painting is optimistic, it speaks of joyous feelings. Landscapes show the changed aspect of the new country. Portraits show its new people. Pictures of complex compositions depict its heroic history, its new Socialist life and work"—or so read the introductory text greeting visitors to the Soviet Pavilion at the 1939 World's Fair.[7]

Because Socialist Realism was less a style than a magical incantation, the categories each example illustrated were identical to those by which it was evaluated: *klassovost* (class awareness), *partiinost* (the expression of the leading role of the party), *ideinost* (the introduction of new thinking as approved by the party), *narodnost* (the celebration of populist sentiments). David Elliott cites Aleksei Vasilev's 1951 *They Are Writing about Us in Pravda* as the embodiment of all four categories plus a fifth, *tipichnost* (the miracle by which a particular individual is universalized, for example, *A Daughter of Soviet Kirgizia*): A group of newly collectivized Moldavian peasants break for lunch, sitting cross-legged on a traditional blanket and beaming at the woman in red babushka who reads aloud the newspaper report that is presumably reflected in the ample harvest surrounding them.[8] And who filed this report? *They Are Writing about Us in Pravda* even suggests a sixth category: *paranoidnost* (the heady sense of instant feedback and total surveillance implicit in all Socialist Realism). For Socialist Realist artworks can barely be considered autonomous objects. They were part of a single, cross-referenced, intertextual, and self-contained multimedia utterance.

Socialist Realism was defined as a "utopia in lifelike forms," differing, for example, from the naturalism of Émile Zola in that, like Lenin, it "dares to dream." And yet, because Socialist Realism was also "the enemy of everything supernatural and mystic, all other-worldly idealism" (according to N. Bukharin), it sought to ground its visionary extravagance in concrete historical circumstance and presented its ideal world as a second reality—reality, that is, as we desire it to be and as it shall inevitably become.[9]

SR = Socialist Realism/Second Reality. Socialist Realism is modernism come to power, a modernism mighty enough to project a new mass consciousness—beyond truth or falsehood. With each canvas a glowing chunk of petrified Stalinism, it would be a mistake to underestimate the mode's seductive power. Soviet art historian Aleksandr Sidorov has noted that the Socialist Realist spirit of social purpose far surpassed the dismal official canvases of the Khrushchev and Brezhnev periods. Stalinist art "never doubted its superiority," asserted Sidorov. "It was permeated by a feeling for a common cause useful to all and by the immutable, optimistic, triumphant basis on which it operated. Right up to the present day, this has had an almost irresistible effect upon us Soviets."[10]

It is thus as a rival of surrealism—a state surrealism—that we should consider Socialist Realism. Surrealism, too, was more than mere art, not so much a new avant-garde movement as a means of knowledge—not to be written or painted so much as lived. Like its near namesake, surrealism was a revolutionary romanticism complete with a pseudoscientific ideology and a radical program: "Today's poet is a magician. It is he who changes life, the world, who transforms man. No concern for art, for beauty. Those are paltry goals, unworthy of attention."[11]

A few weeks into 1927, the same year in which Stalin consolidated power and drove rival Leon Trotsky from first the Politburo, then the Central Committee, and finally the party, André Breton led the surrealists into the French Communist movement, the better to support "that enormous enterprise of recreating the universe to which Lautréamont and Lenin dedicated themselves entirely." A half dozen years later, the surrealists were expelled for, among other things, publishing an article in their journal that excoriated the "wind of cretinization blowing from the USSR" in such proto-SR movies as Nikolai Ekk's *The Road of Life* (1931). Nevertheless, surrealism continued to engage Socialist Realism—in part by forming a tactical alliance with the exiled Trotsky.[12]

Breton's 1937 manifesto "Limits Not Frontiers of Surrealism" employed Freudian categories to attack the rival school:

Above all, we expressly oppose the view that it is possible to create a work of art or even, properly considered, any useful work by expressing only the *manifest content* of an age. On the contrary, surrealism proposes to express its *latent content*. The "fantastic," which the application of a catch phrase such as "socialist realism" excludes in the most radical manner and to which surrealism never ceases to appeal, constitutes in our view the supreme key to this latent content, the means of fathoming the secret depths of history which disappear beneath a maze of events.[13]

The fantastic is where you find it. By setting out to master historical time, to direct the artwork's language, meaning, and reception, SR wound up offering, as Régine Robin put it, the "totally insane dream of explicitly fashioning the social imaginary."[14]

The irony is that, under the rule of capital, surrealism has long since been recuperated as our own social imaginary—instrumentalized in the marketplace as the language of department-store display windows, television commercials, and promotional videos. While contemporary advertising, MTV, and the economy of consumption would be inconceivable without the visual conundrums of René Magritte, Socialist Realism has achieved the exotic and hideous pathos of its lengthy submersion in the dark, dank historical deep.

THE DREAM OF PARADISE

Can it be that, even before Socialist Realism introduced itself as a scandalous digression cum destructive regression in the narrative of modern culture (post-, mass, and otherwise), it was an organic development in Russian art?

This was denied most strenuously by the Russian art historian Margarita Tupitsyn at a roundtable discussion held on April 16, 1994, as part of New York P.S. 1's "Stalin's Choice" show. Yet beginning with the huge Ilya Repin exhibit that opened at Moscow's Tretiakov Gallery in 1936 and subsequently toured the Soviet Union, the school of nineteenth-century naturalist painters known as the *Peredvizhniki* (wanderers) were officially rehabilitated and canonized as the precursor models for Socialist Realism—with the additional suggestion that any and all artistic deviations from such robustly bloodless academic naturalism were indeed foreign to Russian tradition. Although most of the *Peredvizhniki* alive in 1917 had opposed the October Revolution, their vision was transplanted—scientifically—from the populist soil to the proletarian garden.

Furthermore, if, as the historian James H. Billington has noted, Russian painters have historically shown greater concern for the world's spiritual transformation than for its naturalistic representation, then Socialist Realism was also an indigenous and deeply rooted flowering. "Scientific socialism is the most religious of all religions, and the true Social Democrat is the most deeply religious of all human beings," wrote the future

Soviet commissar of enlightenment Anatoli Lunacharsky a decade before the October Revolution.[15]

Long in advance of 1937 (or even 1917), Russia had resisted the secular art of the West. It was the veneration of the holy icon that distinguished the Russian aesthetic—although *aesthetic* may not be the precise word. Converted to Christianity at the height of the Byzantine passion for sacred painted images, Russians would thereafter articulate theology (and ultimately *partiinost*) in visual terms. The icon, collector Ilya Ostroukhov wrote in 1913, "takes us into an absolutely special world, one which has nothing in common with the world of painting . . . a world created by faith and filled with representations of the spirit." More than the stylized image of a saint, the icon was a collective and religious act, "prayer in material form," "a door to heaven."[16]

For Russia's early-twentieth-century avant-garde, the icon was at once manifestation of an ideal national past and inspiration for a transfigured future. Under the rule of Joseph Stalin, who spent his adolescence at a Georgian theological seminary, the icon was recast: Portraits of Soviet leaders greeting happy laborers, planning sweeping industrial victories, inspecting plentiful harvests, and otherwise engaging in the construction of socialism were rendered with a pomp so dogged and extreme that, as the Hungarian art historian György Szücs put it, their perfection "enchants and disarms the viewer."[17]

The icon was the sacred authority that sanctioned the social order; so, too, the guiding images of scientific socialism. "Experts have always wondered at the relative scarcity of themes developed by Socialist Realism," Russian art historian Joseph Bakshtein noted on the occasion of the "Stalin's Choice" exhibition. "The reason is the sacral attitude adopted towards the person portrayed. . . . [As] in traditional Russian icons, canons must be strictly followed in depicting the face, the figure and the posture. It is widely known that a canon to be obeyed in portraying Party leaders and their circle was approved by Politburo resolutions and was to be observed meticulously in copying."[18]

These modern icons were never more modern than in their relation to and reliance on photography.

The objective camera renders the painter's subjective vision obsolete. As with the fabled icons known as *nerukotvornyi*, the painted image was produced not by the artist's hand but by the sacred energy that flowed like an electrical discharge from the subject. Isaac Brodsky, in particular, exploited the authority of the photograph's indexical relation to the physical world. Brodsky took a famous portrait by the Bolshevik photojournalist Pyotr Otsup as the basis for his own *Lenin in Front of the Kremlin,* painted after the subject's death in 1924; his well-known *Lenin in the Smolnyi* (1935) was similarly based on a photograph; while his epic, massively detailed rectangular crowd scene *Lenin's Speech at a Worker's Meeting at the Putilov Factory in May 1917* (1929) drew on multiple Lenin photos, as well as those of individual workers and of the smoky factory yard.[19]

Socialist Realism photographed the project for transforming the world. The improved historical reality provided by Brodsky's masterfully constructed, ideologically airbrushed canvases had its equivalent in the careful removal of Leon Trotsky (among others) from the photographic record, not to mention in the Soviet movies produced from the late 1930s on, under Stalin's close supervision. As early as 1924, Stalin had realized that "film is an illusion which dictates its own law upon life."

Régine Robin considers Social Realism "impossible" because it seeks to eliminate all indeterminacy: Life submits to the logic of Marxism. "A dialectical conjunction between reflection and projection, [SR] constructs reality by developing knowledge of its change."[20]

Not just the past but the future is perfectly evident. To quote K. Radek: "Socialist Realism means not only knowing reality as it is, but knowing whither it is moving." Thus, as Peter Kenez pointed out, the glorious textile factory cum hilltop fairy-tale castle in Grigori Alexandrov's *The Shining Path* (1940) anticipated by a decade the ornate skyscraper spires of the magnificent Moscow State University, constructed on the crest of the Lenin Hills above the city. Similarly, Ivan Pyriev, director of the 1947 superproduction *Siberian Rhapsody,* prided himself on having presented parking lots on the screen well before they were actually introduced to Siberia. (In fact, the movie was made largely in Czechoslovakia.)[21]

Socialist Realism goes beyond a naturalistic representation of current reality to a naturalistic representation of that reality as it will be brightened by the ongoing socialist project. The title of Valentin Kataev's novel *Time Forward!* epitomizes this progressive thrust. Images of youthful motherhood or of factories and hydroelectric installations under construction in the radiant promise of perpetual sunrise express a similar projection. Sometimes it is simply paradise—a cavorting bevy of buxom Soviet houris offering a bouquet of pink and yellow carnations to the beaming dead leader in Aleksandr Samokhvalov's parfait-hued *Kirov at the Sports Palace* (1935). The workers in Alexei Sittaro's *Members of the Young Communist League from the Leningrad Lamp Factory Svetlana* (1937) are fashionably turned out in gauzy rose; the goods produced by Vera Orlova's *Sharikopodshipnik Factory* (1937) sparkle like diamonds.

The world is familiar with the tale of the transportable "Potemkin villages"—flats and facades contrived by Catherine the Great's prime minister to line the banks of the Volga River and thus to conceal from the empress, behind a portable second reality, the actual condition of her people. Is the Potemkin village a principle of Russian history? Marquis de Custine, who visited the empire almost exactly a century before Vera Orlova painted *Sharikopodshipnik Factory*, noted the degree to which the czar's subjects had names for things that otherwise did not exist. "Russia is a country of facades. Read the labels—they have 'society,' 'civilization,' 'literature,' 'art,' 'sciences'—but as a matter of fact, they don't even have doctors. . . . How many cities and roads exist only as projects? Well, the entire nation," de Custine concluded, was "nothing but a placard stuck over Europe."[22]

Certainly, Socialist Realism took its cues from a leader whose characteristic mode of discussion was, according to Moshe Lewin, to present his desire "as accomplished fact" and thus to encourage the party apparatus to come into accordance with "the 'actual situation' as it allegedly existed 'everywhere else.'"[23]

It is in the "Stalin-Gesamtkunstwerk," as Groys calls it, that the grandiose avant-garde desire to remake the world came to fruition. "Life has improved, Comrades, life has become more joyous," Stalin told the First All-Union Convention of Stakhanovite Workers in Moscow, November 1935 (his first public appearance in nearly two years). "Millions of disks record those precious words," exiled oppositionist Victor Serge would report. "Little girls holding bouquets in their arms march across the screen singing: 'Life has become more joyous.' Red calico is hung above the streets, proclaiming that 'life has become more joyous.' Squadrons returning from manoeuvres cry out in a manly voice that 'life has become more joyous.' Tourists stirred by the sights note down in their memorandum books that 'life has become more joyous.'"[24] It was then that the fairy tale became reality and the fantastic age began.

As the prince of Kiev adopted Christianity and liquidated pagan Rus by fiat in 988 A.D., as Peter the Great marked the year 1700 with a decree that his minions become European by shaving their beards and adopting German-style jackets, so the new Soviet Constitution, announced in 1936 as the "most democratic in the world" and distributed abroad under the rubric *A Happy People,* not only included universal suffrage but guaranteed freedom of religion, speech, press, and assembly.

An even more remarkable example of fiction overtaking life was the first Moscow Trial, staged in late August 1936. The plot rivaled any science fiction: Centers of Trotskyite counterrevolution were uncovered in the party apparatus of each and every republic—a vast, hitherto unknown conspiracy of espionage, sabotage, and treason. The terror had begun with the December 1934 assassination of Leningrad party secretary Sergei Kirov, ordered—so the trial would reveal—by no less than Grigori Zinoviev, himself acting on Trotsky's orders. Indeed, since late 1932 the Trotskyites had constituted a clandestine Central Committee. Moreover, as the trial narrative explained, foreign agents were conspiring against the Happy People by cooperating with the Nazi Gestapo to assassinate Lazar Kaganovich, Kliment Voroshilov, Andrei Zhdanov, and even Stalin.

These trials—at which, without material proof, the accused *accused themselves*—produced further revelations. Serge filled an entire page in *Russia Twenty Years After* listing the internationally known veteran revolutionaries, civil war heroes, and former Lenin associates—some of them still editing newspapers, serving as commissars, or heading diplomatic missions—who were implicated in the plot: "It is learned that all these men and many others are terrorists or the accomplices of terrorists! . . . A veil falls, the truth bursts out in full. All the surviving members of the Central Committee that made the October, Stalin excepted, are indicted."[25]

Just as the political show trial was the performative equivalent of the photo-realist canvas, so these paradigms of Stalinist culture could work in concert. Originally scheduled to open in 1937, the Industry of Socialism exhibition was delayed two years while the artists scrambled to repaint— and then re-repaint—their canvases to eliminate portraits of those former heroes who had been exposed as traitors.

The perfected Stalinist trial was actually staged after World War II in Czechoslovakia—despite an extensive rewrite even while the show was in preproduction. The initial fabricated scenario concerned a plot to assassinate Rudolf Slánský, then general secretary of the Czechoslovak Communist Party. Stalin, however, effectively revised the script and recast the production so that the original victim would became the star villain—a Zionist traitor who conspired to return Czechoslovakia to the imperialist camp. The ongoing investigation then uncovered an incriminating letter addressed to Slánský—albeit as the "Great Street Sweeper."

Every aspect of the so-called Slánský trial was designed to contribute to the total effect. (In her memoirs, Heda Margolius Kovály writes that her husband Rudolf Margolius's arrest was "staged like the climactic scene of a spy thriller. The whole street had been lit up by the headlights of black police cars positioned at strategic angles and manned by members of State Security.") The title of the show was the subject of much discussion. "For a long time," according to the chief prosecutor Karel Doubek, "the favorite was *Espionage and Conspiratorial Center*." But this indicated neither the center's "Zionist" ideology nor its relationship to the renegade Tito. New titles included *Conspiratorial Zionist Espionage Center*, but no suggestion ever satisfactorily encompassed the Titoist line: "The final approved name was the *Anti-State Conspiracy Center Headed by R. Slánský*. This was approved by all authorities and accepted by all the defendants, including R. Slánský himself."[26]

Following the method developed by their Soviet advisers, the Czech producers made sure that all testimony was prepared in advance. The trial would follow an exact eight-day schedule, after which some eighty thousand copies of the transcript (or rather, script)—translated into four languages, as well as in Czech—were to be available for immediate distribution. Naturally, those on trial were required to memorize their lines. (According to surviving defendant Eugen Loebl, the only one of the accused who had difficulty learning his part was Bedrich Geminder, hampered by his poor Czech.) The thirty-five handpicked witnesses and alternate witnesses were similarly prepared to recite their testimony by rote.

As a precaution against the sort of lapse that had marred the Kostov trial in Bulgaria, all proceedings were rehearsed in a recording studio. Doubek asked his questions and each defendant, believing he was being tested (rather than tape recorded), answered them. Thus, if one of the accused misspoke during the actual trial, the microphone could be turned off and the tape recorder switched on to provide the correct answer for the benefit of those millions following the proceedings by radio. The preparation paid off. When one of the prosecutors inadvertently skipped a scripted question, the well-rehearsed defendant declined to ad lib, sticking with the answer that should have been given.

Just as the Potemkin villages concealed (while exemplifying) Russian underdevelopment, so Socialist Realism provided a magic mirror for Real Socialism. The unspeakable brutality and mass starvation that had accompanied the great collectivization and the First Five-Year Plan dissolved into the golden harvest of Sergei Gerasimov's canvas *Kolkhoz Festival* (1936) or was rationalized by the orgiastic feast of Friedrich Ermler's *Peasants* (1935)—a movie that also included an animated dream sequence featuring, for the first time in any Soviet film—Stalin![27]

The era of purges and show trials is subsumed in the dreamy prospect of Yuri Pimenov's *New Moscow* (1937). It is, in a way, SR's visual equivalent to that surrealist favorite *Alice in Wonderland*. The viewer of this suspiciously Monet-inspired canvas is effectively placed in the passenger seat of a Soviet convertible roadster, bedecked with a red carnation and piloted, by a fashionably permed young woman in a flowered frock, toward Ilyich Way, the grand boulevard that was to lead to the fabulous, never-built Palace of the Soviets.

Just as SR movies and paintings portrayed a world of superabundant produce, joyous workers, and tireless, charismatic leaders, so a second Soviet capital coexisted with the actual Moscow. While families crammed into decrepit "communal" apartments, queued in drab streets to purchase basic necessities, or disappeared backstage, the state erected grandiose public buildings and organized mammoth public festivals. And as citizens vanished into the dungeons of the People's Commissariat for Internal Affairs (NKVD) or were transported to prison camps a thousand miles away, so the underworld was illuminated by Moscow's labyrinthine Subway of the Revolution. "The Moscow subway makes the New York subway look like a sewer," reported Frank Lloyd Wright of this SR "People's Versailles," where chandeliers cast their glow on the red granite archways and the huge, allegorical mosaics.[28]

The quintessential SR castle was the Palace of the Soviets, intended to be the world's highest building. This grandiose edifice was not only never completed but—despite years of planning—never even undertaken. Perhaps it was sufficient that, in clearing space for the Palace, Stalin demolished what had been the largest sacred object in Moscow—the marble turreted thirty-story Temple of Christ the Savior, built by Alexander I to mark Napoleon's defeat. Or perhaps, as the Russian architects Alexei Tarkhanov and Sergei Kavtaradze suggest, "this non-existent building figured so often and so insistently in architectural drawings and town-planning projects that its actual construction seemed superfluous." It was simply imagined into the landscape.[29]

Always referred to in the present tense, the Palace was to be a combined seat of government and cultural center that would house sessions of the Supreme Soviet, official congresses, concerts, and theatrical performances. The Soviets invited outstanding international architects—Hans Poelzig, Joseph Urban, Le Corbusier, and Walter Gropius, among them—to submit proposals, ultimately deciding in February 1934 on Boris Iofan's plans for a severe monolith to be topped by a statue of a liberated worker several times the size of the Statue of Liberty. A small army of artists began to prepare acres of paintings and fields of monumental sculptures as Iofan continued to perfect his design. For twenty years, new "definitive" plans were regularly exhibited. (In the interim, the architect won contests to build the Soviet pavilions at the 1937 Paris and 1939 New York World's Fairs.) Stalin himself expanded the capacity of the great auditorium from fifteen thousand to twenty-one thousand; proposed setting the Palace amid a landscape of parade fields, boulevards, and grand arches; and suggested that the liberated worker be replaced with an even larger statue of Lenin. Topping this Soviet super–Empire State Building like a victorious King Kong, the leader of earthbound proletariat revolution was elevated to ruler of a heavenly realm.[30]

Milan Kundera has called the period of Stalinist terror a time of "collective lyrical delirium." It is the frighteningly garish representation of official gaiety in Vasili Svarog's *J. V. Stalin and Members of the Politburo among Children in the A. M. Gorky Central Park of Culture and Rest* (1939), where, surrounded by his entourage dead center in the composition, Stalin exerts a force field that commands a mad whirl of bridges, parachutists, and boats. It is the opalescent light of Pimenov's *New Moscow*, suggesting the aftermath of a cleansing spring shower. In the shimmering distance, the new Council for Labor and Defense beckons bright promise, towering over the older structures on either side. The thoroughfare is populated—but uncongested—with automobiles, trams, and strolling pedestrians. All travel together on a collective spatiotemporal voyage as old Moscow melts away into Stalin's new world.

New Moscow vibrates as if with the triumphal melody that grew ever louder and more persistent throughout the period of human sacrifice. The mobilized harmony of the Stalinist pageants, the utopian parades with a million participants and no spectators, the ecstatic odes to the Soviet sun god were variations on a single theme. "Totalitarianism is not only hell, but also the dream of paradise—the age-old dream of a world where everybody would live in harmony, united with a single common will and faith, without secrets from one another," Kundera has pointed out, even recalling a famous passage from André Breton's *Nadja*. "Breton, too, dreamed of this paradise when he talked about the glass house in which he longed to live."[31]

"HE IS EVERYWHERE, HE SEES EVERYTHING"

Despite the fantastic ornamentation of Stalinist edifices—the frilly, fortresslike "triumphalist" skyscrapers, their spires topped with red stars —no art was ever more functional. "Prayer in material form," a "door to heaven," these gigantic stone wedding cakes provided a utopian alternative to shortages and repression; they concealed the cost of socialist construction, even as they dramatized the idea of such "construction" in a country where socialism itself was an ever-receding chimera.

Even ordinary apartment buildings might be adorned with mosaics of ancient cities or gratuitous colonnades. Indeed, expatriate scholar Vladimir Paperny maintains that "long before the American architect Robert Venturi discovered Las Vegas and proclaimed its 'decorated sheds' to be a model for Western architecture, his Soviet colleagues had already broken with the 'form-follows-structure' axiom of constructivism and made the separation of the architectural 'skin' from the 'bones.'" Stalinist architects proclaimed their mastery of the heritage, calling their style Red Doric and Proletarian Classicism, but their creations are actually pre-postmodern masterpieces of "facadism"—if not a more permanent form of the Potemkin village.[32]

The leaden whimsy of the Hotel Moscow notwithstanding—legend has it Stalin signed off on alternate designs, creating a building whose main facade was made up of two boldly unrelated halves—the All-Union Agricultural Exhibition exemplifies the Stalinist baroque. Celebrated in the press as "the mirror of the Stalinist era," the All-Union Agricultural Exhibition was inaugurated on August 1, 1939, by V. M. Molotov and ten thousand guests. Just as Stalin never visited a museum, so he never toured the exhibition. Was it enough for him simply to imagine it? His spirit, in any case, was omnipresent: his words engraved in stone, his name bestowed on machines, his statue an altar at the center of each pavilion.

Vera Mukhina's gargantuan steel sculpture of the forward-striding *Worker and Collective Farm Woman,* which had topped the Soviet contribution to the 1937 Paris World's Fair, guarded the exhibition entrance; its Pavilion of the Mechanization and Electrification of Agriculture was decked out with pop-classical porticoes, gilded candelabra, ornate balustrades; its benches and trash bins were embellished with the hammer and sickle, garlanded by sheaves of wheat. (These stone sheaves, as well as the exhibition's granite cornucopias and bronze fruit bowls, anticipated the stony still lifes that René Magritte, still a member of the Belgian Communist Party, would paint in the early 1950s.) Flower beds groomed and shrubbery sculpted, the exhibition embodied totality. Indeed, it may be usefully considered the world's first theme park.[33] Not unlike the "architecture of joy" with which Morris Lapidus infused the hotels of Miami Beach, Stalinist urban planning was a form of social science fiction. Such "metaphysical cities," as Tarkhanov and Kavtaradze call them, conjuring up the empty immanence of Giorgio de Chirico's urban prospects, "lacked only suitable inhabitants, as ideal as the buildings themselves."[34]

Although not completed until 1953, the year of Stalin's death, the exhibition nonetheless appears as a realized paradise in two classic Socialist Realist operettas, Grigori Alexandrov's *The Shining Path* and Ivan Pyriev's *The Swineherd and the Shepherd,* both released in 1940.

The "shining path" leads to the exhibition where, having been transformed (by the party) from an illiterate peasant to Supreme Soviet deputy, our heroine Tanya finds romance amid the cheerful throngs, sparkling fountains, and alabaster sculptures. Similarly, the eponymous model workers of *The Swineherd and the Shepherd* journey from their respective homes on the shores of the White and Black Seas to meet and fall in love by the Friendship of Nations Fountain at Kolkhoz Square and then, after a year of separation and misunderstanding, find each other once again at the exhibition. "There is nothing more beautiful than Moscow," they sing, but it is the exhibition where these paradigms have their natural home.

Such saints are axiomatic in Socialist Realism, where they are termed *Stakhanovites* and *positive heroes.* The former, actual workers who extravagantly exceeded the norms of production, were named for the miner Alexei Stakhanov, who presaged the new Soviet man when, on August 31, 1935, he cut some 102 tons of coal to exceed the quota by 1,400 percent. The latter, largely fictional but perhaps more ubiquitous, were those party savants who embodied history's forward trajectory and thus became SR's defining feature.

Courageous, intelligent, patriotic, steadfast, selfless, respectful of women, the positive hero is the allegorical personification of Bolshevik ideals and the paradigm of Bolshevik virtue. (In Socialist Realist movies, the positive hero is also impeccably groomed, continually solicitous, and frighteningly cheerful.) The positive hero is that which will be; lesser characters represent what is. For him, there is no riddle that cannot be solved by applying the logic of objective historical necessity; hence the remarkable exactitude of his emotions, judgments, and deeds. Free of doubts, confident in the inevitable, the positive hero is that "peak of humanity from whose height the future can be seen"—or what Scientology would call a perfect clear.[35]

Stalin, of course, is the greatest of positive heroes as well as, in some sense, their creator—screening and approving all movies that were made (often at his suggestion) and released (sometimes with his modifications) in the Soviet Union. "*Not a single article* of a journal or review . . . does not begin and end with quotations from the words of the Leader," Serge observed in *Russia Twenty Years After,* detailing the various invocations found in the August 2, 1936, issue of *Izvestia,* where the editorial "Towards New Victories" managed to cite the "wise thought of Stalin" four times in two columns while capitalizing all personal pronouns pertaining to the Soviet leader:

> The peroration of a speech of the People's Commissar of Transportation, Kaganovich, in two columns, carries this subheading: "Let Us Learn from the Great Locomotive Engineer of the Revolution, Comrade Stalin." In two hundred lines "our great Stalin" is quoted seventeen times and almost every time with several lines of eulogy. "By his Leninist firmness, his wisdom, his stoicism, his great and gifted mind, his perspicacity, his practical work, by the education and organization of men, Comrade Stalin is assuring us the victory over the enemies of our country!" (*Thunderous acclamations, cries: Hurrah!*)[36]

Any "positive" aspect of daily existence is a factor of Comrade Stalin's concern for mankind. Naturally, Stalin is the inspiration for all true Soviet artists—as Komar and Melamid propose in their post-SR Social Realist canvas *Stalin and the Muses* (1981–82), in which a beaming elderly Stalin accepts tribute from the quartet of grateful nymphs who might be a delegation of exotic *kolkhoznitsy* from faraway Uzbekistan: "O great Stalin, O leader of the peoples, Thou who broughtest man to birth, Thou who fructifies the earth . . . "

How to explain the revulsion I experience when confronted by Nazi portraits of Hitler (or even the mild nausea inspired by the illustrations of Frederic Remington or Norman Rockwell) and the amazement mixed with contempt provoked by Mariam Aslamazyan's 1948 *Carpet-Weavers of Armenia Weaving a Carpet with a Portrait of Comrade Stalin*?

Here we gaze on the manifestation of faith, and more: The image within the image has the same effect as the actual television set incorporated into Tom Wesselman's *Still Life #28* (1963). In the midst of *Carpet-Weavers*'s windblown exoticism—cowled women, fragrant cherry blossoms—a chasm opens onto a greater reality. Comrade Stalin is the true subject of all pictures in which he appears—his portrait borne across the threshold *In the New Flat* (1951), his presence imagined *At Lenin's Death-Bed* (1944). Even a Hungarian *Still Life with Pictures and Vase*, presciently painted by Károly Lászlo Háy in 1946, includes a small picture on a parlor table—the likeness more abstract than a child's crude impression of Mickey Mouse, yet the quick dabs of paint unmistakably signify Stalin's face (as reproduced from a reproduction of Aleksandr Gerasimov's 1939 portrait).[37]

Similarly, as Golomstock points out, an ordinary genre painting might be transformed by virtue of a grandiloquent title (*They Saw Stalin*) or a landscape transfigured as the backdrop for, to take one example, *Comrade Stalin in His Early Years*.[38] Throughout the 1930s, the Soviet leader was painted actively participating in the company of other comrades. Pyotr Maltsev's *Meeting of a Heroic Crew* (1936) puts Stalin on an airfield with a group of aviators and two frisky kids, as does Vasili Svarog's distinctively windblown, daringly off-kilter *Comrade J. V. Stalin and Members of the Politburo at Tushino Airfield on Aviation Day* (1938). In Anatoly Jar-Kravchenko's *A. M. Gorky Reading His Work "The Girl and Death" to J. V. Stalin, V. M. Molotov, and K. E. Voroshilov* (1941), the famous writer basks in Stalin's approval. But after World War II, painters typically showed Stalin in awesome solitude—set apart even when in the company of others.

Visiting the Soviet Union in 1947, John Steinbeck noted with wonderment in his diary that Stalin's "portrait does not just hang in every museum, but every room of every museum. His statue marches in front of all public buildings. . . . His bust is also in all school rooms, and his portrait is often directly behind his bust. In parks he sits on a plaster bench and discusses problems with Lenin. . . . The stores sell million upon million of his face—surely the painting and modeling, the casting, the forging, and the embroidering of Stalin must be one of the great industries of the

Soviet Union. He is everywhere, he sees everything."[39] Stalin's portrait likewise appeared daily in every periodical published in the Soviet Union—ubiquitous yet unique. Tarkhanov and Kavtaradze's 1992 *Architecture of the Stalin Era* includes a "forbidden" photograph of a sculpture-house courtyard populated by an irreverent cluster of mass-produced Stalin multiples.

For a time after 1924, the image of Lenin had been emblazoned on porcelain tea sets, candy wrappers, and cigarette packs. But his quaint cult did not survive the tenth anniversary of his death: The Lenin Mausoleum, a triumph of the First Five-Year Plan, erected over the objections of Lenin's widow and other members of the Central Committee, became Stalin's pedestal. "The spiritual atmosphere of Russia changes at a single stroke," Serge wrote. "A mausoleum is built for the mummy of Lenin. Marxian thought congeals into verbal repetitions; formulae must be stereotyped so that their content vanishes, and Leninism, invented yesterday, solemnly substitutes for the revolutionary Marxism of Lenin."[40] Lenin was now cast in the supporting role of Sacred Ancestor: Just as Lenin had been the "Marx of his time," so Stalin became the "Lenin of Today." Founded on the transmigration of political souls, as Isaac Deutscher put it, the history of the Bolshevik Revolution was successfully "rewritten in terms of sorcery and magic."[41]

Leader, Teacher, Friend, painted by Grigori Shegal in 1937, shows an apparent meeting of the Central Committee. An avuncular Stalin stands left of center at the podium. He has patiently heard the question of the earnest-looking peasant woman who sits beside him and is affably poised to answer her. Around them, people in various modes of national garb cup their ears, tilt their heads, pretzel about to catch his imminent words. Revelation or terror? A diagonal vector leads from the strenuous attention of the woman in the foreground through Stalin to the outsized stone Lenin hovering behind, harmonizing the space while bestowing the blessing of history.

Stalin as trademark: Always painted once removed, from photographs rather than life, his portraits are endless variations on a single theme. Isaac Brodsky's 1933 *Portrait of J. V. Stalin,* in which the Soviet leader appears neither benign nor paternal, is a marked contrast to the expansive Stalin of Aleksandr Gerasimov's 1939 portrait. (The artists partook of the power they painted: Brodsky as rector of the All-Russian Academy of Arts and Gerasimov as head of the Moscow Union of Artists.)

For artists, necessity was the mother of invention: Vasili Svarog's severely prismatic *Stalin Reports on the Project of the Constitution at the*

VIII Extraordinary Congress of Soviets (1938), which presents the demiurge from a sinister low angle with something resembling a stage villain's waxed mustache, is no more stylized than the gigantic *Prominent Muscovites in the Kremlin* (1949), a painting created by a brigade of artists under the direction of Vasili Efanov. In the latter, a fantastically individuated crowd of guests throngs the ogre's palace to celebrate Moscow's ninth century, applauding the elderly worker who proudly affixes the Order of Lenin to the city banner under outsized crystal chandeliers and the cold marble gaze cast by a colossal bust of Stalin.[42]

The artist who did the most to dramatize this icon on celluloid was Mikhail Chiaureli. As a youth, Chiaureli had painted frescoes in Georgian churches. At the post–World War II height of his career, he was a deputy to the Supreme Soviet. Chiaureli's first films showed the influence of the European avant-garde, but he soon corrected himself—or rather, enlisted in another vanguard. It was in 1938, in *The Great Dawn,* that Chiaureli introduced the infallible Stalin as a historical character. The next year he began *The Vow,* to confirm Stalin as Lenin's heir. Completed in 1946 (its production delayed by the Great Patriotic War), *The Vow* is named after the great oath of fealty that Stalin took at Lenin's tomb—a declaration suggesting for Isaac Deutscher an "homage to a deceased tribal chief."[43]

The Vow is predicated on a series of sacred substitutions. The journal *International Literature* would declare that "the acclaim accorded the picture by the general public and the critics" could be compared only with that given the two previous landmarks of Soviet cinema, *Battleship Potemkin* (1925) and *Chapayev* (1934). At the same time, *The Vow* "opens up a new page in the history of Soviet cinema." Less a narrative than a succession of friezes populated by a mixture of historical personalities and abstract social types, the movie dramatizes the flow of events from Lenin's death in 1924 through World War II as they course through the mighty figure of Stalin and concern the fate of the Volga port city that from 1925 to 1961 bore his name. And so, "a stirring, poetical narrative of the fulfillment of a dream," *The Vow* replaces history.[44]

Like a messenger from the serfs, sent to entreat their czar, an old Bolshevik sets out for Moscow to deliver a letter that would presciently warn Lenin of the threat posed to the revolution posed by the wealthy peasant kulaks. Scarcely less prescient themselves, the kulaks kill the herald en route, and his grandmotherly wife, Varvara, assumes the mission. But she arrives too late: Lenin is ill—and then, Great Lenin has died. To whom can she entrust the letter now?

As the people weep outside their departed leader's home and the music swells, the film's somber Stalin impersonator appears in majestic close-up, walking alone in the snow, letting his gaze rest sadly on the very bench where he and Lenin last sat and spoke. That the outline of Lenin's form is still marked by the snow seems a gag out of the surrealist film *Un Chien Andalou* (1929), an impression only reinforced by the irrational cut that instantly transports Stalin to his Kremlin office. He sits at his desk, lights his pipe, and is given an epiphany—a thought balloon of Lenin agitating.

Snow is still falling in Red Square as Stalin reemerges to declare that "men like Lenin never die" but "live forever in our hearts." He stands up and swears eternal allegiance. The onlookers are rapt: "Stalin gives his vow and so shall we!" The crowd parts as Varvara advances with the letter. Celestial voices resound as she presents it to Stalin. A banner is raised, the face of Lenin fills the screen, and a maimed herdsman speaks for all: "Now we know that Lenin is still alive."

Aleksandr Gerasimov's 1950 painting of this moment has Stalin standing before a standing audience with a spotlighted, giant stone bust of Lenin already in place behind him. (Can this be what Stalin meant when the "Man of Steel" stood before his predecessor's embalmed corpse and declared that "we Communists . . . are made of a special material"?) The age of miracles continues.

"The only difference between Stalin and Tarzan is that the films about the latter don't pretend to be documentaries," French critic André Bazin would write.[45] The morning after Stalin's vow, the first Soviet-made tractor chugs into Red Square and then, tragically, stalls. Kibitzed by sympathetic bystanders, the desperate driver ineffectually tinkers under the hood. Nothing works. At that moment arrives Stalin, accompanied by a few colleagues. Friendly and concerned, ignoring Bukharin's cynical crack about the superiority of American products, Stalin inquires as to the difficulty and diagnoses it instantly: "The spark plugs, of course."

Comrade Stalin, leader of world revolution, climbs into the driver's seat. Suddenly, a close-up of him piloting the vehicle dissolves into the image of endless tractors plowing the Soviet fields. Film historian Maya Turovskaya calls this the "best sex scene in Soviet cinema." Stalin activates his tractor and impregnates the entire land. Life *has* improved, Comrades![46]

The postwar Stalin was beyond mortal ken. A painting like Feodor Shurpin's pearly, pastel *Morning of Our Motherland* (1946–48) may be something unprecedented in naturalistic art: White dress uniform opalescent in the early light, a grave and solitary Stalin has materialized in the midst of his fruitful domain. His uncannily static figure dwarfs the power lines and tractors in the background. Is it a gigantic statue draped with an overcoat, or has the living God himself appeared in the fields?

Fully achieved Stalinist art eradicated conflict altogether. Earlier representations of struggle were superceded by blandly harmonious depictions of everyday life in an achieved utopia. As the 1946–53 period saw the acme of Socialist Realism, so *The Vow*'s grateful deification of Stalin inaugurated a new era in Soviet moviemaking, according to *International Literature*. Although production dwindled, each film was an a priori "masterpiece." Ivan Pyriev's 1949 *Cossacks of the Kuban,* shot in the midst of famine, drafted every harvester in the Soviet Union for an opening sequence in a vast, fertile landscape animated by an ecstatic torrent of marching, singing farmers.[47]

After Khrushchev cited *The Vow* in his "secret" denunciation of Stalin at the Twentieth Party Congress in 1956, Mikhail Chiaureli also fell. His most famous movies were hidden. For a time, he was reduced to directing educational cartoons—apt fate for one who had made his reputation engineering the psyches of impressionable children. Then, some fifteen years later, Dusan Makavejev's *WR: Mysteries of the Organism* (1971) took advantage of the resources of the Yugoslav film archive to quote several sequences from *The Vow* in the service of the most intense critique of the October Revolution ever produced in a Communist country.

Idolatry infers iconoclasm: *WR* mocks Communist intellectuals, Yugoslav workers, the Stalin cult, and the sacred symbols of World War II partisans, in part by having them rub up against the sexual-political (sexpol) theories of the radical Freudian Wilhelm Reich. (*WR* also stands for world revolution.) In his reckless montage-mongering, employing sound as well as image, Makavejev is the irresponsible heir to Sergei Eisenstein. At his most grotesquely tender, Makavejev conjoins the piercing harmonies of a Yugoslav hymn—"Oh, Communist Party! My fragrant flower!"—with a mock Reichian documentary of a couple making love in an open field and later with an image, evidently taken from a Nazi medical film, of a mental patient banging his head against the wall. At his most blandly provocative, the filmmaker inserts images of shock therapy into *The Vow* and juxtaposes Stalin's proclamation "Comrades, we have successfully completed the first stage of Communism" with a plaster cast of an erect penis.

This crypto-dramatization of Reich's *Mass Psychology of Fascism* also mixes documentary and fiction. In addition to filming interviews with

Reich's American disciples, Makavejev shot travelogue footage among the hippies, drag queens, and weirdos of New York's East Village, to be intercut with a narrative staged in Yugoslavia, suggesting a form of self-conscious Socialist Realism. It's a Communist romance, like *The Shining Path* or *The Swineherd and the Shepherd,* except that characters discuss the most intimate matters in ecstatic Marxist clichés: "As long as you were an apprentice beautician, you used to let me pluck roses in your garden. But now that you've passed a Party course, you snub intimate proletarian friend," an irate shock-worker of Tito complains to winsome sex-pol militant Milena, who responds to his "slanderous lie" by labeling him an "irresponsible element."

WR's narrative concerns the doomed romance between Milena, a modern Yugoslav "positive heroine," and an uptight Soviet "positive hero," the champion ice-skater and people's artist insolently named Vladimir Ilyich. Encased in Reichian character armor, Vladimir Ilych cannot accept Milena's sexual importunings. Indeed, after he responds to her affectionate caress by reflexively knocking her to the ground, he briefly disappears to be replaced by a tearful Stalin in a frozen world, the bereft Stalin of *The Vow.* "That's a beautiful shot," Makavejev told an American interviewer. "Stalin watches the bench in the snow where Lenin used to sit, and he is crying. This is pure demagogy, and I loved this scene for its shallowness." The pathos of the moment in *WR* cannot be fully appreciated, or perhaps even understood, without knowledge of *The Vow.*[48]

Milena loses her head to love, literally. In a final (unseen) burst of sexual violence, Vladimir Ilych decapitates her with his ice skate. Maybe it would be more accurate to say that Milena loses her body, since, in *WR*'s final scene, her severed head addresses the viewer from a tray in a forensic lab: "Even now I am not ashamed of my Communist past," she tells us—speaking, one suspects, for Makavejev as well.[49]

PATHOS AND IRONY

WR was to be the last utopian Communist film; that it was produced at the height of the 1960s in a no longer existent country adds to this fanciful quality. It was, however, the first film to appropriate a Socialist Realist text.[50]

In using SR movies to signify the past, most directors have been more literal-minded than Makavejev. Andrzej Wajda's 1976 *Man of Marble,* based on a treatment first submitted to the Polish Ministry of Culture in 1962, investigates the creation—and subsequent disappearance—of an imaginary Stakhanovite. Just as, in Alexandrov's operetta, Tanya's shining path led inevitably to the achieved paradise of the All-Union Agricultural Exhibition, so the bricklayer Mateusz Birkut in Wajda's film is launched as a public figure by a propaganda short on the construction of the model city Nowa Huta, the greatest project of postwar Poland's Six-Year Plan— and as such, the subject of novels and songs, the "Pride of the Nation," the "Forge of Our Prosperity." (Wajda credits himself as assistant director on this film within the film, *Architects of Our Happiness,* an adroit combination of vintage and newly shot "documentary" footage.)

Cities such as Nowa Huta, the Hungarian Sztálinváros, and the Czechoslovak Nová Ostrava, can be considered Socialist Realist installations. The largest of these, Nowa Huta was a name to conjure with, literally. (As Anders Åman reports in his history of postwar Eastern Bloc architecture, the two words Nowa Huta were "so pregnant with meaning as to require no expositions. The eight letters . . . carried in monumental format on demonstration marches through Warsaw, were sufficient in themselves.")[51] Birkut's career as a Stakhanovite is short-circuited when, in the midst of a work demonstration, he is tossed a scalding-hot brick—double act of sabotage for being a travesty of one of Poland's most celebrated Socialist Realist paintings, Aleksander Kobzdej's 1950 *Pass Me a Brick!*

Like *Man of Marble,* Márta Mészáros's *Diary for My Children,* finished in 1981 but shelved for several years by the nervous Hungarian authorities, not only integrates bits of cold war newsreel footage—anticipatory documentaries of utopian, which is to say nonexistent, events—but extensively quotes the 1950 Hungarian feature *Life Is Beautiful if You Sing.* Originally advertised as a "film-comedy about our sunny, free, happy life," this account of rival factory choirs—one led by a bourgeois conductor, the other by the workers of the Socialist Brigade—is so relentlessly didactic and enlightened, so worshipful of the machine shop where it is set, and so stolidly enthusiastic about the "New World being built in the name of Stalin" that it approaches Kundera's "collective lyrical delirium."[52]

Given the official suspicion of all theatrical revivals, the resurrection of even one scene from *Life Is Beautiful if You Sing* in the Hungary of the early 1980s signified more than mere *temps perdu.* As noted by the Russian writer Boris Kagarlitsky, "For the classical socialist-realist, a theatrical performance is a play which is read from the stage 'in character.' Campaigns were waged against distortion of classical plays."[53] Under the shared delusion of the SR regime, the model citizen would be expected to embody *partiinost,* to quote current party slogans and invoke official clichés—in all sincerity.

In this context, an even more subversive Hungarian movie of the period is the one known in English as *Singing on the Treadmill,* based on the 1957 Socialist Realist operetta *Bástyasétány 77.* The title is the address of a dilapidated Budapest house that four young couples compete to restore. Director Gyula Gazdag and screenwriter Miklós Györffy set the original situation within an elaborate frame: The operetta is being composed by pair of clownishly bureaucratic librettists, Dezsö and Reszö, for characters who have minds—or at least wills—of their own.

Although Dezsö and Reszö write the script, it would be more accurate to say that they transform than that they create. The film's other characters are born in ditches and carried along on an assembly line to the warehouse where their benefactors work. The bureaucrats urge the couples to trust them: "We promise all your dreams will come true. All we ask is patience and discipline." But try as Dezsö and Reszö might to legislate a happy ending, they are confounded by recalcitrant human nature—compelled to replay ruined scenes, revive suicide victims, and forcibly reorient the couples until even their own confidence is shaken.

The movie's satire of the paternal state is no less self-evident than its conflation of romantic and political illusions—in part because the couples are so blatantly childish. (Like Witold Gombrowicz's 1966 play *Operetta, Singing on the Treadmill* may be said to mix "the monumental idiocy" of its chosen genre with "the monumental pathos of history.")[54] The film climaxes in a burst of operetta madness: A chorus, dressed in a wardrobe room's worth of costumes, dances the rumba while singing an ode to a Mexican volcano. Finally, all four couples are permitted to share the house and, swaying in unison, break into the finale from yet another Hungarian Socialist Realist operetta, *The People's Department Store* of 1949: "Life has become so beautiful, our hearts are filled with joy."

Gazdag was informed that no amount of cutting would make *Singing on the Treadmill* acceptable. By the time the movie was released in 1984, a decade after completion, its provocative use of Stalin-era optimism had already been absorbed by the culture of Hungarian Realist Socialism. In 1976, one of Gazdag's associates at the Csiky Gergely Theater in

Kaposvár staged *The People's Department Store,* replicating as closely as possible the costumes, props, and acting style of the early 1950s. When Gazdag proposed a production of a Soviet operetta from the same period, however, permission was refused.[55]

"Irony is the faithful companion of unbelief and doubt; it vanishes as soon as there appears a faith that does not tolerate sacrilege," wrote Andrei Sinyavsky in his pseudonymous *On Socialist Realism.* Under the regime of Socialist Realism (a serious modernism, after all), "irony was replaced by pathos, the emotional element of the positive hero."[56]

But once Socialist Realism was "post-," its icons could be read only as ironic—as well as pathetic. In 1971, the same year that *WR* won the Luis Buñuel prize at the Cannes Film Festival, Eric Bulatov, a Russian artist of the same generation as Makavejev and Mészáros, began to paint what might have seemed an eccentric Soviet version of Western photo-realism—uninflected images of ordinary vistas, rendered spatially ambiguous by imbedded or superimposed political symbols. In *Red Horizon* (1971–72), a brilliant crimson and gold band bisects a beachscape where the sea would otherwise meet the sky. Is it a Suprematist intervention, a mechanical sunrise, or, as Boris Groys points out, the ribbon of the Order of Lenin?

Other canvases of the period exploit the tension between material and representation by imposing the flatness of a political slogan or placard on a naturalistic rendering of three-dimensional space: Bulatov's *Krassikov Street* (1976), for instance, replaces the black or white square that might have charged a Kasimir Malevich composition with a billboard of Lenin. German critic Claudia Jolles has characterized Bulatov's interest as the "energy" behind the painted scene: That "the visible world is little more than a momentary disturbance in the light radiating from the picture" puts Bulatov closer to icon painting (or to Suprematism) than to pop art.[57]

Bulatov's apparent photo-realism seems a form of Social Realism redux. Yet by simply framing his social reality, he subverted it. The red letters of *Welcome* (1973–74) emblazon a Cinerama-shaped canvas showing the Friendship of Nations fountain at the All-Union Agricultural Exhibition. (Bulatov here anticipates the cult of the exhibition that developed among unofficial artists during the mid-1970s.) In *Glory to the Communist Party of the Soviet Union* (1975), the words of the title—

again red and even larger than in *Welcome*—are set against a postcard-perfect blue sky. How could one explain such deadpan overenthusiasm to the cultural apparatchiks of the Brezhnev era?

Soviet Cosmos (1977) suggests a comically bungled obsequiousness. An imposingly decorated Leonid Brezhnev is ridiculously overshadowed by an immense red and gold halo of hammer-and-sickle flags. Here, the simple representation of the icon is itself iconoclastic. This is why Bulatov was bracketed with Sots Art—"Sots" being short for "socialist"—the term coined in 1972 by two younger artists, Vitaly Komar and Alexander Melamid, and subsequently adopted by the painter Alexander Kosolapov and the sculptor Leonid Sokov, their former classmates at Moscow's Stroganov Art Institute. Early work created under the Sots Art rubric ranged from Sokov's paternal wooden mobile *Threatening Finger* (1975), to Kosolapov's crudely surreal juxtaposition of ballerinas, cosmonauts, and monuments under the title *Soviet Myth* (1974), to Komar and Melamid's portraits of patriotic cigarette packs and their red pennants inscribed in gold with standard agitprop exhortations such as "Onward to the Victory of Communism," made extraordinary only by the addition of the artists' names in the lower right-hand corners. (The January 1978 issue of *Artforum* noted that one of these red banners was "one of the only works in Komar's and Melamid's recent exhibition not sold.")[58]

Just as Komar and Melamid equated their pennants with Andy Warhol's Brillo boxes, more than a few European critics present at the 1964 Venice Biennial, won by Robert Rauschenberg, had equated pop art with Socialist Realism. Virtually all the themes in something like Mikhhail Khmelko's *Greeting to the First Cosmonaut, Yuri Gagarin, on His Return to Earth* (1957)—national leaders, space travel, abundant produce, festive flags—can be found, *mutatis mutandis,* in Rauschenberg's *Retroactive I* (1964). Others saw a useful analogy between Socialist Realism and the "capitalist realism" of Madison Avenue. From the perspective of Russian artists, such equivalences provided artists with both a means to subvert Communist pretensions and a point of entry into American culture.

The combining of Soviet and American icons anticipated by Makavejev in *WR* and, several years later, by the Czech expatriate Milan Kunc became the most persistent Sots Art strategy, ranging from Kosolapov's trademark juxtapositions of Lenin and Coca-Cola to Sokov's *Meeting of Two Sculptures* (1987), in which a monumental plaster Lenin shakes hands with a spindly faux Alberto Giacometti figure. Farther afield, the Chinese painter Wang Guangyi's "Great Denunciation Series" emblazoned images of heroic worker-peasants with corporate logos from companies such as Kodak and Maxwell House.[59]

Once provocative, the device has since become commonplace. A T-shirt widely sold in West Berlin after November 1989 conflated the year's two superheroes: The then Soviet leader clad in purple tights, towering over the rubble of the Berlin Wall and the acrostic logo:

GorBATshow
MAN

Within a year of (re)unification, the decomposed ideological landscape of the former East Germany abounded with such inadvertent or vulgar Sots Art juxtapositions, ranging from the flashing Coca-Cola sign presiding over the Berlin boulevard still called Karl-Marx Allee to the posters showing an outsized portrait of Stalin being garlanded by an adoring trio of Young Pioneers, reprinted from 1952 and sold in the lobby of the Deutsches Historisches Museum. By the mid-1990s, the All-Union Agricultural Exhibition had itself become a monumental piece of Sots Art. where, as one observer noted, beneath the engraved words of the Stalin-era national anthem children sat entranced by the video projection of old Tom and Jerry cartoons, while the public address system broadcast advertisements for Mercedes Benz, Ford, and Panasonic products.[60]

Describing the exhibition as Russia's equivalent to the Mall of America, the *New York Times* reported:

> At the cavernous pavilion formerly dedicated to space exploration, late-model Cadillacs and Lincolns are on display under a frayed banner that reads, "Power to the Heroes of Soviet Labor!" Outside, a Soviet-made airplane that was once an object of reverential admiration has been transformed into a video store.
>
> Many pavilions are guarded by oversize statues of muscular laborers and peasants, weeds now sprouting from beneath their feet. In what was once the Pavilion of Agronomy, fading murals depicting an idealized wheat harvest loom over stalls where cameras, leather jackets, skis and Oriental rugs are sold.[61]

In New York, the late days of perestroika and the first flushed excitement of Soviet Communism's collapse brought department-store advertisements for Bolshevik blue jeans and facsimiles of revolutionary porcelain design. (Can we imagine these goods on sale at the People's Department Store?) All that remains is the integration of an exemplary Socialist Realist painting into the permanent collection of the Museum of Modern Art.

After all, the museum has already acquired Komar and Melamid's 1982 *I Saw Stalin When I Was a Child*. But a follow-up purchase would, of course, assume a postmodern revaluation of what a museum of modern art actually is.

KITSCH IN REVERSE

The once-canonical essay "Avant-Garde and Kitsch," originally published in autumn of 1939 as Clement Greenberg's first contribution to the then-Trotskyist *Partisan Review,* attacked Stalinist kitsch—turning to true socialism for the "preservation" of modern art.

On the eve of World War II, as Harold Rosenberg would recall, modernism itself seemed a period style. It was "to all appearances part of the past, suppressed by force in Moscow, Berlin, Rome, silenced in Paris by the conflict between the political right and left." The aesthetic avant-garde had been superceded by another historical vanguard: "A spectator in New York was looking *back* to modern art; new as they seemed, the exhibits at the Museum of Modern Art belonged to art movements that were already extinct."[62] This putative obsolescence was linked to the rise of Stalin, Hitler, and Mussolini, dictators who took it upon themselves to remake the world.

Existing modernism appeared to erode, then, in the face of this supermodernism, and at precisely the moment when art was taken most seriously—or at least, deemed too important to be left to the artist. (Surrealism anticipated this development by characterizing itself as a form of scientific research.) Some forty years later, Sots Art may have seemed to constitute a belated response, one that could be easily drafted into ideological combat as the adversary of Soviet totalitarian culture. It is suggestive that the golden age of New York Sots—beginning in the spring of 1982 with the Kazimir Passion Group performance *Communist Congress,* at the experimental art center P.S. 1; followed by Komar and Melamid's "Sots Art" exhibit at the Ronald Feldman Gallery; and climaxing four years later with the Sots Art show organized by Margarita Tupitsyn at the New Museum of Contemporary Art—coincided exactly with the height of Reaganism, Rabo, and the "evil empire"; the celebration of 1984; the revival of Hollywood anti-Communism and cold war jitters. (Since then, Bulatov's 1989 *Perestroika*—a phalanx of block letters against an El Greco sky, with two hands in the foreground holding aloft an interlocked hammer and sickle—has proven the road sign for an aesthetic dead end.)

As early as 1979, however, Jack Burnham expressed concern for "the artistic future of Komar and Melamed if they [were] deprived of the abrasion and suppression of Soviet dogma."[63] But was that deprivation ever really the question? There is a moment in *Singing on the Treadmill* at which the various schemes, squabbles, and mutual denunciations of the four couples vying for possession of the dilapidated house threaten the Dezsö/Rezsö regime with chaos. At this point the Eternal Goddess of the Operetta graciously appears and restores order by crooning a notorious Stalin-era lullaby: "A better world is being born for you, thousands of working hands watch over your dreams."

The gross, pitiful yearning of this state-sanctioned, scientifically designed, politically correct nursery song is another legacy of Stalinism: For Gyula Gazdag, as for the Kazimir Passion Group and for Komar and Melamid (who, in their 1982–83 *Double Self-Portrait as Young Pioneers*, paint themselves as mustached eight-year-olds ambiguously razzing or saluting a bust of Stalin), Socialist Realism is associated with childhood. Who can gauge the impact on an impressionable fourth-grader of something like the 1953 Hungarian spectacular *Young at Heart*? The movie is a color vision of total mobilization, set in an immaculate vocational training school—at once drably institutional and eerily palatial—where uniformed teachers engage in all manner of mass parades, calisthenics, and hootenannies. At the climax, a shiny-eyed ten-year-old is placed in charge of production: "Join us comrades! Become an iron worker and life will be even more beautiful!"

As if that were possible. Small wonder that in pronouncing Socialist Realism to be among the "best" of all art movements, Komar and Melamid declared themselves not a parody of SR but rather its continuation. They clearly took (or perhaps, mistook) the second reality for usable culture. Their paintings *The Birth of Socialist Realism* and *Stalin and the Muses* make explicit that which is already present in *Kirov at the Sports Palace*. Even Bulatov's *Brezhnev in the Crimea* (1981–85) might seem like a petrified Magritte were it not so obviously modeled on Feodor Shurpin's no less opalescent *Morning of Our Motherland*. If Socialist Realism is kitsch, then Sots Art must then be kitsch in reverse.[64]

"The precondition for kitsch," Greenberg insisted, "is the availability close at hand of a fully matured cultural tradition, whose discoveries, acquisitions, and perfected self-consciousness kitsch can take advantage of for its own ends. It borrows from it devices, tricks, stratagems, rules of thumb, themes, converts them into a system, and discards the rest. It draws its life blood, so to speak, from this reservoir of accumulated experience."[65] This, of course, was the Sots Art program—even if the mature cultural tradition at hand was not the one Greenberg had in mind.

Addressing the World Economic Forum in February 1992, scarcely a year after the Soviet Union dissolved, Václav Havel, then president of the former Czechoslovakia, linked the end of Communism to the failure of master narratives and universal theories, to the death of the idea that the world was ultimately knowable and that such knowledge could be generalized, to rejecting the notions of scientific progress and the primacy of reason—in short, to the passing of the modern age.[66] (At that very moment in Prague, stores were selling a record mixing Communist hymns, among them a disco version of the "Internationale," with the chants of Romania's anti-Ceauşescu demonstrations, the soundtracks of Social Realist movies, the theme from *The Good, the Bad, and the Ugly,* and phrases looped from the radio speeches of Stalin-era party hacks.)

The post-Soviet fascination with Socialist Realism acknowledges that Communism itself was an aesthetic project—perhaps *the* aesthetic project of the twentieth century. Kundera has spoken of the spell cast by Marx's idea that the human era consists of two parts: the prehistoric realm of necessity and the true history that begins—with the proletarian revolution—when humankind becomes master of its destiny. It is this sublime Promethean image, promising complete liberation from all tradition, that served as a beacon for the artistic and political avant-gardes.

The greatest aesthetic project; the most abject, ridiculous, heartbreaking defeat: Marxism, Kundera writes, was "the grandiose attempt to explain the world in terms of total rationality. Having failed, it picked up a lyre and descended into the irrational, just as Orpheus did. . . . A single stanza of this poetry has hypnotized our entire era."[67] The frozen music of its photographed dreams is what passes for Socialist Realism.

CHAPTER 2

Realist Socialism:

Documenting the

Undocumentable

I am obliged to transpose the following statements to the past tense.

Socialism [was] a superior society. This [was] no empty slogan. Artists [knew] what it [meant]. . . . Socialism [needed]
the arts. The state apparatus, the economy, and those in
power [needed] the arts. The socialist state [had] promised to
attend to all basic human needs in order to ensure the loyalty
of the society it [governed]. If, under capitalism, art [was] a
kind of costly adornment, under socialism, art [was] an essential garment.

So wrote the Hungarian dissident Miklós Haraszti.[1]

Between 1979 and 1987, I visited Hungary five times as a journalist, usually in conjuncton with the
National Film Week. Totally susidized by the political system that it (strategically) criticized, the local
film culture was characterized by a unique mixture of idealism and cynicism, as well as a sensibility
I associated less with Hollywood than with certain New York City neighborhoods. This account is
largely drawn from reports published in *American Film, Film Comment*, and the *Village Voice*, as
well as from program and catalog notes prepared for retrospectives devoted to Gyula Gazdag,
György Szomjas, and the experimental Béla Balász Studio.

In neighboring, normalized Czechoslovakia, the raiments of art were still fused with life:

Existing socialism [required], above all, that the appearance of order should reign in the media. . . . The mass media [dressed] up domestic social problems and complex global issues in a sort of uniform by which they [were] easily recognizable.

Everything [was] made to sound trivial and cheerful. . . . These absurdities [were] the most evident sign of order in existing socialism.[2]

And similarly, in People's Poland, the media dutifully constructed a second reality:

There was virtually no crime, and no preventable accidents, no alcoholism, no serious or contagious disease. The cities and countryside were clean and well-maintained. There was no pollution. Factory and farm workers worked happily for good wages under ideal conditions. Women workers had no difficulty holding down a job and caring for families at the same time. Food and consumer goods were plentiful at uninflated prices whenever and wherever they were needed. No one, including political leaders and celebrities, lived better than anyone else. Sportsmen were model citizens. The young were well educated. Families were well provided for; the elderly, adequately cared for.

This "joyous haven" was truly a collective enterprise:

Unconsciously, journalists were their own censors. The majority had been dealing with censors since the Stalinist period. They simply ceased to think in terms of writing critically of the Soviet Union, proposing alternatives to the Polish way of socialism or revealing details of leaders' lives and internal party debates. Even if they had information it seldom occurred to them to even try to use it.[3]

A contradiction, then, between art-recognized-as-art and art-pretending-to-be-life? As another Hungarian intellectual put it, "When your fancies touch barbed wire, the bloodhounds that protect you from yourself begin to bark."[4]

It was after 1956 that, for the first time in thirty years, an anti-Stalinist Communism became possible—or rather, became possible as a possibility.

A time of unbridled revolutionary energy surpassing even the fetishized 1968, 1956 brought the revelations of the Twentieth Party Congress that February in Moscow: Khrushchev's denunciation of Stalin's crimes. Back in the United States, 1956 saw unprecedented African American militancy and youth culture run wild—the bus boycott in Montgomery, Elvis Presley on television, weird doings in San Francisco ("I saw the best minds of my generation . . . ").

For Americans, the revolution of 1956 reached its climax in November. As Dwight Eisenhower coasted toward reelection, *Time* reported that "TV last week hysterically joined the weird posthumous cult of James Dean" by rebroadcasting three undistinguished teledramas in which Dean had played minor parts. The magazine quoted one unnamed executive: "He's hotter than anybody alive."[5]

November 1956 was also the month of the doomed but glorious Hungarian Revolution. Suddenly, the American ideological apparatus turned cheerleader. *Time*'s Man of the Year was a long-haired youth—a crazy, mixed-up kid—with a gun, the perfect sublimation of wild man Elvis and the onslaught of juvenile delinquency that had succeeded Communism as the great internal threat. He was called Freedom Fighter.[6]

Bloody trauma of 1956: Russian tanks crush the legitimate aspirations of Hungarian people, liquidate the modest illusions of the past February—but also, after a time, create conditions for the most modest and humane form of really existing socialism in the Soviet bloc. "People do not exist so that we may test Marxism on them"—or so the Soviet-installed Hungarian leader János Kádár eventually explained.[7]

Kádár was resigned in the knowledge that the pacifying presence of the Red Army was the only reason that such a Marxism existed in Hungary at all. A lifelong Communist imprisoned, even tortured, by his own party at the height of the 1948–53 proletariat consolidation, after having been enlisted by the leadership to secure the false confession of his friend Lászlo Rajk, Kádár was once again recruited—this time by the Russians—to betray his reformist comrades.

Kádár's precursor, Mátyás Rákosi, presided over Eastern Europe's model Stalinist police state—a regimented, Soviet-devoted fairyland of political terror and torture-cell make-believe. But what manner of Communist was Kádár? How did he maintain his faith? Was he the ultimate cynic? A guilt-consumed Macbeth? The hapless agent of a concealed and unnameable power? In any case, Kádárism was a Realist Socialism—strategically depoliticized and founded on the nation's passive acquiescence.

At the very end of 1961, just past the fifth anniversary of the Soviet invasion that installed his regime, Kádár reversed the belligerently paranoid Rákosi-era slogan to declare that "those who are not against us are with us."[8] Finally, in the first month of 1968, after eleven years of rule and two years of careful preparation, cautious Kádár introduced his reform program. The New Economic Mechanism (NEM) was based on market pricing and decentralized planning, introducing the concepts of investment, productivity, and competition. But, cursed Hungarian fate, the heady events in Czechoslovakia overtook this gradualism. Kádár sympathized with Alexander Dubček's humanist socialism, but having collaborated with a previous Russian invasion, the Hungarian realistically argued that the Czech reforms would have to be limited to forestall Soviet intervention—and thus allow him time to legitimize the NEM.[9]

Some say that Kádár's personal popularity was enhanced by the Warsaw Pact's August occupation of Czechoslovakia. At the very least, he had contrived to provide only minimal Hungarian participation, successfully stalling for weeks before expressing his own unenthusiastic acquiescence to the state of affairs. (In the parlance of the day, the party distanced itself from itself.) Czechoslovakia was plunged into the so-called normalization, but like a flickering phantom of the Prague Spring, the Hungarian NEM remained in effect for nearly another four years, until snuffed by major economic difficulties with the Soviet Union.[10]

It was during the period of Kádár's patronage that Hungarian filmmakers came to take a leading role in interpreting their nation's often tortuous history and illuminating the contradictions of its present condition. "In Hungary, or at least in Hungarian culture, film nowadays plays the role of the avant-garde," Georg Lukács told the editor of the Hungarian journal *Filmkultúra* in the course of a celebrated interview held in his shabby, book-crammed Budapest apartment during the glorious May 1968.[11]

Lukács had been particularly impressed by Miklós Jancsó's 1965 release *The Round-Up*. A ceremonially cruel allegory, *The Round-Up* is set in the 1860s, twenty years after Lajos Kossuth's failed revolution, when remnants of his Hungarian army still roamed the countryside and Austrian soldiers detained entire villages to uncover the partisans concealed among them. The film concerns one such mass arrest and the inevitable ensuing round of interrogations and betrayals. Most of the often cryptic action is confined to a wooden fort, the gingerbread concentration camp on a vast plain where Austrian automatons in operetta uniforms play endless cat-and-mouse games with the exotic, impassive peasantry they've corralled.

A laconic succession of fluid takes and elegant compositions that isolate tiny figures in the windswept nothingness of the flat Hungarian *puszta* (central plain), *The Round-Up* synthesized all that Lukács repressed. One could find here the "decadent modernism" of Franz Kafka, Samuel Beckett, Eugène Ionesco, and Michelangelo Antonioni—but even more intriguingly, an imaginative representation of the circumstances under which the philosopher had lived his life. And then, there was the unmistakable (but also unspeakable) evocation of the unrepresentable 1956.

The Round-Up's Hungarian title may be translated as "hooligans," the official term for those whom *Time* had dubbed freedom fighters. And as these captive losers are imprisoned in open space, so the movie maps a particular state of being: "Do you accept this condition?" "Well sir, I must."

If movies suggest how a nation might imagine itself to be, documentaries assume the responsibility of showing things as they really are—or at least, of pretending to do so.

Given the nature of Kádár's Realist Socialism, the documentary film would necessarily occupy a privileged position—if it was to play any role at all. Socialist Realism conjured up that which was acknowledged but did not yet exist. No less paradoxical, Realist Socialism sought to reveal that which existed but could not be acknowledged. Thus, an agnostic icon, the Realist Socialist (RS) documentary was ultimately concerned with representing the ineffable.[12]

The RS documentary was nurtured by the experimental Béla Balász Studio (BBS), named for the pioneer Hungarian film theorist who died in 1949. The studio was established in the still-bleak year of 1958 as a sort of halfway house, allowing recent graduates of the Hungarian film academy an opportunity to hone their skills and develop their ideas before entering the presumably ever-expanding culture factory. One of the more remarkable film institutions to exist anywhere in the world throughout the 1960s, 1970s, and 1980s, this unique agency served first as a training ground for young filmmakers, then as the bastion of a documentary avant-garde, and finally as an equipment collective cum funding agency for a tenacious underground of amateur filmmakers, as well as painters, musicians, and other artists with an interest in cinema.

The earliest BBS productions were mainly short and poetic—although a few had significant impact on Hungarian film culture. Sándor Sára's 1962 documentary short *Gypsies* made a daring departure from the informational films of the 1950s. After centuries of oppression, Hungarian Gypsies articulated their situation in their own words, decrying the threat to their traditional culture posed by insensitive bureaucrats. Thus, as a designated victim class spoke for all society, so Kádárism might allow for the sanctioned expression of unofficial opinions—even suggesting the tantalizing possibility of representing an alternative to the social order that, in fact, underwrote it.[13]

"Artistic alienation is sublimation," Herbert Marcuse declared the same year. "It creates the images of conditions which are irreconcilable with the established Reality Principle but which, as cultural images, become tolerable, even edifying and useful." Did Kádárism, then, propose a form of socialist "repressive desublimation," extending artistic liberty the better to intensify political domination?[14]

Winning prizes at both Hungarian and East German film festivals, *Gypsies* proved a harbinger of the Hungarian film renaissance. For some, that rebirth was embodied by András Kovács's feature-length documentary *Difficult People,* released in 1964. Inspired by the Jean Rouch films he had seen on a study trip to Paris, Kovács sought out and interviewed five Hungarian inventors whose innovations, even when patented and praised, were stymied by bureaucratic ineptitude or professional jealousy. "It was," according to Czech critics Antonin and Mira Liehm, "the first time in years that a Hungarian film expressed ideas and attitudes about cowardice and hypocrisy, tearing down the painted curtains before which rosy *csardas* princesses had for decades been performing their divertive dances."[15]

That the filmmaker was himself an apparatchik, having been the chief of the Budapest Film Studio's script department from the cold war depths of 1951 through the postrevolutionary second consolidation of 1957, only gave the film further sanction. *Difficult People* was awarded the Hungarian Critics Prize for 1965 and attracted attention abroad—particularly in France where Louis Marcorelle, the champion of *cinema verité,* called it "the frankest and most 'direct' film [ever] made in a socialist country."[16]

High praise; but despite this critical success, Kovács's follow-up documentary—another interview with a frustrated innovator, in this case a self-proclaimed "revolutionary" architect—was never completed. As far as documentaries were concerned, the leading role reverted to the younger filmmakers at BBS.[17]

As the first generation of BBS directors (including Judit Elek, Pál Gábor, Zsolt Kézdi-Kovács, and István Szabó) entered the mainstream of the revitalized Hungarian film industry, the studio became more programmatic in its goals. In the spring of 1969, some seventeen months into Kádár's reform economy, BBS announced a new policy—its manifesto published in *Filmkultúra* exactly a year after the Lukács interview—centering on the production of so-called sociological documentaries.[18]

As official culture now produced an officially critical avant-garde, the worker's state incubated its own revolutionary opposition. However, the sociological documentary did not constitute a dissidence. The BBS's rarefied critiques were pushed toward the center of the Hungarian political spectrum for being produced in the context of the Hungarian student New Left—largely the offspring of the Rákosi-era party faithful and even some Kádárist officials.

Imagine the disorienting strangeness of growing up in an embittered Stalinist family—perpetrators or victims?—in a make-believe Communist state! There was the subject for a never-to-be-made BBS documentary. Born into the utopia of achieved socialism and thus programmatically more militant than their parents, these ultrared Red Diaper babies included Gábor Révai (son of Rákosi's culture czar); Anna Szilágyi (daughter of the current vice minister of culture) and her husband, György "Bambino" Pór, as well as the young poet Miklós Haraszti.[19]

This Maoist group attracted police attention by engaging in activities that might be considered a form of Communist performance art. Pamphlets denouncing Kádár's "frigidaire socialism," the rise of a red bourgeoisie, and the Soviet Union were planted between the pages of library books. One member of the Maoist group, traveling on a student visa to the Soviet Union, even managed to seek out and interview the disgraced Rákosi in his Kazakhstan retirement. Pór established illegal contacts not only with China but, thanks to a cadre of hard-line Greek Stalinists living in Hungary, even with Albania. The climax came in the spring of 1968, when some fifty of the Maoists were arrested and put on trial for their conspiracy to build a "true Communist Party." Neither the privileged Révai nor Szilágyi was prosecuted, although Pór was sent to prison.[20]

Intentionally or not, aspects of the Hungarian New Left were reflected in Jancsó's 1969 feature *The Confrontation*—which restaged events from an earlier period of youthful militance with performers wearing blue jeans and miniskirts. The BBS produced its own equivalent, joining the student Maoists as the only groups to mark the fiftieth anniversary of Béla Kun's short-lived Council Republic. In the spring of 1969, a group of BBS members produced *Agitators* (the studio's first feature), adapted by Gábor Bódy from Erwin Sinkó's novel of the 1919 Hungarian Revolution, *The Optimists.*

The clash between groups of voluntary and official propagandists—and their debate on class division under communism—had obvious parallels to the current situation, and the filmmakers clearly enjoyed themselves. running around in leather trench coats toting prop carbines. The anachronistic dialogue included quotations from Mao Zedong and Che Guevara. The wildly posturing cast included László Földes, who later established himself as an indigenous rock star with the Hobo Blues Band (Hungary's onetime answer to the Rolling Stones); Gábor Révai provocatively played his own father, who had been Béla Kun's secretary.[21]

Further inbred culture and generational conflict of Communist Hungary: Documentary filmmaker Pál Schiffer was the grandson of Árpád Szakasits (the Social Democrat politician who merged his party's left wing with the Communist Party in March 1948 to form the Hungarian Workers Party). Schiffer came to BBS with six years of experience at Mafilm's documentary studio and thus a greater awareness than his predecessors of the nonfiction film's historical development. The very title—not to mention the subject matter—of his 1969 *Black Train* recalls the Polish "black series" of the mid-1950s, so called to distinguish them from the rosy-hued films produced during the period of unbridled Stalinism. The black films focused on housing problems, juvenile delinquency, the destitution of rural life, and the situation of urban workers, and when these themes were explored in Hungary, Czechoslovakia, Yugoslavia, and Poland again during the 1960s, the same term was used.

Black Train portrays the impoverished workers brought to work in Budapest from Hungary's poorest region—Szabolcs-Szatmár County, on the northeast border. Like *Difficult People,* the film consists largely of interviews. But because most of these are given either in the station or on the train (where every inch is seemingly jammed with hard-drinking workers and Gypsy violinists), *Black Train* conveys a pungent, vomit-on-the-window quality of lumpen proletarian disorder—underscored by Schiffer's ultraverité, mike-in-frame style. "This tavern is my mistress. I've got a right to do this, don't you agree?" one worker tells the camera with boozed-up sincerity.

Even working for the BBS, the filmmakers represent authority. The subjects ask the camera operator to add more trains or offer Schiffer a fraternal swig from their bottles. When Schiffer and his crew arrive in Szabolcs, however, they are greeted with something less than open arms. "But your husband invited us," the filmmaker explains to one irate mother of six. "Perhaps he was out of his mind," she snaps, slamming shut the hovel door in the film's key moment of revolt. Comparable in its stark poetry to Walker Evans's exposé of rural poverty in the American South, *Black Train* is loaded with unresolved social problems, ranging from alcoholism and broken families to chronic underemployment and state exploitation of a powerless underclass. The film is a portrait of people so beaten down they can't even imagine anything better. Asked about his Lenin poster, a young gypsy explains that the Soviet leader "was the first idea of this thing, this, er, . . . developing world thing."[22]

A prizewinner at the 1971 Pesaro Film Festival, *Black Train* received the ultimate badge of honor when it was compelled to wait another three years before it could be shown publicly in Hungary. By then, the sociological documentary movement was virtually over.

The most original of the BBS documentarians, Gyula Gazdag attracted attention with his 1968 short *The Long-Distance Runner,* a drily comic portrait of a Hungarian athlete who demonstrated his dedication to the socialist ideal by jogging all the way from Budapest to Moscow. (The film title's literal translation is "We can always count on your long-distance running.") With *The Long-Distance Runner*'s deadpan portrait of a somewhat ridiculous national hero, the twenty-one-year-old Gazdag emerged as a significant presence on the cultural scene—and subsequently, with his 1971 *The Whistling Cobblestone,* became the youngest Hungarian director to make a dramatic feature.[23]

Albeit only a fifteen-minute diploma film, *The Long-Distance Runner* proved among the most influential Hungarian movies of the 1960s. György Schirilla, the film's eponymous subject, was a Budapest cabdriver and amateur athlete, famous for taking an annual, eventually televised bath in the icy Danube as well as for several marathon runs. Here, Schirilla revisits the town of Kenderes, where one year earlier he had stopped—en route to Moscow—to request a glass of strawberry juice.

For the town fathers, Schirilla's visit is a great occasion. Just as the workers on the Black Train understand the camera crew as, above all else, authorized, so the villagers take Schirilla as a manifestation of power. As the critic György Báron has observed, "Schirilla is a well-known personality, someone shown on TV, spoken about on the radio: he comes running from the 'circle' where people who make decisions sit. And from this aspect it does not really matter whether the person concerned is a famous TV commentator, humorist, pop singer or a chief executive of public standing." The grandiose rhetoric fuels the comedy: "Swelling with pride, the local notables receive their great guest as though he were the king arriving to celebrate the nation's millennium. 'This is an exceptional event in the life of our country' are the words of the local council chairman. Schirilla also uses words appropriate to the occasion: he is engaged 'with the concept of overcoming great distances.'"[24]

To commemorate Schirilla's pause for refreshment, the town council has resolved to name a restaurant for him. But because Kádárist law—sensitive to the cult of personality and devoted to the naturalization of power—forbids the naming of institutions after living persons, the Sport Bistro must be content to feature only Schirilla's picture. The villagers are not alone in their disappointment. Schirilla afterward complains of the drab ceremony—he is used to being greeted by larger crowds.

Released theatrically during the summer of 1969 as a short subject along with Livia Gyarmathy's Czech-style comedy *Do You Know Sunday-Monday?*, *The Long-Distance Runner* made Gazdag's precocious reputation while inspiring the BBS new wave of so-called sociological documentaries. Gazdag maintains that he was nonplussed:

> I didn't want to make documentaries. I was the youngest student in my class and I wasn't important at all—I felt like a young boy among all the grown-ups. I couldn't understand why this Schirilla film was such a success. For me it was natural to shoot the film this way. But among the others it started a new mood. Still, I didn't really want to make documentaries, I thought that this was an interesting event and I made a documentary but I wanted to make feature films. And then came another interesting event and I made another documentary.[25]

That film was *Selection*. Here, Gazdag turned his camera on a process rich with the material of its own contradictions—namely, the means by which a Budapest oil refinery's Communist Youth Organization (KISZ) chapter decided on a rock 'n' roll group to sponsor. Among other things, *Selection* is testament to the power of then "unofficial" culture. Although KISZ made it clear that musicians would not be paid, some ninety-five bands answered their radio advertisement—which also inspired the film. (This unofficial Hungarian youth culture must be distinguished from the Maoists, who had accused the party of promoting pop music as an agent of depoliticization. Dissociating themselves from most Hungarian rock 'n' roll, the New Left supported a form of Old Left protest singing, as exemplified by the Guerrillas and their so-called Pol-Beat.)

Shot in February 1970, *Selection* shows the influence of two earlier examples of Realist Socialist documentary satire—Milos Forman's *Competition* (Czechoslovakia, 1961–63) and Dusan Makavejev's *Parade* (Yugoslavia, 1963), both of which deal with the issue of power. *Competition*, which Forman produced as an independent 16mm filmmaker, is a *cinema verité* practical joke. The neophyte director was fascinated by open auditions at the Semafor pop-music cabaret: "I couldn't believe the power of the microphone over the girls. They stepped up to it as if it were a magic wand that would endow them with a great voice and beauty. This foot of fat wire got homely young women to vamp shamelessly, tone-deaf singers to wail away at the top of their voices, shy neurotics to put themselves through the torture of public scrutiny. There were moments when the spectacle of the audition became tough to watch."[26]

Having secured the backing of the Barrandov Studio, Forman announced a bogus tryout for a job of female singer at a popular Prague nightclub, then documented the mob of innocent, aggressive, and untalented aspirants who appeared to audition. Not quite *cinema verité*, the film has a simple narrative. One shop girl bombs; another young woman—the future star Véra Kesadlová—watches the proceedings in dismay, then runs away, although she would likely have been given the position. Her integrity underscores the film's fundamental deception.[27]

More straightforward and less sadistic, *Parade* resulted from an assignment to document the quasi-religious spectacle that would be Belgrade's annual May Day festivities. Instead of filming the spectacle, Makavejev humanized the event—concentrating on the preparations and backstage politics with such deadpan sarcasm, abetted by the choice of overenthusiastic background music, that Yugoslav officials reportedly opted for less ostentatious rituals in subsequent years.

A fascinating essay on behavioral tics, applied power, and free-floating anxiety, *Selection* has been called a film about the "terror of false ardor."[28] It soon becomes obvious that KISZ has no interest in rock music per se; their real concern is regulating the leisure time of young workers. Scarcely does the film open before the exuberant KISZ chairman confesses that he attends dances only as part of his job. The film abounds with suggestive, found metaphors: The chairman, who is thirty-five and first appears posed before a portrait of Lenin, turns out to have been a member of KISZ since the consolidation year of 1957.

Made after twenty years of Communist rule, exploring the relationship between music and work, *Selection* suggests a Kádárist remake of Márton Keleti's *Life Is Beautiful if You Sing*—a 1950 Socialist Realist meditation on the importance of music as a means of organizing proletarian leisure. "There was a time when we saw reality not as it was but as we would have liked it," Kádár once said.[29] So it is with *Life Is Beautiful if You Sing*—set as it is in an insanely cheerful machine works. Not only does the entire factory seem to live, sitcom style, in the same apartment building, but all belong to the Silver Lyre factory choir. As the chorus is a metaphor for the nation, so the conductor is a leader—although, as indicated by his preferred term of address (*colleagues* rather than *comrades*), Dr. Réz is a supercilious bourgeois individualist.

When, inspired by the spectacle of marching soldiers, the Silver Lyre democratically decides to try a new harmony, Dr. Réz rejects their optimism, ordering them to sing instead a lugubrious dirge: "We are starving, we are suffering." What reaction can possibly equal the watching positive hero's enlightened amazement at this disgusting performance? Half the Silver Lyre quits to form a New Voice chorus, their places taken by riffraff dressed in the plaid-on-plaid zoot suits of the so-called American fashion. The most absurd of these frenzied jitterbuggers cum saboteurs is a youth named Swing Toni.

Meanwhile, the positive hero leads the New Voice chorus to glory. The music swells like a revelation when he picks up a copy of Zhdanov—he's moved by his own clichés, and so is everyone else. (Because this is a Socialist Realist movie, expressions change in unison.) The iconic statues loom larger with each successive cut as the New Voice extolls the "New World being built in the name of Stalin."

The Silver Lyre is still droning hopelessly on, even as the New Voice inspires a montage of mass enthusiasm: "Singing makes life beautiful—and it's going to be more and more joyful. . . . We are constructing a new world, singing." How to inspire the same proletarian sentiments in 1970? Although the KISZ chapter's desire to sponsor a band is purely pragmatic, its standards are insufficiently cynical (and inherently self-defeating), being predicated on ideological purity rather than on musical talent or audience approval. Confronting this dilemma, Communism can't help but reveal an all-too-human face. Should the rockers appeal only to the young or to all the workers? Should they be able to play Hungarian songs as well as Western rock 'n' roll? Moreover, KISZ is haunted by the specter of Swing Toni: How can they ensure the band won't attract a bad element?

At once indulgent and puritanical, naive and manipulative, the KISZ committee warns all applicants that they cannot expect to receive money for their equipment, cautions them against wearing "hippie crucifixes," suggests they be prepared to perform in uniform—even if only blue jeans and identically colored shirts—and inquires after their marital status ("The KISZ committee cannot tolerate groupies"). Sensing the rules by which the game is being played, several of the musicians make hilariously mealy-mouthed suggestions, offering, for example, to provide literary evenings as well as dance music. Or is it possible? Can they really be sincere?[30]

The climactic audition, a battle of five politically correct bands, has one off-key group after another performing the same lugubrious song for the stern-faced KISZ committee and a meager, expressionless rank-and-file audience. At last, KISZ makes its decision, choosing the Pumps, a group managed by the mother of one of its members (and thus ensured of parental guidance). As the movie ends, Gazdag reprises the band's winning performance. Incredibly, the words are so doleful as to be a lament too gloomy for the Silver Lyre:

> All day I waste my time feeling sorry for myself.
> No one is with me who matters, no one is with me.
> Everyone is against me.

Despite the success of *The Long-Distance Runner*, *Selection* had no theatrical release—it was shown only in film clubs.[31]

Selection served as a warm-up for *The Resolution* (1972), the feature-length documentary that Gazdag and Judit Ember directed at BBS two years later. Considered by some critics to be the most important Hungarian documentary of the Communist era, *The Resolution* and the Polish newsreel *Workers '80* rank as the frankest representations of political power in a Communist state—even if this power is necessarily unshowable.

In the early 1970s, Kádár's greatest economic success story had been the successful development of the agricultural sector, which, under the NEM, had consistently surpassed the rate of industrial growth. Hungarian

cooperatives—occupying about 75 percent of the nation's arable land—
were nearly autonomous, almost free to select their leadership, trade with
the West, and set their own prices.

According to Gazdag, Ember—who served as assistant director on his
first feature, *The Whistling Cobblestone*—conceived the idea of documenting the process by which agricultural co-ops choose their leaders: "I
went with her to help and got more and more involved in the project. We
learned that the way that new chairmen were elected was completely
undemocratic and corrupt. The members of the cooperative had to decide
on a candidate they had never seen—perhaps someone from the other side
of the country with good Party connections. We wanted to find out how
it is possible to persuade people to accept an unknown leader"[32] and
hence, to accept the entire system.

In their search for a chairmanless cooperative, the filmmakers met a
Party secretary named Gyula Estélyi, who had one such a cooperative in
his district. Although Estélyi forbade their making a documentary on that
particular case, telling them that it was currently under police investigation, he suggested an alternative. The party was recommending to the
membership of another cooperative that they recall their leader, one József
Ferenci. Estélyi offered the filmmakers his full support in documenting the
procedure by which Ferenci would be voted out.

What could Estélyi have been thinking? Was he a little Kádár—so
self-confident that he made the filmmakers privy to the party's strategy for
unseating Ferenci? The atmosphere in the smoke-filled room with which
The Resolution opens—the county-level party apparatus deliberating over
the situation—suggests nothing so much as the first scene of *Macbeth*.
Some vague issue of corruption seems to be at stake. One hitch is that,
financially at least, the cooperative is doing quite well and is thus likely to
be surprised by the party's move. The other complication is that, strictly
speaking, the cooperative is not obligated to follow the party's advice.

Sure enough, in the documentary's second act, when the sleek party
bureaucrats confront the gnarled peasants of the cooperative leadership,
the farmers are dumbfounded. Why haven't they heard anything before?
Ferenci is the first good chairman they've had! Who is behind this plot?
The co-op's accountant warns that banks may withdraw credit if the
popular chairman is forced out. As if on cue, Ferenci arrives and immediately begins protesting his innocence. Everything he did was done in
the interests of the cooperative. If he's guilty, then so is everyone else!
(Making reference to the film crew, Ferenci slyly goes on record with the

hope that the accountant's statement will not be cut out of the final print.) Now it is the party that is speechless.

The film's real subject is official rhetoric and, hence, official reality. The dramatis personae—apparatchiks and peasants—do not themselves represent authority. Rather, they attempt to articulate an authority that (like the film itself) has been delegated. Thus, as György Báron writes, *The Resolution*—even more than *The Selection*—documents the language of power "in its extreme form." Nor is this language transparent: "Exclusively based on clichés unrelated to reality, [it] is a language able to argue for and against the same thing without the least logical contradiction. . . . This distorted speech appears all the more awful when compared to the lucid, colorful vernacular of the cooperative members."[33]

"We are wasting the filmmakers' time," one apparatchik finally announces, and it is decided to continue the discussion without Ferenci, who is sent home. That the debate will go on is assumed. But what about the movie? *The Resolution* has managed to document a schism between the public performance and the actual power relations, which will henceforth be staged in secret, thus providing the film with its structuring absence. The filmmakers have reached the border of representation. They have broken their noses on the Berlin Wall. Their fancies have touched barbed wire, and yet the show must go on. Gazdag and Ember continue to document the situation—in effect, to film that which cannot be filmed. (It is the avant-garde search for the ineffable—although not, perhaps, as Georg Lukács imagined.)

The Resolution reaches its climax at the cooperative's general meeting, where the party accuses Ferenci of nepotism and padding his expense account. Such petty corruption hardly seems unusual. Ferenci appears to have hired, in some comically unspecified capacity, a Budapest confidence man named Fischer, who managed to use his position to set up a brothel. Nevertheless, despite a rather peculiar balloting procedure, the vote is ninety-six to sixty-seven against Ferenci's removal. (Stung, the party lamely invokes a two-thirds rule and asks for a second ballot.)

A postscript returns us to the smoke-filled room where the gathered honchos offer their postmortem, deciding to "share the blame" and take solace in their 40 percent of the vote (which, for the Communists, would surely have been a massive show of support back in the parliamentary days of 1947). It's a fascinating coda, which the party secretary Estélyi cuts short by staring balefully at the filmmakers and, with read-my-lips emphasis, pronouncing, "Enough, it is over." The chilling freeze-frame that follows is amply justified. Producer Estélyi has pulled the plug—on camera.

Gazdag and Ember, who were obliged to complete *The Resolution* by the end of 1972, received no additional funding to continue the project. Thus we are left with only an end title revealing that, one year later, Ferenci was voted out "with disciplinary action." But even this does not conclude the story. *The Resolution* was screened twice by Estélyi, who authorized its release—a decision that would later cost him his position. Gazdag told me that a few months after he and Ember showed their film at BBS to great acclaim, "there was a festival for young filmmakers and we wanted to enter *The Resolution*. "An official from the [culture] ministry told me 'I'm sure this film would win all the prizes but it won't get to the festival because that's not the right place for it. This film will circulate in the Party apparatus and after that it will find its right place.' As you don't understand what he meant, I didn't either."[34] What *did* he mean?

The Resolution was shelved for a decade—and even then never accorded a theatrical release. (It surfaced publicly first as part of a 1982 BBS retrospective and had its official "premiere" two years later as part of the national film week.) But this is not to suggest that *The Resolution* went unshown; far from it. According to the filmmakers, the original 16mm print disappeared altogether for two years. They later discovered that it had been screened in a number of closed situations for political scientists, historians, and economists, as well as at various party training schools. This is entirely fitting, for it is authority that is the film's true subject—not only its content but the determination of its form. As every aspect of the production was, in effect, predicated on invisible power's ubiquitous, vigilant gaze, the party was only replaying that which it had already seen. Supported, terminated, and finally shelved, *The Resolution* is the quintessential BBS production.[35]

Much of the BBS membership was purged or forcibly "graduated" in 1975. The postpolitical BBS became an artists' collective. Was this not a socialist dream?

Miklós Erdély, a professional architect as well as painter, writer, and performer, was nearly fifty when he made *Dream Reconstructions* at BBS in 1977. But he, too, raised the issue of representation. Erdély called his film's staged dreams "copies of copies." *Dream Reconstructions* is composed of three such simulacra and a coda. In one, a woman takes a group of actors out to the countryside to reenact her dream, which, although she describes it as "just a scene [that] doesn't even have a story," involves such charged players as a priest, an old couple, and a handsome young man. The woman expresses a naive disappointment when her dream resists staging. "Reality is different from what you dream," one of the actors commiserates in a line that would be Socialist Realist heresy. "As a matter of fact, that's part of the character of dreams."

Erdély mediated his film's sounds and images through his experience of them at the editing table (making copies of copies of copies). Many scenes were apparently refilmed off the Movieola screen, with freeze-frames or lapses into reverse motion keyed to phrases spoken by the film's subjects— thus literalizing the dream work of condensation, displacement, and dramatization. No less than *The Resolution,* Erdély's feature attempted to document the undocumentable—although in this case, it is the workings of the unconscious rather than the party.

Another, less programmatic example presented itself in 1984 when the American artist Peter Hutton was invited to make a film portrait of Budapest under BBS auspices. Hutton was only the second non-Hungarian to make a film at the studio, and the first from a nonsocialist country. Budapest, Hutton observed (his nostalgia matching my own), was a city that was inexorably and irrevocably growing more "European" and thus losing something of its unique character.[36]

Light-years away from the colorful, music-filled environment depicted by Miklós Jancsó in a contemporary television documentary, Hutton's Budapest was a world of moldering apartment houses and massive factories, lonely Stalinist monuments and revolutionary ghosts. (Béla Kun can be glimpsed at one point in an old newsreel film-within-the-film, and an image of Yuri Andropov, who died while Hutton was at BBS, appears at another strategic juncture.) Close-up portraits of two ancient ragpickers and a succession of elderly peasant women aside, virtually every person shown in *Budapest Portrait* is dominated by the surroundings. Human presence is often suggested merely by indexical signs—photographs, shadows, or bullet holes. This relative absence of the figure, together with the harsh chiaroscuro of the winter light, induces a poignant loneliness. Voluptuously gray, worn, and lived-in, the city seems a stage set for an invisible drama.

Another version of *Budapest Portrait,* renamed *Memoirs of a City,* was shown during the 1986 Hungarian Film Week on a program of recent BBS productions. Its title perhaps prudently reinforcing the film's subjectivity, universality, and sense of documenting that which is past, *Memoirs of a City* ran some eight minutes shorter than *Budapest Portrait*. Hutton's images were accompanied by a vaguely jazzy piano score. The work was co-signed by the documentary filmmaker András Mész (who, as a teenager, had appeared in Gazdag's *Whistling Cobblestone*); this certified it as the at least partially Hungarian production that it had to be in order to have been made at BBS at all. Certain images were conspicuous by their absence: *Memoirs of a City* dropped not only the portrait of Andropov but also an ordinary shot of a drab, empty suburban street. Other shots were rearranged.

Budapest Portrait features a series of studies of disheveled men sleeping in the waiting room of the Eastern Railway Station, among them a uniformed official dozing at his post. For *Memoirs of a City,* this sequence was reshuffled so that the official appeared first. No longer was the station master a man among men. Now, the collapse of his authority had permitted the general torpor. The paradox was that the evident tightening and obtrusive music failed to efface the film's pervasive bleakness. If anything, in obliterating Hutton's subtle visual rhythms, the score made the images seem that much more oppressive and overdetermined.

When I asked Mész about these changes, I was told simply that the BBS membership had found Hutton's cut too long and too monotonous. Clearly (or rather, obscurely), there was more at stake. Hutton's film had lost its innocence. But did *Memoirs of a City* politicize or depoliticize *Budapest Portrait*?

As far as I know, the BBS never examined itself—or the larger movie industry. For that we have the Polish director Krzysztof Kieślowski's 1979 *Amator,* released in the United States as *Camera Buff*.

Writing in West Germany a year after Georg Lukács gave his interview to *Filmkúltura,* the poet-sociologist Hans-Magnus Enzensberger noted that "tape recorders, ordinary cameras and movie cameras are already extensively owned by wage earners" and wondered why it was that "these means of production [did] not turn up at factories, in schools, in the offices of the bureaucracy, in short, everywhere where there is social conflict."[37] Over the course of the entire cold war, *Camera Buff* was virtually the only film—in the East or the West—to address precisely this question.

Kieślowski's second theatrical feature after a dozen years making documentaries, *Camera Buff* concerns Filip, an overenthusiastic young buyer for an unspecified industrial plant in southern Poland, who splurges two months' salary on a boxlike Soviet Quarz-2 8mm movie camera in order to photograph his infant daughter. Filip's first experience of censorship comes at home—his wife objects to his filming the baby naked—but his naive fascination with the medium soon takes him beyond home movies. Like the would-be rock stars of *Selection,* Filip is a candidate for the conquest of unhappy consciousness. Casting around for a cultural activity, his bosses encourage him to form a factory cine-club. ("Cinema's the supreme art, so somebody said," one pontificates, quoting Lenin by rote.)

Jerzy Stuhr, who plays Filip, wrote much of his own dialogue, and so wired he can make an anxious, avid spectacle of himself merely by chugging a Pepsi, he gives the film the breathless stumble of a man with one eye shut and the other glued to the viewfinder. Because he is not yet a professional, Filip has not learned how to censor himself. With comic thoroughness, he documents the plant's jubilee celebration—not forgetting to film the entertainers receiving their payment, a flock of pigeons, the trips taken by the various dignitaries to the toilet, and the antics of their drivers waiting outside.

Filip's film is developed, edited, and shown to its producer. The factory director, who has come to the screening prepared with a flashlight pen, suggests adding a commentary and music. Privately, he instructs Filip to delete those shots depicting the interpolated pigeons, the lavatory sequence, the disbursement of money, and particularly the presence of a mysterious man in glasses. Learning quickly how to be an East European filmmaker, Filip makes a deal to keep the pigeons at least but then shows the restored version of *The Jubilee* at an industrial film competition that the judges practically sleep through.

Given the "informational psychosis" cited by Poland's Experience and the Future Discussion Group in 1979, it becomes a heroic task merely to discover and declare a true thing.[38] ("That's quite a brainwave. You mean you film what's there?" exclaims a fellow amateur on seeing *The Jubilee*.) Thus, supported by two cultural apparatchiks—one of them, Jurga, a TV producer playing himself—Filip's film wins third prize, and he consequently finds himself embarked on a second, perilous career.

At times, this mainly comic saga turns so melodramatic as to evoke Stan Brakhage's dark, hyperbolic warning to the would-be artist: "Your mother will never recognize you, your father will disown you, your friends betray you, your loved one live in fear of you."[39] Brakhagian, too, is Kieślowski's understated equation of the newly minted filmmaker and his infant daughter—both seeing everything for the first time, as it were. Filip even makes a frame of his hands as he watches his wife walking out on him: As in the 1960s, life is a movie. The factory director who is his producer, however, demands prior script approval. All plans must be submitted on paper. Doing "what you like, when you like," it's pointed out, is "the amateur's forte."

Full of handheld and high emotion, an unlovely film that's all information, *Camera Buff* addresses itself to exactly the major freedom that Eastern artists had over their Western counterparts—namely, the freedom to be taken seriously by the powers that be. This Rosetta stone of Eastern Bloc filmmaking, replete with cameo performances by several well-known members of the Polish film industry, playing themselves, often hilariously evokes the political economy of socialist cinema—the bargains struck with censorship and cynicism, the degree to which success and provocation are entwined. (Indeed, although *Camera Buff* won first prize at 1979 Moscow Film Festival, it was never actually released in the Soviet Union.)[40]

Filip's subsequent productions include a portrait of a dignified and resigned factory worker who happens to be a dwarf (a found metaphor to be sure). The boss, forever lurking, is upset that his protégé is filming this individual. "You're not going to do any festival with that," he warns, even while upgrading the camera buff to 16mm. Filip, however, manages to get *The Worker* on TV and thus obtain a commission to make a series of documentaries on his hometown.

The first of these is the quintessential Realist Socialist attack on Socialist Realism—an exposé of a recent renovation that consisted entirely of repairing building facades, a sort of Potemkin village. Televised, it has immediate repercussions. The architect is fired—despite the subsequent revelation that there were insufficient funds and material to complete the job—as is the manager of the brickworks. Filip's immediate supervisor, the kindly Osuch, is forcibly retired. The filmmaker is, however, taken into the boss's confidence. (After all, he has demonstrated that he is a filmmaker, an artist, an intellectual. Were the makers of *Resolution* ever so addressed?)

The factory manager explains that his plan to divert money from the building to improve conditions in the local kindergarten was effectively thwarted by Filip's film. Power speaks: The boss reveals that community affairs cannot always be public and that, in fact, the brickworks's major function is to create jobs. Filip sought to show things the way they really are; now he has been made privy to the ultimate social mystery, that which exists but cannot be acknowledged.

Having cut his teeth as a documentarist, Kieślowski is not surprised that the big boys can pull the plug at any time. What preoccupies him is how easily film serves as a pawn in the larger game. "You are young," the boss tells Filip. "You can make mistakes." Osuch puts it in another way: "You must realize this will happen more and more often. You won't know who will take advantage of it." (*Resolution* is, of course, a case in point.)

In effect, Filip is co-opted by the manager's revelation. Without ever desiring it, he has been brought within the circle of power. What can he do now with this particular information? This, presumably, is why—to the amazed horror of his own naive assistant—Filip ultimately censors his film. According to Kieślowski, "He simply realizes that, as an amateur filmmaker, he's found himself in a trap and that, making films with good intentions, he might prove useful to people who'll use the films with bad intentions."

Kieślowski experienced a grotesque variation on that very experience the year after *Camera Buff*'s release, while making a thirteen-minute observational documentary of people waiting in Warsaw's Central Railway Station (a study perhaps not unlike Peter Hutton's). The police confiscated his footage, not for any political reason but because they believed it might help identify a killer: "A girl had murdered her mother, cut her to pieces and packed her into two suitcases. And, that very night, she'd put those suitcases into one of the lockers at the Central Station. . . . If we'd turned the camera left instead of right, perhaps we'd have caught her. And what would have happened? I'd have become a police collaborator. And that was the moment I realized that I didn't want to make any more documentaries."[41] From now on, he, like Filip, would be free to devote himself to dream reconstructions.

Camera Buff's physician-heal-thyself fade-out may be sentimental, but it was evidently heartfelt. In the spring of 1990, Kieślowski visited Hollywood to screen his latest (and what would turn out to be his last) Polish work—the ten-part telefilm *Decalogue*. Was the director auditioning for a contract? Although he now preferred the personal to the political, Kieślowski seemed almost nostalgic for the idiotic literal-mindedness of Polish censorship: "That was the only thing in the country that functioned well."[42] And that was also the main thing that gave *Camera Buff* its significance.

CHAPTER 3

Beyond the Pale:

Soviet Jews and

Soviet Jewish

Cinema

PREVIOUS PAGE:

Poster, *Jewish Luck*. Natan Altman (1925). (Photo by Jennifer Kotter)

*There is an old Talmudic saying: "A Jew
who has sinned still remains a Jew."*

—Isaac Deutscher, "The Non-Jewish Jew" (1958)[1]

I t is Thursday night, November 12, 1925, when—as advertised in
the Yiddish-language Communist daily *Der Emes*—the "magnificent motion picture" *Jewish Luck* has its gala premiere at the
Moscow Conservatory on Gerzen Street, not far from Red Square.[2]

Earlier that week, a million organized workers paraded through
the city to mark the eighth anniversary of the October Revolution.
Somewhere in Moscow, Sergei Eisenstein hastens to complete editing
his *Battleship Potemkin*—shot, like *Jewish Luck*, the previous summer
in Odessa. (By the time *Potemkin* has its first public showings, six
weeks later, the period of "collective leadership" will have fallen beneath the standing ovation and fervent singing of the "Internationale"
that follows the speech to the Fourteenth Party Congress by the first
secretary, Joseph Stalin.)

More communal than Communist, *Jewish Luck* was adapted from
a popular story cycle by the most beloved of Yiddish writers, Sholom
Aleichem. The movie was directed by Alexander Granovsky, founder
of the world's first government-subsidized Jewish theater, the Moscow

---

In the postrevolutionary erasure of religion and nationalism on the one hand and social restrictions
and political anti-Semitism on the other, the only sources for a politically correct Soviet Jewish
collectivity were the Yiddish language and the memory of the shtetl. Optimistically anticipating the
era of Jewish assimilation, the Communist Jewish culture of the 1920s and 1930s was nevertheless
founded on the perverse nostalgia for an obsolete identity. Buried by the Soviets, repudiated by
anti-Communist Jews, the long-forgotten relics of this failed, foredoomed, antichauvinist, interna-
tionalist Communist Jewish culture project an abandoned past into an impossible future.

GOSET (State Yiddish Theater); it stars that theater's leading performer, Solomon Mikhoels, as Menakhem Mendl, the comic, rootless *luftmensh* (air man) spinning hither and yon in response to economic restriction and physical persecution.

Even beyond this, the *Jewish Luck* production was designed by the Jewish painter Natan Altman. The score, a boldly discordant mix of cantorial, klezmer, and Russian motifs, was composed by the erstwhile Bolshoi violinist, Lev Pulver. The zesty, idiomatic intertitles were provided by the newly famous Isaac Babel, whose sardonic tales of the Polish-Soviet War, fought in the Jewish heartland of Galicia and the Ukraine, had recently been published to great acclaim—not to mention in rival Yiddish translations.

Oh, Communism! Not until the version of S. Ansky's *The Dybbuk* filmed a dozen years later, in Warsaw on the eve of oblivion, would so august a group of Jewish artists collaborate on so Jewish a movie. Never again would official sanction imbue Yiddish folk tradition with comparable authority. The gala—complete with Pulver conducting a full symphony orchestra—is sponsored by the Society for the Resettlement of Jewish Workers on the Land (GEZERD), a quasi-public agency closely associated with the Jewish section of the Communist Party (Yevsektsia).

Jewish Luck—the Russian title can also be translated as *Jewish Happiness*—is one more event in Moscow's season of celebration. Three days before, a Red Army soldier drove a rubbish cart through the streets, carrying dummies dressed to represent the ridiculous defenders of the doomed capitalist system. Tonight—in somewhat the same spirit?—leading figures of the new Soviet Yiddish culture gather together to celebrate the liquidation of their ancestral heritage, casting their former selves on the pyre of revolution.

That discarded past is embodied in the person of Menakhem Mendl— quintessential *galos yid* (Diaspora Jew), emblem of exile, dreamer, schemer, combination of Don Quixote and Sancho Panza. *Jewish Luck* opens amid the chaos of Menakhem Mendl's large and underfed family and—shot mainly in exterior and on location, not just in Odessa but even in Yakti, the tumbledown Jewish quarter of Berdichev, itself the Ukraine's archetypal Jewish town—documents the perimeters of his world.[3]

Obsequious yet irrepressible, the diminutive Mikhoels cuts an endearing figure, giving Menakhem Mendl a Chaplinesque aura of shabby gentility and scurrilous pathos. (Unlike the Little Tramp, however, Menakhem Mendl is never permitted to triumph—even temporarily—over his social betters.) The *luftmensh* leaves Berdichev for Odessa, where he hopes to sell corsets. After the comic failure of even this modest enterprise, he stumbles on a book containing a list of prospective brides and grooms and decides to become a matchmaker: "*Shadkhn*—that's a real profession!"

In the film's set piece, shot in and around the Odessa harbor, Menakhem Mendl dreams that he is a *shadkhn* of international proportions—recruited by the Jewish philanthropist Baron de Hirsch to "save America." As Menakhem Mendl mobilizes Berdichev, the vision grows increasingly elaborate in its extravagant plenitude of marriage-minded women. In waking reality, however, his new career goes spectacularly awry when the would-be "King of the *Shadkhonim*" inadvertently arranges a match between two girls. Although this blunder serves to unite the film's young lovers, Menakhem Mendl is betrayed by his employer and left to wander off alone.

"For us," critic Viktor Shklovsky will return home to write, "*Jewish Luck* is almost an historical film. Such Jewish life no longer exists." War, pogroms, starvation had already devastated the shtetl (Jewish market village). Now, Shklovsky maintains, "the Revolution [has] removed all limitations from the Jews and destroyed the most essential trait of the Jews—the Pale of Settlement."[4]

Shklovsky's defining Jewish characteristic is negative and geographically determined. But thanks to the revolution, Russian Jews may be fully deterritorialized, float free of their former identity, become a new sort of *luftmensh*. Even today, *Jewish Luck* cannot but inspire a certain ambivalence—that which was liberated was also doomed. If Shklovsky seems a bit defensively smug, to read Babel's 1920 war diary is to recognize a modern nostalgia for the lost world of the shtetl: "What a mighty and marvelous life of a nation existed here."[5]

Marvelous life or impoverished captivity? The prerevolutionary economy restricted Russian Jews to the Pale of Settlement, forbade them to own land, and compelled most to eke out a living as small traders, artisans, and middlemen, exchanging goods with neighboring peasants in the Pale's hundreds of shtetlekh—activities that, before the revolution, all Jewish radicals regarded as "unproductive." For prerevolutionary Yiddish writers, the shtetl had been a subject of satire; for postrevolutionary Jewish Bolsheviks, it was, as historian Zvi Gitelman put it, a leper colony. (Nor did Zionists, themselves striving to create a new Jew in a new Jewish territory, feel any different.) For Russian Marxists, the underdeveloped, impoverished, obscurant Pale epitomized what Lenin called the "primitive residues of Russian life." For anti-Semites . . .[6]

But now! Thousands of Jews had moved and were moving to once-forbidden Moscow. "No need to pity the torn umbrella of Menakhem Mendl, no need to look for romanticism in the past," Shklovsky wrote. Where, then? Was there to be a Jewish romanticism of the radiant future?[7]

> A directive to a propagandist lay next to the notebooks of a Jewish poet. The portraits of Lenin and Maimonides were neighbors—the gnarled iron of Lenin's skull and the dim silkiness of Maimonides' picture. A lock of woman's hair marked a page in a bound volume of the Resolutions of the Sixth Party Congress, and crooked lines of Hebrew verse were crowded into the margin of political pamphlets.
> —Isaac Babel, "The Rabbi's Son"[8]

January 1918, not four months into the October Revolution, the new Bolshevik regime gave Jewish nationality legal status, and later that year, the Communist Party formed the Yevsektsia to implement policy and orchestrate propaganda on what was termed "the Jewish Street."

But there were scarcely any Yiddish-speaking Communists. Outsiders had to be hired to translate Bolshevik material into *mameloshn* (mother tongue). Elections held that June in the newly established local Jewish governing *kehillas* (communal organizations) made clear that Zionists owned the Jewish Street, while the left opposition was represented by the Jewish Labor Bund, which—expelled in 1903 (by the young Leon Trotsky himself) from the Russian Social-Democratic Labor Party for its insistence on organization autonomy—had, as recently as its December 1917 party congress, condemned the Bolshevik's October Revolution.

And yet, during the civil war, hundreds of thousands of Jews were won over to the new regime. Why? First was the anti-Semitic violence of the counterrevolution. An estimated two hundred thousand Jews were murdered in White or Ukrainian Nationalist pogroms. (And had not a Jew built the Red Army?) Second were the opportunities created when the Russian intelligentsia fled abroad. Third (can we deny it?) was the millennial promise of a classless society, to be followed by the withering away of the state and the sense that redemption, when it came, would be a public event—not so much on the stage of the Moscow Conservatory as on the stage of history.[9]

After the Jewish Labor Bund was suppressed, its left wing joined the Communist Party, contributing substantially—along with former Labor Zionists—to the Yevsektsia leadership. (By the Third Yevsektsia Conference in July 1920, ex-Bundists were the majority.) In the bright new Bolshevik world, anti-Semitism was a state crime. And for the first and only time in history, Yiddish was the language of official culture. Feeble, tawdry attempts to take charge of Jewish history? In the predominantly Jewish city of Vitebsk, Marc Chagall was appointed commissar of art; in besieged Petrograd (where Commissar Altman, designer of the first Soviet postage stamp, directed the reenacted storming of the Winter Palace), Alexander Granovsky was authorized to form the revolutionary Yiddish theater that, two years later, would move to Moscow.

The cosmopolitan Granovsky had conceived his theater as Yiddish in form but universal in content. But in Moscow, where the GOSET took residence in the ninety-seat auditorium of a "liberated" bourgeois town house, Granovsky realized that to set apart his theater from the dozens of new companies competing for an audience, he needed a distinctive repertoire. The non-Yiddish-speaking Jew who had been recruited to revolutionize the not-then-existing Yiddish theater would have to re-deterritorialize himself, working his way back into—rather than out from—the fading Yiddish folk tradition. Was this unprecedented Jewish realm an authentic Yiddish modernism or a just new form of *galos yiddishkeyt*?[10]

Whereas Russia's leading exhibition group of the early teens, the painters known as the Knave of Diamonds, had split into rival groups of folk-nativists and cosmopolitan "Cezannists," Yiddish modernism was defined by the struggle to integrate these two tendencies. "Our first imprimatur is our modernism, our leftism, and our youth. Our second imprimatur is our orientation towards the people, our traditions, and our antiquity," the young critic Abram Efros proclaimed in his 1918 essay "Aladdin's Lamp."[11]

While such active ambivalence gave Yiddish modernism its particular incandescence, this striking out on two apparently contradictory paths had its equivalent in the political sphere: "crooked lines of Hebrew verse crowded into the margin of political pamphlets." For Jewish artists, neoprimitivism was as fraught with revolutionary implications as cubofuturism. The preservationist impulse valorized a popular folk tradition in addition—or in opposition—to both the high culture of Hebrew clericalism and the rival Zionist modernism exemplified by the Hebrew-language theater HaBima.[12]

A dedicated opponent of HaBima, Efros served as GOSET's *shadkhn*, bringing together the assimilated, "universalist" Granovsky with Chagall, the shtetl-born child of Hasidim. ("Granovsky's always-sleepy eyes opened with a start and rounded like the eyes of an owl at the sight of meat," Efros recalled.) Emblazoning the GOSET's interior walls and ceilings, Chagall's eight allegorical paintings created a festive atmosphere suggesting the Jewish carnival of Purim. The new theater's first success, *A Sholom Aleichem Evening,* which opened on New Year's Day 1921, was a kind of three-dimensional Chagall, replete with frozen tableaux. Audiences were dazzled by Mikhoels's stylized clowning amid the painter's prismatic sets. This initial collaboration would prove decisive. Mikhoels was a *luftik luftmensh* — lively and nimble — and so was Granovsky's new theater.[13]

As the Yevsekstia implemented the party's campaign against religion, the *luftmensh* theater was privileged as a Jewish domain untainted by clericalism. Raising the GOSET's subsidy, the authorities provided Granovsky with a five-hundred-seat auditorium in a building that included living accommodations, a school, and a museum. As a director, Granovsky downplayed the text, emphasized the nonverbal, and applied Vsevolod Meyerhold's "biomechanics" — stylized units of movement — to the characteristic gestures of shtetl life. GOSET's 1922 production of Avrom Goldfaden's quaint operetta *Koldonye: or, the Witch,* transformed the sentimental tale of a beleaguered orphan and her evil stepmother into a Yiddish *commedia dell'arte* — not to mention a self-conscious blasphemy that went so far as to use the Kol Nidre prayer for the witch's spell.

Jews riffing on Jews: Removing all limitation, revolution set the signifiers free. "Spellbound" by the "sophisticated" handling of such hackneyed material, the Russian-born American artist Louis Lozowick thought that "the exaggerated makeup, the near frenzied movement, the acrobatic grotesquerie, and the background music" all but "obliterated whatever message the play meant to convey." In contrast, *Koldonye* was criticized by *Der Emes* for drawing on antiquated theater and elsewhere compared (unfavorably) to HaBima's *Dybbuk,* which had opened on the last day of January 1922.[14]

In April 1923, the Twelfth Communist Party Congress created a Council of Nationalities, proposing legislation that would implement the use of indigenous languages by those state agencies serving the national minorities. The next few years brought numerous such cultural and political institutions: Yiddish-language schools, courts, and publishing houses; additional GOSETs; even a few Jewish municipal soviets in the Ukraine and Belorussia, the two republics encompassing the former Pale. That year as well, in a conciliatory attempt to "productivize" tens of thousands of "declassed" Jews and persuade surviving "petit-bourgeois elements" to participate more fully in the socialist construction, the Yevsektsia announced its own version of Lenin's New Economic Policy: A face to the shtetl.

October 1923, month of the failed German Revolution, GOSET premiered its most enduring and frequently revived production: a Bolshevized version of Sholom Aleichem's *200,000* in which the impoverished tailor Shimele (Mikhoels) wins the lottery and—living high until the bubble bursts—attempts to transcend his class. Slapstick tragicomedy of absurd Jewish bourgeois aspiration! Or pitiful prophecy of Jewish Communist delusion?[15]

GOSET's exuberantly grotesque—if not alienated—vision of shtetl life struck a responsive chord with Moscow's swelling Jewish community. "Comrade" Shimele's songs and sayings, his speech patterns and walk were widely imitated. One of *200,000*'s most famous bits had the performer who was playing the unctuous *shadkhn* literalize his *luftmensh* status by actually making his entrance out of the air: To the delight of the audience, actor Venyamin Zuskin "floated" onstage, using the marriage broker's traditional umbrella as a parachute. Naturally, *200,000* included a parody of *The Dybbuk*. If HaBima depicted a ritual exorcism, then the GOSET was one. HaBima was "mere mirage," Efros would declare; the GOSET was "a historical reality."[16]

Actually, the reverse was closer to the truth.

GOSET turned the idiom of the shtetl against the shtetl—as Efros provocatively put it, "Granovsky really unfurled the 'Yid.' . . . From dross he spun gold."[17]

Jewish reaction to the GOSET was, understandably, complex—and not just because of the theater's hard-line anticlericalism. Even more than most vanguards, Yiddish modernists marched ahead of their constituency. The Yiddish audience that had only recently entered the secular realm of art was scarcely prepared to see its naturalistic precepts inverted. But there was something else. Visiting Moscow only weeks after *Jewish Luck* opened, Walter Benjamin was decidedly unimpressed with Granovsky's theater—"a farcical, anti-religious, and, from outward appearances, fairly anti-Semitic form of satirical comedy, a parody of [Yiddish] operettas."[18]

The Soviet vanguard felt itself living out the future. The collapse of old Europe seemed imminent (at least until the abortive German October). In this heady atmosphere, the GOSET's youthful performers might well imagine themselves red Purim players, liberated by Communism. Most ferocious was the controversial 1925 production of Y. L. Peretz's previously unstageable poetic drama *Night in the Old Marketplace,* which, in Lozowick's words, represented the "dying world of priests and rabbis, traders and prostitutes, writhing in its last agonies and clinging desperately to its old superstitions." Lozowick paraphrased Marx: "The dead regulate the customs of the living and the living are putrid with the germs of decay."[19]

Mikhoels played Menakhem Mendl once more in Granovsky's last Soviet stage production, *Der Luftmensh,* which had its Moscow premiere in early 1928 and was performed by the GOSET in various European capitals when they made their first international tour later that year. Even before departing Moscow, the GOSET was under political scrutiny for its alleged chauvinism. When Soviet authorities canceled the tour after three months, Granovsky chose not to return with his troupe. Thereafter, the GOSET directorship passed to Menakhem—or rather, Mikhoels—along with the task of guiding the theater through the perilous shoals of the Stalinist cultural revolution.

The Yiddish Communist journalist Melech Epstein, arriving in Western Europe in GOSET's wake, reported the disgruntled response of the local Jewish Communists: "Instead of scenes of the civil war, of Jewish revolutionary heroes, of the efforts to reconstruct Jewish society, they were treated to cheap satires of the old pattern of Jewish life. The stylized presentation accentuated the mocking effect. That the bourgeois press praised the performances for the strange and exotic flavor—all plays included singing and dancing—added insult to injury."[20]

But if the shtetl vanished, why should Yiddish remain?

I tell them fairytales about Bolshevism—the blossoming, the express trains, Moscow's textile mills, universities, free meals. . . . I captivate all these tormented people.

—Isaac Babel, *1920 Diary,* July 24

The tragic holiday Tishebov finds Communist propagandist Babel spinning yarns for a family of Galician Jews: "The lamp smokes, the old woman wails, the young man sings melodiously, girls in white stockings, outside—Demidovka, night, Cossacks, all just as it was when the Temple was destroyed."[21]

And just as it was when Russia's Jews made their convulsive entry into the modern world; for some modernisms are more modern than others. No less than the Yevsektsia, the new Soviet Yiddish culture labored beneath a double burden, for where Soviet Russian literature might simply direct Russian workers and peasants across the threshold of the future, a Soviet Yiddish literature needed first to transform the Jewish masses into workers and peasants.

The first Soviet nationality films were preoccupied with the civil war and the detritus of prerevolutionary tradition. After 1927, a year in advance of the First Five-Year Plan, emphasis shifted to the new life of the present. No subsequent film would have the gaiety and the pathos of *Jewish Luck*. Sholom Aleichem, designated Jewish Pushkin, remained a standard of the state Yiddish stage and a talismanic figure in *Der Emes*, but his writings provided material for only one further film: Grigori Gricher-Cherikover's *Through Tears,* released in 1928 by the All-Ukrainian Photo-Cinema Administration (VUFKU).

The *Jewish Luck* of 1927, *Through Tears* most thoroughly elaborated the critique of the pre-1917 shtetl. Shot, like its precursor, with near-documentary verisimilitude, it is mainly concerned with depicting the bitter marginality of shtetl life. The Jewish hamlet is a ramshackle backwater—if not a purely ideological landscape—where, like Menakhem Mendl, young people attempt a series of foredoomed get-rich-quick schemes. Here are neither community rituals nor fanciful dreams—only the plight of the *luftmensh* globalized into a universal principal.[22]

Along with *Through Tears* (originally written for the Moscow GOSET), VUFKU inherited a pair of projects developed by Isaac Babel— an adaptation, now lost, of Sholom Aleichem's novel *Wandering Stars* and a script based on Babel's stories of Odessa's Jewish underworld and its "king," Benya Krik. Filmed in Odessa during the summer of 1926 by Vladimir Vilner, *Benya Krik* created problems by presenting its flamboyant criminal hero as a victim of the Bolshevik regime—as well as by evoking the image of the Jew as profiteer. Thus, if the film's final sequence offended party ideologues, the often-grotesque picture of Odessa's demimonde proved no less disturbing to image-conscious Jews. A letter written to *Der Emes* by one S. Daytsherman in the name of the Soviet Jewish public decries both the paucity of appropriate Jewish films and those few that are made; witness *Benya Krik*, which suggests that "thieves, prostitutes and speculators created the Revolution, fought for it, defended it and—took advantage of it. . . . The poison and hatred such a film spreads is obvious."[23]

Inevitably, the harshest critics of the new Soviet Yiddish culture were Jewish Communists—more self-conscious and less secure than their Russian comrades. When VUFKU's monthly journal *Kino* published several articles on Jewish cinema in March 1928, soon after Stalin had declared war on the kulaks and liquidated the New Economic Policy, Ukrainian critic M. Makotinsky praised *Through Tears* and *Jewish Luck* for helping the "village masses" understand the "roots of anti-Semitism."[24]

Criticism was offered Jew to Jew (in Yiddish, without Ukrainian translation) by Itzik Fefer—poet, ideologue, and secret member of the NKVD (People's Commissariat for Internal Affairs). Sick of *luftmenshn,* Fefer wanted to see positive images of Jewish workers, even if they did not yet exist:

> The workers ask, "Why do you only write about *Jewish Luck?* About *Benya Krik* and *Wandering Stars?* Why don't you write about us?"
> They ask, "Is Benya Krik more interesting than we are?"
> The working class wants to see itself, its struggle and its life in the new art.
> The working class is right.[25]

Similarly, American visitor Melech Epstein claimed to have stunned a reception for the Moscow GOSET by challenging the theater to transform itself into a mirror of postrevolutionary Jewish life: "Pointing at some of the younger artists who portrayed comical old Jews, I asked why they could not portray young Jewish Communist builders. Not a hand moved when I finished."[26]

Desire for oblivion: The first Jewish film to attempt the new line, emphasizing class struggle and revolutionary heroism on the Jewish street, was Grigori Roshal's *His Excellency,* shot in 1927 at the Belorussian studio Belgoskino's temporary Leningrad facilities. According to Roshal, his subject matter was so delicate that Commissar of Enlightenment Anatoli Lunacharsky personally oversaw the production—for *His Excellency* had taken as its protagonist Hirsh Lekert, executed in 1902 after his attempted assassination of the Vilna governor-general Viktor Von Wahl. While Lekert was an authentic proletariat folk hero, he was also the most celebrated martyr of the suppressed Jewish Labor Bund.

A Bundist return to Jewish nationalism, *His Excellency* makes no mention of the Bund. The film shifts Lekert's act forward several years to the period of the 1905 revolution and sets it in an unspecified city. The protagonist, who here successfully shoots the governor, is identified only as "the Jewish fighter." Roshal carefully stresses the solidarity between Jewish and Russian political prisoners, while making a programmatic comparison between honest Jewish workers and cowardly Jewish reactionaries. He stigmatizes the latter with a number of politically incorrect traits: They are not only bourgeois but seemingly Germanized. They meet beneath a portrait of Theodor Herzl and yet are beholden to a traditional, orthodox rabbi whom the film implicates a Jewish religious leader in the reactionary status quo.[27]

Thus, in spite of itself, *His Excellency* explicates a Russian Jewish dilemma, existing under the Soviets no less than under the czar. The bourgeois Jews are terrified that they will be blamed for the disturbance created by their proletariat coreligionists—"We're not revolutionaries, we're Zionists," one protests in vain—and send a delegation to the governor to plead for protection from the anticipated pogrom. As feared, these law-abiding Jewish leaders are held accountable and ordered to punish the revolutionaries themselves or else face the consequences. (Soon, outside the cinema, leading Jewish Communists come under fire for "idealizing" the prerevolutionary Jewish labor movement. Eventually, "Zionist" becomes synonymous with "Jew."[28])

The first example of a Soviet Yiddish Socialist Realist movie was *The Land Is Calling,* a postrevolutionary shtetl drama set on one of the new Jewish collectives in the Crimea, released in 1928 and since lost. Natan Altman codesigned this tale of a rabbi's daughter who spurns the son of a rich landowner for love of the young blacksmith who has organized an agricultural cooperative to work the kulak's confiscated property. Ignoring the presence of so fabulous a creature as a Jewish kulak, M. Makotinsky considered *The Land Is Calling* a sequel to *Through Tears.* Makotinsky praised its "bright picture of determined work," calling for a final section of the "trilogy" that would show the lives of those "sons and grandsons of Sholom Aleichem who work in the factories, the ports, and all other branches of our socialist construction."[29]

In May 1928, the Ukrainian Communist Party held a special conference on anti-Semitism. Among the resolutions was one that VUFKU prepare an "appropriate moving picture" to deal with the problem. Gricher-Cherikover's *Suburban Quarters* (1930) is likely that film. Directed from a script by *Kino's* twenty-five-year-old editor, the futurist poet Mykola Bazhan, this contemporary shtetl story criticized both anti-Semitism and Jewish chauvinism while privileging the role of the Komsomol (Young Communist League).

A young Jewish girl—hair bobbed and heroically stubborn, the only modern creature in a typically tumbledown village—flouts her religious parents to marry a Ukrainian boy. A beautiful park, replete with waterfalls and strolling comrades, blooms in the mist of the miserable shtetl. Having endured the monumental disapproval of the shtetl's old people, the Jewish girl encounters the anti-Semitism of her in-laws. But *Suburban Quarters* ends happily when a cheerful Komsomol athlete intervenes. A public court criticizes the husband's insensitive behavior, his wife defends him, and all happily recognize the evil of petit-bourgeois religious prejudice.

And yet . . .

Visiting the Soviet Union in 1930, Melech Epstein compared the Yiddish milieu—schools and cultural institutions—of Minsk favorably to that of Moscow and Kharkov. The Belorussian Soviet Socialist Republic was organized as a multinational state, with Yiddish one of four official languages. Many non-Jewish Belorussians spoke some Yiddish, which was extensively used on posters, street signs, and facades. "Jews were everywhere in the Soviet apparatus. The very climate of the city was Jewish"—the very air. "The first thing a visitor saw on alighting from the train in Minsk was the name of the city in big Yiddish letters, alongside Byelorussian and Russian, above the main gate of the railroad station."[30]

Belgoskino's first short sound film, released in 1931, featured traditional Belorussian, Polish, and Yiddish songs. The next year, the studio went further and produced a feature-length Yiddish talkie, *The Return of Nathan Becker,* starring Solomon Mikhoels in a scenario by Yiddish poet Peretz Markish. After twenty-eight years in America spent "laying bricks for Rockefeller," Nathan Becker leaves the land of breadlines and depression for his Belorussian hometown and thence, having reunited with his aged father Tsale (Mikhoels), for the new industrial center of Magnitogorsk. "Mayke, we are going home," Nathan tells his dubious wife.[31]

Like *Jewish Luck, Through Tears,* and *Suburban Quarters, Nathan Becker* opens in a decrepit shtetl populated mainly by old men, stray dogs, and ragged children. The sense of entropy is emphasized by the mournful score and accompanying montage of crooked roofs and empty mud streets. Nathan's arrival draws a crowd of urchins, layabouts, and beggars. A ragged klezmer plays his clarinet and sings a toneless song. But even as old Becker greets the returning son, the town is honored with another distinguished visitor. When a pretty young *komosolka* appears in an official car to recruit workers, an enthusiastic mob abruptly materializes, falling over themselves in their desire to leave the shtetl for the city of steel beyond the Urals—Magnitogorsk!

"A fever of moving has gripped the disturbed and famished population," Victor Serge wrote of the First Five-Year Plan. "You travel in order to find shoes, tea, bread, soap, to flee excessive exploitation; you travel because wherever you are you feel bad. . . . The cities grow before your very eyes, at least so far as population is concerned, faster than Chicago not long ago, faster than San Francisco: for the villages have become uninhabitable."[32]

Magnitogorsk is a victory for the Bund rather than the Labor Zionists. Here the shtetl Jews are educated in progressive work methods by enthusiastic young Communists. Nathan is assigned to the Central Institute of Labor as an instructor—"We'll make a professor out of you!" the merry comrades promise—along with a German specialist imported to teach the workers a regimen of movements combining efficiency, artistry, and pleasure. Suddenly, Nathan is unconvinced: "The piano they play? Why don't you hire musicians then? *Meshugoim* [lunatics]!" Unpacking his trowel, he proposes an "American-style" competition: "I will show them who works better, *Sovetishe klezmer* or American bricklayer."

When the Yiddish version of *Nathan Becker* opened in New York in April 1933, the *Daily Worker* would note that "28 years of intense economic struggle to live have left their mark on Nathan Becker. He has become a machine, an automatic robot. . . . The new type of Soviet worker whom he now meets, a new man with a new outlook on life, is incomprehensible to him." The *Worker*, however, missed the nuance: Nathan is not robotic enough.[33]

Despite its schematic narrative, *Nathan Becker* is surprisingly playful. A circus ring provides the site where, for a seven-hour shift, Nathan competes against a Soviet worker. (As befits a robot comedy, the competition is framed, cut, and scored as entertainment.) Old Becker watches the contest intently, as do the other bearded Jews, some of whom have signed up for the shock brigade. By the seventh hour, Nathan is exhausted. As the unflustered Russian forges ahead, the American vainly remembers the class in mechanical movement.

Humiliated by defeat, Nathan decides to leave the workers' paradise. Mayke reminds him of the American unemployed fighting for soup, but he is determined to depart until his Soviet supervisor firmly reminds him, "You're not in America. We're not going to fire you. We're going to learn from you. But you should learn from us too." Thus, Nathan takes his place on the Great Conveyor Belt. The synthesis of American and Soviet techniques will increase production, and the movie ends with a hymn to labor: "We must win. We will win," the chorus sings. "Long live the Day of Victory!"

Home at last, the *galos yid* is here doubly liquidated.

Long ago when men were still very foolish, they had rulers who waged war and murdered one another. Our ancestors were then called aliens. They were beaten up, tortured and were driven away from land to land.

Then came a man who was very wise, who had a broad forehead, fiery eyes and a smile upon his lips, and he freed men from all their kings.

And this man's name was Lenin.

Formerly, there were many different lands with various languages and boundaries, but when mankind liberated itself from all its kings, they called the whole world: Leninland.

And the Jews settled in that part known as Biro-Bidjan and there built a fine country, where all have an equal amount of work and live as equals, as indeed is the case with the whole of Leninland.

—Solomon Davidman, *Jewish Children in Biro-Bidjan*[34]

As far as Soviet filmmakers were concerned, the shtetl was obsolete—if the issue of Jewish resettlement was not.

In 1926, one year after the first Jewish agricultural colonies were established in southern Ukraine and Crimea, the undeveloped, sparsely populated region of Birobidzhan—an area the size of Switzerland, bordering China in the Soviet Far East—was proposed by the Soviet president M. I. Kalinin to the GEZERD as a national Jewish homeland. Inspired— who knows?—by *Jewish Luck,* this would be the most elaborate of Soviet Jewish fictions: epic location, elaborate sets, a cast (so it was hoped) of millions.

Birobidzhan was opened to Jewish settlers in 1928, the first year of the First Five-Year Plan. Whereas relocation to Magnitogorsk promised

Jewish industrialization, the Birobidzhan project was a counter-Zionism (and in some cases, a crypto-Zionism): not the River Jordan but the River Amur! Despite a concerted propaganda campaign, however, the remoteness of the region and its primitive living conditions discouraged immigration. By 1933, a year when more settlers actually left Birobidzhan than arrived, there were but eight thousand Jews in the region; the original timetable had called for six times as many.

Indeed, Jews constituted less than 20 percent of the region's total population when, in May 1934, Birobidzhan was declared a Jewish autonomous oblast (subdivision of a republic), with Yiddish its official language. That year, the distinguished Yiddish novelist David Bergelson published his *Birobidzhaner,* an idealized report on Jewish pioneers who transform the taiga as well as themselves—ex-*luftmenshn* chopping down the primeval forest, draining swamps, laying down streets, putting up schools, and constructing homes. Nothing can deter these sturdy young enthusiasts who "come to build something new." No trial is too great—neither the constant rain and mosquito swarms of summer nor the freezing winds and fierce blizzards of winter: "The sifting snow has stopped, the wind has died down, and everywhere you look the snow lies smooth as a counterpane. And the sun . . . The sun, above you, below you, on the hillocks and in the sky, so bright—could it possibly be any brighter?"[35]

Under that great sun, Birobidzhan offered the most radical mutation yet: Ben-Zion Goldberg, an important American Jewish fellow traveler (as well as Sholom Aleichem's son-in-law), visited the autonomous oblast in 1934, reporting back that "instead of being built up by Jews in what we call a typical Jewish manner, Birobidzhan is being reclaimed with that Soviet efficiency which came into play in the construction of Dnepotrostroi and Magnitogorsk."[36]

To a certain degree, Birobidzhan, like the Moscow GOSET, was a production made for export. Years later, Goldberg would acknowledge that the Soviet Jewish homeland had inspired greater enthusiasm in New York and Buenos Aires than in Moscow or Kiev. Publicity was a necessary part of the package. The prospects for peaceful settlement, the friendliness of the indigenous population, and the existence of government support were favorably contrasted to the difficult lot of the Jewish settlers in Palestine, caught between Arab hostility on the one hand and British imperialism on the other.[37]

The years 1935 and 1936 marked the high point of immigration to Birobidzhan—although many (if not most) of the sixteen thousand new arrivals were non-Jews. The propaganda offensive gathered momentum as the Nazis continued to disenfranchise German Jews. Birobidzhan was a crucial component of the Popular Front and thus of the binding of American Jews to the Communist Party. Just before the opening of the first Moscow Trial, the Soviet Central Committee announced that "for the first time in the history of the Jewish people its burning desire for the creation of a homeland of its own, for the achievement of its own national statehood, has found fulfillment." It was predicted that by 1940, the Jewish population of Birobidzhan would reach 150,000.[38]

This fulfillment was illustrated by Belgoskino's *Seekers of Happiness*— its Russian title echoing that of *Jewish Luck* (or *Jewish Happiness*). Codirected by Vladimir Korsh-Sablin and I. Shapiro, including songs by the enormously popular Isaac Dunayevsky, not to mention a star turn by the GOSET's Venyamin Zuskin, *Seekers of Happiness* was cited—well in advance of its September 1936 release—by the new film production chief Boris Shumyatsky as one of the best Soviet movies of the year.[39]

As an appeal to Jewish nationalism and as a criticism of Jewish life in the Diaspora, *Seekers of Happiness* went far beyond *The Return of Nathan Becker*. A poor family of foreign Jews—perhaps even American—undertake a journey to Birobidzhan's Royte Feld (red field) *kolkhoz,* a collective farm where a relative has already happily settled. A Yiddish lament is heard on the boat that carries the long-suffering Dvoira (people's artist Maria Blumenthal-Tamarina); her son, Leva; her daughters, Rosa and Basya; and Basya's husband, the incorrigible *luftmensh* Pinya Kopman (Zuskin): "The world is pale, great and strange, for he who has no place, no work for his hands. I am weary of wandering. What does the Bright Land hold for me, happiness or sorrow?"[40]

What indeed? The quintessential *galos yid*, Pinya is always humming, forever calculating, constantly complaining. Brother-in-law Leva asks him to stop: "You interfere with my thinking." "Interesting," Pinya replies (his trademark expression), "What could you be thinking about?" Leva, a bit of a wise guy, responds that he's thinking about where Pinya might possibly fit in, "what kind of work you could do." Pinya tells him not to worry. It turns out that he's read a newspaper article about a farmer named Katz who discovered gold in Birobidzhan.

Life at Royte Feld is celebrated with a brief, quasi-documentary passage showing Jewish settlers blowing up trees to clear the land. (Inevitably, they will raise pigs.) But addicted as he is to *luftgeshekt* (airbusiness), Pinya cannot help but imagine Birobidzhan as one more shtetl get-rich-quick scheme. He is, in effect, too Jewish to appreciate the Jewish oblast—whose enemies, according to a pamphlet published to mark the tenth anniversary of Jewish settlement, attack the Bright Land as if "it were some sort of real estate venture concerning which the bargain of the transaction is the point at issue—the question as to whether or not one has overpaid; whether it will be salable, when the time comes; or whether, possibly, a poor bargain has been struck. Such a consideration is ridiculous as well as malicious, in the light of what the Soviet Union has done during the years to transform the Jews into productive workers."[41]

While the *kolkhoz* harvests, the *luftmensh* (still wearing city clothes) digs for treasure and, in a grotesque parody of Menakhem Mendl, spins the fantasy of Pinya Kopman the Suspender King. Finally, after nearly killing Leva in a struggle over what Pinya imagines to be gold, the Suspender King attempts to cross the border into China—but not before the truth is discovered. Dvoira, her hands "calloused from working," excoriates her son-in-law Pinya: "We tore ourselves away from where they did not consider us people, we took you out of filth and poverty, we tried to make a man of you and you, you learned nothing."

Thus, the *luftmensh* is exorcized and excommunicated. To complete the happy ending, Rosa overcomes her mother's misgivings and marries the young Cossack who had been wrongly accused of assaulting Leva. *Seekers of Happiness* concludes with a lengthy, joyous wedding scene in which individuals representing a variety of nationalities serenade the couple and present them with gifts. (Nor, in a since-excised shot, does Dvoira forget to thank Comrade Stalin.)[42]

Seekers of Happiness received an extraordinary amount of publicity in the English-language *Moscow Daily News*. Solomon Mikhoels—who earlier that year had crooned a Yiddish lullaby written by Dunayevsky for Grigori Alexandrov's musical extravaganza *Circus*—was credited as "acting consultant." But Korsh-Sablin took credit for the film's transformations: "I have straightened up the stooping Jews, shaved off the beards and cut their hair and have shown them as healthy, good-looking people, full of life and energy."[43]

On that hygienic note, Russian Jews vanished from the Soviet screen. Such was Soviet efficiency that, within a year of the movie's release, the NKVD became responsible for transportation of Jewish settlers to Birobidzhan, and the oblast's entire leadership was purged in the Great Terror.[44]

POSTSCRIPT: THE CASE OF *COMMISSAR*

> Dubno synagogues. Everything destroyed. . . . There are no adorn-
> ments in the building, everything is white and plain to the point
> of asceticism, everything is fleshless, bloodless, to a grotesque de-
> gree, you have to have the soul of a Jew to sense what it means.
> But what does the soul consist of? Can it be that ours is the
> century in which they perish?
>
> —Isaac Babel, *1920 Diary,* July 23[45]

An eternity passes, and then another. Like Pinya's treasure, every one of
these movies is long buried. So are many of their authors.

Babel, arrested as a Trotskyite spy in May 1939, is held for eight
months in NKVD dungeons, tortured into confession and then—after a
twenty-minute trial—executed. Mikhoels—who served with Markish and
Eisenstein on the wartime Jewish Anti-Fascist Committee and has become
the unofficial leader of the Soviet Jewish community—is sent on a fool's
mission to Minsk to award a Stalin Prize to the local GOSET. There, on
the night of January 13, 1948, he is murdered by NKVD agents—his
bloody corpse dumped in the snow behind the railway station so admired
by Melech Epstein.

Mikhoels is accorded a state funeral, but for Soviet Jews, his death is
the equivalent of the assassination of Leningrad party secretary Sergei
Kirov—the signal for a new terror. (Scarcely a year later, the actor's image
will be removed from all prints of *Circus* even as he is resurrected in the
NKVD files as the leading figure in a vast Zionist conspiracy.) By
summer's end, while the Moscow GOSET is on tour, Mikhoels's successor, Venyamin Zuskin, disappears—arrested at the hospital where he is
being treated for nervous exhaustion.[46]

On November 20, 1948, six months after the state of Israel is proclaimed, the Jewish Anti-Fascist Committee is dissolved. The Birobidzhan
GOSET is shut down—not even the name of Lazar Kaganovich can protect it. Christmas Eve 1948, the NKVD knocks on Itzik Fefer's door. In
January, 144 Jewish writers are arrested, including Markish and Bergelson. One month later, Yiddish literature is effectively banned. In the summer of 1949, when the visiting Paul Robeson inquires as to Fefer's whereabouts, the poet is produced for a brief meeting. On August 12, 1951,

after a secret trial at which only Fefer pleads guilty, Zuskin, Markish, Bergelson, and Fefer are shot, along with a dozen other Yiddish writers.

Even this is not the end. On January 13, 1953, *Literary Gazette* breaks the story of that a dozen Kremlin doctors, most of them Jews, have conspired to murder the Soviet leadership. The planned show trial for these "murderers in white gowns," is derailed only by Stalin's death on March 5—as are the plans that many feel were in the works to deport Russian Jews en masse to Birobidzhan or beyond.[47]

> First only Stalin was the heavy, then Marx, then Hegel; but the truth is there are no heavies and no heroes here, only fate and history. The earth moves under our feet, the ceiling caves in, and we try to climb out from under the rubble.
>
> —George Konrád, *The Loser*[48]

The Russian earth has begun to shift. Soon it will quake. Now we have one more premiere—Alexander Askoldov's hitherto unknown *Commissar*. Extraordinary relic, it is the final Soviet Jewish movie and the last film to emerge from the film agency Goskino's vault, proscribed for twenty years before its unscheduled appearance at the 1987 Moscow Film Festival.[49]

Commissar had gone beyond the Pale by returning to it. Set in the southern Ukraine at the time of the civil war, the movie was based on a once-famous story, "In the Town of Berdichev"—first published in *Literary Gazette* in April 1934 and subsequently praised by Isaac Babel, Mikhail Bulgakov, and Maxim Gorky—that had effectively launched the late, long-banned writer Vasily Grossman's literary career.[50]

Commissar's eponymous protagonist is a beefy, severe woman, first seen meting out revolutionary justice to a deserter who broke ranks to visit his wife. The irony is that family ties are about to put the commissar herself out of commission—she's in her sixth month of an unwanted pregnancy. Glum and wordless, built like a refrigerator and scarcely warmer, this paradigm of Bolshevik discipline is left behind in Berdichev to have her baby, billeted with a poor Jewish family in its tumultuous, tumbledown shack. It is just her Jewish luck.

Shot in wide-screen black and white and distanced by Alfred Schnittke's modernist, contrapuntal score, *Commissar* is a closet drama with a confident surplus of showy style. Askoldov choreographs the action and dances around it with sudden swish tilts or bombastic, handheld camera moves.

The bullet that kills a Red Army deserter passes in slow motion through a clay vessel of milk; the epic shot that catches a column of Red Army soldiers as they march toward the camera swings back to follow them away, mixing up mud and soldiers in one long, sinuous take. (Twenty-four years after the film wrapped, the camera operator Valery Ginsburg would receive an award for his work from the Union of Cinematographers.)

Even in 1967, *Commissar* was something of an archaeological expedition. Askoldov had not only reworked the rhetoric of the Soviet silent film; in deliberately excavating the state Soviet Yiddish culture that had been terminated with Mikhoels's murder, he portrayed the Soviet cinema's first village Jews since the mid-1930s. Given the circumstances, it's scarcely an insider's portrait: At once earthy "little folk" and denatured philo-Semitic stereotypes, these Jews are exotic Others, lovers rather than fighters—constantly eating, talking, washing, working, complaining, as the camera prowls around their teeming courtyard.

Perverse nostalgia for an obsolete identity: The tinker Yefim (Roland Bykov) speaks Russian with a Jewish accent and makes fanciful, ironic Jewish jokes. Bykov, who went on to a notable career as an actor and director, strains to represent the hitherto unrepresentable. His forehead bulges over his expressive, homely—and beardless—face. His performance seems modeled on a Mikhoels or Zuskin *luftmensh*—or more likely, the idea of one. Yefim greets the morning with an elaborate ritual, an expressive yawn, a shrugging chant, a relaxing piss (on his doorstep, yet)—then wipes his face with his shirt, kisses his wife, smooches the baby's *tukhes*, and ruefully dances off to work.[51]

The tinker's wife, Maria (Raisa Nedaskovskaya), is a girlish earth mother—dark and sexy, with six children frisking at her feet. There's also the grandmother (Ludmila Volynskaya), possibly the only adult Jewish member of the cast, who speaks nothing but Yiddish—heard once more in a Soviet film. Well-intentioned minstrelsy, without a hint of religious practice; and yet, conjured out of the past in the context of *Commissar,* Yefim and his brood are humanity. The *luftmensh* is here a positive hero; the *luftshlos* (castle in the air) is the commissar's dream of October.

Commissar shifts Grossman's time frame forward, from the Polish-Soviet War of 1920 to the late stages of the civil war, and eliminates the commissar's climactic vision of Lenin. Askoldov also incorporated elements of Babel's "Gedali," including a specific conversation: When the tinker invokes an "international of kindness," the commissar (embodiment of what Gedali familiarly refers to as "Mrs. Revolution") can respond only with Bolshevik platitudes: "The foundation of the International Community consists of worker and peasant blood."[52]

Blood in *Commissar* is both abstract and visceral. As the Russian film historian Elena Stishova put it, the pregnant woman is "Clio herself, the muse of history," and the child in her womb is the revolution. As the commissar gives birth, Askoldov's montage juxtaposes her maternal agony with images of a desert campaign in which the men and horses of the Red Cavalry strain to dislodge a cannon stuck in the sand. The fatally wounded officer who appears is understood to be the father of the commissar's child; his death is marked by a maddened stampede of riderless horses.[53]

This frenzied sequence is scarcely the film's last domestic apocalypse. Yefim's ramshackle courtyard is both heaven and hell, and as White soldiers advance on Berdichev, the impending pogrom is evoked by his children's play: Ganging up on one sister ("Got you, Jew-bitch"), they rip her clothing and bind her to a swing. This brutal scene sets up the movie's eerily subdued centerpiece. Hiding with the family in their cellar, the commissar has a prophetic vision.

The Nazi massacre of Russian Jews began in Berdichev on September 15, 1941; as described by Grossman in *The Black Book of Soviet Jewry,* the town's Jews are marched off to their death. The commissar walks uncertainly behind them, clutching her newborn son. The cinematic equivalent of Yevgeny Yevtushenko's "Babi Yar"—published in 1962 and unpublished a year later—*Commissar* is the lone Soviet film to acknowledge Jewish suffering during World War II, let alone suggest any measure of Russian complicity.

In the end, the commissar returns the front, perhaps to die—leaving her child behind with the Jews. On paper, this must have seemed the ultimate revolutionary sacrifice. Reading Askoldov's script, veteran director Mikhail Romm expressed his enthusiasm for this expression of universal brotherhood, not to mention the revolution's "elevated humanity."[54]

On screen, however, the effect would be quite different: Did *Commissar* propose that Communist authority merge with Mother Russia and board with a shtetl *luftmensh* to learn about suffering? Who had appointed this family of oppressed, doomed Jews the guardians of revolutionary hope? What Jewish Communist was left to dare?[55]

The remarkable thing about *Commissar,* which opens under the sign of the Holy Virgin and closes with a supremely mournful and possibly perfunctory rendition of the "Internationale," is not that was banned but that it was ever approved at all.

In late 1988, Elena Stishova located two hefty volumes in the Goskino archives that—stamped with injunction "Store indefinitely"—detailed the official proceedings on the film *Commissar* from October 15, 1965, when the scenario was submitted by the Gorky Studio to Goskino, through the end of 1967, when the movie was shelved in perpetuity. Better almost than the film itself was this narrative of its tortuous relationship to Soviet power.

Forty years after *Jewish Luck* and *Battleship Potemkin* received their premieres and Stalin his standing ovation, the *Commissar* script was approved for production. But that same fall in 1965 the dissident writers Andrei Sinyavsky and Yuli Daniel were arrested, and early the next year, they were tried in the first show trials of the post-Stalin era. The Khrushchev thaw was officially over: The two writers were sentenced to terms of seven and five years. (At this time, too, the future Nobel laureate Joseph Brodsky was jailed for "social parasitism.")

The *Commissar* script was accused of being unheroic, as well as distorting "the humanitarian essence of the proletarian revolution." One sharp-eyed reader criticized Askoldov for grafting Babel onto Grossman. Another protested his adding the scene in which the commissar shoots the deserter. Nevertheless, the script was approved; production began the next summer; editing was completed in spring of 1967. And then—HaBima's revenge.

A few weeks after *Commissar* was finished, Israel defeated Soviet client states Egypt and Syria in the Six-Day War. What to do with the movie now? The Soviet government openly identified with those whose announced desire was to destroy the Jewish state—and who had abjectly failed to do so. The rhetoric machine went into high gear: A major media offensive used the basest anti-Semitic caricatures to represent Israel (while describing Israeli leaders as neo-Nazis), repeatedly insisted on the existence of a Zionist fifth column, and, at its most virulent, characterized Judaism as a religion that "calls for genocide."[56]

All remaining illusions were liquidated. As the Soviet media made no distinction between Jews and Zionists, Soviet Jews were effectively converted to Zionism. The last Communist Jews were driven from Poland. (In New York, even the Yiddish communist daily the *Morgn Frayhayt* broke with the party.) *Commissar* had been overtaken by another world-historic event. Leonid Trauberg, whose career was wrecked in 1948 when he was labeled among the film industry cosmopolitans, had been Askoldov's teacher: "I want to see a film about a commissar," he blandly told a meeting convened to discuss *Commissar*'s disposition. "I don't need a film about the unpleasant fate of the Jewish people." (After all, such Jewish life no longer exists.)[57]

At the same time, clever Trauberg proposed a strategy to save his student's project. Released now, *Commissar* might innoculate the Soviet Union against current charges of anti-Semitism: "I would be happy if [*Commissar*] premiered today to inform the world as quickly as possible, that if we are angry about what is being done [by Israel to the Arab states] in the Middle East, then this is not a nationality issue but a social one; for our country is the first to call for equality among nations, and the film proves this." It was a vague memory of the cover once furnished by Birobidzhan or the Moscow GOSET. Another participant agreed: *Commissar* "provides us an ideological weapon for the present situation."[58]

The debate continued into the winter of 1968, when it was finally resolved that *Commissar* took a deviant view on questions of "proletarian internationalism and humanism." Citing Askoldov's "nihilistic view of our Revolution's history," as well as his scandalous portrayal of a Bolshevik commissar as "a Cossack chieftain," Goskino director Alexei Romanov clinched the decision. He reported discussing *Commissar* "with some Jewish individuals who study cinema, individuals whom I deeply respect, and they say that this is an anti-Semitic film." (At which point, according to the transcript, an anonymous voice chimes in, "But Russians say that this is an anti-Russian film.")[59]

Askoldov would recall that Romanov paternally advised him that he might yet salvage his film if he changed the family's nationality and cut the flash-forward. After the director refused, "the film was simply taken away. The editing room was sealed off." Studio officials accused Askoldov of "preaching cynicism," but as film journalist Anne Williamson has suggested, his real crime was less cynicism than its absence.

As far as his colleagues were concerned, the most aggravating of Askoldov's sins may have been his fervent, idealistic Communism. Given his identification with writers such as Bulgakov, Grossman, and Babel, not to mention Eisenstein and Trauberg, Askoldov represented a distinctively Soviet counterculture. (His code name for this was "internationalism.") Askoldov actually believed he was right. He not only refused to compromise, he acted as if he imagined that his view would prevail! Throughout 1968, the director continued to petition the party cinema committee meetings and write letters to Romanov, the Central Committee, and even the Kremlin's supreme ideologue, Mikhail Suslov.[60]

Having refused to compromise, Askoldov appealed *Commissar*'s suppression so vehemently that, in March 1969, he was dismissed (for reasons of "professional inadequacy") from his position at the Gorky Studio and physically removed from the premises. "Obviously Askoldov is a unique specimen if neither actions nor outside influence have any effect on him—not that of his comrades and colleagues, nor that of the high authorities and the Party collective," one exasperated apparatchik complained. By 1970, the specimen was purged from the Communist Party and the Cinematographers Union; over the next twenty years, he made but two TV documentaries, only one of which actually aired.[61]

Perhaps the most taboo film in Soviet history, *Commissar* is a monument to a thrice-vanished world—the abandoned Pale of Settlement where it is set, the impossible future of Soviet Jewish culture that it evokes, and the historical moment at which it was made. All have disappeared beneath the waves, along with the system only within and against which *Commissar*'s passion can be fully appreciated. A number of movies were consigned to the vaults during the freeze of 1967–68; *Commissar* alone was reduced to unfilmhood. (Askoldov was told that the single print had been burned.)

The author would maintain that it had been merely his duty to make this unseeable movie: "It is the philosophy of my religion." And what was that? Alexander Askoldov reinvented himself as the last Soviet Jew—the *non-Jewish* non-Jewish Jew.[62]

CHAPTER 4

Who Was Victor
Serge (and
Why Will We
Have to Ask)?

*I welcome all signs that a more virile,
warlike age is about to begin . . . the age
that will carry heroism into the search for
knowledge and that will wage wars for the
sake of ideas and their consequences.*

—Friedrich Nietzsche, *The Joyful Wisdom* (1882)

Victor Serge (1890-1947) is an author whose work is not included in any literary canon—however assiduously it may have
been collected by the Soviet security apparatus. A Russian novelist who wrote in French, Serge was born into one political exile and
died in another; his homeland was a succession of prisons and left-
wing political parties.

It was some sort of twentieth-century career: Serge dwelt in millennial expectation and catastrophic loss, living dangerously alongside
three generations of European anarchists, syndicalists, Bolsheviks,
Trotskyists, independent communists, and unaffiliated leftists—in Belgium, in France, in Spain, in Soviet Russia, in Germany and in Austria, back in the Soviet Union, once more in France, and, finally, in
Mexico.

An organizer and agitator—which is to say, a professional revolutionary—as well as a journalist, pamphleteer, and historian, Serge
turned seriously to writing fiction only after being purged from the
Communist Party. He was nearly forty when he finished his first novel,

His significance as a political novelist indistinguishable from his role as historical actor, Victor Serge
had a certain Communist totality—at least until the (second) collapse of the October Revolution.
Does the Serge oeuvre now annotate the historical text, or vice versa? Written for the *Voice Literary
Supplement*, this chapter appears largely as published in November 1984. Serge's novels have become
even harder to find—although *Russia Twenty Years After* has since been republished, as has Serge's
correspondence with Trotsky and even a book of poems. The circle of Anglo-American Serge scholars, headed by Richard Greeman, remains small but devoted.

Men in Prison (1930), composed in fragments and mailed to his friends so that, if its author was arrested (as he eventually was), the assembled manuscript might be published abroad.

The decade that Serge spent as a member of the Soviet government (and as a Comintern agent) seems almost a fluke; his politics were those of the permanent oppositionist. Did Serge embody only what Slavoj Žižek has called the "narcissism of the lost cause"? His "instinct," wrote Peter Sedgwick, translator of Serge's *Memoirs of a Revolutionary,* "was always to swim against the stream. In the full flood of Bolshevism he stood for Anarchy, during the Stalinist bloodbath for the Left Opposition, in the rising Cold War for the integrity of Bolshevism's past." The reality was a bit more complex than that—but then, Victor Serge is also a myth.[1]

Neither a theoretician nor a leader, Serge participated in three revolutions (Barcelona 1917, Petrograd 1919–20, Berlin 1923) and wrote, for the most part, from a rank-and-file perspective. Political knowledge seeps from the pores of his work: An apartment where a black-market deal is transacted in *The Case of Comrade Tulayev* (1950) is "not a place where anyone lived, it was a place where someone was waiting to vanish, in a confusion like a station platform during the rout of an army." Serge's observations are often too unexpected to be anything but genuine. "What is the point of being incorruptible," asks a syndicalist leader in *Birth of Our Power* (1931), "if you don't take the money?"[2]

Hard-nosed but generous, at once a realist and a utopian, Serge functioned most eloquently as a conscience of the Left. He was also, by some accounts, an unlikely figure. Claude Lévi-Strauss, who shared passage with Serge when both were escaping from the Nazis in 1940, found him startlingly incongruous—a kind of Buddhist monk. Serge's association with Lenin "was all the more intimidating, because it was difficult to reconcile it with his looks."[3]

Serge was, at one point and in some circles, the most celebrated political prisoner of his day. In June 1935, his case rocked the European intellectual community when it was raised in Paris at the International Writers Congress for the Defense of Culture. "Immediately," according to one participant, "the audience was divided between Trotskyites and Stalinists. Adversaries insulted each other in the jargon and with the arguments of the two political positions that had also divided Russian opinion." The uproar bade to become violent when André Malraux melodramatically threatened to expel from the hall anyone who uttered the words *Victor Serge.*[4]

This political antipathy notwithstanding, Serge's novels have a generic resemblance to those of Malraux. But unlike the future French culture minister, Serge never seems descended from Alexander Dumas—his books aren't invented tales of derring-do in exotic climes. The worm's-eye view came to him naturally. Although given to occasional sentimentality or patches of stilted dialogue, Serge was an ironist with an appreciative ear for the lumpen *bon mot:* "What—you really believe that the day will come when men won't have lice?" sneers an anonymous member of *Tulayev's* crowd. "True Socialism—eh?—with butter and sugar for everybody? Maybe to increase human happiness, there'll be soft, perfumed lice that caress you?"[5]

Perfumed lice: At times, Serge's authorial voice recalls that of his contemporary B. Traven, another international revolutionary anarchist (of the Wobbly persuasion) who wound up in Mexico. Serge, too, was a genuine proletarian writer, drawing his language and metaphors from the experience of his class. "Powerless oaths fell about them like flaccid gobs of spit," he could write with sardonic affection.[6]

Like the George Orwell of *Down and Out in Paris and London,* Serge exhibits a striking solidarity with the human wreckage of European cities. Indeed, Orwell was one of the few contemporary commentators to consider Serge in a literary context—Orwell's 1946 essay on Arthur Koestler cites Serge as a key figure in "the special class of literature that has arisen out of the European political struggle since the rise of fascism." Serge, Malraux, Koestler, and Ignazio Silone, Orwell noted, were alike in their "trying to write contemporary history, but *unofficial* history, the kind that is ignored in textbooks and lied about in the newspapers."[7]

To be ignored in textbooks—if no longer lied about in the newspapers—has been Serge's fate ever since. A year after Orwell's essay, Jean-Paul Sartre spun his own theoretical web around the same group of writers, *sans* Serge. "Forced by circumstances to discover the pressure of history, as Torricelli discovered atmospheric pressure," Sartre wrote in the final chapter of *What Is Literature?* "we have a task for which we may not be strong enough." Sartre called for a literature that reconciled the "relativity of the historical fact" with metaphysical absolutes— a formula, not unsuggestive of Socialist Realism, that charged political struggle with spiritual commitment. In a footnote, Sartre elaborated: "What are Camus, Malraux, Koestler, etc. now producing if not literature of extreme situations? Their characters are at the height of power or in prison cells, on the eve of death or of being tortured or of killing. Wars, coups d'etat, revolutionary action, bombardments, massacres.

There you have their everyday life. On every page, in every line, it is always the whole man who is in question."[8]

The year of his death, Serge was already forgotten by the city where, a dozen years before, the mere mention of his name had nearly incited writers to riot.

PORTRAIT OF THE REVOLUTIONARY AS A YOUNG MAN

Our Victor Lvovich enjoyed a unique heritage. History was his birthright—and the idea of making history. "From Russia, swarming through the whole world, came men and women who had been formed in ruthless battle, who had but one aim in life, who drew their breath from danger," Serge wrote in *Memoirs of a Revolutionary.*[9]

Among these Russians were the writer's parents. Serge's father, a noncommissioned officer of the imperial guard, had sympathized with People's Will, the tiny underground party that, in 1881, managed to assassinate Czar Alexander II—indeed, Sergei's father's assignment was to shoot the czar should Alexander survive the first attempt on his life. From 1878 through 1883, political assassins had attacked numerous European heads of state, including the kings of Spain and Italy, the German kaiser, and the French prime minister; only Alexander was killed. Serge's parents escaped to the West, although their gentle, scientifically inclined cousin Nikolai Kibalchich was hanged as the chemist who constructed the bomb that blew away the czar.

The refugee Kibalchiches set up house in a Brussels slum, nursing their firstborn on politics and deprivation. "On the walls of our humble and makeshift lodgings there were always the portraits of men who had been hanged." It is scarcely an exaggeration to say that Victor Kibalchich grew up starving. There were times when his family lived on stale bread soaked in black coffee; his younger brother died of malnutrition.[10]

The child Victor imbibed a heady mixture of class resentment, immigrant alienation, and revolutionary fervor: "Even before I emerged from childhood I seem to have experienced, deeply at heart, that paradoxical feeling which was dominate me all through the first part of my life: that of living in a world without any possible escape, in which there was nothing for it but to fight for an impossible escape. I felt repugnance, mingled with wrath and indignation, towards people I saw settled comfortably in this world. How could they not be conscious of their captivity?"[11]

The earth was a prison.

Serge was largely self-taught; his father despised the "stupid bourgeois instruction for the poor" and could hardly afford to pay for his education. Where other boys read Karl May or James Fenimore Cooper, young Victor fantasized over Louis Blanc's *History of the French Revolution.* By age fifteen, he was living on his own; he became a photographer's apprentice, then a draftsman and a linotype operator, organizing all the while for the Belgian Socialist Party. A few years later, having read Peter Kropotkin's *Appeal to the Young,* he toured various utopian colonies in Belgium and France, havens for Tolstoyans, tramps, and apostles of free love: "buzzing of bees, golden summer, eighteen years old, and the doorway to Anarchy!"[12]

Having attained his majority, Serge took his place among the "subproletariat of declasse 'emancipated' men." At nineteen, he moved to Paris—"an immense jungle where all relationships were dominated by a primitive individualism"—and, working intermittently as a printer and translator, threw himself into the fringe political scene. As remembered three decades later, his milieu included "young vegetarians involved in pointless struggles against the whole of society," philosophical tramps "fanatical in affliction," militant nonsmokers, teetotalers, revolutionary bandits, intellectual criminals, and charismatic personalities such as the Catalan organizer-orator-fixer-revolutionary Miguel Almereyda (an anarchist martyr, whose baby son would grow into the filmmaker Jean Vigo).[13]

Thus, a precursor of the New Left before he had even joined the old one, Serge wrote in his memoirs that "anarchism swept us away completely because it both demanded everything of us and offered everything to us." Disgusted by the mellow, academic antistatism of Jean Grave, Serge followed anarchism's most extreme line—which, through the logic of its particular dialectic, had succeeded in discarding the necessity for revolution altogether. Class warfare was not the engine for change but rather the individual's total revolt against the strictures of society.[14]

The extreme "individualism" to which Serge subscribed derived as much from Max Stirner and Nietzsche as from Mikhail Bakunin or Kropotkin. His guru was the crippled spellbinder Albert Joseph, also known as Libertad, an emaciated, hirsute protobeatnik who lived in destitution and preached a dogma of absolute freedom, exhorting his unkempt, agitated followers to live their lives as though the millennium had already arrived. The proper anarchist Grave accused the individualists of being tools of the police. His charges may have been paranoid, but the offices of *L'Anarchie,* the journal founded by Libertad and, after 1911, edited by Serge, were frequented by a criminal element that the paper was polemically prone to glorify. *L'Anarchie* exalted the outsider and the outlaw; "work, marriage, military service, voting [were considered] to be vices." Publishing his manifestos—he was even then a writer first—under the name *Le Rétif* (the unbroken), Serge was soon the most notorious of Libertad's disciples.[15]

Pre–World War I Montmartre was a spawning ground for both the aesthetic and political avant-gardes: "Our Montmartre adjoined, but never met, the Montmartre of artists' taverns." Along with Pablo Picasso, Serge favored the notorious Lapin Agile, popularly known as "the Assassin's Cabaret," a hangout for crazy painters and political loudmouths as well as a picturesque lowlife made up of criminals and whores—thus incubating twentieth-century Europe's cultural vanguard. Serge at the Lapin Agile anticipates by several years the confluence of Lenin playing chess in the same Zurich café at which Tristan Tzara claimed to have discovered the word *Dada*.[16]

The anarchists' Montmartre was a milieu of incessant discussion in shabby offices, occasionally punctuated by bloody shoot-outs. But once Serge became editor of the faction-ridden *L'Anarchie,* he shifted the newspaper's emphasis from individualism to social action. Specifically, *L'Anarchie* glorified the violence of the Bonnot Gang, which included two of Serge's Belgian comrades. The so-called desperadoes of the *tragique bande* were modern bank robbers who made their getaways in automobiles and, professing an ideology, defied bourgeois society as well as the police. "Je suis avec les bandits!" *L'Anarchie* proclaimed in December 1911, after Bonnot shot and robbed a bank messenger in Paris. Serge's alleged taste for shouting down speakers at public meetings notwithstanding, he engaged in neither criminal activity nor armed resistance. He did, however, briefly shelter two of Bonnot's associates and continued to justify their crime, reiterating his position in *L'Anarchie*'s January 4, 1912, issue that "to shoot, in full daylight, a miserable bank clerk proved that some men have at least understood the virtues of audacity."[17]

By April, Bonnot met his end, wrapped in a bullet-riddled mattress and killed in a gunfight with the French authorities. "The outlaw-anarchists shot at the police and blew out their own brains," Serge later wrote. "I saw the whole movement founded by Libertad dragged into the scum of society by a kind of madness; and nobody could do anything about it, least of all myself. The theoreticians, terrified, headed for cover. It was like a collective suicide."[18] Nor was this the last time he would watch a revolutionary movement self-destruct.

FROM ANARCHY TO BOLSHEVISM

In January 1912, the police had found two revolvers while searching L'Anarchie's offices. Serge was arrested and charged with harboring the criminals whom he had publicly defended. He refused to cooperate with the police and was sentenced to five years in solitary confinement, to be followed by another five in exile.

Thus, Serge fulfilled his childhood destiny. "Of prison I shall say here only a little," he would write in his memoirs. "It burdened me with an experience so heavy, so intolerable to endure, that long afterwards, when I resumed writing, my first book (a novel) amounted to an effort to free myself from this inward nightmare." It was after leaving prison that Victor Kibalchich—Le Rétif—took for himself the name Victor Serge.[19]

Serge was still incarcerated when world war "burst suddenly out of the void." The inmates were forbidden to know anything about the conflict, but soon the first military prisoners began to arrive. "A strange joy glittered in their eyes, 'Stop complaining!' they said. 'You can't imagine how well off we are here!' 'I'd rather do five years than go back to living that life at the front.'" The sensation of discovering, while in prison, that the world had gone mad was one Serge would evoke repeatedly: "We were the only men on earth forbidden to know about the war, but, although we read nothing and could only glimpse, through the double smokescreen of war and administrative stupidity, the general outline of events, some few of us were blessed with exceptional clear-sightedness. . . . Long before Europe ever dreamt it, we were discussing, in whispers, the coming Russian Revolution. We knew in what part of the globe the long-awaited flame would be born. And in it we found a new reason for living."[20]

Released in 1917, Serge made his way to neutral Barcelona, a hotbed of spies and political agents, refuge for all manner of international criminals. As a noncombatant, Spain was enjoying the greatest export boom in its history, although prices were rising faster than wages. By summer, the city was a prerevolutionary pressure cooker. Junior officers agitated for reform of the army while even large industrialists had joined the socialists and other left-wing parties in open opposition to the Spanish monarchy.

Haunting the Ramblas cafés, waiting for news of Russia, Serge broke with his individualist comrades, fell in with the syndicalist organizer Salvador "Sugar Boy" Seguí—reader of Nietzsche, leader of the most effective anarchist movement in twentieth-century Europe—and took part in preparations for a general strike. But when the government provoked a crisis, the alliance of liberal bourgeoisie, Catalan nationalists, industrial workers, and military reformers proved illusory: The "liberals took fright at the last minute and refused to join the struggle," while the soldiers reverted to form and turned their guns on the strikers. "We fought alone, in a day of sunshine and shouting, of impetuous crowds and chases in the streets, while the cautious black-hats charged lazily and pursued us without enthusiasm."[21]

Seguí went into hiding to organize the next offensive, but Serge, now more than an intellectual, could wait no longer. "I had lost all hope of victory hereabouts, I was weary of discussions with militants who often seemed to me no more than great big children." When the rebellion broke out (and was crushed) that August, Serge was already en route to Russia, where the Bolsheviks were poised to seize power. Or rather, he was already on his way to the French prison camp where he would be detained for over a year as a Bolshevik agent.[22]

The uprising in Barcelona, the world war, and his abortive journey home provided Serge with material for his second novel, *Birth of Our Power*. The book's epiphany comes during an air raid: "Civilization reaches its high point in this senseless combat above the Louvre. . . . The bombing plane closes the circle that began with the victory at Samothrace." The narrator experiences the aerial battle as the apotheosis of western civilization, then—in a remarkable passage—absorbs its mechanical fury into himself and the revolution, sounding amazingly like both the right-wing Italian futurists and the leftist Russian constructivists.[23]

"We must be precise, clear-sighted, strong, unyielding, armed: like machines, you see," the anonymous narrator muses, identifying a particular essence of the twentieth-century worldview.

> To set up a vast enterprise for demolition and to throw ourselves into it with our whole being because we know that we cannot live as long as the world has not been made over. We need technicians, not great men or admirable men. Technicians specialized in the liberation of the masses, licensed demolition experts who will have scorn for the idea of personal escapism because their work will be

their life. To learn how to take the mechanism of history apart: to know how to slide in that extra little nut or bolt somewhere—as among the parts of a motor—which will blow the whole thing up. There it is. And it will cost whatever it costs.[24]

Whatever it did cost, the Russian Revolution was the supreme event of Victor Serge's life. In the first month of 1919—"the year of ice"—he made his way to red Petrograd, capital of the motherland he had never seen, hub of the cataclysm for which his parents spent their lives waiting: "We were entering a world frozen to death . . . the metropolis of Cold, of Hunger, of Hatred, and of Endurance. . . . Never until now had any of us known such a horrid diet. Girls with red head-bands joined with young bespectacled agitators to give us a summary of the state of affairs: 'Famine, typhus and counter-revolution everywhere. But the World Revolution is bound to save us.'"[25]

World revolution was not immediately forthcoming, however, and the Russian Revolution, as Serge would later write, was "at once grandiose in its inner necessity and pitiful in its outer helplessness." This was the civil war's decisive moment: Petrograd blockaded and the Western powers prepared to descend. Fuel was so scarce that virtually all the city's wooden houses had been torn down for firewood. Families burned their books, furniture, and flooring to keep warm. (Viktor Shklovsky noted in his memoirs that "everything was now divided into two categories: combustible and noncombustible.") Abandoned children joined in criminal gangs. Prostitutes demanded the right to organize a trade union. Old people starved to death in the streets, amid mounds of frozen sewage. The population that year decreased by nearly one-third.[26]

Maxim Gorky, who had, in his youth, known Serge's mother, welcomed the young seeker to his apartment ("as warm as a greenhouse") on Kronversky Prospect. The Bolsheviks, the writer told Serge, were "drunk with authority" and "cramping the violent, spontaneous authority of the Russian people." But just as he had in Barcelona, Serge threw in his lot with the revolution: "I was neither against the Bolsheviks nor neutral; I was with them, albeit independently, without renouncing thought or critical sense."[27]

By May Day 1919 (red-painted airplanes circling overhead), the former anarchist had joined the Communist Party. Serge criticized the Leninists' intolerance, their "faith in statification," and their propensity for centralism and bureaucracy, but he was also a realist—or so he thought. The "gravest and most impermissible error that the Bolshevik leaders committed" was precisely, he realized, the most tragic and understandable. This was the creation of the Special Commission for the Suppression of Counter Revolution and Sabotage, known as the Cheka, to preserve the revolution by any means necessary, including terror.[28]

"A notable saying of Lenin kept rising in my mind," Serge would remember. "It is a terrible misfortune that the honor of beginning the first socialist revolution should have befallen the most backward people in Europe." Nevertheless, it *was* socialist revolution: "Within the current situation of Europe, bloodstained, devastated, and in profound stupor, Bolshevism was, in my eyes, tremendously and visibly right. It marked a new point of departure in history."[29]

Serge fought in the defense of Petrograd—attacked twice that year by General N. N. Yudenich's army, which both times reached the city's suburbs. As a Communist, Serge taught political education courses to the workers. Eventually, he went to work for Grigori Zinoviev, then chairman of the Petrograd soviet: "Clean-shaven, pale, his face a little puffy, [Zinoviev] felt absolutely at home on the pinnacle of power . . . all the same there was also an impression of flabbiness, almost of a lurking irresolution." Zinoviev seemed pleased when informed by Serge that, back in Europe, he had a "frightful reputation for terror."[30]

Setting up the Comintern publishing house and running the Romance language section while editing international journals, Serge was also responsible for cataloging the archives of the czarist secret police—a sort of postgraduate education in political espionage in which, among other things, he discovered the file of student informers who had betrayed People's Will. Typically, Serge appreciated this material as literature. "Where does sincerity begin in these letters?" he wrote in *What Everyone Should Know about State Repression*. "Where does duplicity end? We do not know. We have before us a complex, painful, blemished, prostituted, naked soul."[31]

Serge also found time to compose a number of pamphlets in defense of the revolution, many of them directed at his friends in Western anarchist circles. Such hyperactivity was, he would assert, merely the Bolshevik norm: "Every Communist and participant in the revolution felt himself the unimportant servitor of an immense cause. The greatest compliment one could pay such a man was to say: 'He has no private life.'"[32]

As a member of Petrograd's ruling circles, Serge knew everyone from Lenin (with his "amazingly fresh and pink face," "surpassing air of geniality and cheerful malice") and Trotsky ("we had admiration for him but no real love" for "his sternness, his insistence on punctuality in work and battle, the inflexible correctness of his demeanor in a period of general slackness"); through the two other "brains of the Revolution," Nikolai Bukharin ("habitually surrounded by crowds of smiling young listeners, who drank in all his incisive observations") and Karl Radek ("thin, rather small, nervous, full of anecdotes which often had a savage side to them, realistic to the point of cruelty") to the American journalist John Reed ("tall, forceful, and matter-of-fact, with a cool idealism and a lively intelligence tinged by humour") and Hungarian leader Béla Kun ("a wholly unattractive personality . . . dominated by his sense of failure" and, according to Serge, publically characterized by Lenin as an "imbecile").[33]

In addition to this galaxy of history-making revolutionary stars, Serge also consorted with Mensheviks, left social revolutionaries, members of the so-called Workers' Opposition, and worse. He was the lone Bolshevik who was permitted to attend Kropotkin's funeral. "I was the only member of the Party to be accepted as a comrade in anarchist circles. . . . I belonged to the last free thought society; in all probability I was the only Communist member."[34]

Serge watched as the victorious Bolsheviks first courted and then arrested their erstwhile allies. The end of the civil war brought a storm of left-wing protest against the so-called War Communism. Strike-beset Petrograd was placed under martial law. When, in March 1920, the sailors of the Kronstadt naval garrison—an island fortress at the mouth of the Neva—declared their solidarity with the strikers, Lenin and Trotsky opted to subjugate the garrison at a cost of more than four thousand lives.

For Serge, as for others, this event was traumatic:

After many hesitations, and with unutterable anguish, my Communist friends and I finally declared ourselves on the side of the Party. This is why. Kronstadt had right on its side. Kronstadt was the beginning of a fresh, liberating revolution for popular democracy: "The Third Revolution!" it was called by certain anarchists whose heads were stuffed with infantile illusions. However, the country was absolutely exhausted, and production practically at a standstill; there were no reserves of any kind, not even reserves of stamina in the hearts of the masses.[35]

The revolution was to be professionalized by a full-time elite. In 1922, Serge was sent west to Berlin to edit for the Comintern's European press service. When he arrived, the German mark exchanged at four hundred to the dollar. The next year brought the worst inflation in modern history. Breakdown! "Seen from here, the Russian Revolution appeared as a superb exploit," Serge wrote. "In this decomposing bourgeois world we recovered our confidence."[36]

By the summer of 1923, the German mark was trading at 4.5 million to the dollar, and Bolshevik leaders, Trotsky in particular, saw their longed-for German revolution nearly at hand. Mad theater of the moment, the Russians had even scheduled the uprising to coincide with October's sixth anniversary. But once it became clear that the local red units were pathetically underarmed, everything had to be canceled. (Counterorders failed to reach Hamburg in time, and three hundred Communists led a two-day uprising.) The most notorious insurrection of the season wasn't even Communist-inspired: On November 8, Adolf Hitler and his National Socialists staged their futile Munich putsch.

For the Russians, the collapse of German Communism came as a nasty shock. The isolation of the Bolshevik Revolution was now a foregone conclusion, inadvertently presaging Stalin's formula for "socialism in one country." Serge's account makes his frustration with both the Germans and Russians palpable—although he is surprisingly taciturn in analyzing the debacle. Surely among the obscure turning points of history, the failure of the German proletariat in 1923 paved a path not only for Hitler but also for Stalin.[37]

Serge was spirited out of Berlin and into Vienna, where "blood and despair hovered in the giddy air." Watching from afar the battle for succession that followed Lenin's death in January 1924, he encountered such distinguished Western Marxists as Antonio Gramsci ("an industrious and Bohemian exile, late to bed and late to rise . . . losing his way at night in familiar streets, taking the wrong train, indifferent to the comfort of his lodging and the quality of his meals") and Georg Lukács ("a first-class brain which could have endowed Communism with a true intellectual greatness if it had developed as a social movement instead of degenerating").[38]

Returning to the Soviet Union in 1926, Serge found Stalin in the driver's seat. The writer's first night in "dark" and "inhospitable" Leningrad is a scene out of *Nosferatu*: "It is raining; the jetties are black. Two rows of dotted lamplight extend far back into the night. Between them, the black waters of the Neva." Emerging from customs, "we are met by a run-down cab advancing over puddles of mud; a ghost-horse and a rattling carriage."[39]

There was a new atmosphere of despair. The revolutionary citadel of 1919 has become its own haunted house. Leningrad lived "at the cost of ten to fifteen suicides a day, mainly among the under-thirties." The New Economic Policy, which had reinstated some free enterprise in the wake of War Communism, seemed to Serge nothing more than "one big confidence trick." As led by Trotsky (who would be exiled the next year) and joined now by Stalin's former ally and Serge's erstwhile supervisor Zinoviev, the party's so-called left opposition was in confusion.[40]

The Bolshevik opposition crystallized around three issues: the collectivization of agriculture, the role of democracy within the party, and the Chinese Revolution (a last hope that, as Serge wrote, "galvanized us all"). In 1927, Serge openly criticized Stalin's China policy, publishing a series of articles in a French journal that advocated support for Mao Zedong rather than Chiang Kai-shek. For this, he was expelled from the party.

"At the beginning of 1928," wrote Serge, Trotsky's first wife "Alexandra Bronstein and myself were the only known Oppositionists in Leningrad still at liberty." Soon, Alexandra Bronstein was all alone.[41]

FROM OPPOSITION TO EXILE

Serge was arrested and, for eight weeks, interrogated by the Cheka's successor, the State Political Administration (GPU). After little more than a decade, he again found himself in prison, that "subterranean world" where people live like "larvae in a kind of slow delirium."[42]

Whatever brutality Serge suffered at the hands of Stalin's secret police in his refusal to make a confession, he nearly died of an intestinal occlusion twenty-four hours after his release. It was then that he resolved to become an artist, mentally sketching a series of documentary novels about what he had seen and what he knew best—the extreme circumstances of prison, revolution, and political terror.

Once free, Serge turned madly productive. He began a history of the Russian Revolution and a study of proletariat culture; completed his first novel, *Men in Prison* (which he had begun writing in German while in Vienna); and composed two others, *Birth of Our Power* and *Conquered City*. Unable to publish in the Soviet Union, Serge sent his manuscripts to Paris, where, he would say, they "lived out their lives tenaciously," appearing between 1930 and 1932, ignored by bourgeois and leftist critics alike.[43]

Denied a ration card during the famine of the First Five-Year Plan,

Serge scraped by doing French translations for the Lenin Institute, which were checked, line by line, for "possible sabotage in the disposition of semicolons." He lived, in a shabby communal flat, under constant, almost comic, surveillance. One GPU agent and his family were installed across the courtyard; another crouched in "a hidey-hole next to the bathroom." A student was stationed in the corridor to eavesdrop on Serge's telephone conversations. Finally, "a sham Oppositionist, who was visibly annoyed at the role he had to assume, visited me once or twice a week for confidential political discussions."[44]

March 8, 1933, the inevitable happened: Serge was rearrested and deported beyond the Urals to Kazakhstan. "Sun-scorched, exciting, picturesque . . . overwhelmed with heat, poverty, and sand," suffering famine as well, the town of Orenburg was nevertheless considered a privileged spot in the Gulag. Serge's fellow politicals included social revolutionaries, Zionists, anarchists, and oppositionists. Serge (who managed to have his denunciation of Stalin's totalitarian regime published in Paris that spring) saw these comrades as something like holy martyrs: "Journeying over the years from prison to prison, from exile to exile, tormented by privation, these comrades kept their revolutionary faith, their good spirits, their sparkling political intelligence."[45]

Orenburg would be the setting for his near-religious novel, the hauntingly titled *Midnight in the Century* (1939). Serge continued to mail chunks of manuscripts either to his family—most already imprisoned—or to friends abroad, who raised his case in Paris at the July 1935 International Writers Congress for the Defense of Culture. The congress was a watershed in the creation of a Popular Front (Soviet delegates included, by Stalin's orders, both Boris Pasternak and Isaac Babel). Left-wing critics of the Communist Party—namely, the surrealists and the Trotskyists—were deliberately marginalized. The anti-Fascist historian Gaetano Salvemini was first to invoke Serge, but others followed. When the surrealist-turned-Stalinist Louis Aragon later commented that even permitting Salvemini to mention Serge had been "too much consideration for a counter-revolutionary," the conference reached critical mass.[46]

Serge's name was proscribed, but the uproar put his case on the international agenda. The following April, as Stalin's boon to the noted French fellow traveler Romain Rolland, Serge was deprived of his citizenship and expelled from the Soviet Union. (Again, this remarkable good fortune was made possible by Serge's refusal to confess to any criminal behavior.) Two complete novels—*The Lost Ones*, an account of the prewar French anarchists, and *The Torment,* a sequel to *Conquered City*—as well as a book of poetry and a history, *Year Two of the Russian Revolution,* were confiscated by the GPU on his way out.

Serge would never return. "Oh, our great Russia of agonies, how hard it is to tear ourselves away from you," he wrote without irony, adding, "So ended my seventeen years' experience of victorious revolution."[47]

THE DEATH OF A LEFTIST

Refused a visa by France, Great Britain, Denmark, and the Netherlands, Serge settled first in Brussels, then moved to Paris—amid a campaign orchestrated against him in the Communist and Popular Front press. "For a short while I was the most calumniated man in the world." For a somewhat longer time, he was also the leading Trotskyist publicist in France.[48]

Serge's impact was comparable to that of Alexander Solzhenitsyn some thirty-five years later. Only weeks after Serge's arrival, the Spanish Civil War broke out, and soon after that, Stalin charged his old Bolshevik comrades with treason. That summer, the first major show trial opened, with Zinoviev, Lev Kamenev, and fourteen co-conspirators accused of the Kirov murder, planning the death of Stalin, and other crimes.

One of the few oppositionists to survive the purges (and perhaps the only one to escape to the West), Serge was once again in his element—putting out pamphlets, addressing rallies, dealing with the "pidgin agitprop" of Communist hecklers. Along with other independent leftists, Serge set up a Committee for Inquiry into the Moscow Trials, while writing inside accounts of the Soviet system—*From Lenin to Stalin* and *Russia Twenty Years After*—as well as *Midnight in the Century.* (Could this have been what Trotsky had in mind when, in July 1936, he cautioned Serge against addressing the political problem of Stalinism as an artist or a psychologist? And could that have been what Serge was remembering when, writing *The Case of Comrade Tulayev,* he had Stalin address an old comrade with affectionate contempt: "Always the writer! You ought to go in for psychology.")[49]

France and the Soviet Union signed a pact of mutual aid. French Stalinism would never seem closer to the center of power—the nation's first socialist premier, Léon Blum, was no longer a "social-fascist" but a hero of the Popular Front. Serge, meanwhile, was an oppositionist within the opposition. (Spain's independent Communist POUM was probably closest to his heart.) Highly critical of the sectarian feuding of Europe's Trotskyist parties, he denied that the oppositionist movement had been Trotskyist: "We regarded the Old Man only as one of our greatest comrades." Soon afterward, he quarreled with the old man himself; the Kronstadt uprising was now fifteen years past.[50]

The satirical journal *Le Crapouillot* had devoted its entire January issue to Serge's *From Lenin to Stalin*. *Russia Twenty Years After* was published in the context of the International Exposition that opened in the center of Paris that May. In a key moment of modern times, Boris Iofan's Soviet pavilion faced Albert Speer's German pavilion, the Nazi eagle peering down on Vera Mukhina's forward-striding *Worker and Collective Farm Woman*. (The Spanish pavilion exhibited Picasso's *Guernica*.) As the anarchists and POUMistas were being liquidated in Barcelona, so the Stalinist terror resumed in Moscow: "Black was the spring of 1937."[51]

Serge corresponded with a number of New York intellectuals associated with the then-Trotskyist *Partisan Review* (*PR*), including Dwight Macdonald, Sidney Hook, and William Phillips. *PR* published Serge's essay "Marxism in Our Time" in late 1938, followed by a section of *Conquered City*. Yet, despite the relative success of *Midnight in the Century* (appearing in 1939, it likely kept the writer from being interned as a foreign national), Serge was almost totally isolated in Paris. Proscribed by the Popular Front, denounced by the Trotskyists, he supported himself and his family by working as a typesetter. Then, Stalin and Hitler came to terms, and there was war. Serge escaped Paris ahead of the German army in 1940: "We fled with a feeling of relief that verged at moments on light-heartedness."[52]

Hiding out in Marseilles, Serge worked on *The Case of Comrade Tulayev*, hoping that Dwight Macdonald (who had ties to the Emergency Rescue Committee, organized by Eleanor Roosevelt) would successfully organize visas for himself, his companion Laurette Séjourny, and his son, Vlady. Serge shared his house with surrealist leader André Breton; his wife, Jacqueline Lamba; and their daughter. The writers had worked together in the French section of Trotsky's International Federation of Independent Revolutionary Artists; indeed, Breton had been a teenage reader of *L'Anarchie*.[53]

Casablanca time: March 25, 1941, the Breton and Serge families, along with novelist Anna Seghers, painter Wilfredo Lam, and another 350 passengers, sailed on the SS *Capitaine Paul Lemerle*, a boat with cabin space for seven, described by Serge as "a can of sardines with a cigarette butt stuck on it." Claude Lévi-Strauss, another passenger, likened the embarkation to "the departure of a convict ship."[54]

The "scum," as the French police called the refugees, crossed the Mediterranean to Oran, steamed along the African coast to Dakar, then crossed the Atlantic to Martinique. There everyone was subject to interrogation, with Lévi-Strauss and Serge, a Jew and a Communist, held for several days in a former leper colony. Denied a U.S. visa, incarcerated briefly in Cuba, Serge was finally granted asylum in Mexico, where, just one year before, Stalin's agents had finally succeeded in murdering Trotsky—albeit still a country that, in providing the Europeans with refuge, asked relatively few questions regarding their nationality and politics. Shortly before Serge's arrival in the summer of 1941, Hitler turned on Stalin: "For weeks I find it impossible to think of anything else but the nightmare sweeping over Russia."[55]

Serge spent the remaining six years of his life in isolation and poverty—for a time, living with the British surrealist painter Gordon Onslow Ford, who had renovated an abandoned mill in a remote Tarascan village. Dodging the sporadic attacks of Mexican Communists and the NKVD (successor to the GPU), Serge wrote his memoirs (on Macdonald's suggestion), finished *The Case of Comrade Tulayev* (without hope of publication), and commented on the international situation for the benefit of his New York comrades.

Had Serge been allowed into the United States, might he have become the godfather of the New York intellectuals? To judge from his American publications, Serge's wartime politics oscillated between the left-wing social democracy of the *Socialist Call* and the right-wing social democracy of the *New Leader*. Dismissive by now of non-Russian Communist parties, Serge even published an attack on Ho Chi Minh as Kremlin stooge in Macdonald's journal *Politics*.

The essay "Thirty Years after the Russian Revolution," written during the summer of 1947, finds Serge still seeking history's secret mechanism. It was, he argued, the War Communism instituted during the summer of 1920, along with the failed attempt to take Warsaw and the suppression of the Kronstadt uprising the following winter, that created the conditions that spelled October's doom: "Proletarian revolution is no longer to be our aim: the revolution that we are waiting to serve can only be socialist—in the humanist sense of the word—or, more precisely, *socializing*, through democratic, libertarian means."[56]

That Serge planned to return to France explains the ambiguous letter he wrote to his onetime enemy Andre Malraux, now a hero of the French resistance as well as an adviser to Charles de Gaulle: "Had I been in France I would myself have been among the Socialists collaborating with the movement you are in. I consider the electoral victory of your movement a great step towards the immediate salvation of France."[57]

It hardly seems likely that Serge would have repudiated the politics of a lifetime to wind up a cold war liberal, but who can know? In November 1947, the fifty-seven-year-old revolutionary hailed a Mexico City taxi, got in, sat down, and, before telling the driver his destination, died.

SERGE IN PRINT

One can only speculate how Serge would have assessed the postwar world or what he might have accomplished if he'd had the luxury of fully developing and polishing his novels. *Men in Prison,* the book over which he labored longest, has the greatest conventional literary merit. As much an essay as a story, it is a work of fantastic introspection. Serge details the prisoner's inner life with an exactitude and sensuality that anticipates Jean Genet, focusing particularly on the state of sensory starvation.

When the anonymous narrator relates "the profound drama of the appearance and disappearance of a ray of sunlight" or speaks of developing "an obsessive *desire for color,*" the reader appreciates the discipline that Serge derived from this experience. Confronted with the execrable prison library, Serge's narrator has a poststructuralist epiphany: "I learned, alone with those books, that the most mediocre printed page can have its value. Everything is in knowing how to read and how to make the book a pretext for meditations. Even if only on human stupidity . . . "[58]

Men in Prison is grimly poetic. Its set piece—a dreamlike account of the narrator's transfer from one prison to another—takes its title as well as some of its imagery from Rimbaud's *The Drunken Boat.* But Serge was, above all, an observer. Apparently blessed with total recall, he excelled at character vignettes. Although largely written in the first person (with an anarchist narrator who could hardly be anyone other than the author), *Men in Prison*—like Serge's later novels—is remarkable for its swarming cast of characters. Indeed, this is one of its organizing principles.

Serge took seriously the notion of a collective hero. "Individual existences were of no interest to me—particularly my own—except by virtue of the great ensemble of life whose particles, more or less endowed with consciousness, are all that we ever are," he explains by way of a literary manifesto in his memoirs. "And so the form of the classical novel seemed to me impoverished and outmoded, centring as it does upon a few beings artificially detached from the world."[59]

The narrator of *Men in Prison*, *Birth of Our Power*, and even *Memoirs of a Revolutionary*—itself a succession of snapshot characterizations—is primarily an eye. *Men in Prison* "is not about me, but about men," Serge told his friend Panaït Istrati, the Romanian poet and sometime revolutionary who introduced the book's first edition. "It seems to me that the time has finally come for literature to discover the masses, the link between the individual and his fellow man, where the problem of the individual's destiny will exist only in terms of every man."[60]

However programmatic this aesthetic, it served to populate Serge's novels with vivid, economical portraits. (It also resulted in a virtual suppression of his personal life: Serge's memoirs mention only one of his three wives, and even she doesn't appear on the scene until already pregnant.) Written mainly in the first person plural, *Birth of Our Power* sweeps from one end of Europe to the other—opening in Barcelona on the eve of an abortive uprising, tarrying in a French concentration camp, and ending in revolutionary Petrograd. In a chapter bluntly called "Us," Serge celebrates the revolutionary fellowship of assorted American Wobblies, Polish Zionists, Russian Leninists, Mexican followers of Pancho Villa and Emiliano Zapata, thrown together with miscellaneous, less easily characterized malcontents: "We formed a world apart within this city. It sufficed for one of us to call the others together with that magic word 'Comrades,' and we would feel united, brothers without even needing to say it, sure of understanding each other even in our misunderstandings. . . . Saint-Just, Robespierre, Jacques Roux, Baboeuf, Blanqui, Bakunin were spoken of as if they had just come down to take a stroll under the trees." It is the heaven of perfumed lice—as utopian as these discussions sound, they are still being held in a concentration camp. "A nice little piece of Europe," one of the prisoners says of their home. "Authentic. Every man a suspect."[61]

Serge's distinctive blend of revolutionary idealism and sardonic realism would find its supreme subject in the new Soviet state. *Conquered City* inaugurates what could be called his Bolshevik trilogy. The first-person narrator has gone; the writer has now found a theme to subsume all others. *Conquered City*, *Midnight in the Century*, and *The Case of Comrade*

Tulayev teem with characters, although one—the good Bolshevik Ryzhik, a workhorse with an unconscious as well as a conscience—wends his way through the trilogy, the personification of revolutionary enthusiasm. Serge hardly shies from portraying ideological enemies in human terms. Stalin himself appears in *The Case of Comrade Tulayev,* and Serge's grasp of political psychology is never so acute as in his portrait of the chief as a canny political animal—bluff, hearty, and vibrant with suspicion.

In *Conquered City*—an almost Boschian evocation of revolutionary terror—Ryzhik is a reluctant member of the Cheka, whose creation Serge believed to be the Bolsheviks' worst blunder. This novel, less polished than *Men in Prison* but arguably Serge's greatest, anticipates the bitter first-hand knowledge of post–World War II East European film directors Miklós Jancsó and Andrzej Wajda. "Do you by any chance imagine that we won't all end up like that?" a member of the Special Commission mocks his colleagues after they have painfully sentenced one of their number to death.[62]

The horror of *Conquered City* is that the revolution has already gone wrong; by the time the novel ends, most of its protagonists have been dispatched. *Midnight in the Century* is another sort of tragedy, which, despite the overwhelming bleakness of its situation, is actually less despairing that *Conquered City;* for now, once again, the good guys are on the outside—shattering in their purity. In fictionalizing Serge's Orenburg experience, *Midnight* recounts the story of five "files"—veteran Bolsheviks exiled to Central Asia. ("Five of us—and not one informer!" Ryzhik exclaims. "Do you think that's possible?") Serge's most lyrical novel is not only mystical in its celebration of the doomed prisoners but pantheist in its evocation of the Russian steppe: "The sky takes on a pearly, almost azure hue; a kind of peace descends from it. You might mistake it for hope."[63]

Midnight in the Century was the first novel Serge wrote outside of Russia; its cosmic yearning may well be a function of his homesickness. *The Case of Comrade Tulayev,* his novel of the purges (and the only one he wrote without firsthand knowledge), has a more polemical thrust—modeling its central incident on the 1934 assassination of the Leningrad party secretary Sergei Kirov, which provided Stalin with a pretext for the party purge and first Moscow Trial. (The book is set in 1938–39, after the third Moscow Trial—thus proposing itself as an account of a mythical fourth show trial, as well as allowing Serge to depict the Stalinist war against the POUMistas in Spain.)

In these two novels, the experience of the old Bolsheviks grows closer to that of an underground religion. It is difficult to imagine another writer suggesting, as Serge does almost ecstatically in *Midnight in the Century,* that "if the Interim Director of the Department of Inner-Party Deviations had a touch of the poet about him," he might gaze down at his map of Stalin's Soviet Union and see the concentration camps and exiles of the Gulag radiating like stars from which "the heresy shines out again over the whole USSR."[64]

Serge may be an uneven stylist, but he is capable of astonishing extended and multilayered metaphors—not only Marxist but worthy of Marx. In *Birth of Our Power,* for example, he simultaneously (and effortlessly) evokes the dustbin of history to dispose of the old ruling class and celebrates newborn revolution by describing it as if through a child's eyes. At the novel's climax, the narrator finds himself in what once was a counselor of the empire's study, where an entire wall is covered by glassed-in bookcases holding the massive volumes of the czarist legal code: "One could easily imagine the late master as he appeared on a photograph which had been used to pick up sweepings in the next room: narrow forehead, stern monocled eye; an intelligent, egotistical industrialist, resembling a Roman senator; and a little girl bursting into that austere study clapping her hands: 'Papa, little Papa, it's the revolution! If you knew how happy everyone is in the streets. I saw some soldiers with red ribbons, how pretty it is!'"[65]

Similarly (if to opposite effect), *Conquered City* opens in "prehistoric gloom," with Serge visualizing revolutionary Petrograd as a settlement of cave dwellers living amid piles of frozen excrement, which are covered with delicate crystals of frost. Virtually the rest of this dense, ferocious novel takes place in the "primordial night" of Marxist prehistory, as overtaxed Bolsheviks huddle in "oases of electricity" and attempt, through the primal bloodletting of the terror, to preserve their beleaguered revolution.[66]

In the penultimate chapter of his 1957 *Politics and the Novel* (a chapter that begins by invoking the Russian Revolution as "the central event of our century"), erstwhile Trotskyist and lifelong socialist Irving Howe concludes a discussion of three disillusioned revolutionaries—André Malraux, Ignazio Silone, and Arthur Koestler—by citing *The Case of Comrade Tulayev,* "a second-rank novel" that is "not quite as successful in its effort to absorb modern politics into fiction."[67]

Without elaborating *Tulayev*'s failure, Howe cites two exemplary incidents from the novel—a snowball fight among a trio of doomed old

Bolsheviks and Ryzhik's death-house meeting with another comrade. A line from *Tulayev* is even given as a prescription for the political novel: "Amidst the clamor of ideology—the indispensable, inescapable clamor—listen to your nerves."[68]

Perhaps Howe (like Sartre?) saw Serge only as a journalist. But if Serge is something less than a *litterateur,* he is also something more. *Darkness at Noon* was written to demonstrate Koestler's thesis of the Moscow Trials (and by extension, the Russian Revolution); *The Case of Comrade Tulayev* seems to have been written to feel out the complexity of these events—or at the very least, the complexity of the Bolsheviks' response to them. An absence of self-abasement distinguishes Serge's novels from the disillusioned confessions of ex-Communists such as Koestler and Silone (the latter of whom, in fact, published a hostile review of *Midnight in the Century* in 1940).

Chancing on Trotsky's widow in Mexico, Serge noted in his diary that they were "the sole survivors of the Russian Revolution here and perhaps anywhere in the world. . . . There is nobody left who knows what the Russian Revolution was really like, what the Bolsheviks were really like."[69]

Serge elaborated on the conceit in *The Case of Comrade Tulayev.* As the Spanish Republic goes down, a doomed Trotskyist tells his lover that "there are not more than fifty men on earth who understand Einstein; if they were all shot on the same night, it would all be over for a century or two—or three, how do we know? A whole vision of the universe would vanish into nothingness. Think of it: Bolshevism raised millions of men above themselves, in Europe, in Asia, for ten years. Now that the Russians have been shot, nobody can any longer see from the inside what was the thing by which all those men lived, the thing which constituted their strength and their greatness; they will become undecipherable and, after them, the world will fall below them."[70]

So it is with Victor Serge, who even in his most difficult years kept the faith of 1919. His last published essay reminded *Partisan Review* readers of "the most important psychological aspect of the Russian Revolution." Throughout history, Serge maintained, "the poor and the exploited had been eternally beaten. For the first time, through the advent of Bolshevism, this harsh 'natural' law appeared annulled. The masses' feeling of inferiority gave way to confidence, pride, a new optimism. *Some roots of Stalinism are still embedded in the soil of these feelings.*"[71]

Serge never forgot what the revolution was about. He made no apologies; he simply hung his experience of the twentieth century out on the line. Serge did not become a novelist until his days of practical activism were curtailed, but unlike Koestler and Silone (as well as Malraux), he was not writing about a former self. This, as much as anything, derailed his literary reputation. Whereas Malraux worked steadily toward the very center of power, Serge's equally determined career took him to the obscure margin of the political spectrum.

"For Malraux," Harold Rosenberg once observed, "the individual is an actor in history, but history is organized by totalitarian professionals." For Serge, one might add, the individual is an actor in history, *even though* history—"that vile scholar's lie among whose printed lines not a single drop of spilled blood can be found, where nothing remains of the passion, the pain, the fear, and the violence of men"—is organized (if we can call it that) by totalitarian professionals.[72]

In the final analysis, it is neither Serge's inconsistent prose nor the obscurity of his final exile that consigned him to unpersonhood. Rather, it is the fierceness with which he remained unreconciled. *Pace* Sartre, Serge is arguably the key practitioner of the "literature of extreme circumstances." You might say that Serge's very disinclination to separate his life, his writing, and his politics was an extreme circumstance in itself.[73]

Lost in the Gulag, where he will deliberately starve himself to death, the old Bolshevik Ryzhik hallucinates a powerful collective intelligence—the brain that "brought together thousands of brains to perform its work during a quarter of a century, now destroyed in a few years by the backlash of its own victory, now perhaps reflected only in his own mind."[74]

Here the dialectic evaporates. An individual dies and the historical universe implodes: Bonnot, Barcelona, 1919, Kronstadt, Stalin. The lost cause is lost once more. What does it mean to be the negation of that which no longer exists?

CHAPTER 5

Life in

Czechoslovakia,

or a Cage in

Search of a Bird

At the height of the Reagan era, in the years just before and immediately after our long-dreaded 1984, Penguin Books published a uniform series of mainly post–World War II novels and short story collections under the tantalizing rubric "Writers from the Other Europe." Writers, to be sure; but Other? How? To whom?

Suggestive of an alternative universe or at least a parallel world, the Other Europe was both a geographical entity—the erstwhile Soviet satellites plus errant Yugoslavia—and a particular state of mind. "This city," wrote Tadeusz Konwicki of his native Warsaw, "is the capital of a people who are evaporating into nothingness."[1]

Writers from the Other Europe considered themselves part of an endangered species and they were—albeit not, it turned out, in the quite way they imagined. Konwicki and the others were connoisseurs of entrapment and experts on authority: it went with the territory (or rather, its disappearance). Since lurching into recorded history some

---

The political landscape was nowhere more phantasmagorical than on the western marches of the Soviet sphere—poor in material goods, rich in ideological complexity, a world of subterfuge and bureaucracy, where the memory of police terror mixed with nostalgia for the wrecked Hapsburg Empire, and the radiant future sought its foundation in the swampy killing fields of World War II. One had to be a bit of a Communist to appreciate the anti-Communist literature, less straightforward than the writings of Victor Serge, produced in cold war Eastern Europe—as well as to enjoy the paradox in which writers were taken so seriously that they might be subsidized by the regimes they satirized, and forty years after his death, an author could be magically resurrected as a dissident. A shorter version of this piece was published as "Closely Watched Books: At Home in Eastern Europe" in the November 1983 issue of the *Voice Literary Supplement*, on the occasion of Franz Kafka's centennial.

fifteen hundred years ago, their domain had passed, in whole or in part, back and forth between brief periods of autonomy and lengthy incorporations into the Roman, Holy Roman, Ottoman, Hapsburg, and Russian empires, the Third Reich, and the Soviet sphere.

Thus, for all the peripheral connotations of Other Europeanness, the world of these writers hardly seemed provincial. On the contrary: The alert Other European had something closer than a ringside seat on the zeitgeist. These were voices from the ring. "It is here, in Central Europe, that modern culture found its greatest impulses," Milan Kundera told the Penguin series editor, Philip Roth, in the interview that served as an afterword to the Czech writer's 1979 *Book of Laughter and Forgetting:* "psychoanalysis, structuralism, dodecaphony, Bartók's music, Kafka's and Musil's new esthetics of the novel."[2]

And then, of course, there was socialism, surely modern culture's most noble impulse—if linked in its really existing form to an oppressive set of historical circumstances. "The postwar annexation of Central Europe (or at least its major part) by Russian civilization caused Western culture to lose its vital center of gravity," Kundera explained. Living in loss was the Other European's vanguard position. The Asiatic conquest of the former Hapsburg Empire was nothing less than "the most significant event in the history of the West in our century." Nor, the writer warned, could we "dismiss the possibility that the end of Central Europe marked the beginning of the end for Europe as a whole."[3]

But, as we all know, something else ended instead.

Writings from the Other Europe encompassed the hallucinated prose poems of Bruno Schulz and the laconic tales of what Tadeusz Borowski called "Auschwitz Our Home." Some books, such as Jerzy Andrzejewski's searing *Ashes and Diamonds* and Bohimil Hrabal's sweetly comic *Closely Watched Trains,* had been the bases for celebrated movies. There was even room for an antediluvian fossil such as Géza Csáth—a pre-World War I Hungarian decadent who savaged the Hapsburg bourgeoisie and took refuge in drugs.

The series also included some of the strongest authors of editor Roth's own generation—men (as all the Writers were) who came of age after World War II and during the period of Stalinist consolidation. Kundera (with four books, the Other European heavyweight) was then the best known of these; the somewhat younger Danilo Kiš and the slightly older

Konwicki were two more writers of international stature whose fictions on life with socialism eluded easy political classification.

Kundera, Kiš, and Konwicki were disillusioned Communists—and yet they were recognizably men of the Left (not the least in temperament). Theirs, however, was a homeless Left. Unlike professional anti-Communists in the United States, Kundera, Kiš, and Konwicki had opted out of, rather than into, the local power structure. But paradoxically, this had rendered them positively cosmopolitan. Not a few writers from the Other Europe went to live in Paris (and some never returned). Others received one-term teaching fellowships at Ivy League universities. Translated into English, their work was praised by Irving Howe in the *New York Review of Books*—a new literature of extreme situations. Understood by contributors to *Dissent* and *Partisan Review* as heirs to the European political writers of the 1930s, the Other Europeans were lionized in PEN and championed by Susan Sontag. Intellectuals from the West Side of Manhattan found them—glamorous.[4]

"We are wolves, all right and true adults," exulted the narrator of *The Loser* (1980)—*chef d'oeuvre* by Hungarian novelist George Konrád, the leading contemporary Other European author not published by Penguin. "Compared to us our Western friends are sheep and adolescents. They prove with their articles they know what socialism is; we prove it with our ulcers."[5]

Konrád's macho bravura, Kundera's historical fatalism, and the sardonic tolerance with which Konwicki regarded the vagaries of human nature seemed to confound the pieties of Western as well as Eastern ideologues. Kiš's *A Tomb for Boris Davidovich* (1976)—an oblique but devastating worm's-eye view of self-devouring Stalinism—survived the attacks of party conservatives and Serbian nationalists alike to win a Yugoslav literary prize. The struggle left Kiš in a state of what was euphemistically termed "nervous shock."[6]

Although a bout of nervous shock is admittedly less severe than a trip to the Gulag, Other European writers were understood to play for high stakes. Unlike their Western colleagues, they enjoyed the dubious distinction of being taken seriously by their rulers; their work received recognition with a vengeance. Western authors might worry about finding an agent or landing a book contract; Other Europeans were concerned with losing their livelihood or their citizenship. "There nothing goes and everything matters," was Roth's elegant formulation. "Here everything goes and nothing matters."[7]

Ocher and grey labyrinths, the Other European capitals of the 1970s and 1980s afforded authentic adventure. The winter air was acrid with soot, the food as heavy as the lowering sky, the brandies no less exotic than the official jargon. Scaffolding supported the decomposing office buildings. The excitingly drab streets, devoid of advertising billboards (save for signs promoting the consumption of milk or a local lottery game), led to meetings in overheated restaurants or book-stuffed apartments. It was a sociopolitical acid trip.

Could anything in the West compare to the heady brew of ironic double-talk and naive sincerity, the brain-twisting politics and no less incestuously convoluted personal-professional relationships? "Left was right, right was left" is too simple a formulation. Who could resist the thrill of possible police surveillance, the atmospheric drizzle, the haunting Jewishness of these places? What had Irving Howe had written of Victor Serge? "The material is so close to us, the point of view so congenial, the pathos so unbearable" as to render us "emotionally defenseless."[8]

Roth made an annual pilgrimage to Communist Prague throughout the 1970s. (How many times has he returned since 1990? one wonders.) There, his principal "reality instructor" was the dissident novelist Ivan Klíma: "In his car he drove me around to the street-corner kiosks where writers sold cigarettes, to the public buildings where they mopped the floors, to the construction sites where they were laying bricks, and out of the city to municipal waterworks where they slogged about in overalls and boots, a wrench in one pocket and a book in the other."[9]

During the so-called normalization, Klíma himself had been compelled to work as a street cleaner—an occupation described in his novel *Love and Garbage*. Klíma was a talented and persevering writer, a courageous dissident, a Jewish child who had been transported to the concentration camp Terezin, a survivor of the Holocaust *and* Stalin, a publisher of illegal samizdats, a participant in both the glorious Prague Spring and the Velvet Revolution. He was more than familiar with extreme situations. Perhaps Roth envied Klíma his résumé—and perhaps not only Klíma, and perhaps not only Roth.[10]

In Other European terms, the Penguin series offered a particular mode of literary appreciation—a fascinating mix of what, in Kádárist Hungary, would have been termed the *sanctioned,* the *tolerated,* and the *prohibited.*

These volumes were steeped in arcane knowledge. They not only demanded to be read but, at times, begged to be decoded against the hazy patterns of a shifting party line, a bureaucratized culture, an intensely political history. Some were written on state grants; others were best-selling samizdats; a few seem to have been both. Living or dead, every writer in the Other Europe was engaged in a permanent chess match with the powers that be. As George Konrád and Ivan Szelényi slyly pointed out in their proscribed treatise *The Intellectuals on the Road to Class Power:* "For intellectuals, Eastern Europe over the past century has been an excellent school in the virtues of being good subjects."[11]

The local weather conditions might, of course, vary. The hometown availability and official reputations of even prewar writers like Csáth and Schulz gave some idea of the barometric pressure in Budapest or Warsaw. Visiting Budapest in February 1983, I wasn't too startled to find an indigenous punk-rock movie, *Night Song of the Dog*, packing the big Red Star Cinema on the since-renamed Lenin *körút*. It was the National Film Week, and Hungary had a long punk tradition. As early as 1976, semi-official sources were complaining about the "boorish" English-language slogans ("Long Live War," "I Wish I Was Dead," "The Best Sex Is Homo Sex") embellishing the T-shirts of local rock fans. Moreover, it had been twenty years since the rehabilitation the *fin de siècle* decadent Csáth, whose tormented life and pharmaceutical visions would scarcely leave the most hardened reader of *High Times* unmoved.

Jan Kott would joke that there was no censorship in Poland because "the word 'censorship' [was] censored."[12] (In fact, as demonstrated in the "black book" smuggled to the West in 1983, Poland was the Communist nation with the most detailed and exhaustive list of taboo subjects, as well as the largest censorship bureaucracy.) Czechoslovakia was more orderly: The books by Kundera, Hrabal, and Ludvík Vaculík were openly banned. All three writers first began to publish during the early 1960s; Hrabal's *Closely Watched Trains*, written in 1948, was published during the early 1960s thaw and filmed amid the Prague Spring. (It is an indigenous irony that because Hrabal—unlike Kundera and Vaculík—never joined the party, he was, in 1984, far less an unperson than his younger peers.)

Penguin's jacket copy called Milan Kundera "the most important writer from behind the Iron Curtain since Aleksandr Solzhenitsyn." But Kundera was not a symbol of opposition in quite the Solzhenitsyn sense. Among his other distinctions, Kundera was a man twice expelled from the Czech Communist Party—once in 1950 and again two decades later. *The Joke*, published in Prague in 1967 (several years after Kundera first submitted his manuscript), was the fruit of the first expulsion and the cause of the second.

The literary act that provided the title for Kundera's novel was an anti-Stalinist jape so unambiguously tasteless that the book could never be tolerated—only supported or prohibited by an orthodox Other European regime. "The plot of *The Joke* is itself a joke," Kundera explained in his introduction to the book's second English translation. "And not only the plot. Its 'philosophy' as well: a man caught in the trap of a joke suffers a personal catastrophe which, seen from without, is ludicrous. His tragedy lies in the fact that the joke has deprived him of the right to tragedy. He is condemned to triviality."[13] Such marginality might be the bitterest joke of all; for Kundera, *The Joke* was less some Upper Slobovian anecdote than the essence of literature and the story of the century.

Kundera's protagonist, Ludvik, had been a student Communist during "the years of revolutionary enthusiasm"—the spring that followed the Victorious February 1948, when Czechoslovakia's was the largest Communist Party (relative to its population) in the entire world. But although an idealistic true believer, Ludvik was cursed with a caustic sense of humor and consequently irritated by the discipline of puritanical joy. His crisis occurred when the girl he fancied left for a two-week party training session. She sent him a letter "chock-full of earnest enthusiasm for everything around her. It was all so wonderful: the early-morning calisthenics, the talks, the discussions, even the songs they sang; she praised the 'healthy atmosphere' that reigned there and diligently added a few words to the effect that the revolution in the West would not be long in coming."[14]

Actually, Ludvik quite agreed with what she wrote. But he was peeved that, despite their separation, she could sound quite so happy—and to tell the truth, he was a bit bugged by her shallow clichés. By way of a reply, he composed a sort of satiric haiku, which he mailed to her inscribed on a postcard: "Optimism is the opium of the people! A healthy atmosphere stinks of stupidity! Long live Trotsky!" Sots Art *avant la lettre*, Ludvik's blasphemous jape ruined his life. When the postcard was read by the humorless faithful, his girl was forced to denounce him, and his comrades drummed him out of the ranks. He was expelled from the university, drafted into the army, and sent to work in the mines.[15]

Jumping back and forth in time from an unraveling past to a precipitously unfolding present, shifting from Ludvik's consciousness to that of other principals and back, *The Joke* is less a historical novel than a comedy of sexual frustration and revenge. (The bitter movie that Jaromil Jires

directed in 1968 from Kundera's script is an even more cynical and absurdist vision of alienation in a drably decrepit worker's paradise.) Fifteen
years after his fall from grace, Ludvik finds himself in his Moravian hometown, carrying through a scheme to seduce the wife of Comrade
Zemanek, the party chairman who presided over his excommunication.

Such ploys are the staple of Kundera's not inconsiderable erotic imagination. Like D. H. Lawrence or Sigmund Freud, he is a philosopher
of the bedroom. Sex, in Kundera, is a means of rebelling against authority; often, it is the only means. Too bad that sex is equally a game in
which the powerless (mainly men) attempt to exercise their domination
over the gullible (usually women). Sexual strategems are fundamental to
Kundera's sense of humor; his stories were collected in 1969 as *Laugh-
able Loves*. And often as not, his seductions backfire. The role-playing
that preoccupies the couple in "The Hitchhiking Game" is so exciting
that it results in genuine estrangement. The horny hero of "Edward and
God" fakes a religious conversion to woo a pious young schoolteacher,
but—shades of *The Joke*—his newfound Catholicism queers him with
the authorities. Instead of bedding his love, Edward finds himself
boffing his boss, a Communist crone with a secret yen for religious
perversion.

Ludvik's conquest is scarcely less grotesque; for while he has remained
lost in the past—the frozen moment in "that lecture hall with a hundred
people raising their hands, giving the order to destroy my life"—a thaw
has occurred. The first buds of Prague Spring have bloomed and Comrade
Zemanek is still in the vanguard—he even has a twenty-two-year-old
girlfriend to prove it. Far from being humiliated, Zemanek is overjoyed—
it almost seems a miracle—that Ludvik appears to be taking his wife off
his hands. Amid a sodden apocalypse of fights, botched suicides, and
heart attacks, Ludvik flees: "There was nothing else I could have done: I
had to put an end to the whole sorry episode, the bad joke which, not
content to remain itself, had monstrously multiplied into more and more
stupid jokes."[16]

The quintessential Other European was a joker, a trickster, a puller of
pranks—heir to an attitude already highly developed in the work of such
pre-Communist writers as Géza Csáth or Witold Gombrowicz. "We are
bad boys, skeptics, rogues, con artists, wheeler-dealers, survivors," the
irrepressible Konrád boasted in a 1981 "Letter from Budapest" published

in the *New York Review of Books*. "Deep down we love destruction and derision; our historical legacy, our stock in trade, is cynicism."[17]

His sensibility split between the bad boy and the scientist, Konrád's countryman Csáth enjoyed a tale of bureaucratic humiliation as much as the next Hapsburg citizen—although his most vigorous vignettes were medical school legends fraught with blatant Oedipal ironies. In one story, two goonish morgue attendants beat up on a generalissimo's corpse; in another, an earnest American comes to claim the classroom skeleton as his dad. The best of these is a fondly malicious portrait of an absinthe-sodden surgeon—"lost and drifting steadily toward the DTs"—who proposes to stop the flow of time by lobotomizing his patients, cutting the "evil hornets' nest of grief from their brains."[18]

Exemplifying Csáth's adolescent glee in the face of degenerate authority, the slyly delusional "Black Silence" is a classic chiller describing the metamorphosis of an adorable toddler into a raging maniac who pillages the neighborhood and roasts the family kitten alive. Csáth wrote some raw accounts of rural savagery, but by and large, his boldest satire shows the bourgeois home to be as filled with murder and mayhem as the tabloid press. In "Matricide," two fatherless teenagers stab their plump, indolent mother to death and give her jewelry to a prostitute. In "Murder," a rich young socialist defends his father's home against a terrifying burglar and discovers that he has strangled a "poor, weak little peasant" with his bare hands. In "Little Emma" (a feuilleton that went full circle when Roth introduced it in the *New York Review of Books* as "A Great Horror Story"), a group of six-year-olds hang the prettiest of their playmates on a makeshift gallows.

Optimism is the opium of the people! A healthy atmosphere stinks of stupidity! Long live . . .

Sigmund Freud published *The Interpretation of Dreams* in 1900 and *The Psychopathology of Everyday Life* a year later. Well before World War I, his scandalous theories of sex, patriarchy, and the unconscious had begun to ripple across Hapsburg Europe. In Prague, Franz Kafka noted "thoughts of Freud, of course," when describing in his journal the night he wrote "The Judgment."[19]

A Budapest hipster like Géza Csáth was breathing the same crepuscular air. Indeed, what greater prank could a young neurologist play on the local bourgeoisie than to follow (perhaps top) his Viennese colleague's deadpan assertions that, without even being aware of it, they all wanted to fuck their mothers and kill their fathers—and what's more, so did their sons. Like Dr. Freud, Dr. Csáth meditated on authority and turned his case histories into something like adult *kindermärchen*. Indeed, the child killers of "The Black Silence," "Matricide," and "Little Emma" express an infantile rage that goes beyond Freud.[20]

More than opium fumes haunted the "hornet's nest of grief" that Csáth offered up for dissection. Illuminated by the power of unconscious drives, the crimes of "The Surgeon," "Murder," and "Little Emma" were blueprints for the mass slaughter that would become banal as the twentieth century wore on—and might thus be tolerated, if not sanctioned, as period pieces.

The slender, orange-backed volumes of Writers from the Other Europe were generally prefaced by important Western authors (Philip Roth, Heinrich Böll, Angela Carter, or—welcoming Bruno Schulz to America—John Updike). Was it overdetermined that the same name would be evoked in each essay, again and again? "One could try to discuss *The Guinea Pigs* without bringing up Franz Kafka," Neal Ascherson hazarded in his introduction of Ludvík Vaculík's novel, "but it would be a useless exercise."[21]

A useless exercise indeed. Roth, who made his first visit to Prague in search of Kafka, refers to Konwicki, Kiš, and Kundera, as the "three 'K's who have crawled out from under Kafka's cockroach." Schulz translated *The Trial* into Polish. In his introduction to *A Tomb for Boris Davidovich*, Joseph Brodsky compared Kiš to both Kafka and Schulz—why not Babel?—suggesting these writers foreshadowed Kiš's own particular "blend of doom and nostalgia." Of course, while Kafka and Schulz pondered the condition of that most endangered of Western assimilators, the Other European Jew, Kiš's protagonists were, more pointedly, rootless cosmopolitans lucklessly assimilating the Eastern religion of Stalinism. (The tragic-ironic-understated political case histories—or "files"—that make up *Boris Davidovich* actually suggest the amalgam of Kafka and Victor Serge.)[22]

If, in the exception that proves the rule, Jan Kott avoids any mention of Kafka (no, not even "In the Penal Colony") when introducing Tadeusz Borowski's shatteringly matter-of-fact accounts of moment-to-moment survival amid quotidian genocide, it may be because it was unnecessary. For one thing, Borowski, like Kafka, "never moralizes, only relates." For another, as Prague's own Nostradamus, Kafka can be shown to have humorously anticipated every twentieth-century atrocity from the Holocaust to Stalinism to World War III. As Roth remarked to Klíma, "Kafka's prescient irony may not be the most remarkable attribute of his work but it's always stunning to think about it."[23]

"A Fratricide," Kafka's most savagely Csáth-like story, encapsulates the ecstasy of shedding blood with the thrill of watching a street crime unfold from the safety of an upper-story window. Where either condition would be horror enough for Csáth, Kafka goes further: The joy of transgression is not only squelched but socialized by a force whose instant punishment seems almost comforting. In the modernist lexicon, the terms *Joycean* and *Proustian* are popularly used in reference to literary techniques. But the much abused *Kafkaesque*—even when employed to denote the dreamlike or nightmarish—typically refers to something in the world, an actual situation that is most often a posture of ridiculous defeat before some unknowable authority.[24]

Order, as defined by Freud in *Civilization and Its Discontents,* is a "kind of compulsion to repeat which, when a regulation has been laid down once and for all, decides when, where, and how a thing shall be done, so that in every similar circumstance one is spared hesitation and indecision."[25] A professional cog in a doomed social system, Kafka held a view that was even more bleak: The authority of the established order was at once distant and ubiquitous (as in Freud), absurdly potent (as in Kundera), and absurdly decrepit (as in Csáth). Kafka, our contemporary, wrote about the bureaucratization of daily life, and he showed this awesome form of organization to be, in a word, internalized.

The bedridden father in Kafka's "The Judgment" is an unkempt, toothless giant who changes in a matter of moments from a huge infant idly playing with his grown son's watch chain to an "erect" and "radiant" accuser who commands his son to jump in a lake. The luckless son takes this injunction literally—as only the unconscious can—and straightaway hurls himself off a bridge. Kafka, Theodor Adorno once wrote, "snatches psychoanalysis from the grasp of psychology," exhibiting "a skepticism toward the Ego which, if anything, exceeds that of Freud."[26]

As is well known, there are no proponents of order greater than victorious revolutionaries. Thus, like all Writers from the Other Europe, Kafka enjoyed a volatile reputation east of the Elbe. And not just there: A year after World War II ended, the French Communist weekly *Action* published an essay that posed the question "Should Kafka Be Burned?"[27]

The Communists understood the intolerable Kafka all too well.

Whereas their announced goal was to change reality, the Czech writer had advised that, "in the struggle between you and the world, back the world." Kafka's metamorphosis was the very negation of an optimistic transformation. "Very near the top of what I have, in the past, rather indelicately called 'the cultural dung heap of reaction' sits Franz Kafka," boomed the American Communist writer Howard Fast in 1950.[28]

Kafka was, what is more, the darling of the Trotskyist *Partisan Review,* and the Stalinoid line articulated by Fast—enforced for thirty years with somewhat greater sophistication by Georg Lukács—was to castigate Kafka for his "decadent modernism" and lack of "realism."[29]

For one, however, who experienced the purge trials and self-denunciations of the Stalinized 1950s, or even life under existing socialism, Kafka had another meaning. "I have the feeling that in a world whose realities were more and more approximating Kafka's own metaphors and images, Kafka is accepted in quite a different way than in a world where reading him is primarily an aesthetic experience," wrote the Polish critic Roman Karst. "Kafka has an absolutely explosive effect for anyone who lives in a world that is founded on untruth and lack of freedom. Despite their bizarreness, Kafka's settings—his cages in which man is confined, the staircases leading off into infinity, the narrow corridors, dark cellars, secret galleries—compose a twentieth century landscape."[30]

Just as the mental state to which defendant Joseph K. is reduced (searching himself for the unknown crime that he has committed) anticipated the Communist practice known as self-criticism, and just as the last sentence of *The Trial* predicted the exact punishment called for those comrades charged with treason, so the political trials of People's Czechoslovakia again willed Kafka into existence. When, for example, the Slovak Communist and economist Eugen Loebl, at that time deputy minister of trade, was arrested in 1949, he was told that he had already been sentenced by the party. All that was required was his complete confession of his crimes and the names of his accomplices: "I could not believe my ears. There were no specific charges whatsoever against me, only a request that I confess. There were no facts, no witnesses." Loebl's interrogator explained that everyone in prison was a priori guilty: "We don't arrest innocent people. . . . We know you are a traitor, a spy, and a saboteur. If we didn't have proof of that, you'd still be deputy minister."[31]

In Czechoslovakia, Kafka's *Amerika* had been printed but destroyed after the Victorious February. In part because his champion and confidant Milena Jesenká had been expelled from the Czech Communist Party as a

Trotskyist, Kafka was unable to secure his posthumous citizenship in the Czecho-Slovak Socialist Republic. (Roth, for his part, could imagine a miraculously escaped, sixtyish, sour-breathed "Dr. Kishka" teaching Hebrew in a Newark *talmud torah* and courting his maiden Aunt Rhoda, with predictably disastrous results.) But when the *New York Times* reporter Harrison Salisbury visited Prague in October 1957, he discovered that the Writers Publishing House was planning to publish Pavel Eisner's Czech translation of *The Trial*.[32]

Issued July 3, 1958, on the occasion of the author's seventy-fifth birthday, in an edition of ten thousand (with Eisner's afterword, describing his own experience of the 1950s political trials), *The Trial* sold out before publication. But despite the secretary of the Czech Writers' Union, who had told Salisbury that he was "a Kafka enthusiast," the author was again proscribed: A 1961 history of Prague that made mention of Kafka was published by the state imprint Ardis in German and English "for export only." Then, at the Moscow Congress for Peace and Disarmament in July 1962, Jean-Paul Sartre brought up the question of Kafka, explaining that "a double injustice has been committed against this author. In the West, he is distorted and misconstrued and in the East, he is passed over in silence."[33]

The subject was again broached at a symposium on contemporary prose organized by the Czech and Slovak writers' unions early the next year, around the time that *The Joke* is set; Kundera denounced Socialist Realism, and the philosopher Karel Kosík argued for Kafka's rehabilitation. That May (a month after the young reformer Alexander Dubček was elected general secretary of the Slovak Communist Party), the Czechs convened an international academic conference in Liblice to reopen the Kafka question.

Has any academic conference since the invention of Socialist Realism held mere fiction in greater regard? Pavel Reimann, director of the Institute of the History of the Communist Party of Czechoslovakia, began the proceedings by introducing as evidence of potential tolerance the 1924 Kafka obituary that ran in the Communist daily *Rude Pravo:* "A German poet has passed away, a delicate and pure spirit, who abhorred this world and dissected it with a sharp knife of reason." Reimann, one of the founders of the prewar Czech Communist Party, went on to contrast Kafka unfavorably with the Communist journalist Julius Fučík, an official symbol of optimism, martyred by the Nazis.

But picking up the defense, conference organizer Dr. Edouard

Goldstücker termed Kafka one more "victim of the personality cult."[34] A contemporary of Howard Fast who had joined the Czech Communist Party as a student during the 1930s, served as ambassador to Israel in 1947, and was consequently sentenced to life imprisonment as a Jewish bourgeois nationalist in a 1954 show trial, Goldstücker shouldered the burden of assigning Kafka a vanguard position: The Prague Germans, and especially their Jewish majority, he explained, "were the first social group of the bourgeois world whose writers felt their world heading for the abyss."[35]

Austrian Communist Ernst Fischer requested that Kafka be granted the "permanent visa" of a resident alien. Fischer emphasized Kafka's satire and polyvalence—strategies that had served other Other European writers and filmmakers well (perhaps too well)—before tackling Lukács and the "realism" issue head on: "Kafka refers hundreds of times to the available (even if incredible) world of the Hapsburg monarchy as a model of a world going to ruin."[36]

Although Kafka's particular realism is hardly an example of nineteenth-century naturalism, he evidently saw his method in much the same way. "The office is not a dull institution," he wrote to Milena Jesenká after a dozen years at the Workman's Compensation Department of the Kingdom of Bohemia. The office is actually "more related to the weird, to the supernatural, than to the dull." As Kundera has observed, what Kafka did with *The Castle* (1922) is take "a most ordinary story about a man unable to get the job he wanted"—the story, in fact, of most men's lives—and turn it into "a work on a mythological scale, an epic of unprecedented beauty."[37]

In Kafka, utterly mundane experiences—going to work, getting married—are subject to the tyrannical whims of mysterious and absolute authority. As in the office (or at the Liblice conference), this vast force operates through a convoluted and sometimes circular chain of command. The world is an office where the regulations are incomprehensible and, in any case, locked in the files. We are but the shadows cast by our dossiers, deducing our crimes by the punishment meted out. Human institutions have displaced their creator from the center of his universe—and this, naturally enough, is subject for comedy.

Participants at Liblice, who included a number of Western—albeit no Soviet—Marxists, were soon polarized into factions either for or against Kafka, with another line drawn between those who regarded Kafka as essentially historical and those who deemed his work timeless and universal. For the conference was not just an attempt to rehabilitate a particular author but a test of whether literature could be analyzed through any lens save the ideological.

Playing every side of the issue—Kafka's vision of the old Austrian monarchy, the Nazi occupation, the postwar capitalist world—was also way to speak of alienation. Thus, from a political point of view, the boldest approach to Kafka was advanced by Alexej Kusák: "Kafkaesque situations are the model for particular situations in socialist countries during the time of the personality cult" and even, per Jiří Hájek, for "some essential characteristics of the reality of a socialist society in the throes of formation." Indeed, "the will to a complete and truthful confrontation with Kafka in the socialist world is becoming synonymous with a commitment to truth and completeness in socialist life ideals."[38]

Reimann, who had written an introduction to Kafka's *Amerika* declaring the author a "shipwrecked explorer," concluded his presentation with the ringing declaration:

> We cannot force our concept of life on anyone who does not have an optimistic faith in life, who, like Kafka, does not achieve an inner harmony. But I do not believe that Kafka's position can be the normal feeling of a person who is actively participating in building the new socialist society.
>
> The conflicts which defeated Kafka are already largely part of the past. And we will overcome the new conflicts too. . . . We have had storms; often our ship has pitched dangerously in heavy seas; but our course is sure, and we sail straight to the shores of tomorrow![39]

The rhetoric would surely have driven Ludvik screaming from the hall.

"**A**n Old Manuscript" (published during Kafka's lifetime but rarely annotated) opens as an Aesopian burlesque of an anti-Semitic diatribe: The empire must be declining because the capital has been overrun by nomads. "Speech with the nomads is impossible," the narrator tells us. "They do not know our language, indeed they hardly have a language of their own. They communicate with each other much as jackdaws do. A screeching of jackdaws is always in our ears."

A screeching of jackdaws: Kafka had the knack of turning all of human history into *his* history, and what begins as a hostile description of the

Jewish ghetto soon mutates into something else. The nomads refuse to understand even sign language; any comprehension would complicate their simply taking whatever it is they want. "You cannot call it taking by force," Kafka's narrator, a cobbler, explains. "They grab at something and you simply stand aside and leave them to it. From my stock, too, they have taken many good articles. But I cannot complain when I see how the butcher, for instance, suffers across the street."

The nomads are intoxicated by meat; even their horses are carnivorous. One day, the butcher thinks to spare himself the chore of slaughtering and brings a live ox into the shop: "He will never dare do that again." The nomads simply begin rending and eating the ox with their bare hands. (The butcher, it turns out, is subsidized by the other merchants because his misery makes their lives that much easier.)

A nightmare primal ghetto has invaded—not really the capital but another ghetto, home of the uneasy petite bourgeoisie. What obscure authority has caused this state of affairs? Or rather, what absent authority? "The Emperor's palace has drawn the nomads here but does not know how to drive them away again," the manuscript concludes. "The gate stays shut; the guards, who used to be marching in and out with ceremony, keep close behind barred windows. It is left to us artisans and tradesmen to save our country; but we are not equal to such a task; nor have we ever claimed to be capable of it. This is a misunderstanding of some kind; and it will be the ruin of us."[40]

This ruinous "misunderstanding" telescopes the experience of the Hapsburg subject peoples—Czechs, Jews, Poles, Hungarians, Serbs, Slovaks—in the twenty-five years after the story's publication. The collapse of Hapsburg authority left a vacuum of bourgeois democracy (Czechoslovakia) or bourgeois fascism (Hungary) to be filled by successive invasions from the North (Germany) and the East (Russia). In the Other Europe—which had undergone yet another wrenching shift in authority from West to East, from feudalism to socialism—life may have been elsewhere (to borrow the title Kundera borrowed from Rimbaud), but living was Kafkaesque.[41]

A few years after the Liblice conference, Goldstücker pointed out that the ban on Kafka had the effect of transforming his writings into "forbidden fruit." There was now, especially among the youth, a Kafka craze. "As soon as any new Kafka book or article appeared, people lined up to buy it."[42]

Imagine that! The dead victim of the personality cult had become a best-selling dissident. Philosophy professor Roger Garaudy, then the chief ideologist of the French Communist Party, named this phenomenon "Prague Spring" when he published a report on the conference. His opposite number, Fritz Kurella of the East German Communist Party, responded with a lengthy denunciation of Professors Garaudy and Fischer in an East Berlin cultural weekly. As a sort of a joke, a translation of Kurella's diatribe appeared in the liberal Czech journal *Literární Noviny*. According to then coeditor Antonin Liehm, the article's "dogmatism and vulgarized version of Marxism, not to mention its language, were like a voice out of another century." Meanwhile, "readers in Prague were shocked and the censors were delighted. They had never expected such cooperation and understanding from the editors of *Literární Noviny,* of all people. But Kurella's article had been published with a footnote, inviting rebuttal by those whom he had attacked. Their replies were already on the editor's desk."[43] Thanks to Kurella's challenge and *Literární Noviny*'s prank, the Kafka controversy reached a far wider audience than would have otherwise been possible—"a newspaper debate which started out about an author who had evidently lived in the same kind of society as they did."

According to Liehm, the "Kafkaesque" became a Czech idiom even before the first volume of Kafka's collected works was published: "People had never even heard of *The Trial, The Castle,* or *Metamorphosis,* but now, when they got together in their offices or shops or in the streetcar and confronted man's complete alienation and the way they were all being manipulated by society in their daily lives, they would cast up their eyes and confide in a whisper to the first stranger they met, 'This is just like Kafka!'"[44] And so, enchantment of Prague Spring (chestnut trees and blooming forsythia), literature came to life.[45]

For artists, the mid-1960s were the "Kafka years," bringing the first Czech productions of Beckett, Ionesco, and Václav Havel. Thus reborn in Czechoslovakia, Kafka did double duty—representing indigenous culture as well as embodying high modernism. Edward Albee's *Who's Afraid of Virginia Woolf?* (1962) was introduced to Prague under the title *Who's Afraid of Franz Kafka?* Scarcely a year after the Liblice conference, three Czech feature films dealing with the Nazi occupation and the period of Stalinist terror—Zbyněk Brynych's *The Fifth Horseman Is Fear,* Jiri Nemec's *Diamonds of the Night,* and Pavel Juráček's anti-bureaucratic satire *Josef Kilián*—were openly Kafkaesque.

Three decades later, President Havel would tell an audience at the Hebrew University in Jerusalem that he sometimes felt as though he alone understood Kafka: "I'm even secretly persuaded that if Kafka did not exist, and if I were a better writer than I am, I could have written his works myself."[46]

The "restoration of order" that followed the August 21, 1968, military occupation of Czechoslovakia resulted in Kafka's conviction of various posthumous offenses, not least of them having inspired the Prague Spring. Barely a month after the Warsaw Pact invasion, the East German journal *Neues Deutschland* cited the Liblice conference as "an important milestone in the spread of revisionist and bourgeois ideology." It was then that the "revisionist" Fischer-Goldstücker thesis that alienation was no less characteristic of socialism than of capitalism "came out into the open on a mass scale in Czechoslovakia."[47]

With normalization, Kafka's crimes grew increasingly sinister. More than a dissident, he verged on the counterrevolutionary. The Soviet tract *Zionism* (published in Czech and Slovak editions in 1970) identified Liblice as the start of "a long-term operation" devoted to the "ideological subversion" of Czechoslovak youth. "Anti-socialist forces considered the Kafka discussions as an effective instrument which could legally transform itself unhindered into an attack against socialism in the realm of ideology and politics."[48]

In June 1972, František J. Kolár made it clear who was behind Operation Kafka: "If we are to discuss the influence of Zionism on the events in Czechoslovakia in 1968—and particularly on what led up to them—then we must make a detailed analysis of 'Kafkaism' and of the 'alienation' connected with it. Those who propagate his fashionable ideology, which was deviously introduced into this country from the West, have always emphasized the Jewish and Judaic origins of 'Kafkaism.'"[49]

Milan Kundera was a man who invented a joke and who, through some alchemy of desire and happenstance, lived to become its unending butt. No less than Ludvik's imaginary life, Kundera's career in Czechoslovakia was determined by three lines of prose—a joke, comrades, and a memorable dossier—that could never be retracted.[50]

Kundera had warned Philip Roth of the loss of Western culture's vital center of gravity. But what would ever restore it? Delightful Middle European theme park (as it had once been a romantically broken-down and dank Communist Disneyland), Prague was now truly a backwater—no longer on the border of anything. Kundera has not returned from Parisian exile. No longer behind the no-longer-existent Iron Curtain, he now writes in French and is referred to by his publisher as a Franco-Czech writer. On the fifth anniversary of the Velvet Revolution, Ivan Klíma bitterly informed the readers of the *New York Review of Books* of "the waning interest in dissident literature."[51]

The end of the cold war erased the Other Europe and submerged its artifacts, including, of course, Czechoslovakia itself. The corollary to this Kafkaesque fate is Tadeusz Konwicki's mocking lament in *The Polish Complex*. Konwicki was born in Vilnius, a once-polyglot city that has gone from Russia to Lithuania to Poland to Lithuania to Russia to the Nazis back to the Soviets and now once again Lithuania. So "how did it happen that I am an author of Polish books, good or bad, but Polish?" Konwicki howled. "Why did I accept the role which I renounced forever? Who turned me, a European, no, a citizen of the world, an Esperantist, a cosmopolitan, an agent of universalism, who turned me, as in some wicked fairy tale, into a stubborn, ignorant, furious Pole?"[52]

The answer is history—one more human creation with a mind of its own. Konwicki was pursued by Poland, the most peripatetic nation of the Other Europe. Indeed, Poland can be said to have discovered him in a comic inversion of the blind, cosmic force that drove Columbus to "discover" America. If Americans once believed themselves to be destiny's darlings, the Other Europeans knew that everyone was history's stooge.

Géza Csáth may ultimately have more in common with Edgar Allan Poe than with Franz Kafka, but the Kafkaesque (and Freudian) notion that men are less the subject than the object of their history was hardly foreign to him. "Musicians" takes a detached but not uncompassionate view of the ragtag orchestra imported by a Hungarian town from "far off Czechoslovakia." After twenty years in Hungary, these middle-aged failures still can't manage the language, and they drink to revive dreams of success and the ambitions of youth in their "fatty, alcoholic hearts." Their alienation is their very identity. They are called merely "the musicians" by the townspeople, who get their foreign names mixed up.

At the end of the vignette, Csáth shifts to long shot. These musicians, he explains, "had no way of knowing their misfortune was to arrive in Hungary in the latter half of the nineteenth century—a time of provincialism and poverty when no one was in the mood to bother over music, nor had time to." The musicians' lot is one more common confusion. "They never knew they'd been victimized by an uncultivated Hungary," Csáth concludes, with a damning lack of patriotic fervor, "ruined by a nation that could appreciate only gypsy music."[53]

Only gypsy music! As in some wicked fairy tale or old manuscript, these terminal Other Europeans (other even to themselves) had "been deprived of music's pleasures, which they"—naturally—"had a right to, despite their mediocrity." Drawn to Hungary by some mistake, some misplaced memo, "they'd been robbed of their ambition, and driven to drink, forced to lead lives of misery and die disillusioned and poor." So a dissident lost his dissidence. Who even dares take it personally? A wandering identity assumed a man. A standing joke discovered its butt. Or, as our comrade Kafka put it, "A cage went in search of a bird."[54]

CHAPTER 6

Report to the Communist Cell
tomorrow morning.

A History of

Communism in

Twenty-four

Scenarios

1. *OCTOBER* (Sergei Eisenstein and Grigori Alexandrov, USSR, 1928)

For years to come people will study the methods by which Eisenstein has in this instance raised the art of newsreel to the level of a film poem.

—Anatoli Lunacharsky, *Kino* (3/20/28)

An imaginary document projected on actual locations, Sergei Eisenstein's *October* is the Soviet equivalent of the Sistine Chapel—an artist commissioned by the state has represented the sacred origins of the universe.

Woodrow Wilson had famously hailed D. W. Griffith's *The Birth of a Nation* (1915) as "history written with lightning," but Eisenstein's cosmic newsreel cum theoretical film poem goes beyond *The Birth of a Nation*, as well as his own *Battleship Potemkin*, in drafting the past to serve the requirements of the present. No less than the revolutionaries who made October, Eisenstein understood himself as history's tool. Thus consecrated to the Bolshevik faith, his *October* is a perfect tautology—it clarifies and improves on history in the service of objective historical necessity.

Establishing a precedent for the Socialist Realist narrative, *October* illustrates, even as it annotates, the Soviet foundation myth—successively showing how the Russian bourgeoisie usurped the worker-peasant uprising of February 1917 and how, the next summer, after the Bolsheviks thwarted General L. G. Kornilov's reactionary coup, Lenin returned from exile to orchestrate the October Revolution

---

Drawn from twenty years of film reviews, program notes, and classroom lectures, these two dozen movies (largely undiscussed in other chapters) are put forth here as one continuous history, from the October Revolution through the dissolution of the Soviet Union, projected from a variety of national, historical, and ideological perspectives.

against the grotesque, supercilious leaders of the ridiculous provisional government.

Just as the revolution is spontaneous yet organized, an expression of the masses even as it is orchestrated by a revolutionary elite, so Eisenstein's highly choreographed and densely edited movie has no actors—or rather, it proposes the masses as actor. The ten thousand extras included witnesses of—and even participants in—the actual events. Nikolai Podvoisky, one of the three Bolshevik commanders who took the Winter Palace, not only consulted on the script but played himself. Lenin was impersonated by a worker named Nikandrov. This typage was criticized both by Lenin's widow Krupskaya and by Vladimir Mayakovsky, who prophetically noted that "Nikandrov doesn't resemble Lenin, but a statue of Lenin." Elsewhere improving on reality, *October* relocates the dramatic toppling of the statue of Alexander III in February 1917 (in fact, the czar's statue was dismembered, at Lenin's orders, as part of the May Day 1918 festivities) and raises the storming of the Winter Palace to world-historic importance.[1]

Partially based on John Reed's firsthand report *Ten Days That Shook the World* (published in 1919), *October* was written during late 1926 and early 1927; filming began on April 13, 1927. Leningrad was, in effect, Eisenstein's movie set. Not just the Winter Palace but much of the city and its citizenry were placed at the filmmakers' disposal. The Red Army furnished the appropriate uniforms as well as supplying the production with necessary military hardware—including the battle cruiser *Aurora*. Due to a critical shortage of electricity, the film was mainly shot by night. (Even so, the city suffered from power outages.)[2]

October was in production during the period that Victor Serge calls the "Deadlock of the Revolution." In May 1927, Trotsky attacked Stalin for supporting the Kuomintang over the Chinese Communists, even as the Kuomintang massacred tens of thousands of Shanghai workers. Such was the political atmosphere that Eisenstein was forced to deny rumors that he belonged to Trotsky's opposition. According to codirector Grigori Alexandrov, Stalin dropped by the editing room to screen a rough cut—ordering one of Lenin's speeches excised and making the cryptic remark that "Lenin's liberalism is no longer valid today."[3]

Nor was that all: "By a significant coincidence of dates, the Soviet Thermidor was realized in November 1927, the anniversary of the seizure of power," Serge wrote in his memoirs. "In ten years the exhausted Revolution had turned full circle against itself. On 7 November 1917 Trotsky,

Chairman of the Petrograd Soviet, organized the victorious insurrection. On the second day of November 1927 *Pravda* published the report of his latest speech, delivered in October to the Central Committee beneath a hail of shouting." Only excerpts from *October* were ready to be shown on November 7, 1927, while Serge and others participated in violent street demonstrations, outside the Winter Palace and elsewhere in Leningrad.[4]

On November 16, it was announced that Leon Trotsky and Grigori Zinoviev had been expelled from the Central Committee. Still, although Eisenstein ultimately cut his first version of *October* by one-third of the film, the erstwhile chairman of the Petrograd soviet and creator of the Red Army was still visible in several scenes when the finished *October* had its Moscow premiere on March 14, 1928. The movie was not a popular success. "Every Wednesday in the Central House of the Arts there are regular screenings of films for the cultural activists in the trade unions," the journalist T. Rokotov would note. "*October* was shown at one of these screenings. The Cultural Section of the Leningrad Regional Trade Union Council has introduced at these screening a system of carefully monitoring audience reactions while the film is being shown. The dry statistics record in the minutes: 'During the fourth and fifth reels there was a loud sound of snoring in the front rows on the left.'"[5]

It was while completing the editing of *October* in early 1928 that Eisenstein had his most visionary experience of montage and, grasping the nature of Communism's ongoing project, began making notes for a never-to-be realized film version of Marx's *Capital*.

2. *AELITA* (Yakov Protazanov, USSR, 1924)

We *must be precise, clear-sighted, strong, unyielding, armed: like machines. . . . We need technicians, not great men or admirable men. Technicians specialized in the liberation of the masses.*

—Victor Serge, *Men in Prison* (1930)

Flashback of gilded optimism: *Aelita,* the October Revolution's first cultural export, reaches its giddy climax with a proletarian revolution on another planet. What previous political movement had ever devoted itself to the liberation of the entire globe? And now: "Follow our example, Comrades! Unite into a family of workers in a Martian Union of Soviet Socialist Republics."

Combining several popular genres with a sense of everyday constructivism, *Aelita* was directed by Yakov Protazanov from Count Alexei Tolstoy's 1923 best-seller, itself published at the end of a twenty-year cycle of utopian fantasies including Proletkult founder Alexander Bogdanov's 1908 *Red Star,* in which a discouraged activist—not unlike the author—recovers from the failure of the 1905 revolution by discovering a Communist utopia on Mars.[6]

Tolstoy and Protazanov were both newly returned émigrés: Those who fled the revolution returned to celebrate its accomplishments in a spectacular modern film, produced by the Mezhrabpom-Rus Studio—created during the New Economic Policy (NEP) and partially capitalized by the Berlin-based Workers International Relief. Boasting a cast of thousands and a prodigal eight-to-one shooting ratio, *Aelita* was designed to be the Soviet equivalent of *The Cabinet of Dr. Caligari*—the 1920 thriller that put post-World War I German cinema on the international map. Where *Caligari* popularized an already passé expressionism, *Aelita* made use of a particularly Soviet cubo-futurism, including a heavy infusion of Meyerholdian avant-vaudeville.

Like more than one ancient religion and many subsequent science fictions, the original Soviet blockbuster is predicated on a cryptic transmission from outer space: "Maybe someone on Mars is wondering about us," wonders the engineer Los, in charge of Radio Moscow. How could they not, given October's worldwide and world-historical import? The new Soviet Union has begun the transformation of our home planet into a scientific workshop to produce the new Soviet man—an individual perhaps destined to alter the very cosmos. Scientific excitement is, however, quickly subsumed in the soap opera of daily life. Los suspects his wife, Natasha, of carrying on an affair with the sleazy speculator Erlich—this imagined erotic intrigue played out in the new Soviet capital's distinctive milieu of committees, communal apartments, and ration tickets. Meanwhile, as a title informs us, "jealousy was no stranger to the Martians."

Studying the red planet Earth through a high-powered telescope located atop the Tower of Radiant Energy, the Martian princess Aelita has fallen in love with Los, much to the disgust of her consort, Tuskub. Little does Aelita realize that, to escape from his increasingly sordid domestic melodrama, which has escalated to the point of gunplay, the Soviet engineer will soon commandeer a rocket headed for Mars—accompanied on this expedition by the rough-hewn Gusev, a veteran (like Isaac Babel) of Semen Budyonny's Red Cavalry, and the detective Kravtsev.

The movie needs eighty-five minutes to get to Mars, but then—feudal yet hypermodern, madly geometric, the planet is a world of petrified rays, total deco; its denizens would have been the best-dressed nightclubbers in 1980s New York. Dressed in Alexandra Exter's geometric aluminum-and-glass tutus, the female Martians more than match the curved stairs and translucent columns of Isaac Rabinovich's ultraconstructivist sets (which, as in *Caligari,* turn out to be a subjective hallucination). Aelita, a sensuous pixie in a slinky metallic evening gown, her bobbed hair crowned by a hundred antennae, commands Los to "touch my lips with your lips as those Earth people did."

In the finale, everything gets mixed up—Los imagines that Aelita is his (not really) unfaithful wife, and Gusev incites the local proletariat to put "an end to a thousand years of slavery" and "unite into a family of workers in a Martian Union of Soviet Socialist Republics," the set suddenly crammed with battling soldiers in square helmets firing flashlight ray guns. A primitive montage shows the breaking chains, the hammered sickle, the word *October* in flames.

Aelita was the most elaborately realized space opera since Georges Méliès's 1902 *Voyage to the Moon.* (The vision of stunted subterranean workers in boxy helmets sweating over star-shaped gears anticipates Fritz Lang's 1927 *Metropolis,* even as the mixing of conjugal paranoia with delusions of extraterrestrial revolutionary grandeur oddly forecasts the 1990 Arnold Schwarzenegger vehicle *Total Recall.*) Still, no less evocative than the Martian sets are the scenes filmed in the streets of Moscow during the winters of 1923 and 1924.

The shoot opened in February 1923 and wrapped over a year later—the German Revolution failed and Lenin died while *Aelita* was in production. Although the period represented is slightly earlier—from December 4, 1921, into 1923, "before the advent of bureaucracy," as Victor Serge put it—the movie is a portrait as well as an expression of the NEP. The bundled-up extras, the mob of speculators attending a "secret high-society ball," with winter coats over their tuxedos; the steam shovels and scaffolding; the agitational posters; the interpolated footage of people's nurseries and revolutionary pageants (there's a parade through Moscow the day that the rocket leaves); the semidocumentary plot devices hinging on food shortages, housing problems, and queues—all are bizarrely juxtaposed against the constructivist extravagance of Mars.

In the spirit of the NEP, *Aelita* even incorporates its own publicity: Not only is the story revealed to be a dream, but the mysterious transmission is an advertising slogan for a new brand of automobile tire. Like *Caligari*, *Aelita*'s release was preceded by a carefully orchestrated, deliberately enigmatic ad campaign. Moscow was plastered with the Martian message "ANTA . . . ODELI . . . UTA"; other cities were leafleted from the sky. When *Aelita* had its gala premiere on September 30, 1924, Moscow's Ars Cinema was decked out with geometric shapes and raked by shafts of light. The unprecedented demand for tickets evidently kept the director himself from reaching the theater.[7]

Abroad, *Aelita* was the most publicized Soviet film before *Potemkin* concretized the revolution in 1925. At home, where its release was restricted to urban centers, it was at once a popular success and the most reviled movie of the mid-1920s. A target for vanguard film critics and doctrinaire politicos alike, *Aelita* was attacked as too expensive, too Western, too bourgeois, and too convoluted, not to mention anti-Soviet and antiproletariat. After the establishment of "socialism in one country" in 1931, space fantasy was no longer legal, and soon after, *Aelita*'s innocently Trotskyist fantasy of interplanetary solidarity was forbidden altogether.

3. *WE THE LIVING* (Goffredo Alessandrini, Italy, 1943/1968/1988)

We the Living is *Aelita* in reverse. Produced in Fascist Italy, this three-hour Cinecittà vision of émigré Ayn Rand's red Petrograd is lavish and gloomy—a film of fiery titles and perpetual snow flurries that's not quite nutty enough to qualify as camp but more than worthy of its source. Unique combination of Adam Smith, Friedrich Nietzsche, and Jacqueline Susann, Ayn Rand (born Alice Rosenbaum in St. Petersburg, 1905) wrote seven-hundred-page potboilers to illustrate her philosophical doctrine—an engagingly solipsistic mix of free-market fundamentalism and right-wing anarchy, spiked with heavy-breathing hero worship.

Rand left the Soviet Union in late 1925 and wound up in Hollywood—working for Cecil B. DeMille, marrying a minor actor, managing the RKO wardrobe department, and writing unproduced screenplays with titles such as *Red Pawn* and *Penthouse Legend,* as well as the best-selling *We the Living.* Called as an expert witness before the House Un-American Activities Committee (HUAC) on October 20, 1947, she usefully defined Communist propaganda as "anything which gave a good impression of Communism as a way of life." Much of her testimony concerned the 1943 wartime extravaganza *Song of Russia* (produced by Metro Goldwyn

Mayer [MGM] at approximately the same time that *We the Living* was shooting in Rome). Although MGM's Louis B. Mayer had just assured the committee (and even swore to God) that *Song of Russia* had no political implications, Rand pointed out that the movie began "with Robert Taylor playing the American national anthem [which] dissolves into a Russian mob with the sickle and the hammer on a red flag very prominently above their heads."[8]

Rand found America at the movies, but the movies first discovered her in Mussolini's Italy, where—for reasons far from clear—an adaptation of her anti-Communist novel, originally published in 1936, was adapted to the screen in 1942. Although *We the Living* was a major production and even a popular hit, its memory was so repressed that in 1988, when the restored print had its premiere at the Telluride Film Festival, not one English-language history of the Italian cinema had even mentioned it.[9]

The heroine of Rand's quasi-autobiographical fantasy is the individualist counterpart to the new Soviet woman. Arriving in revolutionary Petrograd with her now-impoverished bourgeois family, teenage Kira has shining eyes and, beneath her stylish beret, a head full of plans for skyscrapers and aluminum bridges. She enrolls at the State Technology Institute and, no less than Aelita, princess of Mars, becomes a science-fiction construct—the indomitable "Kira of Steel," as her lover will say. Kira's dreams of becoming an engineer, however, are confounded by the fools and knaves of the Communist Party, extending each other "hearty proletariat greetings" while hypocritically wheeling and dealing on the black market. As coolly played by twenty-one-year-old Alida Valli, Kira drives these Komsomol Quasimodos mad by her mere existence. Her grave, far-away look suggests a heritage and a destiny far more noble than their miserable ideal. "Every honest man lives for himself—alone, absolute, an end in himself."

We the Living makes much of the persecution of the old Russian ruling class, but primitive living accommodations notwithstanding, Kira does not suffer indignity until cousin Victor, a class renegade who has joined the party, becomes overfamiliar. She flees into the sleaze district and there—struck by the thunderbolt—meets the aristocratic Leo (Rossano Brazzi), counterrevolutionary love of her life. Leo initially mistakes Kira for a prostitute, which, by the end of the movie, is what she will become—albeit not in the way he imagines.

Shot mainly in close-up and entirely in the studio, *We the Living* evokes an atmosphere of total, demoralized corruption. As directed by

Goffredo Alessandrini, a filmmaker with some Hollywood experience, the movie does not lack for *mise-en-scène*. The grim sets are scrawled with hammer-and-sickle graffiti and Cyrillic exhortations, emblazoned with menacing posters of proletarian ape-men and encephalitic Lenins. That everyone is always layered with clothing adds to the sense of unpleasant crowding, just as the already high fog quotient is significantly augmented by a constant sucking on cigarettes. The atmosphere is as gray as the dialogue is purple. Caught *in flagrante* with Leo by some Bolshevik neanderthal, Kira is brutally dismissed: "We don't fight children, especially those who find time for love on a spewing volcano."

Nothing matches Kira's disdain for the leather-coated Commies running the show. She falls into a sadomasochist affair with one, the seasoned, taciturn GPU man Andrei (Fosco Giachetti), who haunts her campus. "I know," he says in a typically dour attempt at flirtation, "you admire our ideals but you hate our methods." Guess again, Comrade. "I loathe your ideals," Kira haughtily replies. (Following Rand's lead in the novel's 1959 edition, the subtitlers omit the girl's coy Zarathustran kicker "but I admire your methods.") Andrei's jealous associates call him "a saint who sleeps with the red flag," but his weakness is love—or at least, this upper-class cutie.

After Leo develops tuberculosis, Kira goes to Andrei's room and gives herself to him—subsequently bilking the amorous Bolshevik for cash to keep Leo in a private sanatorium. More risqué than the novel, the movie has Kira rushing from Andrei's bed to Leo's arms. As in a whole subgenre of gothic romance, she is torn between two lovers—one flighty and well-born, the other devoted and down-to-earth. In this class-conscious triangle, everybody is somebody's fool. Presenting Kira with a sheer negligee, Andrei proposes marriage and defection. "Andrei, you were their best," she says reproachfully, then runs back to the permed and sneering Leo to make him the identical offer and discover that the monkey business that interests him has less to do with black lace than the black market.

Things come to a splendidly melodramatic head when Andrei has to arrest Leo and finds Kira's dresses hanging in the criminal's closet. "I'm proud of what I've done—yes, proud!" she cries when confronted. The realization that the red regime has made Kira a whore prompts Andrei's conversion. Having obtained a print in 1968, Rand composed a speech that was dubbed for the revised *We the Living*: The GPU man turns vehemently anticollectivist, abruptly adopting the objectivist creed that every honest man lives for himself. Then, after expressing his scorn for a particularly scummy lot of comrades, he burns Kira's sacred nightie and shoots himself.

In its morbid fatalism, *We the Living* suggests a more engagingly tawdry equivalent to the German movie industry's 1945 Götterdämmerung, *Kolberg*. The rondo of hopelessness comes full circle when Leo rejects Kira—although Rand again modified the original film, which, following the novel's ending, had Kira perish in an attempt to cross the Soviet border.

First shown eleven months before Mussolini's fall, at the 1943 Venice Film Festival, *We the Living* received a minor award and was released that November as a two-part epic. The film ran for five months—despite German criticism that it was "too mild" in its representation of the Russians—and was then withdrawn from circulation.

Rand told her onetime lawyers Erika and Mark Holzer about her "lost" film in 1966 or 1967. The couple went to Rome during the summer of 1968, located the movie, and brought back a print. Rand and producer Duncan Scott then substantially recut the picture from four and a half to three hours and added subtitles. It was another two decades before *We the Living* would be released in the United States—six years after Rand's death, and represented as an anti-Fascist story made under the regime's nose. Perhaps it was taken as such, but one doubts that was the filmmaker's intention. Among other Fascist propaganda, Alessandrini (one of only three directors punished for collaboration with the Fascists by a postwar film industry commission) directed the popular *Lucian Serra-Pilota*, a 1938 allegory of a bitter stunt flier who redeems himself in the Ethiopian War and, according to producer Vittorio Mussolini, "vividly symbolizes today's Italian, who was beaten and then won out over forty-two nations."

Indeed, the junior Mussolini helped authorize *We the Living*, and given the young Rand's anti-Communism, isolationism, and temperamental futurism, one wonders if she wouldn't have approved the adaptation herself. According to the Holzers, she preferred it to King Vidor's 1949 version of *The Fountainhead*.[10]

4. *MY FRIEND IVAN LAPSHIN* (Alexei German, USSR, 1982)

Elusive even by the standards of East European cinema, *My Friend Ivan Lapshin* is a movie where narrative is secondary to atmosphere—the evocation of provincial Russia on the eve of the Great Terror. Alexei German wrote the screenplay for *My Friend Ivan Lapshin* in 1969. The project was delayed for over a decade and, although finally completed in 1982, withheld from release until the 1985 Moscow Film Festival.[11]

German's father, Yuri, was a well-known literary figure and (unlike his son) a precocious success. The elder German's early novels, one of which was published by Knopf in 1938, ostensibly concerned the everyday lives of ordinary Soviet citizens. In addition to celebrating the quotidian, Yuri German specialized in portraying heroic cops—although in this he was hardly alone: It is estimated that two thousand Soviet books devoted themselves to extolling the security organization known successively as the Cheka, NKVD, OGPU, GPU, and KGB, in a dogged attempt to imbue its agents with the friendly glamor of Canada's Royal Mounted Police.[12]

The virtuous and energetic NKVD man Ivan Lapshin was the hero of two Yuri German novellas, one providing the basis for Alexei German's film. In a sense, the Lapshin stories were the more "naturalistic" Stalin-era successor to the utopian science-fiction and red detective novels of the 1920s—projecting a rational vision of collective social order. Thus, the NKVD men live in a commune, and their leader's greatest concern is to "reform" those criminal elements he pursues. The most optimistic character in the movie, Lapshin is prone to statements such as "We'll clear the nation of scum, plant an orchard, and still have time to take a walk." That the movie's characteristic landscape is bleak and snowy renders the metaphor grotesquely self-deluded.

Set (more specifically than the novel) during the winter of 1935, transposed from Leningrad to a fictional backwater Volga port somewhere in the great Russian north, *Ivan Lapshin* concerns men who were in their early twenties during the revolution and civil war. Lapshin is the same age as Isaac Babel and Solomon Mikhoels; he might have been Aelita's lover, Kira's class-renegade brother. After a brief, present-day prologue that establishes the movie proper as a flashback from the perspective of a then nine-year-old boy, the narrative kicks in with Lapshin's fortieth birthday party, held in the cramped communal flat where the Chekist, his men, and an unhappy journalist named Khanin make their home. (Dimly aware that the times are changing, they comfort themselves by singing, only half ironically, the proletarian anthems of their youth.)

Lapshin's plot is scarcely more than an anecdote: A mediocre theatrical company arrives in town to present a fourth-rate production of Nikolai Pogodin's *Aristocrats,* the once hugely popular (and subsequently proscribed) Socialist Realist comedy about the "regeneration" of criminals—bandits, thieves, prostitutes, kulaks—forced to build the White Sea Canal. Such is the redemptive power of this collective enterprise that the most extravagantly antisocial of the outlaws is ultimately converted into a Stakhanovite zealot.

No less paternalistic than the security police on stage, Lapshin takes an interest in the production. Along with the firewood he less than legally gives the troupe, their obliging friend furnishes an actual whore for the untalented Natasha to study. (If she's the closet Stanislavskyite in this sub-Meyerhold company, Lapshin is the true believer who mistakes theatrical illusion for idealized reality.) Indeed, the good-natured, ungainly NKVD man falls for Natasha, only to discover that the high-spirited actress is in love with gloomy Khanin.

Aristocrats literally comes apart midperformance, and so, too, albeit landing with a softer thud, do Lapshin's ideals. His disappointment is only somewhat tempered by his capture of the supposedly dangerous Solovev—the mysterious criminal whose gang runs the town, or at least the local black market. A hysterical mixture of violence and farce, replete with a visual reference to the Odessa Steps sequence from Eisenstein's *Battleship Potemkin,* this complex sequence in which Lapshin and his men trap Solovev in the miserable, overcrowded farmhouse that serves as his lair has been described by Russian critic Oleg Kovalov as "the imagistic essence of the 1930s."[13]

Solovev surrenders when, in a shocking bit of business invented by the younger German, Lapshin shoots his captive point-blank. "Lapshin acts as if he were a god," the filmmaker said of this summary justice. He is "convinced that he holds a key to happiness for all mankind."[14] This lapse is all the more startling in that, for the most part, *My Friend Ivan Lapshin* is subtle to the point of obscurity. Even given familiarity with its subject, the film can be difficult to follow. German's lack of orthodoxy extends to his style: Space is highly variable; the geography and population of Lapshin's communal apartment are forever shifting. The movie, which employs a variety of tinted film stocks, is characterized by a virtual absence of reverse-angle or reaction shots.

Probing the landscape (whether the suggestively vague geography of the communal apartment or the stark rural squalor of the brigand's lair), making tentative maneuvers and then abruptly doubling back, German's camera almost never stops moving; when it does, the actors are usually in motion themselves. Every scene is elaborately choreographed; the frame is less an image than an intersection, often glimpsed through a veil of smoke or snow. (As the visuals eschew an overt point of view, so the largely martial soundtrack refuses to cue appropriate responses.) As in a Socialist Realist canvas, *Ivan Lapshin*'s real drama is obscured by optimistic rhetoric, happening offstage and behind the scenes. In the aftermath of the December 1, 1934, assassination of Leningrad's party secretary Sergei Kirov, the Great Terror had already begun. Some two to three thousand party members were arrested during the winter of 1934–35.

February brought the purge of Leningrad. As recounted by Victor Serge, "The TASS agency communicates to the press that two hundred former nobles, superior officers, gendarmes, and policemen of the old regime have been expelled from the city for infraction of the law on passports. The TASS agency lies, as usual. *Thirty, fifty, perhaps a hundred thousand persons* are not just expelled from Leningrad; they are deported from it to regions of the Volga, the Urals, Central Asia, Siberia." What is more, "they are not former servitors of the old regime, but engineers, scholars, artists, functionaries, workers, in a word, collaborators of the new regime." The official purging of the party, which began that summer, would send another 150,000 to 200,000 Communists to prison. *Lapshin*'s protagonists are thus the potential victims, as well as the agents, of the Terror.[15]

Not overtly anti-Stalinist (let alone anti-Communist), *Lapshin* could easily be seen as a whitewash. Why, then, did German's film cause such enthusiasm among Soviet intellectuals? For one thing, there was the surface naturalism and fanatical attention to detail. *Lapshin* is a Soviet contribution to the postmodern nostalgia film. The sharp-focused, high-contrast images suggest an exhumed, unexpectedly beautiful example of *cinema verité*. But German's painstaking reconstruction of an erased period goes beyond the use of thrift-shop clothing and furniture to reconstruct attitudes, if not delusions. Filled with iconic portraits of once-revered Soviet leaders who failed to survive the 1930s (Kirov, Marshal M. N. Tukhachevsky, the NKVD head G. G. Yagoda), *Ivan Lapshin* represents Bolshevik idealism as a lost dream.

German (who would not complete another movie for sixteen years) described *Lapshin* as "a film about solitude." Having expressed doubt that his movie could really be understood in the West, German linked it to the experience of his parents and their generation—"their faith, their melancholy, the fact that they go straight ahead, towards Communism, without understanding that the road is long, and even very dangerous. . . . On one side you have the sad collectivization and the burgeoning trials against the Trotskyites and the Zinovievists; on the other, there is the powerful industrialization of the country and the unshakable faith in Stalin. My father believed happiness would come the following day!"[16] Lapshin is in a similar state of denial.

Whereas the father's stories romanticized the work of the NKVD, the son's movie emphasizes the squalor of provincial life—poverty, crime, fuel shortages, overcrowding, coughing, illness, intimations of famine and cannibalism. Even the police are closeted in rude, bedbug-ridden quarters, and as the film makes abundantly clear, the thieves, whores, and lumpen riffraff at society's margins live under even more primitive conditions. For a Soviet movie, *Lapshin* was shockingly raw—the English subtitles give little indication of the language's unprecedented coarseness in some scenes—and its critique of representational styles extends into the narrative.

Ivan Lapshin ends in muddy spring with a burst of rueful pageantry. The actors are leaving this godforsaken hole, hopefully for Moscow. Lapshin, wearing a white dress uniform, has been called into the party shop for an ideological tune-up. It is at this moment that the film's first portrait of Stalin appears—the image of the Great Locomotive Engineer absurdly nailed to the front of the ramshackle trolley that carries the townspeople into a less-than-radiant future. Chekhov meets the Cheka: The spirit of *Uncle Vanya* hovers over German's laconic, ambiguous narrative and oblique pathos—if pathos is the word to describe these innocent monsters, drinking their tea (as was said of Ayn Rand's Kira) on the lip of Vesuvius.[17]

Postscript

A dozen years after *My Friend Ivan Lapshin*, Nikita Mikhalkov—like German, the son of a popular Stalin-era artist—took a Chekhovian approach to the Great Terror, with considerable popular (and international) success.

Set during the summer of 1936, precisely the time of the first Moscow show trial, Mikhalkov's 1994 *Burnt by the Sun* collapsed Soviet history into a bloody domestic quarrel while conflating nostalgia for the prerevolutionary gentry with the Terror's onset. As a further complication, the movie was a psychodrama in which the director cast himself as an indulgent father (named for his own), a Bolshevik war hero, and a political martyr heedlessly enjoying his last day of freedom. Simultaneously glib and resonant, heartfelt and sleazy, the movie employs several of

German's tropes—similarly withholding Stalin's image, here emblazoned on a hot air balloon, until the final moments.[18]

5. *THE SHINING PATH* (Grigori Alexandrov, USSR, 1940)

Set in a world where lovers sing, tough guys dance, and work is defined as putting on a show, the musical comedy is a taste of paradise—it presents, in Richard Dyer's formulation, "what utopia would feel like rather than how it would be organized."[19]

Show business, as Dyer suggests in his essay "Entertainment and Utopia," is essentially compensatory, with the musical in particular offering audiences an "image of 'something better' to escape into," something that "our day-to-day lives don't provide." Scarcity is countered by abundance, exhaustion by energy, dreariness by intensity, manipulation by transparency, fragmentation by community.[20]

The musical may be the most millennial of movie genres, but it is not necessarily the most American. Utopia also required utopia. The notion of revolutionary song and dance is usually associated with the humorless model operas of the Chinese Cultural Revolution. ("After a week's work, people want to go to the theater to relax. Instead, with this thing, you go to the theater and find yourself on the battlefield," was Deng Xiaoping's unwise review of the militant ballet *The Red Detachment of Women,* filmed in 1967.) The Stalinist musical, by comparison, was almost giddy.[21]

Grigori Alexandrov pioneered the mode. Sergei Eisenstein's assistant from *Strike* (1924) through the unfinished *Que Viva Mexico,* Alexandrov accompanied Eisenstein to Hollywood in 1931, where both were under contract to Paramount. On their return to Moscow, Alexandrov accepted an assignment the maestro had turned down. Thus, the same year Fox released *Stand Up and Cheer,* a musical in which the American president charged Secretary of Amusement Warner Baxter with tap-dancing the nation out of its Great Depression, Alexandrov directed *Jolly Fellows* (1934), a vehicle for the reigning Soviet jazzman, Leonid Utyosov.

Synthesizing Western developments that ranged from surrealism to scat singing, cutting scenes to prerecorded sound and staging them on streamlined, modernistic sets, interpolating cartoon gags, and anticipating Spike Jones in the movie's climactic musical brawl, Alexandrov produced a Soviet cousin to Paramount musicals such as *Love Me Tonight* or the anarchic comedies *Million Dollar Legs* and *Duck Soup.* (Indeed, the mountain that was the Paramount logo insinuates itself into the theatrical backdrop in the movie's madcap Bolshoi finale.)

Jolly Fellows premiered to acclaim at the 1934 Venice Film Festival but was dismissed by the Soviet *Literary Gazette* as a "vulgar mistake." Still, young people adopted the movie, and after a command Kremlin screening, so did the leadership. *Pravda* endorsed *Jolly Fellows* and rebuked its critics. Alexandrov would later claim to be the only Soviet civilian awarded the Order of the Red Star—Stalin thought him "a brave man to do a humorous picture." (This courage notwithstanding, playwright Nikolai Erdman was arrested while working on *Jolly Fellows*'s screenplay.) The movie's success made singer Lyubov Orlova a star (as well as Mrs. Alexandrov), while creating the vogue for composer Isaac Dunayevsky, whose affirmative "mass songs" for the follow-up *Circus* (1936) were widely distributed in advance of the movie's release.[22]

Where *Jolly Fellows* was essentially apolitical, *Circus* opens with a frenzied Kansas mob chasing the aerialist Marion (Orlova) and her mulatto baby out of town. Cut to a Soviet circus, complete with resident Chaplin impersonator and Russian Rockettes. Marion, a visiting artiste whose German manager is a proto-Nazi, falls for a handsome Soviet acrobat. To thwart this romance, the German exposes her "racial crimes." Surprise! The Russians don't even understand the problem. Performers of various nationalities, including Yiddish actor, Solomon Mikhoels, take turns serenading the child—"Here you will grow up safe"—and the movie ends with Marion marching on May Day, alongside her Soviet comrades. (Unlike *Jolly Fellows*, which opened in New York in March 1935 under the title *Moscow Laughs*, *Circus* was not exported to the United States.)

Made at the height of the Great Terror, Alexandrov's 1938 aggressively populist *Volga Volga* is said to have been Stalin's favorite movie. Invited to send a delegation to the Moscow amateur music festival, the officious manager of a small-town musical-instrument plant opts for a mediocre classical orchestra. A postal worker, played by Orlova as a vigorous exponent of the People's Song movement, insists that her band also make the trip. Spurred on by the leading lady's piercing soprano, the comrades engage in all manner of pixilated song-and-dance routines. Such manic cavorting is an Alexandrov specialty—as is the grand finale, which, as in *Circus*, transposes the performance onto a wider stage. Arrived in the continual festival that is the Moscow of their dreams, the actors directly address their movie audience: "Laughter conquers evil!"

Volga Volga's vision of Paradise Regained might almost have been conceived to demonstrate Dyer's thesis. Despite perfunctory day jobs, the movie's characters are exclusively devoted to their amateur music making—alienated labor has been abolished. Meanwhile, the continual festival that is the Moscow of their dreams suggests that achieved Communism is an idealized form of Hollywood. Yet Alexandrov's next musical, *The Shining Path,* was even more utopian in transforming factory work to exalted play. The original title was *Cinderella;* Stalin objected, making no fewer than twelve alternative suggestions. But no movie better illustrated the official dogma that "the fairy tale has become reality." Indeed, *The Shining Path* recapitulated the Stalin era, spanning the 1930s in tracking the transformation of Tanya Morova—an illiterate, shapeless potato sack played by Orlova—into a Stakhanovite heroine of labor and her eventual ascension to a decorated Supreme Soviet deputy.[23]

Employed as a drudge by the silly and self-important proprietress of a provincial rooming house, Tanya—like her employer—is smitten by a handsome young guest, engineer Alexei Lebedev. The jealous proprietress throws Tanya out but (life has grown more joyous!) the girl has a fairy godmother—namely, the local party secretary, Maria Pronina. A merry, middle-aged woman, she takes Tanya in and enrolls her in an adult education course, pointedly held in a former church that has been deconsecrated (or is it reconsecrated?) with new icons. Maria Pronina (whose magic wand, in the words of the *Daily Worker,* is the Soviet Constitution) further arranges for Tanya to attend the "prince's ball"—our Cinderella dreams that Maria guides her to an enchanted castle guarded by giant statues of heroic workers. Tanya is entranced—it is a vast, airy, magnificent textile mill. Suddenly, it's back to "reality"; the factory is vast, noisy, and filled with scraps. The wide-eyed girl is presented with a broom.

Tanya graduates to operating a loom. She is given the worst machine in the factory, which the manager then accuses her of breaking. (This is inexplicable until it is revealed that he is in league with the wreckers.) Tanya suffers but, thanks to Alexei, gets another chance to demonstrate her capacity for joyous labor. No different from Disney's Cinderella, Tanya sings as she sews. Unlike her cartoon counterpart, however, she is obsessed with productivity. Inspired by an article in *Pravda,* Tanya goes from operating eight to sixteen looms. To overcome the manager's opposition, she writes to the chairman of the Council of People's Commissars, V. M. Molotov himself. Ultimately, the mill must be expanded so that the ecstatic

Tanya can operate 150 looms, bursting into Dunayevsky's popular "March of the Enthusiasts" as she dances from one to another.[24]

From here on, the movie grows increasingly dreamy and glamorous. As a Stakhanovite, Tanya herself becomes an icon—her image is reproduced on a poster and placed on a kiosk outside the factory. Ultimately transported to Moscow to receive the Order of Lenin, Tanya finds herself alone in the Kremlin's operetta palace. There, she sings to her old babushka'd self in a magic mirror, then—in a sequence cut from the American version—takes a flying automobile to travel over Moscow and the Urals into the future.[25]

An engineer and a deputy to the Supreme Soviet, Tanya is reunited with her Prince Charming in the deco Stalinist heaven of Moscow's newly opened All-Union Agricultural Exposition (where she has inaugurated the Textile Pavilion). Dunayevsky's score becomes a Rachmaninoff rhapsody. Radiating happiness, the couple stand together before a misty fountain, Mukhina's heroic forward-striding couple visible behind them—icons of petrified fertility in a utopia of abundance, energy, intensity, transparency, community.

Postscript

The Exposition also serves as the setting for *The Swineherd and the Shepherd* (1940), directed by Alexandrov's only peer, Ivan Pyriev. School friends from Yekaterinburg, Alexandrov and Pyriev both acted with Eisenstein at the Proletkult. Alexandrov, however, was a something of a cosmopolitan. ("I was very conscious of the deep impression which his years in America had made on him," a coworker later wrote. "His sincere admiration for the United States was evident in his clothes, his constant smile, and his descriptions of what he had seen in America.") Pyriev was more of a nativist—his concern, film historian Maya Turovskaya says, was with the "great Russian soul."[26]

In 1938, five years before *Oklahoma* opened on Broadway, Pyriev invented the *kolkhoz* musical. *The Rich Bride* starred his wife, Marina Ladynina, singing a folksy Dunayevsky score. It was followed by the singing title figures of *Tractor Drivers* (1939) and *The Swineherd and the Shepherd,* both enormously popular—and, what's more, correct. While allowing that some shots in the latter reminded him of "lacquered snuffbox paintings," Eisenstein nevertheless asked, "What other picture has hymned the indissolubly united friendship between our country's peoples with such verve, optimism and exuberance?" (What other picture opened with its joyous heroine running through a soundstage birch wood, serenading her hogs?) Indeed, Eisenstein would publish a slyly prudent tribute: "Snobs and aesthetes may splutter that Pyriev's work is not always refined. But even they find it difficult to deny that it has a quality that rings true. . . . The fact stares us in the face: Ivan Pyriev has won the Stalin Prize four times."[27]

The Soviet musical sputtered during the postwar period, but not before Pyriev won a fifth Stalin Prize for *Cossacks of the Kuban* (1949), written by Nikolai Pogodin (the author of *Aristocrats*) and scored by Dunayevsky. In *Cossacks's* fantastic opening scene, a peaceful golden landscape is suddenly animated by Pyriev's mobile camera and a small army of marching, singing, working peasants, operating (legend has it) every harvester in the Soviet Union. The movie manifests a new theory: Communism has been built, art must be free from conflict. There are no more saboteurs; the kulaks are gone. All characters on the *kolkhoz* are positive. The narrative is to reflect the competition between good and better—in this case, the Red Partisan *kolkhoz* and its (friendly) rival, the Testament of Ilyich *kolkhoz*, chaired by the ever-smiling war widow Galina.

Gordey, the Red Partisan chairman, is a bit too dense and macho to grasp the new situation. Galina, meanwhile, urges her comrades to be even more optimistic: "We're going to run our whole farm by electricity." (Having played a shock-worker in *The Rich Bride*, a brigade leader in *The Tractor Drivers*, prizewinning pig breeder in *The Swineherd and the Shepherd*, and a kindergarten teacher turned antiaircraft gunner in *At Six o'Clock after the War*, Ladynina was more than qualified to run a *kolkhoz*.) Although Gordey and Galina don't seem to know it, all the other characters understand that they are destined to wed—there is even a variety-show skit to that effect performed in the midst of the movie's obligatory feast of plenty (a riot of colorful goods and produce, with heaps of books, decorative balloons, and exciting music issuing from futuristic radios).

The conflict, such as it is, is resolved by marriage. "We sought the land of happiness and now it's something we possess!" is the movie's final line. Evil distortion or a cheerful ray of sunshine? When the young Mikhail Gorbachev saw *Cossacks of the Kuban* in the early 1950s, he reportedly told a companion, "It's not like that at all." In contrast, on New Year's Eve 1995, Russia's largest television network broadcast a slick three-hour, three-million-dollar special in which the nation's leading pop stars re-created scenes from *Cossacks* and other Stalinist musicals. "Everyone is sick of American movies and tired of having an inferiority complex," the youthful TV star and coproducer Leonid Parfyonov told the *New York Times*.[28]

6. *MISSION TO MOSCOW* (Michael Curtiz, U.S.A., 1943)

"I want a sound American businessman to get the hard-boiled facts behind the most dangerous situation in history," President Franklin Roosevelt (back to the camera and voice dubbed by the Vaughn Meader of the day) instructs Ambassador Joseph Davies (Walter Huston). Then it's off to investigate a Soviet Union that, as constructed by the Warner Brothers art department, resembles nothing so much as a glamorized Pittsburgh.

America's ambassador to the Kremlin from 1936 through 1938, Davies—like all things Soviet—was rehabilitated in the aftermath of the 1941 Nazi invasion of Russia. Encouraged by President Roosevelt, who permitted him access to classified State Department files, and aided by ghostwriters, Davies began pulling together an account of his time in Moscow. the *New York Times Magazine* ran an excerpt from Davies's *Mission to Moscow* a week after the bombing of Pearl Harbor; the book was officially published on December 29. By early summer, Warner Brothers had purchased the screen rights.

Although the first scriptwriters were Sherwood Anderson and Erskine Caldwell, the studio soon drafted Howard Koch, fresh (or rather exhausted from) his work on *Casablanca*. Thus, written by Koch (a prominent Hollywood fellow traveler) and directed by Michael Curtiz (whose politically scarlet past had long since been forgotten), *Mission to Moscow* was created by the same writing-directing team responsible for the quintessential World War II romance—Hollywood's greatest expression of the Popular Front.[29]

Davies, who was granted script approval, kept Roosevelt apprised of the movie's progress. A belated sequel to *October, Mission to Moscow* went well beyond Davies's original account of the Moscow Trials, which he had then interpreted as manifesting a power struggle within the Kremlin. The book, however, was revised to explain the presence of Trotskyist traitors within the Soviet Union. All possible ambiguity was eliminated during production (while the compression of the three Moscow Trials into one enhanced the magnitude—and perhaps even the believability—of the supposed conspiracy).

Thus, made to rationalize the trials, the Hitler-Stalin Pact, and the invasion of Finland while introducing the American public to their new wartime ally, *Mission to Moscow* is, in a certain sense, the most political film ever to come out of Hollywood. Isolationist congressmen are excoriated while Stalin is depicted (by stage actor Manart Kippen) as a kind of Slavic leprechaun, and the American president is presented as virtually precognitive in his wisdom. A stock shot of the White House is accompanied by Davies's voice-over: "There was one man who foresaw what [these events] meant."

Featuring everyone from Yiddish theater impresario Maurice Schwartz to noir axiom Mike Mazurki to the young Cyd Charisse and the strongman from *Freaks* (1932), *Mission to Moscow* features such ineffable moments as Paulina Molotova, commissar of cosmetics, telling Walter Huston's wife that, *Ninotchka* notwithstanding, "feminine beauty is *not* a luxury." This scene, added after the film wrapped, was one of several created to satisfy Mrs. Davies's desire for a larger role. "Yes, I guess women are the same all over the world," the actress who plays the ambassador's wife replies. "Primarily, they want to please their men."[30]

Although *Mission to Moscow* does contain one scene—a diplomatic ball where the band is playing "Dancing in the Dark" while a bucktoothed, contemptuously anti-U.S. Japa-Nazi runt plots with the Trots—with the familiar Warners zip, the studio would have created a more surefire crowd pleaser had it dispatched Humphrey Bogart to Stalin's court. Still, the Office of War Information was more than enthusiastic. An internal memo terms *Mission to Moscow* "a magnificent contribution. . . . The producers of this picture are to be congratulated for the forthright courage and honesty which made its production possible." A special White House screening was followed by a gala Washington, D.C., premiere. The movie opened in New York on the eve of May Day, April 30, 1943.

Warner Brothers spent a record $250,000 on promotion alone: "As American as YANKEE DOODLE DANDY!" As it was, *Mission to Moscow* proved both unpopular and controversial—causing a storm, for example, when it was named "Motion Picture of the Month" by the New York City Transit Authority. John Dewey, who had headed a commission of inquiry into the Moscow Trials, wrote to the *New York Times,* calling *Mission to Moscow* "the first instance in our country of totalitarian propaganda for mass consumption—a propaganda which falsifies history through distortion, omission or pure invention of facts."[31]

The movie was attacked by both the Hearst press and the Socialist Workers Party. There were Republican demands for a congressional investigation, while on the anti-Stalinist Left, Dwight Macdonald initiated a letter-writing campaign that enlisted Max Eastman, James T. Farrell, Sidney Hook, and Alfred Kazin. Worse, *Mission to Moscow* would return to haunt Warner Brothers as a prime example of red subversion during the October 1947 HUAC investigation of Hollywood. Jack Warner (who had ordered the destruction of all release prints) defended himself by maintaining that President Roosevelt had personally commissioned the movie. Although, as Stephen J. Whitfield has pointed out, no one chastised the *Reader's Digest* for its wartime *Mission to Moscow* serialization, Koch was subsequently blacklisted in Hollywood for a decade.[32]

7. THE RUSSIAN QUESTION (Mikhail Romm, USSR, 1947)

As a cold war genre, the so-called publicist film was less interested in verisimilitude or probability than in polemicizing (sometimes satirically) on—and providing the correct interpretation of—the developing world situation. The first example was *The Russian Question,* adapted and directed by Mikhail Romm from Konstantin Simonov's widely produced agitprop play.

The project brought together two leading Soviet artists. Romm had established his reputation—as well as the standard characterization of Lenin as merry Spirit of Revolution—with his 1937 *Lenin in October,* one of the first movies to include Stalin as a character, and his 1939 *Lenin 1919.* The younger Simonov, recently appointed undersecretary of the Writers Union and soon to become editor of the influential biweekly *Literary Gazette,* was a poet and journalist famous for his wartime reportage.

A sequel of sorts to *Mission to Moscow,* designed to expose the depraved and amoral nature of American journalism, *The Russian Question* offered a Soviet prophecy of anti-Communist blacklisting. (At the same time, it allowed the filmmakers the opportunity to project, consciously or not, something resembling their own situation onto an imaginary America.) Even before *The Russian Question* was released, Drew Middleton cited the movie in the July 27, 1947, issue of the *New York Times Magazine* as evidence of a new Soviet bellicosity.

On his return to New York from the Soviet Union, American journalist Harry Smith is hired by the Hearst-like media mogul and warmonger McPherson to write a book exposing the Communist threat to peace. Despite the enormous advance he is given, Smith refuses to become a paid

mouthpiece for Wall Street's anti-Soviet campaign. As result, he is perse-
cuted by the authorities, vilified in the press, and deserted by his wife.

Like *The Return of Nathan Becker, The Russian Question* opens with
an "American" montage. Skyscrapers are juxtaposed with slums, breadlines with high society, Negro shantytowns with the Rockettes. The sequence incorporates 1930s footage of a police riot as well as a number of
tabloid headlines and a newsreel sequence of pet dogs receiving mani-
cures: the America of 1946! Not only do his fellow reporters wait for
Smith at an empty airport, but ordinary people recognize the returned
journalist and are eager to discuss the Russian Question. Even his barber
is curious about the Soviet practice of "collective marriage." (Haven't
they seen *Song of Russia*?) But Smith's wife, Jessie (Romm's wife, Yelena
Kuzmina), is longing for material comforts. As the taxi courses through
nocturnal Times Square (shown in rear-screen projection), she discusses
the hardship of her life during the war, expressing a desire to move out
of New York City.

Everyone is selling out. Smith asks one colleague why he wrote anti-
Soviet lies and is told that the man needed money to buy medicine for his
children. Another reporter, Bob Murphy, is drinking himself to death
because he is compelled to work for Hearst: "Every day I dictate and
broadcast so much filth that I have to keep disinfecting my throat."
Meanwhile, the cynical McPherson (who runs phony reports of Soviet
aircraft over Eritrea on page 1, then buries the Russians' honest denial on
page 20) tells Smith that he's the only person who can write this book.
People will believe him.

Smith takes McPherson's money and buys a suburban dacha—the
neighborhood a peculiar mixture of Levittown and Switzerland. There,
Jessie happily bustles about the kitchen as he works on his book. Yet,
remembering the heroic and positive Russia of World War II, Smith cannot bring himself to say that the Soviets don't desire peace. Because Mc-
Pherson (a proponent of a "preventive" attack) insists that the Russians
are preparing for war, Smith will have to choose between honesty and
happiness. Specifically, he will have to change his final chapter—which he
does, in a montage of heroic redictation.

The sympathetic Murphy warns Smith that, within in a year, "people
like you will be in prison," and advises him to restore his manuscript.
Smith refuses, and McPherson reads it in a rage as he is transported
through the expressionist rear-screen projection city. Even as Jessie orga-
nizes her husband's book party, Smith is called on the carpet and told that

what he has written is unpublishable. McPherson informs him that—once branded as a foreign agent and investigated by the House Un-American Activities Committee—he will lose everything and never find another job. Then he instructs his assistant to turn over the task of writing *The Russians Want War* to another journalist with a "good reputation."

For his part, Smith offers his honest reporting to a small progressive newspaper (whose editor tells him that even he can't take the risk). He returns home—dramatic music—to find his furniture being carted out. The radio is reporting on an American pilot's attempt to break the world altitude record; somehow, Murphy is on board the test plane. As the last furniture disappears, so does Jessie, telling Smith that he's too good for her. Just then, a news bulletin carries the message that the airplane, which Murphy had intentionally goaded into flying too high, has exploded.

Murphy, it turns out, has redeemed himself by willing his belongings to Smith. The movie thus ends with Smith addressing a public meeting, explaining that no one would publish his honest book, citing the two Americas—Lincoln and Roosevelt versus Wall Street and the corrupt media—and warning that "America's enemies are not in the Soviet Union but in Washington!"[33]

Postscript

The Russian Question was nuanced compared to the movies that would follow. (Perhaps the time Simonov had spent in the United States accounts for his play's residual fondness for a now dangerously misled wartime ally.) Once Hollywood had responded with *The Iron Curtain* in May 1948, Soviet filmmakers were directed to combat American culture, blow for blow.

A year after *The Russian Question*'s release, at the December 1948 Writers Union plenum in Moscow, Simonov denounced the persistence of formalism, aestheticism, and bourgeois liberalism and the inability to use Socialist Realism. That January, the same month that 144 Jewish writers were arrested, the Central Committee initiated a campaign against "rootless cosmopolitanism." The new line was explicated in Abram Room's 1949 *Court of Honor*. The "rage of Moscow only twenty-four hours after its opening," the *New York Times* reported on January 27, 1949, *Court of Honor* attacked both duplicitous American "cultural spies" who steal Soviet discoveries in the guise of scientific exchange and naive Soviet scientists who believe that their knowledge belongs to the world but are, in truth, only "groveling before the West."

It was Simonov who, at a February 24 meeting with Moscow literary critics, revealed this cosmopolitan conspiracy and, at the next meeting of the Cinematographers Union, attacked those "little people [who] got on Hollywood's bandwagon and compromised the great name of Soviet film." V. I. Pudovkin and Ivan Pyriev further denounced the cosmopolitan and antipatriotic ideas of filmmakers such as Ilya Trauberg, whose crimes included his failure to praise *The Russian Question.*

In addition to Trauberg, the most prominent cosmopolitan targets were Dziga Vertov and Sergei Yutkevich. All three were Jews—as were Room and Romm. A dozen years later, Romm would write that although, after the October Revolution, he had completely forgotten that he was a Jew, he was reminded of the fact during the period that immediately followed World War II: "This took place in connection with cosmopolitanism, in connection with organizing courts of honor, at the time of organizing my filming group and on the occasion of the case of the 'killer doctors'."[34]

8. *THE RED MENACE* (R. G. Springsteen, U.S.A., 1949)

I *always heard Commies peddled bunk. I didn't know they came as cute as you.*

—Bill Jones, *The Red Menace*

Soon after J. Edgar Hoover's March 1947 report on Soviet espionage to the House Un-American Activities Committee, Twentieth-Century Fox studio boss Darryl F. Zanuck announced plans to produce "a semidocumentary" on the subject.

The Iron Curtain (1948) went into production within a few weeks of HUAC's first Hollywood hearing and opened the next spring at five hundred theaters, a month after Communist screenwriter John Howard Lawson was found guilty of contempt of Congress. The sober saga of a Soviet spy ring operating in Canada during World War II, it enjoyed two weeks as the nation's number-one box-office attraction, complete with a nationally reported clash outside the Roxy Theater in New York City between Henry Wallace supporters and the members of the Catholic War Veterans.[35]

Now every studio had to have an anti-Communist manifesto. Sprinting to the theaters ahead of RKO's troubled *I Married a Communist* (1950), Republic's *Red Menace* was the first to focus on the American Communist Party. Released, with "unusual pride," by the low-budget studio in late spring of 1949; personally supervised by Republic owner Herbert J. Yates; and directed by the veteran of twenty-five Roy Rogers westerns, *Red Menace* opens with a terrified young couple fleeing Los Angeles. Their car is a nest of shadows, the atmosphere viscous with paranoia. "What are they running from?" asks the disembodied voice of Los Angeles councilman Lloyd G. Davis.

Basically, *Red Menace* is the story of Bill Jones, a disgruntled World War II veteran led by his libido into the "service of the worldwide Marxist racket." Sex, not ideology, is the selling point. Conveniently located across the alley from the downtown building housing their newspaper the *Daily Toiler,* the Communists operate a secret bar, Club Domino, that is stocked with Venus's-flytraps. Bill, who has been picked up by the Communist Party steerer, who observes him registering a noisy complaint at the Veterans Administration office, is immediately seduced by the red barfly Mollie. He really falls hard, however, for the film's nice girl, Ninotchka-type Nina Petrovka — "a real swell looker," in the words of the Texas sheriff who wanders onto the set for the surreal denouement.

Nina, a Russian Red Diaper baby and lifelong Communist, is in charge of Marxist instruction. But just as Viveca Lindfors would discover that *No Time for Flowers* (1953) was nowhere, just as Cyd Charisse would don *Silk Stockings* (1957), and just as Katharine Hepburn would doff her *Iron Petticoat* (1956), Nina chucks foreign-inculcated class consciousness for the love of an all-American guy. Of course, romance does not triumph before *Red Menace* has treated the viewer to a tour of red Los Angeles. In addition to Club Domino and Molly's supposedly posh apartment (where Bill seems astonished to find actual books — for reading!) there is Nina's basement classroom, as well as the entropic offices of the *Daily Toiler.*

In the course of exposing the Communist milieu, *Red Menace* spends a surprising amount of screen time explicating Marxist dogma. (*Variety,* which praised the film's "bold melodrama" and "documentary flavor," thought that the script bespoke "lengthy research.") Indeed, in exposing the party leadership as cynical and manipulative, the movie comes close to suggesting that the Communists are betraying their own ideals. In one tumultuous scene, the cell's resident Jewish poet Henry Solomon is attacked for denying an immaculate conception view of Communism: "We contend that Marx had no basis in Hegel!" the fat, sweaty party secretary tells him. Subject to this criticism, Henry tears up his party card, denouncing his erstwhile comrades as a pack of "trained red seals" and "psychopathic misfits" before taking a swan dive out the *Toiler* window.

An interesting contradiction, in view of the party's free-love come-on, is that the most villainously crazed Communist turns out to be a sexually frustrated German refugee, Yvonne Kraus. Having eyes for Bill herself, La Kraus works to purge both of the red cuties for whom he's fallen—then, exposed as an illegal alien with phony papers, flips into a breakdown of screaming hysteria, hallucinating the drumbeat of revolution, calling the police "fools," and ranting that she is Commissar Bloch. (As Jack Smith wrote of the lead actor in the 1938 exploitation film *Reefer Madness,* actress Betty Lou Gerson is "given every opportunity to disintegrate to the point of gilded splendor.")[36]

That the Communist Party is a haven for nymphos and neurotics has already been made clear one confused evening when, in a paranoid paroxysm of mutual surveillance, half the cell turns up on the Sunset Strip. (Several of the Communists have disapproving parents operating under the spell of their own religious leaders.) Not only do the Communists spend most of their time spying on one another, but they liquidate one of their own dissidents and then ineptly try to pass off the murder as an anti-Communist hate crime. Indeed, the L.A. cell seems so self-destructive that it is difficult to ascertain just what exactly *is* the red menace. As the sheriff tells Bill and Nina, "You folks have been running away from yourselves."

No doubt, however, that whatever the menace may be, it can be combated by the sheriff's final words of advice: "Get yourself hitched and raise a couple of normal American kids." As if to illustrate his injunction, a seven-year-old boy materializes, dressed—like a true Republic fan—in complete cowboy regalia and toting a toy six-gun.

9. *THE CONFRONTATION* (Miklós Jancsó, Hungary, 1969)

Miklós Jancsó's bleak, antipsychological studies of groups under pressure are distinguished by one of the boldest styles to emerge anywhere in Europe over the first quarter century since the end of World War II—a personal idiom based on long, intricately choreographed tracking shots, copious nudity, and narratives that pivot on cryptic betrayals. His strong-est films dramatizing the seizure of power and the exercise of terror at cusp moments of his nation's tumultuous history, Jancsó has no equal in the metaphoric representation of the encircled Hungarian condition.

Born in 1921, the son of a Romanian mother and a Hungarian father, Jancsó was raised in Vác (twenty miles north of Budapest along the Dan-ube). He received a Catholic education and converted to Communism during World War II, joing the party in 1945. Something of a perpetual student, having variously applied himself to law, art history, and ethnog-raphy (including a period of fieldwork in Transylvania) before entering the Academy of Dramatic Art, Jancsó was also active in the People's College (NeKOSZ) movement that, two decades later, became the subject of his most controversial film, *The Confrontation*.[37]

Jancsó's first color film—as well as a musical, complete with period anthems—*The Confrontation* was set in mid-1947 but produced in the aftermath of the French May and Prague Spring. (Invited to Cannes, Jancsó was unable to screen his 1967 *Silence and Cry* when militants closed the festival; *The Confrontation* shoot was interrupted when Hungarian tanks rolled by en route to Czechoslovakia.) Thus, Jancsó ambiguously portrays his own generation at the zenith of its youthful idealism wearing the blue jeans and miniskirts of the 1960s.

The mood is ambiguously festive. It is only a few months since the Communists engineered the demise of Hungary's most popular political party, the Smallholders, and shortly before the national elections in which the Communist Party would emerge, with 22 percent of the vote, as the largest partner in a new ruling coalition. Mock utopian, *The Confrontation* stages politics as a source of pleasure—or at least as a game. Opening with a close-up of one girl, Jancsó pulls back his camera to show a group of students playfully blocking an army jeep. Mediating between two groups, a young police officer, Kozma, orders the soldiers to remove the demon-strators. Instead, the high-spirited students unexpectedly push the soldiers into the river—then strip off their own clothes and jump in.

The screenwriter Gyula Hernádi was also a member of NeKOSZ, and the film's Hungarian title, *Fényes Szelek* (Bright winds) is taken from one NeKOSZ anthem: "Our banner is blown by bright winds and what it says is Freedom. Tomorrow we will transform the entire world." (While the film adaptation of Milan Kundera's *The Joke*—in production around the same time as *The Confrontation*—makes ironic use of a May Day 1949 newsreel showing official costumed folk dancing in the streets of Prague,

Jancsó is more ambiguous in his nostalgia for the Stalinist folk culture.) The wind is heard when, singing and dancing, the exuberant students invade a nearby Catholic seminary, scaling the fence to drape their red banner over the stone cross, in an attempt at friendly reeducation: "We've come to debate with you."

The student leader, Laci—resplendent in an unambiguously red shirt— is an advocate of persuasion who considers Communism the "first decent power in history." There are two simultaneous debates. One, within the group, concerns revolutionary tactics and reflects a division between the urbanist Communist Laci and a group of radical populists; the other is the ideological discussion with the seminarians. The students initially dominate the seminarians, encircling the bewildered Catholics—as if to emphasize their own freedom and unity. In particular, Laci seeks to engage a Jewish student—an intellectual—who escaped Fascist persecution by taking refuge in the seminar. What, Laci asks, is the role of the individual in history? The Jewish boy rejects the Communists (although it is evident that he is attracted to their community) because of their use of force.

A masterful tour de force, *The Confrontation* consists of only thirty-one shots. Jancsó's ever-moving camera integrates the singing, dancing radical students; the continual parting and regrouping of crowds; the small struggles within the cadre; and the sudden flare-ups of violence into a fantastic political ballet, where meaning is generated as much by action as speech. The narrative unfolds without apparent heroes or villains—initially abstract characters developing through their behavioral responses to the changing situation.

Throughout, the students circle-dance around their adversaries. "This business of 'holding hands,'" the political philosopher Ferenc Fehér wrote in *Filmkultúra*, is "visible presentation . . . that the most decisive organization power is still very definitely that of the people." Perhaps: In *The Book of Laughter and Forgetting*, Milan Kundera describes a news photo showing a row of armed police in riot gear, glaring at a group of youthful demonstrators "wearing T-shirts and jeans and holding hands and dancing in a circle." Kundera, eight years younger than Jancsó, also came of age in the brave new world of East European Stalinism. "I think I understand them," he writes of these youthful demonstrators whom he imagines dancing to "a simple folk melody." "They feel that the circle they describe on the ground is a magic circle bonding them into a ring. Their hearts are overflowing with an intense feeling of innocence: they are not united by a *march*, like soldiers or fascist commandos; they are united by a *dance,* like children. And they can't wait to spit their innocence in the cops' faces."[38]

In *The Confrontation,* the Catholics remain sullen and unresponsive until the Communists bring in a folk band. (At this point, the near-continuous music and dancing proves contagious: "Even God forgives a merry sinner," someone says.) But along with the band comes police support. When the pragmatic Kozma—scarcely more than a student himself, albeit the class-conscious son of a peasant family—takes this opportunity to arrest five suspected counterrevolutionaries, the irate Catholics surround and overturn his jeep.

It is irrelevant to the movie whether Kozma's warrants are justified. Under idealistic Laci, the students refuse to cooperate with the police. Hence, the scrupulously rational Kozma criticizes Laci as overly romantic and insufficiently tough-minded. (Separated by his uniform from his former comrades, Kozma sometimes joins in their dances, other times manipulates them.) Whereas this straightforward policeman is the film's most politically aware character, the neurotically self-doubting Laci is the most sympathetic. When, as a protest against Kozma's tactics, he attempts to resign his leadership position, he is accused of a bourgeois deviation and dismissed.

Now, as suggested in the movie's first image, the students turn to the ousted Laci's adjunct, the rigidly sectarian Jutka—a peasant rather than an urbanist, sometimes referred to as the Girl in Trousers. Borne on her supporters' shoulders, Jutka returns to the seminary and further harangues the pupils: "There can be no democracy for the enemies of democracy. He who is not with us, is against us." Thus anticipating the Hungarian Communist Party's subsequent line, as well as articulating its burgeoning attack on Catholic institutions, she demands that the priests renounce their allegiance to the church, even as her followers stage provocations and break windows.

Jutka is the film's most idealistic and ideologically consistent figure, as well as the most authoritarian and intolerant. (She is, as Kundera wrote of Ludvik's lost love, "naive," "strict," and "full of joy"—like the spirit of the time.) A heroine out of a Chinese revolutionary opera, Jutka is deliberately harsher than the cops. Her methods—burning "reactionary" books, threatening to shave the seminarians' heads until they remember Auschwitz, making them march in dunce caps—suggest Fascism as well as the Chinese Red Guards, a taboo subject in 1969 Hungary.

Jancsó provocatively called *The Confrontation* "a warning to all revolutionary movements in the process of being born and to those which have not yet triumphed that the Revolution carries certain dangers within itself." Jutka's reign of terror lasts only until a group of slightly older Communists arrive and—belying the independence of the people's colleges—assert their own control over both the situation and the student cadre. The party is both cynical and expedient: Jutka and her few faithful followers are summarily expelled from college, although as Jutka defiantly observes, she never cast anyone out.

When Laci objects, the party leaders relent. Jutka may remain. The film ends, as it began, with a close-up of Jutka—in this case, the back of her head—as Kozma observes that she might yet become a leader.

Postscript

Released in February 1969, *The Confrontation* anticipated by a decade the anti-Stalinism of Hungarian films such as *Angi Vera* and *The Stud Farm,* arousing unprecedented popular debate (as well as conflicting appraisals in the official press). "On the one hand," wrote sociologist Iván Vitányi, *The Confrontation* articulated "the basic line of democratic socialism, on the other hand the extremist movement of Maoism and Cohn-Benditism."[39]

After the party daily *Népszabadság* called *The Confrontation* "a defense of church and reaction" (even while favorably citing its "political realism" as an alternative to the now-discredited Czech allegory), the debate over the picture reached an extraordinary pitch. Angry critics stalked out halfway through the screenings. Press and cultural weeklies discussed *The Confrontation* at length, disputing its historical accuracy, with former NeKOSZ students taking positions on both sides of the controversy.[40]

Fehér's *Filmkultúra* piece ended with the prudently italicized Kádárist assertion that *The Confrontation* "certainly does not accept any alternative to socialism." But there were others who suggested that the movie be banned, or at least—as the youth newspapers proposed—given some kind of X certificate, indicating a nonrecommendation for young people. Playing theatrically all through the spring of 1969, *The Confrontation* was the subject of two organized conferences—one for party officials and teachers, the other attended by an assortment of students, historians, pedagogues, critics, philosophers, and housewives.

10. *ANGI VERA* (Pál Gábor, Hungary, 1979)

> **N**o *one is ever born a Communist. . . . Becoming a Communist can only be achieved, the party chiefs have often declared, through an intense process of self-transformation—a process that may never be relaxed without the risk of sliding back into an earlier condition of being.*
>
> —Harold Rosenberg, "The Heroes of Marxist Science" (1947)

A close-up compared to *The Confrontation*'s dance of historical forces, *Angi Vera* is something like *Ninotchka* in reverse—the story of how a beautiful and enigmatic woman is transformed into a Communist.

Society is changing, and at a staff meeting in a Budapest hospital once administered by the Catholic church, a meek eighteen-year-old nurse's aide named Vera Angi finds the courage to speak out. Vera denounces the system as corrupt, as well as rife with privilege. She complains bitterly about hospital hygiene, and she holds the hospital director himself responsible: "Where is the New World? Everything is as it was."

Vera's diatribe makes a small sensation. Afterward, the angry (and frightened) director confronts her, accusing the girl of ingratitude, reminding the poor orphan that the hospital had sheltered her, as well as her late mother, throughout the war. But that night, another force seeks out Vera: "We can take care of your life from now on." The comrades are impressed with her potential. Vera's attack on the hospital director was brave—as well as useful.

Adapted by writer-director Pál Gábor from Endre Vészi's novella *Chapters from the Life of Vera Angi, Angi Vera* opens in the autumn of 1948, six months after the Social Democrats merged with the Communists to form the Hungarian Workers' Party. Where the wartime underground Hungarian Communist Party had only two thousand members in 1944, its successor organization now boasted well over a million. Vera's class background is ideal, as is her gender. (In 1948, the Hungarian Workers' Party had more women—nearly one-third of the membership—and fewer middle-class cadres than any Communist party in Eastern Europe.) The next spring, Vera—like many another fictional heroine—is sent to a provincial town to take a three-month party course.

The men and women selected for the party bunk in military-style dorms. (In fact, the school is a requisitioned convent.) Overawed and unsure of herself, Vera is drawn to two women—the vibrant and earthy Mária Muskát, a dedicated Communist in her mid-twenties, and the veteran cadre, Anna Traján, who is twice Mária's age—as well as much impressed by her idealistic young teacher, István.

Angi Vera is populated by all manner of Communists—among the film's distinctions is that virtually all have their human moments. While the girls in the dorm talk trash, Vera flatters Traján—listening to the older woman reminisce about her romantic past, including the Communist martyr who is her lost love. Feeling competitive, Mária bursts in with the tale of her own, more recent amorous adventures, embarrassing the militant, who weeps—and then moves out of the dorm, leaving Mária to fume that "we differ from the nuns in that we're not hypocrites."

The Communist, Harold Rosenberg argued, was an invented type, "a new coherent entity purposefully constructed." Indeed, the Communist was produced in Lenin's image—modeled on "the man who lives in a world of continual combat, who 'struggles 24 hours a day,' and even in his dreams," to create the revolution.[41]

As the vehicle for this awesome transformation, the party is filled with nervous little people. The camaraderie of group songs and discussions mixes with discipline. The leader Sas, a slight and self-important figure with a generic resemblance to Julius Rosenberg, compels the rough-hewn miner Jószef to make a public apology for being absent without leave. Vera's spontaneous solidarity—she offers to help Jószef with his studies—suggests that she is a natural Communist. But Jószef misunderstands; he asks Vera to go canvassing with him in advance of the May 15 election that will bring the Hungarian Workers' Party to full power. Vera protects herself by going with Anna Traján.

In the course of visiting various homes to mobilize the vote, Anna and Vera are privy to the indiscreet complaints of a "right-wing" Social Democrat. (Adding insult to injury, he cites the number of former fascists who have opportunistically joined the Communist Party.) Lying to further draw him out, Traján takes down his name just as the exposed class enemy realizes to whom he has been so injudiciously speaking.

Fleeing this uncomfortable situation, the women take refuge in a café. Traján indulges an unproletarian taste for sweets while ensuring that Vera signs the statement that incriminates the luckless Social Democrat. At the heart of the movie, then, is a conspiracy—or perhaps another Faustian bargain. Vera agrees to a lie because there can only be one truth. In an allegorical sense, her continued success is linked to the Communist betrayal of the democratic Left. ("Reversals of judgment and feeling are the very key to the Communist's morality and the fullest expression of his constructed character," writes Rosenberg. "His judgement is that of history itself.")[42]

Midway through the course, the party itself holds a party. The comrades sing decorously at their tables. The ridiculous Sas has restricted them to one bottle of beer apiece, though they may dance until midnight. "We're like one big happy family," Traján enthuses. Vera sees István with his wife and child. She asks Jószef to dance but then, thanks to a bit of subterfuge engineered by Mária Muskát, finds herself partnered with her teacher. It is a silly contest to see which couple can dance the longest while balancing a Ping-Pong ball on their pressed-together foreheads. Mutually intoxicated by their proximity, Vera and István win.

An innocent heartbreaker, Vera is desired by two men dissatisfied with their lives. The next day, Vera bumps into Jószef at a café. He has been drinking, and he is about to make a declaration of love when István joins them: What seems to be the trouble? he wonders. "The trouble, Comrade," Jószef replies, "is that first one choses a wife and then . . . one realizes what beauty is. If a man's a Communist," the miner asks pathetically, "can he never change his life?" Having articulated István's own feelings, Jószef is off, leaving Vera to confess her feelings for István, István to interrupt with his protestation of love, and Vera to offer to come to his room that night.

She does. István is overwhelmed by her beauty; but on her way back to her dormitory, after they have made love, Vera imagines that she has been seen by Traján. She is in conflict, and her paranoia merges with the climactic self-criticism session. A soldier confesses that he was soft on Titoism. One woman is accused of arrogance and reduced to tears. Another woman articulates her fear of being wrong. After a break for lunch, the exam continues: "We must transform ourselves. . . . No one can accuse us of lacking in patience." When a veteran of the 1919 Soviet is chastised for sectarian arrogance, Mária Muskát rises to his defense.[43]

Vera, whom the leadership considers to be "accommodating," is terrified that she will be exposed. After thanking the leadership for even bothering about someone so insignificant as herself, she goes on to confess her night with István—and even names his name (while blaming herself). Has Vera gone too far? Her protective patron Traján desperately tries to silence the girl, even lapsing into discredited Freudian categories to cite a "typical hysterical fantasy." But in the crazy confusion, István, too, makes an admission: "For once the truth must be told."

The public humiliation suffered by Ludvik when he is unanimously expelled by his comrades in *The Joke* is here globalized. Protesting, for good measure, against the whole regime of self-criticism ("Surely we Communists don't want to produce masochists, sick liars"), gallant István proclaims his love for Vera. But with her innate *partiinost*, Vera has grasped the situation far better than he—she replies that she was, in fact, deluded. She did not love István, she only loved his authority. From the party's point of view, Vera is—in her objective analysis—perfectly enlightened. The aspiring Communist, as Rosenberg put it, must "conquer every personal sentiment." In any case, the confession of sin is far superior to the absence of sin. The latter, after all, might be construed as pride.

Symmetrically framed by two public meetings at which the heroine's honesty spontaneously destroys a man's career, the novella *Chapters from the Life of Vera Angi* ends here at the self-criticism session. Gábor, less sardonic than Vészi, adds a coda in which István is replaced as group leader and Vera (who was so shaken by her own performance that she contemplated suicide) receives an award at graduation. On hearing herself compared to a "beacon of truth in a fog" she collapses, wailing, "I'd rather go on cleaning and scrubbing floors." But she also refers to the comrades as her family.

Confronted with Vera naked, István had whispered that she was the most beautiful woman he had ever seen. Heartbreaking femme fatale, Vera represents the hopes of 1948. She is the dream of paradise. What makes her tick? Is it class resentment? idealism? opportunism? Does her naive desire for approval mask her ruthless ambition? Is she an angel of truth or an actress? ("I told her to think of herself as a kitten," Pál Gábor said of his direction of Veronika Papp, "a cold and forlorn kitten who will rub up against anyone for warmth.")[44]

Empathetic yet drawn to authority, Vera is something miraculous—a natural Communist. "How did you know that was exactly what to do?" Anna Traján asks her in amazement after the self-criticism session. In the final irony, Traján tells Vera that Vera has been selected for a job in the press. The truth is instrumental and relative. It was Stalin who founded *Pravda*. As George Konrád and Ivan Szelényi noted, the party is, for workers and their children, the prime channel of upward mobility. Once recruited, they cease to be workers and become intellectuals.[45]

The movie's last image has Vera riding in Traján's car, passing the unseeing Mária on the bleak road (to socialism?) as she pedals her bicycle against the wind.

Postscript

Shot in 1977, *Angi Vera* was held up for a year before making a sensational debut at the Cannes Film Festival. The movie's release coincided with János Kádár's comeback (and the restoration of his economic policies) and presaged a number of subsequent films that safely condemned the Stalin period, including András Kovács's *The Stud Farm* (1979), Sándor Simó's *My Father's Happy Years* (1978), and Péter Bacsó's *The Witness* (1979, having been shelved since 1969).

Asked if his film could be considered pessimistic, Gábor replied that "the surgeon is optimistic when he operates, and he does something positive when he makes an incision to remove a malignancy." This was, in fact, the same metaphor Rosenberg had employed to explain the Communist's acceptance of political terror: "We do not feel horror at the agony inflicted by the surgeon because we know why he 'attacks' his patients."[46]

11. *THE WITNESS* (Péter Bacsó, Hungary, 1969/1979)

Banned for nearly a decade, *The Witness* is hardly the comic masterpiece some called it when it was released in the West in 1983. Overlong, chintzy, and saddled with a rinky-dink *Pink Panther* score, *The Witness* is a mediocre film at best. What makes it fascinating is writer-director Péter Bacsó's weirdly inappropriate—or not—"swinging sixties" cum slapstick vision of Hungarian Communism's self-devouring Stalinist reign of terror.[47]

Opening in 1949, *The Witness* follows the absurd career of a bemused dike keeper named Jószef Pelikan. Ostensibly a simple peasant, the slyly obedient Pelikan is shunted from job to job while being groomed as an official witness at the show trial of the former party leader beside whom he had fought in the anti-Fascist resistance. Just as Pelikan resembles the Czech literary hero, the good soldier Svejk (strategically bungling his testimony at the climactic trial), so the Communist fall guy suggests László Rajk, the relatively popular and seemingly powerful minister of interior who was arrested on May 30, 1949, barely two weeks after the single-list election that put the final stamp on Hungarian Workers' Party rule. Rajk was accused of a Titoist deviation, put on trial in September, and executed a month later—the most celebrated victim of Hungary's purges and show trials.

The year 1950 was the year that the First Five-Year Plan was implemented, that the Federation of Working Youth (DISZ) and the Pioneer movements were launched, that the Communists arrested their erstwhile Social Democratic ally Árpád Szakasits, and that *Life Is Beautiful if You Sing* opened. From the perspective of twenty years, the facade had become sufficiently tattered for *The Witness* to represent the Rákosi period as one of food shortages ("Coat those ration cards in bread crumbs," somebody orders) and regulation of the peasantry. The Pelikan family sings a Young Pioneer anthem to drown out their illegal slaughter of a pig.

But from the scene of a dog urinating on a vast floral sign reading "Long Live Our Great Wise Leader" through an official attempt to pass off a lemon as the "new Hungarian orange," *The Witness* is mainly successful as a roistering burlesque of Communist platitudes. Mouthing inane catchphrases such as "the international situation is mounting," party members are depicted as a gang of bloodthirsty clowns or goonish enforcers in leather trench coats. Not only is Rákosi painted in the ludicrous guise of a medieval knight, but anticipating any number of post-1989 fantasies, Bacsó even contrives an amusement-park spook house—"Down with Bourgeois Pseudo-Culture" emblazoned over the entrance—in which patrons are menaced by the specter haunting Europe and mechanical representations of workers rattling their chains.

The first inside accounts of the Rákosi regime had appeared in Hungary in 1966; three years later, Miklós Jancsó's *The Confrontation* and Sándor Sára's *The Upthrown Stone* brought the period to the screen. In the meantime, Rajk himself had been fully rehabilitated. It was in this liberal climate that *The Witness* went into production. Like all Hungarian films dealing with the early 1950s, *The Witness* is implicitly pro-Kádár, since Kádár, too, was a victim of Stalinism. (His arrest came in May 1951—some eighteen months after he persuaded his jailed comrade Rajk to confess his guilt for the good of the party.) Indeed, Virag, *The Witness*'s morosely ascetic villain, is modeled on Rákosi's chief of secret police, Gábor Péter, a onetime tailor who took particular relish in torturing his former comrades, including Rajk and János Kádár. "Show me one person in this lousy country who I'm not able to prove guilty," Virag boasts. Toppled at the end of the movie, he directly addresses the audience: "These are the people I got a stomach ulcer for. You'll all be begging me to come back."[48]

Bacsó had evidently worked for years on *The Witness*'s script. But unlike Jancsó, he scarcely meant to rock the boat. His blunder was a matter of bad luck. By the time *The Witness* was completed, Czechoslovakia had been invaded by its Warsaw Pact allies. Conceived as safe satire of Stalin's crimes, *The Witness* ended up pointing a discomfitingly apt finger at Brezhnev's; hence the netherworld—neither totally banned nor officially released—to which the movie was consigned.[49]

12. *LARKS ON A STRING*
(Jiří Menzel, Czechoslovakia, 1969/1989)

Earth in upheaveal: A product of successive ice ages and thaws, the application (and release) of fantastic pressure, Jiří Menzel's *Larks on a String* is a film of almost geological striation. The action is set in frigid 1951; the script was written during the Prague Spring but shot in the early months of the normalization that followed the August 1968 Soviet invasion. Completed that winter, the film was immediately consigned to the Barrandov Studio's deepest vaults, emerging only after the Velvet Revolution in 1989.

Larks on a String is certainly Menzel's most affecting film—more desperate and tender than his 1965 *Closely Watched Trains,* the movie that, presented with an Oscar in April 1968, epitomized the Czech new wave, at least for American audiences. *Larks* employs many of the same actors as appeared in *Closely Watched Trains* (one can only imagine their thoughts, working now under occupation—a condition but dramatized in the earlier film) and, also like *Closely Watched Trains,* is based on a story by Bohumil Hrabal, the best-loved Czech writer of the post–World War II era.[50]

Not nearly as harsh as the movie version of *The Joke,* which was shot earlier in 1968 and completed in time to be shelved, *Larks* embodies everything that had at last become possible in the Prague Spring—even forgiveness. Menzel's is a conciliatory temperament. He told a press conference at the 1990 Berlin Film Festival that he had intended *Larks* to be "a gesture of peace towards the old line Communists who were in power in Czechoslovakia at the time. They had made serious mistakes, but I still believed in their aim of building a humane form of socialism."[51]

Where *The Joke* includes several scenes of conditions in a reeducation quarry, *Larks* is set almost entirely in an epic industrial junkyard—a section of the huge Kladno steelworks converted into forced-labor camps for former "bourgeois elements." As with Socialist Realism, the allegory is overwhelming: In postwar Czechoslovakia, as in the Soviet Union during the original Five-Year Plan, steelworks were a potent form of iconography—the forging of the nation and the new man.

At once scrap heap of history, replete with mounds of old typewriters and metal crucifixes, and crucible of the New Czechoslovakia, the junkyard is also a Garden of Eden. Here, an all-male team of erstwhile class enemies (including a philosophy professor, a former public prosecutor, a barber, a saxophonist, and a hotel cook) redeem themselves through manual labor while kibitzing, joking, and gazing longingly at the female prisoners, "imperialist agents," who—beautiful, innocent, childlike in their sensuality, and bursting with eager affection—work the same slag heap, just across the fence.

This lovingly shot, extravagantly grim landscape provides the most extreme backdrop imaginable for Menzel's distinctive brand of sentimental humanism. None of his other films exhibits so severe a disjunction between the sweetness of the tale and the harshness of the circumstances. *Larks* is a love story founded on the pathos of men and women passing each other scrap metal without gloves. The schizoid quality extends to the political realm: *Larks* is suffused with the rhetoric and illusions of Socialist Realism, evoking even as it satirizes the stupid poignance of the exhortatory slogans, optimistic posters, and heroic music.

Seen in long shot, waving from a crane, the prisoners are a parody of the optimistic proletariat. At one point, a class of Young Pioneers march singing into dump with their proud young teacher—"These, children, are our workers." Overcome with patriotic enthusiasm, her dutiful charges attempt to tie their red scarfs around men's necks. Observing the scene, the prisoner women beam with vicarous maternal pride—until the teacher labels them "imperialists."

While Menzel exhibits a particular affection for children, Gypsies, and gnarled, impassive peasants, there are no evil characters. The Communists are more ineffectual and self-deluded than vicious. Indeed, not for nothing is the almost-lovable party functionary (Rudolf Hrušínský) known as Angel. "I can't wait to see Paris businessmen sweep the roads and workers kick their butts," he tells the camera. Arranging a marriage between two prisoners, Jitka and Pavel, Angel benignly notes that, given the new socialist regime, "even the impossible is possible here." Unfortunately, before the union can be consummated, the hapless groom is drafted to meet a visiting dignitary and, thanks to his naively inopportune question as to the whereabouts of certain prisoners, is arrested and sentenced to the coal mines.[52]

In the final sequence, the now-imprisoned Pavel and the Jewish phi-losophy professor are marched to the mine shaft. "One day we will see where truth is," the professor says as they step into the elevator and descend into the earth. "I married truth," Pavel tells him. The philosopher is unaccountably happy. "I have found myself," he says as the sky disap-pears and they are, once again, buried alive.

13. *THIS CAN'T HAPPEN HERE*
(Ingmar Bergman, Sweden, 1950)

"Here" is Sweden, and "this" could almost be Ingmar Bergman's *film maudit*—omitted, at the director's request, from all retrospectives.

Bergman's "secret film," as it was termed by the Swedish archivist who screened it for me, was adapted (and presumably updated) by one Herbert Grevenius from a 1944 Danish espionage novel, *Within Twelve Hours*. The extent of Bergman's personal and ideological investment in the project—shot during the Korean War's first summer and released the following October—is shrouded in mystery. Did the then twenty-eight-year-old writer-director accept a commercial assignment? Did he assist, uncredited, in the screenplay? Does the movie reflect Bergman's seldom-articulated politics? How seriously was it intended? Who recut and dubbed the British version, released in 1952 under the title *High Tension*? Whatever its provenance, *This Can't Happen Here* is not only unlike any other Bergman film—characterized as it is by noir lighting, moody jazz, and a climactic automobile chase—but an exemplary cold war thriller.

The cautionary tale opens with a close-up of stormy skies and a voice-over noting that the movie is "set in a small peaceful country that wanted to make itself indistinguishable. . . . Any similarity between this story and real events is *not* accidental." The engineer Atkå Natas arrives in Stock-holm from his native Liquidatzia—the film's stand-in for Soviet Estonia. Planning to defect, Natas attempts to contact first the U.S. embassy and then his estranged wife Vera, herself a refugee from Liquidatzia.[53]

Vera, who has taken up with an honest Swedish cop named Almkvist, returns home to find Natas in her apartment. Bizarrely, he expects to win her back by boasting that he has denounced her parents to the Liquidat-zian authorities. (Although currently a Communist, Natas previously worked in a Nazi death camp and already has thousands of lives on his conscience. Spelled backward, his name is Aktå Satan—meaning the "real

Satan.") His naive father-in-law, Natas explains, "didn't realize that all revolutions are won by the dark elements, the professional murders." Vera, who works in a medical laboratory, proves no less pragmatic than her husband, and perhaps even more ruthless. After going to bed with him, she injects his neck with poison—the moment of horror accentuated by a suddenly ringing telephone.

Vera flees with Natas's briefcase, full of "secrets" he intended for the Americans. She is one step ahead of the Liquidatzian agents who have been shadowing the renegade engineer, when not otherwise engaged in sowing terror throughout the émigré community. ("Refugees!" one pamphlet warns, "Don't imagine that you are safe. The Third World War will soon break out.") The agents manage to spirit Natas away before the medics arrive—but not before one of the Liquidatzians, whose language is backward Swedish, pauses to look out window: "I like this country, it is full of beautiful sleepwalking people who think that *this can't happen here*."

In the most remarkable sequence, suggesting that the movie is some sort of dark comedy, Vera goes to a movie theater—meeting her compatriots behind the screen, on which Donald Duck and Goofy cavort through some Arabian adventure. At issue: Who among the expatriate community is the informer? Vera is accused (background quacks, Goofy laughing, a wacky arrangement of "How Dry I Am"). She reveals that the informer is actually a newly arrived young man, who is then beaten by the Liquidatzians until their priest calls a halt.

In the confused grand finale, Natas recovers his briefcase and is pursued by both the Swedish police and the Liquidatzian agents. Again, the film verges on comedy in the mad, slapstick quality of the chase—replete with people falling down, cars blowing out tires, streets blocked by inconvenient parades. Attempting to escape across a skyway, Natas is trapped and jumps to his death. As his corpse lies on the pavement, one agent seizes the briefcase—it's empty (and promptly trampled by the heedless crowd).

All that remains is to free Vera, held captive aboard a sinister Liquidatzian boat, the *Mrofnimok Gadyn*. (Spelled backward, it is *Kominform Nydag*—*Nydag* [New day] being the name of the Swedish Communist Party newspaper.) The film's final image is framed by one of the ship's lifesavers: Thus Vera escapes, returning to the grim, terrorized land that Bergman would depict, a dozen years later, in *The Silence*.

14. *THE HIJACKING*
(Ján Kádár and Elmar Klos, Czechoslovakia, 1952)

Written in 1951 and filmed in Czechoslovakia the next year, *The Hijacking* materializes something of the Slánský terror. An opening disclaimer announces that the movie is not based on an actual event but might as well be—similar things are going on. In other words, *The Hijacking* is a hypothetical docudrama.[54]

The movie opens in the Czech steel center (and model Five-Year Plan town) Ostrava. Located near the West German border, it is a locus for cold war tensions. Spies are everywhere—in an early scene, one is trapped while paying a visit on a local priest. Newspaper headlines inform us of the latest antisocialist provocation (a speech by the Chilean representative) at the United Nations.

Regarded as if under surveillance by the suspicious camera, the passengers on a Prague-bound airline constitute a cross section of Czechoslovakian society. Among them are a young couple en route to study in Moscow, a jazz musician, a boxer, a simple villager, and an insurance agent. The film's positive hero is a Communist member of Parliament, while the protagonist Prokop is a somewhat disaffected—or "neutral"—engineer from the steel plant, his briefcase (like that of his professional colleague Atkå Natas's) stuffed with top-secret vital plans.

Predating by at least a year Hollywood's air disaster epic *The High and the Mighty*, *The Hijacking* places considerable emphasis on the paraphernalia of flying—especially since the copilot is part of a CIA conspiracy to divert the plane to West Germany. As pilot and copilot battle in the cockpit, American soldiers track the flight—bits of excited phonetic English, "Hi!" "OK?" "OK!" Surrounded by newshounds, the expansive, tough NATO general makes his thrilling announcement: Mass defection![55]

The passengers are suitably agitated as the plane makes its descent over Munich. "This isn't Prague," the peasant protests. "They brought us somewhere in the Western Zone!" His observation is validated by the crazy music, English signs, and overall frenzy that greet them on the airstrip. As the honest Czech pilot is forced through the aisle at gunpoint, he is accosted by a reporter in turned-up hat, loud tie, and shades: "Just a moment, c'mon, what's your name?" The avuncular American general welcomes the Czechs to his base. In a sinister bit of business, they are invited to choose between the new cars on their right and the police wagon on their left.

At once disorderly and mobilized, the West is a realm of gum-chewing, simian military cops and hot jazzy blues. (The movie incorporates actual broadcasts of the American Armed Forces Network.) Not all the Americans are apes—one soldier is the son of Czech immigrant, as well as a former coal miner. The Czechs are tempted with food but refuse even a sandwich—except for the jazz musician, who naturally is a weak link. The positive hero advises Prokop to destroy his papers.

Back at the United Nations, the Soviet delegate tells the world about the political situation. The American delegate, who is watching the speech on television, telephones the general to request evidence of political terror in Czechoslovakia—that is, to mimic the actual situation by forcing confessions and obtaining testimony from the captive Czechs. Although the general and his intelligence officer have already targeted Prokop, NATO may not be as popular as it believes.

The engineer is brought to a BMW plant filled with new tanks (on the soundtrack, a few bars of the "Horst Wessel Song"). "Is this a tractor?" Prokop asks. "Our customers are our masters," the Germans explains, "We have to obey" (on the wall, the fresh graffito "Ami Go Home"). Meanwhile, the worker member of Parliament is being interrogated by American intelligence officer. Pinups are ubiquitous, including one of General Douglas MacArthur. A strategically missing sign suggests that this was formerly Gestapo headquarters; the Americans employ war criminals to do their dirty work, including a sinister Sudeten German in a leather trench coat. ("Don't you realize we've been at war for the last four years?" the general asks the member of Parliament).

As a more benign form of persuasion, the Czechs are taken to see an open-air production, *The Munich Follies.* It's an all-American show: Against a giant Coca-Cola sign and to the sound of Dixieland, a pair of cops take turns beating on a blackface clown. The comedy act is followed by a precision line of bikini-clad, rifle-touting chorus girls. The gum-chewing audience is delighted ("Swell isn't it?"), albeit puzzled by the Czechs' silent response: "Don't they like it?"

American newspapers, including the *New York Times,* are already reporting their defection. Indeed, Prokop is about to go over to the West when the American general boasts of having bombed Ostrova during World War II. Little does he know that Prokop's family perished during those raids. They are in the base canteen, and the engineer's mental state can be deduced by the poster with cartoon dancers inviting us to "See the Ruins of Berlin." The filmmakers contrive to have a statue of praying nun "looking" at the wild jitterbuggers.

Invited to speak, Prokop denounces the Americans for "murdering" his wife and child. As if by magic, military police appear and arrest him—although the Czech boxer takes advantage of the melee to deck one. The clear-headed Parliament member, who has already managed to substitute a girlie magazine for the plans that Prokop is carrying, manages to escape, hitching a ride to Munich and crossing back into the East. (In a key fraternal moment, he makes a question mark on windshield; the driver crosses it with a hammer.)

Fed up with NATO chicanery, the captive Czechs start to hum and then sing the "Internationale." The patriotic women have even stitched a Czech flag. The disgusted Americans are prepared to let them go—all except one. When a Tatra arrives, the Czechs are cheering. But where is Comrade Prokop? "Either all of us or no one will leave." The Americans are still interrogating the engineer when the East German newspaper *Red Flame* breaks the story—Communists organize petitions and protests: Prokop must be freed! The smiling Czechs execute an optimistic folk dance and prepare to return home—all except for the jazz musician, who is already miserable in a refugee camp.

In the triumphant postscript, the Czech delegate to the United Nations decries American cynicism and war preparations, refering to "thousands" of similarly provocative incidents. There is a vote on the Chilean delegate who wants to censure Czech mistreatment. A final dissolve returns us to the Klement Gottwald steelworks, where a factory meeting is in progress: Who wants to open the factory one month ahead of the plan? Everyone happily raises his or her hand, especially Prokop.

Although completed in 1952, *The Hijacking* was held up for release, before opening in three theaters on January 30, 1953. In a conversation with Antonin Liehm, codirector Ján Kádár called *The Hijacking* "an extremely naive, dogmatic, cold-war type of film." Nevertheless, it was not without controversy: "Even our modest effort to make things at least a little believable, probable, was the voice of heresy. The tag they applied to that was 'bourgeoise objectivism.' Finally, the old Russian film pioneer and director Pudovkin, who in spite of everything had not lost his feeling for film, helped get [*The Hijacking*] into movie theaters despite its being banned."[56]

15. *RED PLANET MARS* (Harry Horner, U.S.A., 1952)

*T*his is a story not yet told.

—Narrator, *Red Planet Mars*

Given the widespread expectation of nuclear war between the United States and the Soviets, the American science-fiction films of the 1950s could hardly be anything other than political allegories. With the cold war further conceptualized in theological terms, as a struggle to the death between Godless Communism and Godful Capitalism, this was also a period for religious movies—not just huge biblical spectaculars but also small productions such as *The Miracle of the Bells* (1948), *The Next Voice You Hear* (1950), and *The Miracle of Our Lady of Fatima* (1952).

As the movie that dared to ask the question "Is the man from Nazareth the man from Mars?" *Red Planet Mars* was both—the most visionary of the anti-Communist films released during the science-fiction genre's high-water mark as well as the nuttiest of religious films. Stimulated generally by a shooting war in Korea and the often reiterated warning that this might be the prelude to World War III, not to mention by the spring 1951 second round of the House Un-American Activities Committee's investigation into Hollywood, one-third of all the anti-Communist movies produced between 1948 and 1954 were released in the presidential election year 1952.

While the *Red Planet Mars* ads promised "The World Torn Asunder by a Threat from Outer Space," the danger was neither an oncoming comet nor a fleet of flying saucers piloted by carnivorous carrots but, as in *Aelita,* a transmission from our neighboring planet. Using plans for a "hydrogen tube" recovered from the rubble of Nazi Germany, independent scientists Chris and Linda Cronyn (Peter Graves and Andrea King) are trying to establish radio contact with Mars. So, too, it would seem, is the tube's bitter, ranting inventor—a German scientist named Calder (Herbert Berghof), who is now in the service of the Communists.

Thanks to Calder's trick transmissions, bounced off Mars from his secret hideout—a hut high in the Andes Mountains, beneath a giant statue of Jesus Christ—and picked up by the Cronyns, the world learns that Mars is far more technologically advanced than Earth. Knowledge of this supercivilization triggers a worldwide economic panic (shown on a futuristic wall-sized television set). Like the 1930s all over again, the Kremlin is ecstatic while the U.S. president is so concerned that he invokes national security to shut down the Cronyns' transmitter. But then, Radio Mars sends a new sort of signal, quoting from Jesus' Sermon on the Mount. Linda, who, although a scientist, suffers from acute anxiety and technophobia, wants to broadcast this holy message to the world. So does the president: "Now we're following the star of Bethlehem."

Although internal evidence suggests that *Red Planet Mars* is set several years in the future, perhaps 1956 or 1957, the movie took its cues from the rhetoric of the day. In February 1950, Senator Joseph McCarthy's epochal Wheeling, West Virginia, speech had predicted all-out war between Christianity and "atheistic Communism." J. Edgar Hoover regularly defined Communism as "secularism on the march" and called Christianity its "moral foe." The American Legion was sponsoring a Back to God movement. The evangelist Billy Graham—most admired American of the era, four times on the cover of *Life* between 1949 and 1955—characterized Communism as an invention of Satan and advised his fellow citizens that to "be a true patriot, . . . become a Christian."

In effect, God seems to be speaking from Mars, using the Voice of America to address the people of Earth—or at least some of them. (The montage of worldwide radio receptions features only white listeners.) The transmission has its greatest impact on Soviet Russia; China is never mentioned. Now, it is the Communists' turn to panic. "Speak English, you fool," the Russian leader screams at one of his agents. "Anything is preferable to your atrocious accent." The enormity of the crisis is indicated by mysterious stock footage of Russian peasants ripping portraits of Stalin off their walls and digging up ecclesiastical vestments buried in 1917. Then, in a scene eliminated in most TV prints, an Orthodox priest is placed on the once-Romanov Russian throne.[57]

While it is possible that Russia may yet again become a theocracy, *Red Planet Mars* was more immediately prophetic. Shot during the winter of 1951/52, the movie opened a few weeks before the Republican National Convention that would nominate General Dwight Eisenhower to run for president. The movie's president is, similarly, a former military commander, and the actor Willis Bouchey strongly resembles Eisenhower. Indeed, Eisenhower—identified by the Republican National Convention as "the spiritual leader of our times"—began his inaugural address with a three-paragraph prayer addressed to "Almighty God" and subsequently became the first American president to be baptized in the White House.

Red Planet Mars was produced and cowritten by Anthony Veiller (who worked on the 1946 Hemingway adaptation *The Killers,* as well as Orson Welles's 1946 *The Stranger* and Frank Capra's 1948 *State of the Union*). Veiller's collaborator John L. Balderston had, twenty-some years earlier, adapted both *Dracula* and *Frankenstein* for the stage, subsequently writing the screenplays for *The Mummy, Bride of Frankenstein, The Lives of a Bengal Lancer, The Last of the Mohicans,* and *Gaslight.* Balderston, brought up as an orthodox Quaker, had been a passionate advocate for American involvement in World War II.

The movie was directed by Harry Horner, a Czech-born onetime assistant to Max Reinhardt who came to the United States during the 1930s. Having worked mainly as art director, Horner was perhaps responsible for touches such as the ritual masks that decorate Calder's hut and the Cronyns' surprisingly elaborate lab. These are important because, despite its title, *Red Planet Mars* never leaves Earth or, for the most part, even California.

Although *Red Planet Mars* borrows a few homey notions from MGM's *The Next Voice You Hear,* in which God commandeers the radio for six successive nights to endorse the American way of life, it has an earlier source in the play *Red Planet,* cowritten by Balderston and J. E. Hoare. Opening on Broadway in December 1932 (perhaps the worst winter—at least economically—in American history), *Red Planet* was set in London. An astronomer couple establish radio contact with Mars and receive a message that sounds like the Sermon on the Mount. The characterizations are similar: He is "a cold agnostic," and she "is a warm Episcopalian." The ensuing tumult is somewhat different: The streets of London are filled with hymn singers, a Jewish financier attempts to option the Bible and convert New York's movie theaters into churches, and an opportunistic British politician makes himself world dictator. The endings, however, are the same: God works in mysterious ways.

In the play's last act, the radio transmissions are revealed to be a hoax, perpertrated by a hunchbacked scientist broadcasting from the Alps. In the movie, an avalanche sweeps away Calder's shack, yet he turns up at the Cronyn's lab to inform them gleefully of his cosmic prank. "What were you after?" they cry. His answer: "Shall I say . . . amusement?" Realizing that Calder is less a Commu-Nazi than a Satanist, the Cronyns contrive to blow up their lab, sacrificing themselves to destroy the Antichrist. That this is done to secure the future of the baby boom is implicit in Chris's declaration that their two young sons belong to a "blessed generation."

Red Planet Mars opened in New York City at the Criterion Theater on June 14, 1952—the same day that President Harry Truman dedicated America's first atomic-powered submarine, the *Nautilus,* and declared it the "harbinger of a new age." I am haunted by the image of that kindly lawyer Emmanuel Bloch, schlepping the two young sons of Julius and Ethel Rosenberg up to Sing Sing or out to Brooklyn for some Committee to Secure Justice in the Rosenberg Case meeting and then, as a special Saturday treat, to this educational documentary on our celestial neighbor.

Manny nods, but Robby and Michael are entranced. Moments before the explosion that martyrs the Cronyns, there is a final transmission from Mars. The smoke clears on the president. To the sound of tolling church bells and celestial choirs, he reveals that the ultimate message was "Ye have done well, my good and faithful servants." Then he smiles upon the newly orphaned Cronyn kids: "Lucky boys—you're their sons."[58]

16. *SILVER DUST* (Abram Room, USSR, 1954)

The work of two potential cosmopolitans, director Abram Room and screenwriter August Jacobson, *Silver Dust* was something of a cold war zombie, completed (and released) well after Stalin's death in March 1953. Nevertheless, this lavishly gloomy, full-color publicistic comedy earned a four-page spread in the October 11, 1954, issue of *Life:* "Reds'-Eye View of Us: Russians Make Crude, Effective Hate-America Film for Home Consumption."

Like *The Russian Question, Silver Dust* is notable for being entirely set in an imaginary America. However effective the movie was as propaganda (the filmmakers can never quite solve the problem of making the United States both prosperous and evil), Americans will naturally treasure such details as the blue Coca-Cola signs; advertising billboards planted neatly side by side, parallel to the highway; and the sight of a family gathered in their parlor drinking highballs through straws as they listen to the radio that's perched atop their TV.[59]

Working on behalf of the Eastern Chemical Trust, General McKennedy (played, with a perpetual grin, by popular Jewish comic Rustaslav Platt) is dispatched to the small Southern town of Fortskill, where the nuclear researches of the solitary superscientist Professor Steel (!) are funded by the rival Southern Chemical Trust. McKennedy visits Steel's mansion—complete with pampered lap dogs—as well as the vast laboratory that the professor operates in his basement. Assisted by the unreconstructed Nazi chemist Dr. Schneider, Steel is developing a deadly radioactive toxin that has no fallout and is hence undetectable. McKennedy is impressed, particularly after watching a monkey die minutes after exposure to the silver dust.

More than a simple saga of capitalist science run amok, Jacobson's script has elements of a Socialist Realist *Hamlet:* Professor Steel is a usurper who has poisoned his teacher, the "great humanist" Dr. O'Connell, then married O'Connell's widow. Now the O'Connell son has returned from the army—an idealistic crypto-Communist who addresses an integrated, worker-organized civil rights rally on Main Street. After this peaceful meeting is disrupted by a Salvation Army choir under the direction of the reactionary priest Gideon Smith, police attack the progressive demonstrators, arresting a number of them, including the son of Steel's black servant Mary, Ben.

When the news arrives that Ben—who has committed the crime of collecting signatures to protest racism—is in the hands of the police, Steel's distraught daughter Jane cries that she feels ashamed to be white. Not so her beau, Dave, or teenage brother, Harry, or General McKennedy, who holds forth on how "the entire world will be America." With this in mind, McKennedy has interested the Pentagon in Steel's discovery.

That the Pentagon first wants to test the silver dust on humans creates additional intrigue: After a representative of the Southern Chemical Trust calls the state governor, who suggests importing some Chinese or Korean POWs for the experiment, McKennedy proposes using criminals. Moving quickly now, McKennedy approaches Dr. Schneider, promising instant war with the Soviet Union if he steals the secret for him. The conspiracy to secure the necessary guinea pigs will involve framing a group of black prisoners—including Ben—for rape. But this cannot be done in secret: A montage, replete with spinning (misspelled) headlines and mass protests, punches across the story of these Fortskill Six.[60]

Mobilized as they had been for the wrongly accused Scottsboro Boys in the 1930s, American Communists are evidently circulating a petition, which McKennedy and Steel refuse to sign—even though, as someone helpfully points out, the ramifications of the case are international; Soviet writers are also protesting! In vain, faithful Mary begs the Steel family to help her Ben. The ensuing, unusually philosophical family debate raises the issue of peace, the responsibilities spelled out at the Nuremberg Trials, and, as in *The Russian Question,* the idea of the two Americas—to no avail. Leaving, Mary predicts that the day will come when Dr. Steel and General McKennedy will plead to be saved from the wrath of the poor.

As the soiree continues, Gideon Smith wonders when anti-Communist jihad will start—Jesus has already blessed the American army. After leading Mrs. Steel in singing a hymn meant to suggest "Onward, Christian Soldiers," Smith reveals that he is in spiritual communion with her late husband's ghost. Meanwhile, the Ku Klux Klan has burned a cross, spreading terror throughout the Negro shantytown. After parading down Main Street (where they are turned back by a human wall of silent leftists), the KKK attack the prison. Fearing that their prospective guinea pigs may be lynched, the conspirators dispatch the police to assure the Klansmen that the jailed blacks are destined to die in the electric chair. The prisoners, referred to as "material for experiment," are then transported to Steel's lab, where the assistants are puzzled that there are no monkeys on which to test the silver dust.

Hoping to secure Dr. Schneider's war records, Harry (who has become the Nazi's acolyte) steals the key to the laboratory from his father and inadvertently exposes himself to the silver dust. Steel backs off as the contaminated youth staggers out, amid a flashing red alert. McKennedy attempts to take advantage of the odd inertia in the face of disaster to talk business—binding Professor Steel to a chair and demanding the silver powder. Just as Steel shouts that he'll never reveal the formula, a group of honest citizens led by O'Connell storm the lab and free all prisoners, leaving the villains to face the wrath of the people's justice.

In his memoir *Child of Communism*, Ede Pfeiffer describes seeing *Silver Dust* in a Hungarian cine-club sponsored by the Federation of Working Youth (DISZ):

> Another film pictured an American atom-physicist making experiments with a new kind of exterminator. Not even his wife knew of the hideous work he did in the basement laboratory of his house, but his son discovered his awful secret. Negroes were kept in the cellar as guinea pigs for his revolting researches. The boy, after a struggle with his conscience, told his father that his work was no longer a secret, but not having the facilities of Soviet freedom he could not pick up the telephone and call the secret police. He had to content himself with the devious and doubtful means open to a capitalist country. He aroused public opinion against his wicked father, and the film ended with pictures of the people of

America making mass demonstrations of solidarity with the policies of the Soviet Union.

The effect of such a film was incalculable. Some of us were dumfounded [sic], some bewildered, some muttered in doubtful disbelief, a few laughed—their laughter was smartly reprimanded. We had to write an essay on this film too. Our DISZ representative got top marks.[61]

17. INVASION OF THE BODY SNATCHERS
(Don Siegel, U.S.A., 1956)

The adjusted are those who reflect their society, or their class within the society, with the least distortion.

—David Reisman, *The Lonely Crowd* (1950)

This country has become a laboratory for the dark and insidious science of modern revolutionary propaganda. It is difficult for the American to realize that the ideas, the prejudices, the convictions he holds may have been deliberately—though slyly—planted in his mind by men who have a settled purpose in performing that operation, who possess the instruments of thought control and understand how to operate them.

—John T. Flynn, *While You Slept* (1951)

As much as anything, the original 1956 *Invasion of the Body Snatchers*—produced by Walter Wanger, directed by Don Siegel, and adapted (mostly) by Daniel Mainwaring from the Jack Finney novel—has been a source of outrageous simile.

The most famous B-movie allegory of the 1950s, *Invasion of the Body Snatchers* gave the familiar cold war scenario of extraterrestrial conquest an additionally paranoid twist: Drifting down from the sky, seedpods from outer space replicate human beings and replace them (as they sleep) with perfect, emotion-free, vegetable doubles—thus successfully colonizing Earth with the asexual, other-directed drones of a harmoniously single-minded mass society.

Ever since the Truman administration began stoking the Red Scare in the spring of 1947, Communism had been visualized as a disease, a germ, a form of alien mind control. By the time *Invasion of the Body Snatchers* appeared, however, the nation had submitted to the soothing presence of President Eisenhower—embracing a consciousness exemplified by the psychologically homogenizing combination of the tranquilizer Miltown and the suburb Levittown. So which was which? Was the conformist organization man an analogue to the master of deceit?

If *High Noon* (1952) managed to attack Hollywood cowardice while providing justification for America's cold war foreign policies, then *Invasion of the Body Snatchers* offered an all-purpose metaphor for the nation's domestic life. Like *High Noon, Invasion of the Body Snatchers* lent itself to both right- and left-wing readings—a drama alternatively of Communist subversion and of suburban conformity, unfolding in a hilariously bland atmosphere of extreme hypervigilance. The script originally ended with a tight close-up of the distraught, solitary pod fighter, Dr. Miles Bennell (Kevin McCarthy), screaming at the audience: "There's no escape . . . no time to waste. Unless you do, you'll be next!"

Given its maximally lurid title (Finney had simply called his work *The Body Snatchers*), the movie is all the more enjoyable for the podlike quality of its impassive performances and cheap, open-air noir naturalism. Nor is this the only source of deadpan humor. An innocuous small town is the very fount of contagion; the cops are actually criminal; love has become a source of terror; tranquilizers must be prescribed by creatures from another planet; psychology is identified with brainwashing, adjustment made synonymous with conformist coercion; the family has been infiltrated by inhuman enemies; the telephone is an instrument of surveillance. In short, normality is rendered sinister. Put another way, overwhelming anxiety fed a powerful desire for security, a longing to merge with the group, whether in suburbs or party cells, even as this urge to merge was experienced as a threat to the individual.

The transformation of ordinary Americans into soullessly Sovietized Babbitts was a pop *1984,* complete with the notion of subversive sex crime. More than any other cold war fantasy, *Invasion of the Body Snatchers* showed America alienated from itself: The "good" motherland is experienced as a nearly identical "bad" one.

First appearing as *The Body Snatchers* in the November 26, December 10, and December 24, 1954, issues of *Collier's* magazine, Finney's pods had been anticipated by the eponymous "puppet masters" of Robert Heinlein's novel, originally serialized in the September 1951 issue of *Galaxy*. In the Heinlein scenario, giant slugs from Saturn's moon Titan travel to Earth by flying saucer and attach themselves to American citizens, whom they transform into zombies controlled by an unfeeling, communal mind.

Although set after World War III, *The Puppet Masters* was totally contemporary—resembling in some respects a two-fisted, kisser-mashing Mike Hammer thriller. There is a suggestion that the slugs have already conquered Russia (thus making it, in effect, its own "puppet regime"). In the United States, these disgusting aliens actively seek to take over government officials—including army brass, member of the president's cabinet, and congressmen. Given this crisis, civil liberties must be suspended. The question of the hour (Are you now or have you ever been a slug-zombie spy?) is superceded by the vow of constant vigilance articulated by the book's intelligence-agent hero.

Finney's novel is less overtly McCarthyite, particularly as it has been revised several times—first when published as a Dell paperback in February 1955 and again twenty-three years later, reissued to coincide with Philip Kaufman's remake of the Siegel movie. As originally published in *Collier's, The Body Snatchers* was set during the summer of 1953, soon after the execution of Julius and Ethel Rosenberg capped a six-year hunt for Communist traitors and immediately after the Korean armistice. It was a moment when the American press was preoccupied with stories of GIs subjected to Communist "brainwashing," and there are other cold war markers as well. Going into battle, Miles Bennell invokes Winston Churchill: "We shall fight them in the fields, and in the streets, we shall fight in the hills; we shall never surrender." In *Collier's*, the story has a happy ending: The FBI successfully beats back the invasion.

As imagined by Finney, the collectivized pods suffer from apathy. They let the town they infiltrate fall into a state of seedy decline, so that the stores are as empty of produce as those in a drab East European city. ("You can hardly even buy a Coke in most places," a traveling salesman complains to Miles. "Lately, this place has been out of coffee altogether, for no reason at all, and today when they have it, it's lousy, terrible.") Still, for Finney's hero, the pods suggest something beyond Communism. As Glen M. Johnson has pointed out, Finney's *Body Snatchers* provides an even more comprehensive catalog of topical anxieties than Siegel's film. At one point in the book, Miles compares the pods' false human personalities to the exaggerated servility of the middle-aged black man who runs the town shoe-shine stand; elsewhere he refers to himself as a "puppet," who married and divorced as if devoid of will. Thus, America is already a land of masked rage and zombie automatons.[62]

Sorting out the politics of the men who filmed *Invasion of the Body Snatchers* is no less convoluted. Siegel has described himself as a liberal, although his oeuvre is more suggestive of an antiauthoritarian libertarian belief in rugged individualism. Wanger, a producer with an interest in topically political material, was responsible for both the crypto-fascist *Gabriel over the White House* (1933) and the prematurely antifascist *Blockade* (1938), as well as such New Dealish genre exercises as *You Only Live Once* (1937), *Stagecoach* (1939), and *Foreign Correspondent* (1940). A brief stretch in prison for jealously shooting the agent representing his wife, Joan Bennett, resulted in the reformist *Riot in Cell Block 11* (1954), directed by Siegel.

Although working on a budget of less than four hundred thousand dollars, Wanger treated *Body Snatchers* as an important production. Scarcely had *Collier's* finished running Finney's serial than Wanger, Siegel, and Siegel's erstwhile collaborator Daniel "Geoffrey Homes" Mainwaring met with the author to discuss the movie version. Mainwaring, a man of left-wing associations who'd begun his career writing socially conscious journalism and pulp fiction, is credited with Miles's speech on the changes he's noted in American society: "People have allowed their humanity to drain away . . . only it happens slowly rather than all at once. They didn't seem to mind."

Invasion of the Body Snatchers went into production in late March 1955. As a further complication, the script was reworked by Richard Collins, author of *Riot in Cell Block 11* as well as one of the most ambiguous figures of the blacklist era. A former Communist Party functionary, the coauthor of the once-notorious *Song of Russia* (1943), and an announced unfriendly witness first subpoenaed among the original Hollywood Nineteen by the House Un-American Activities Committee in autumn 1947, Collins subsequently reversed fields—first becoming an FBI informer and then the namer of twenty-six names before the HUAC on April 12, 1951.

Having wrapped after a brisk twenty-three day shoot, *Invasion of the Body Snatchers* further evolved over the course of a lengthy postproduction debate on how best to position the narrative. Wanger thought to preface the movie with a recent quote from Winston Churchill and, as he had in *Foreign Correspondent,* add a didactic final warning. The necessity for a framing story, to be set up by an onscreen narrator, was perceived as increasingly urgent after a series of unsuccessful previews during the summer of 1955. Wanger's first choice for narrator was Orson Welles, establishing an obvious link to *The War of the Worlds* (which had been filmed, as a ready-made allegory of U.S.-Soviet atomic war, in 1953); the alternatives were a trio of World War II radio correspondents—Edward R. Murrow, Lowell Thomas, and Quentin Reynolds.

A framing story was ultimately shot—*sans* celebrity narrator—in late September, thus providing the movie a marginally more optimistic ending. Finally, the title presented a problem. *The Body Snatchers* was too similar to Val Lewton's 1945 *The Body Snatcher*. The distributor, Allied Artists, proposed the generic *They Came from Another World*. Siegel strongly objected, offering instead *Sleep No More* and *Better Off Dead*—titles suggesting the familiar cold war metaphor of sleep versus wakefulness and the cold war mantra "Better Dead than Red"—before the idea of "invasion" was finally affixed to the threat of "body snatchers."

Even without Welles, Wanger was committed to the movie's liberal interpretation. In November, he told the American Booksellers Convention that his still-unreleased *Invasion of the Body Snatchers* was a picture on the subject of "conformity," showing "how easy it is for people to be taken over and to lose their souls if they are not alert and determined in their character to be free." Just as European commentators were quick to recognize *High Noon*'s foreign policy implications, so the Italian critic Ernesto G. Laura was apparently the first to link *Invasion of the Body Snatchers* to the anti-Communist rhetoric of J. Edgar Hoover and the *Reader's Digest*. Two years after *Body Snatchers*'s release, the anti-Stalinist leftist Seymour Stern wrote program notes for a revival at Los Angeles's Coronet Theatre that took an epigram from a recent item in the *Los Angeles Times*: "India's communists today began a crucial special congress called primarily to perfect their new political technique—the attainment of absolute power through respectability."[63]

Tracing *Body Snatchers*'s lineage back to D. W. Griffith's *The Flying Torpedo* (1916), Stern gave the movie an unambiguously universally antitotalitarian reading: "Long ago, the natives whose bodies are snatched by the pods had cancelled or forfeited their own birthright of sexual freedom based only on mutual consent; they had lost their liberty in meek submission to their own conservative authority. If all brands of sovietization seem here, then all forms of Fascism are here too—clerical fascism, economic fascism, political fascism, sexual fascism, social fascism, name-the-brand."

So familiar has the *Body Snatchers* metaphor become that it's worth noting that, back in 1956, *Variety* found the movie sometimes "difficult to follow due to the strangeness of its scientific premise." As film theorist Noel Carroll has pointed out, however, *Invasion of the Body Snatchers* offers a near-textbook illustration of the rare condition known as Capgras syndrome—the delusional belief that close relatives or associates, sometimes including one's pets or oneself, have been replaced by sinister doubles.[64]

The original *Invaders from Mars* (1953) and the British *I Married a Monster from Outer Space* (1958) are related examples of Capgrasoid sci-fi. The latter's title echoes the similarly premised *I Married a Communist* (also known as *Woman on Pier 13*, 1950), and a study of the syndrome's case histories shows that imagined Communist conspiracies were scarcely unknown during the heightened suspicion of the cold war. Capgras syndrome has been variously analyzed as a paranoid projection (if a familiar person no longer elicits the same affective response, the person must have changed—not the subject's feelings) and as a form of denial (accounting for certain negative traits in one with whom the subject has strong emotional ties). As Capgras syndrome suggests the need to idealize a particular individual, it makes sense that the original *Invasion of the Body Snatchers* appeared soon after the 1948–53 period of maximum mobilization—once it was safe to dramatize the recent hysteria and meditate on the Pod That Failed.

The original *Invasion of the Body Snatchers* provided an imaginative visualization of the national security state and reckoned its psychic cost to America's self-image. Thus, looking back on the cold war from the post-McCarthy period, Siegel and company not only naturalized the Red Scare but imbued it with Darwinian angst—the fear that, as the Reds themselves suggested, Communism might actually be a higher stage on the evolutionary ladder.[65]

18. *I AM CUBA* (Mikhail Kalatozov, USSR-Cuba, 1964)

History barely records that *I Am Cuba*—Soviet director Mikhail Kalatozov's deliriously stodgy two-hour-and-twenty-minute paean to the Cuban Revolution—was one of three fraternal projects that the then-fledgling Cuban Film Institute (ICIAC) coproduced with its new Warsaw Pact allies as a means of educating homegrown moviemakers.

Two of these productions were banal genre pieces: *Prelude 11*, by the intermittently distinguished East German director Kurt Maetzig, was a thriller about CIA-sponsored counterrevolutionaries; *For Whom Havana Dances*, by the Czech hack Vladimir Cech, set a story of contemporary Cuba against the picturesque backdrop of Havana's carnival. *I Am Cuba*, which has the rapturous quality of a Bolshevik hallucination, is less easy to categorize. A throwback to the red modernism of the 1920s or belated tribute to Sergei Eisenstein's incomplete *Que Viva Mexico*, Kalatozov's sunstruck evocation of life before and during the Cuban Revolution was a critical and commercial failure—never shown outside the Soviet Union or Cuba until it surfaced as part of a Kalatozov tribute at the 1992 Telluride Film Festival.

A veteran director and former camera operator, the Georgian-born Kalatozov (1903–73) enjoyed a varied career before venturing out into Havana's searing tropical light. His first feature was the experimental, staged-ethnographic documentary *Salt for Svanetia* (1930). *Nail in the Boot,* a 1932 treatment of the Russian Civil War, was banned, but his 1941 *Valery Chkalov,* a fictionalized biography of the Soviet pilot who made the first flight from the Soviet Union over the North Pole to the United States, capped a popular cycle of films that celebrated "Stalin's falcons."

Kalatozov served as Soviet consul in Los Angeles during World War II, shored up his credentials with the cold war publicist melodrama *Conspiracy of the Doomed* (1950), then signaled the post-Stalin "thaw" with a visually stylized, almost hysterically poignant, and extremely popular World War II romance, *The Cranes Are Flying* (1957). This last feature marked the beginning of a three-film partnership with virtuoso cinematographer Sergei Urusevsky (1908–74), a former combat cameraman as well as a disciple of the cubo-futurist painter–photographer–graphic designer Alexander Rodchenko.

I Am Cuba's episodic script was cowritten by two young poets, Soviet bard Yevgeny Yevtushenko and Cuban writer Enrique Pineda Barnet. Sent by *Pravda* to newly revolutionized Cuba as a "poetry correspondent" during the spring of 1961, Yevtushenko spent six months on the island in the aftermath of the abortive, CIA-sponsored Bay of Pigs invasion—learning Spanish, traveling the countryside, and hanging with Fidel.[66]

Although, according to Yevtushenko, the September 1961 publication of his anti-anti-Semitic poem "Babi Yar" made it more difficult for Kalatozov and Urusevsky to secure his services for their planned Cuba project, the poet traveled again to Havana with the two filmmakers during the winter of 1962 to work on the script. Yevtushenko was still in Cuba at the height of the Missile Crisis. The front page of the October 25, 1962, issue of *Pravda* featured his editorial in verse, a "Letter to America," phoned in from Havana the night before:

> *America, I'm writing to you from Cuba,*
> *Where the crags and the cheekbones*

Of rigid sentries shine anxiously tonight
In the gusting storm. . . .

A tobacconist, carrying a revolver,
    prepares to leave for the harbor,
A shoemaker cleans an old machine gun,
A showgirl from a cabaret, wearing army
    boots,
Goes along with a carpenter to stand
    guard.[67]

When *I Am Cuba* began shooting in January 1963, however, the poet was no longer on the scene—once again, he says, in official disgrace. Moreover, in the wake of the Missile Crisis, relations betwen Castro and Soviet premier Nikita Khrushchev had cooled precipitously. Interestingly, Yevtushenko had only recently held up Cuba to Khrushchev as a model. "My recent work has been very closely connected with Cuba," the poet told the premier in a celebrated public exchange on the value of modern art. "I like Cuban abstract painting very much. . . . Cuban abstract art enjoys great popularity among the Cuban people and their leaders. Fidel Castro is keen on it. Cuban abstract art helps the Revolution."[68]

Relentlessly visual if not completely abstract, *I Am Cuba* employs relatively sparse dialogue in the service of four narrative vignettes, more or less delineating the progress from prerevolutionary despair to armed struggle. The movie opens with a bird's-eye view of pristine beaches and primordial palm trees, the contrast between sand and sky intensified by the use of infrared film stock, the wide-angle lens warping space and elongating the Cuban natives. "Ships took my sugar and left me in tears," a female narrator sonorously intones (first in Spanish, then in Russian).

Almost immediately, however, suffering is upstaged by aestheticism. Using a specially constructed external elevator and handing off the production's single Eclair from one operator to another, Urusevsky contrived for the camera to swoop among Havana's skyscrapers; land on the deck of a luxury penthouse, insinuate itself amid a gaggle of bikini-clad jet-setters; and then, still in a single, continuous shot, plunge beneath the chlorinated water of the rooftop swimming pool.

Downstairs is the cabaret—designated site of Cuban degradation and American imperialism, here visualized as something out of *La Dolce Vita*. (Interestingly, the filming of *I Am Cuba* coincided with a fierce debate in both the Cuban press and the United Cuban Revolutionary Socialist Party regarding the suitability of the Federico Fellini film, among the most popular movies released 1963, as entertainment for Cuba's newly enfranchized working class.) Two slick rockers—one an ex-member of the Platters—croon a ballad in praise of "loco amor" as American tourists ogle writhing dancer-prostitutes, when not rendering them in suitably degenerate Picasso-like sketches. Treating the nightclub interior like the material of a taffy pull, bobbing and weaving through a foliage of foreground clutter and masklike faces, Urusevsky films the orgiastic floor show. For all the contorted performers, the Eclair is the star: Throughout the movie, the wildly tilted, often filtered, sometimes spinning, almost always handheld "emotional camera" keeps the viewer in a permanent state of vertigo. Some shots feel as if filmed from a hammock, others from a dolly whose tracks are laid across the sky. (The cranes are really flying here!)

The second, shorter episode leaves decadent Havana, where even the taxis are Cadillacs, for the countryside—although even here, a farmer's humble hut offers ample arena for Urusevsky's loop-the-loop camerawork. The dispossessed peasant sends his teenage children to town (where they spend his last peso swilling Coca-Cola and playing the jukebox), then torches his sugar crop—the camera spinning like a corkscrew through the flaming cane field.

Maintaining the fiery metaphor while picking up the revolutionary pace, the movie's third and longest section returns to Havana. A newsreel of Cuba's pre-Castro dictator Fulgencio Batista is revealed, as the camera tracks back, to be projected on a drive-in movie screen. A group of student Fidelistas hurl firebombs at the image, setting it aflame. When the police shoot a student distributing antigovernment leaflets from a campus balcony, the swirling camera accentuates the trajectory of his fall—shadows of fluttering leaflets caress him as he lies on the pavement. Topping even this overheated symbolism, a dead dove drops down from the sky as the young Fidelistas march toward the waiting fire hoses of Batista's officers.

The murder of another student leader provides material for one more visual tour de force—the victim advancing into swirling smoke and spattered by water even as he is gunned down. The most extraordinary shot is, however, reserved for a funeral procession. As the young martyrs are borne through the narrow streets of downtown Havana, the camera ascends over the crowd to a fifth-story loft, to observe a group of cigar workers leaving their tables in order to unfurl a commemorative banner from their window, and then—still in one unbroken take—it floats out into space to follow, overhead, the parade of mourners.

Finally, having established the traditional worker-peasant-intellectual triumvirate, *I Am Cuba* visits the rebel stronghold of Oriente Province for a minidrama of revolutionary conversion. A peon family shelters a fugitive Fidelista—although his attempt to raise their consciousness fails, until they are subject to gratuitous bombing by Batista's air force. Saturation bombast is the operative strategy here. *I Am Cuba* is a movie in which drunken American sailors saunter past Havana's illuminated storefronts, leering at Cuban schoolgirls and declaring themselves the "heroes of old Uncle Sam," while stalwart guerrillas march singing into battle, smiling through the explosions. (When captured and interrogated as to the whereabouts of their leader, the revolutionaries paraphrase *Spartacus* (1960), individually proclaiming, "I am Fidel.") As the narrator informs us in a burst of official bluster, "These are the people about whom legends will be told."

History is made with the monument in mind. For all its splendid expressionist frenzy, *I Am Cuba* is formidably static—memorializing, as if in granite, the hopes, illusions, and hysteria of 1960. At once stirring and stultifying, the movie is as hubristic as its title. *I Am Cuba* petrifies the moment when an already moribund Socialist Realism dared to cha-cha-cha.[69]

19. *ONE, TWO, THREE* (Billy Wilder, U.S.A., 1961)

A knowingly cartoonish return to high cold war anti-Sovietism, Billy Wilder's *One, Two, Three* celebrates as it satirizes U.S. cultural imperialism. The great gangster of the early 1930s has here gone legit. James Cagney plays a comic version of the Ugly American—the megalomaniacal boss of a Coca-Cola bottling plant in West Berlin, dreaming of a deal with the Kremlin bosses that will open new territories behind the Iron Curtain.

At once hysterical and ironic, sophisticated and vulgar, *One, Two, Three* updates a one-act Ferenc Molnár farce that Wilder saw, as a youth, in Berlin. In the original, the daughter of a Swedish industrialist—a houseguest in the Paris home of a banker who hopes to become her father's business partner—elopes with a socialist cab driver. The banker then has but one hour in which to turn the cabbie into an appropriate son-in-law—a miracle accomplished, in part, by a well-deployed battalion of tailors. In Wilder's version, cowritten with I. A. L. Diamond, the political stakes have been raised. The cab driver is a belligerent East German beatnik Communist (Horst Bucholtz), who must be transformed into the appropriate mate for the dizzy teenage personification of American capital (Pamela Tiffin), daughter of Cagney's superior at the Coca-Cola home office in Atlanta.[70]

Pure elixir of democracy, Coca-Cola was synonymous in 1959 with American culture. Twenty years earlier, the soft drink had scarcely been a national trademark, let alone an internationally known icon. Coke was then regional: Outside the South, Americans used it mostly as a mixer. Only during World War II did the drink become mother's milk for uprooted GIs. Indeed, recognizing Coke's morale-boosting importance, General George Marshall (himself a Southerner) accorded the cola special status: He exempted it from sugar rationing and, in a foretaste of the Marshall Plan, requested an expanded overseas operation to keep the front supplied—thus creating the framework for postwar Coca-Colanization.

An artifact from the era of geopolitical competition and nuclear crisis, sufficiently prescient to evoke the idea of Soviet missiles in Cuba, *One, Two, Three* further anticipates pop art in its ambiguous treatment of the American mass culture that would eventually defeat Communism. The East German police torture Bucholtz by subjecting him to repeated playings of the American novelty song "Itsy Bitsy Teenie Weenie Yellow Polka Dot Bikini." When Cagney cries, "The hell with Khrushchev," Bucholtz waits a beat before replying, "The hell with Frank Sinatra."

One, Two, Three was shot during the summer of 1961, its script in continual revision. "Every morning, before leaving for the studio," recalled Diamond, "we would tune in anxiously on the American Forces Network to hear the latest developments in the Berlin crisis. Every evening, on returning to our hotel, we read the international edition of *The New York Times*, and then rewrote the script." The production was working in Berlin, when the Wall went up in the early hours of August 13.[71]

When *One, Two, Three* opened in December 1961, the *New York Times* cited it as a rare reversion to anti-Soviet filmmaking (and thus a test case), while the *New Yorker* somewhat dourly accused the filmmakers of "pitching a circus tent on grounds that threaten to become a cemetery." Abby Mann, who wrote the screenplay for *Judgement at Nuremberg* (the season's other cine-statement on post–World War II Germany), deemed *One, Two, Three* so tasteless that he felt obliged to apologize for it at the 1963 Moscow Film Festival.[72]

Such publicity notwithstanding, *One, Two, Three* proved a financial disappointment, grossing only five million dollars. Commercially rereleased in West Germany during the mid-1980s, Wilder's comedy became something of a cult film. Reportedly, the youthful audiences of West Berlin (which had seen a recent stage adaptation) interacted with the projected image as though it were *The Rocky Horror Picture Show*.[73]

20. *TIME STANDS STILL* (Péter Gothár, Hungary, 1983)

Q: *"Why, or how, did you become a film director?"*

A: *"When I was 16, two things happened to me: I lived through 1956 in Budapest, and I heard rock 'n' roll."*

—interview with György Szomjas (1986)

The most complex and successful example of *le mode retro* produced in Eastern Europe, Péter Gothár's *Time Stands Still* conflates the revolution of 1956 with the youth-culture hopes of 1963. The film, made when Gothár was thirty-six, is a generational self-portrait with marked affinities to Hollywood "movie brat" productions such as *Mean Streets* (1973) and *American Graffiti* (1973). The 1963-64 period is the same, and the use of rock 'n' roll is even more affecting. But because the film is set in Budapest, the big beat isn't the normal pulse of teenage life but the siren song of the mythical West.

For an American of Gothár's age, *Time Stands Still* suggests an alternate universe: A remade *Zéro de Conduite* scored by a manic DJ and transposed to a Communist Party–administered housing project. Gothár and his childhood friend, cinematographer Lajos Koltai, depict a milieu of overcrowded apartments and moldy institutions with an expressionism that is simultaneously muted and garish. *Time Stands Still* makes dreariness hallucinogenic. All Budapest, inside and out, is enveloped by a perpetual clammy mist. Light comes from the least likely sources: Neon reds and oranges glow in the fog, offering a promise of warmth as baleful as the film's pervasive sexual callousness. The worn faces of the solitary boozers in a shabby bar are illuminated as though the floor were paved with kryptonite, their amber drinks like radioactive beacons.

Youth has found, if only temporarily, another solution: "Teenage Party." (This two-hour radio broadcast from Radio Free Europe in Munich would eventually be countered by Radio Budapest's "For Young People Only.") Dini, the film's protagonist, shambles down the snot-green corridors of his dilapidated high school with the stridently poignant 1958 Paul Anka anthem "You Are My Destiny" pounding in his brain. Down in the basement—where a bottle of the capitalist elixir Coca-Cola, brought back from London and passed around a sweaty party, produces the narcotic stupor that the official press always promised it would—a twisting rock combo mumbles "Don't Be Cruel" in phonetic English, giving the vintage Elvis hit a slow, hyperbolic beat that renders it as ritual an anthem as the "Internationale," as funky a performance as a Delta blues.[74]

High school may be a universal regime, but less than evident to the Western viewer is *Time Stands Still*'s evocation of a political thaw. The film opens with black-and-white newsreel footage dated November 5, 1956—the day after the Soviet army invaded Budapest. Images of streets filled with tanks and burning barricades (scored to incongruously lilting music) segue into an individual drama whose heroic lighting and angles ironically suggest the Soviet war movies of the early 1950s. A desperate freedom fighter, Dini's father fails to persuade his frightened wife to flee with him to Vienna. As he chooses an unknown world outside Hungary, she and their two small sons remain to face the equally unfathomable world within.

Jumping ahead seven years, *Time Stands Still* represents a key moment in Hungarian history. The year 1963 was when Kádárism prevailed—the last prisoners of 1956 were released, the first critical accounts of the pre-1956 Stalinist regime published, travel restrictions relaxed, economic experimentation begun, and the party sanctioned rock 'n' roll. (By 1966, Hungary boasted over seven hundred pop groups; by 1969, just before Gyula Gazdag conceived *Selection,* there were four thousand, half of which had played in public.) Thus, while Dini struggles with adolescent sexuality and his older brother worries that their father's counterrevolutionary past will keep him out of medical school, the film's adult characters—a well-etched gallery of rehabilitated freedom fighters, discredited Stalinists, party reformers, and bitter conservatives—scramble to find their places in the new political climate.

The ambivalent antiauthoritarian attitude of Dini and his pals is partially the result of no—or perhaps, too many—adult role models. Enter a leather-jacketed hooligan nicknamed Pierre, whose pompadour alone is sufficient to throw his teachers into a state of consternation. It is as though Swing Toni, the ridiculous jitterbugging saboteur of the sternly optimistic

Socialist Realist musical *Life Is Beautiful if You Sing,* had returned as a sort of subversive positive hero. In one of *Time Stand Still's* most memorable sequences, Pierre disrupts the headmaster's speech commemorating the arrival of the Red Army in 1945 by commandeering the school public address system and broadcasting a liberation message of his own: "Long live idiots! Let there be nothing! Blueberry Hill! Pussy! Let's twist again!" Chuck Berry couldn't have put it more bluntly; Pierre is last seen heading for America in a battered, stolen car.

Time Stands Still includes a brief postscript, set on New Year's Eve 1968. Dini's father is now able to revisit Hungary, but the film's sense of closure is more ominous. In the final scene, Dini is wearing a soldier's uniform, and although here he's drunkenly relieving himself against the wall, the unmistakable inference is that, seven months later, he'll be pissing on Czechoslovakia.

21. *WHEN JOSEPH RETURNS*
(Zsolt Kézdi-Kovács, Hungary, 1975)

Perhaps the most brilliant Hungarian film of the inter-NEM period, Zsolt Kézdi-Kovács's *When Joseph Returns* ponders the Kádárist depoliticization of daily life, imbuing a straightforward look at everyday existence in a Communist state with extraordinary clarity and allegorical richness.

Writer-director Kézdi-Kovács worked as Miklós Jancsó's first assistant throughout the 1960s, but surgical precision aside, his style is Jancsó's antithesis—quiet and static rather than bravura and fluid, punctuated by judicious megaclose-ups rather than shock imagery. A subtle editor who never holds a shot too long and seems congenitally incapable of overstatement, Kézdi-Kovács achieves a documentary hyperrealism akin to Yasujiro Ozu and Chantal Akerman, two other poets of boredom and routine. "This is the real Hungary," one of Kézdi-Kovács's colleagues told me when I first saw the movie in Budapest in 1979.

When Joseph Returns gives a world of stultifying factories, crammed clinics, shaggy recreational parks, and posh "red bourgeois" flats the quality of an illumination. (Is it Socialist Realism or not when Kézdi-Kovács and cinematographer János Kende treat an assembly line as a subject for Vermeer?) *Joseph's* method allows for contemplation of its plot. Marika, the new bride of the young Hungarian merchant-seaman Joseph, is left to stay with her mother-in-law, Agnes, while Joseph goes on his yearly voyage. "I thought he'd become a worker like we were," Agnes explains. "His teachers pressed him to study on. He didn't say a word. I told him: 'The workers are the masters now, education is within your reach.'" But such positive slogans notwithstanding, it would appear that Joseph just wanted to escape.

Joseph and Marika are the children of socialism—indeed, Marika is an orphan, a former ward of the state. But where the absent Joseph is an abstraction, the terminally depressed and engagingly disheveled Marika (indelibly played by Lili Monori) is all too human. Playing hooky from work, she turns on the radio and dances before the mirror, singing, "To be with you among the flowers would be fine" (this addressed to herself rather than another). Then the song turns lugubrious: "No matter who says so, don't believe that all is well. Don't believe that everything is fine. Do not believe that we can just be ordered to change."

Marika's disapproving mother-in-law (Éva Ruttkai) is her antithesis—an impeccable, controlled, severely attractive woman. The two spend their days working in separate factories, their evenings watching the TV that is the ubiquitous third presence in their immaculate two-and-a-half-room apartment, and their lives waiting for inane postcards from seafaring Joseph. Mutual dislike presently turns visceral—when Agnes falls asleep in front of the television, Marika maliciously turns up the volume—and inevitably, the sullen girl is acting out. Fired from her job at a Budapest shipyard, she falls into a casual affair with the driver for a government official.[75]

Tender rather than cynical (despite the general absence of idealism), *When Joseph Returns* is nonetheless filled with oblique and sometimes savage social criticism. Life is just short of pleasant; petty corruption is as natural as breathing. Like *A Worker in a Worker's State* (Miklós Haraszti's banned account of conditions in a Hungarian tractor factory), *When Joseph Returns* addressed a major East European taboo—namely the life of the proletariat under its official dictatorship. Marika's factory Communist Youth Organization (KISZ) leadership perfunctorily tries to save her job by forging a doctor's certificate to explain her repeated absences. ("I did a lot of shirking for your sake," she reminds the KISZ committee.) Meanwhile, practical Agnes brings her foreman home to bed one night and is soon decorated as a "distinguished" worker.

In a nightmare out of Makavejev's *WR*, the bosses regulate the workers' sex lives. When Marika gets a job cleaning house for her lover's employer, the boss orders an end to their affair. In the film's hyperbolic instance of worker revolt, the enraged girl smashes up her new employer's lavish apartment, complete with *Playboy* calendar in the kitchen. Of course, Marika is as devoid of political consciousness as her mother-in-law, and just as emotionally starved. She becomes pregnant, spontaneously aborting the fetus; this miscarriage is the most devastating scene in the movie, particularly as it come back in a dream.

Marika wages war against Agnes and her fate until she is exhausted. By the time the two women come to terms—Marika ultimately takes a job docilely packing pharmaceuticals opposite Agnes—the viewer has come to appreciate the meshing of needs that underlies their mutual security pact. Hungary is landlocked, and so the notion of Joseph sailing the sea is at once poignant and metaphorically suggestive. If women define the limits of working-class expression, Joseph's presumed freedom casts an almost mystical spell over their lives. The film is about loneliness and yearning and the compromises one makes with social necessity.

There may be no choice other than accommodation, but things could be worse, and they have been. A framed photograph of the title character—uniformed and smiling, a ridiculously boyish signifier of patriarchal order—presides over the living room like a Stalinist icon. When Joseph returns, indeed.

22. *RED DAWN* (John Milius, U.S.A., 1984)

Made for 1984, John Milius's *Red Dawn* is the quintessential cine-celebration of Cold War II. Indeed, it was while *Red Dawn* was in release that Ronald Reagan delivered his infamous sound check: "My fellow Americans. I'm pleased to tell you today that I've signed legislation that will outlaw the Soviet Union forever. We begin bombing in five minutes."[76]

No less than the president's gag, *Red Dawn* has a half-intended camp quality that belies its macho posturing. Given the premise—a Soviet invasion of the United States stopped cold by eight teenage guerrilla fighters in the Colorado Rockies—one wonders if the film's real audience wasn't so much the Middle America that Milius purported to celebrate as the aging hippies and limousine liberals of the film industry. Who else but some UCLA-educated nuclear-freezenik was likely to notice that *Red Dawn* opens in the clouds like *Triumph of the Will,* or that, after the Russian takeover, Sergei Eisenstein's 1938 nationalist epic *Alexander Nevsky* is playing at the local bijou (for free, yet)?[77]

After a terse title card announcing the escalating world crisis, *Red Dawn* gets down to business, with Russian, Cuban, and Nicaraguan (!) paratroopers descending on the postcard-pretty Colorado town. "Wow, check it out," an excited high schooler exclaims as bursts of machine-gun fire send his classmates scrambling for their cars. This classic propaganda opening—during which a half dozen boys spend a brisk twenty minutes eluding Russian tanks—is as mindlessly exciting as any of the chases in *Indiana Jones and the Temple of Doom* (1984). But once the boys make the mountains, *Red Dawn* turns turgidly didactic: The high school quarterback handily deposes the sniveling class president as undisputed führer of this newly constituted militia (named the Wolverines, after their football team), and immediately begins instructing his followers in the drinking of deer blood and other fine points of survivalist lore.

Avenging the fatherland is literalized when the Russians execute the quarterback's own dad (Harry Dean Stanton) as he defiantly sings "God Bless America," while several forays into town reveal the horrors of a Soviet America—the drive-in transformed into a reeducation camp, posters of Lenin on Main Street, police spies and Cubans everywhere. On one such trip, the boys even meet some girls: "I got some heirlooms I want to hide with you," old Ben Johnson chuckles, unveiling a pair of virginal cuties. "Them sons of bitches tried to have their way with them," he explains, coyly adding, "I don't even want to know where you're going." Sounds like an invitation to an orgy in the woods; but as it turns out, the girls are two tough little Valkyries—chaste warriors and not cheerleaders.

Somewhat more exotic—at least, coming from an ostensible right-winger like Milius—is the identification of these American insurgents with various Third World liberation struggles. Milius is in love with the idea of guerrilla warfare (in theory, anyway; asthma kept him out of the army), right down to its fashion accessories. By the end of the movie, his heroic quarterback is even wearing a homemade burnoose. Huge chunks of *Red Dawn* are reversals of scenes from *Apocalypse Now* (1979)—the labor of love that Milius turned over to Francis Ford Coppola—with Americans enacting the role of Vietcong partisans, and Cubans and Russians playing the part of American invaders.[78]

While the Russians compare Colorado to Afghanistan, the Cubans—whom Milius sees purely as guerrillas—are less at ease in their imperial role, not to mention depressed by the frigid *yanqui* winter. By the end, the film's main Cuban (Ron "Superfly" O'Neal) is so taken with the gutsy

Wolverines that he actually gives them his blessing: "*Vaya con Dios.*" (Proof that he's really a liberal wimp: Imagine a Green Beret similarly saluting some black-pajamaed Vietcong.) This identification ultimately poses a contradiction that Milius can resolve only in territorial terms. After the Wolverines summarily execute a traitor in their ranks, one of the more timid boys asks the quarterback, "What's the difference between them and us?" "We live here" is the reply.

Although, *Nevsky* in a nutshell, the notion of America for Americans is about as subtle as *Red Dawn*'s politics ever get, the movie's explanation for what got the United States into this pickle is steeped in a right-wing paranoia more xenophobic than anti-Communist. Rather than blaming insufficient defense spending, *Red Dawn* invents a new form of sneak attack. In this grim extrapolation of the survivalist worldview, the Soviets are starving for want of American grain. The initial invasion force came disguised as commerical airliners—an armada of Aeroflot planes stacked up over New York's JFK International Airport. This is followed by a few "selective nuclear strikes." The coup de grâce, however, has been the years and years of illegal infiltration from Mexico—the wetback Commies have even managed to insinuate themselves into military installations, thus providing the filmmaker with a means to deny the existence of nuclear weapons and indulge his yearning for conventional warfare.

Some thirteen years after *Red Dawn*'s release, *Variety* editor Peter Bart attributed this back story to the influence of Reagan's newly resigned secretary of defense, Alexander Haig. According to Bart, a former MGM/United Artists senior vice president for production, the studio's then chief executive officer Frank Yablans enlisted Haig as a consultant to the project. "Yablans declared in no uncertain terms that he wanted to make the ultimate jingoistic movie and that Al Haig would take him there."[79]

There is a sense in which *Red Dawn* is a less imaginative version of Joe Dante's *Gremlins*—another desecration of Main Street by some uncouth foreign invader, released in Reagan's America during the summer of 1984. Like the gremlins, the Russians are often figures of fun, and in both films, interestingly enough, the first casualty of the enemy invasion is a black schoolteacher. The difference is that *Gremlins* offers some hint that the monsters come from us, while *Red Dawn* blithely projects its own hostile impulses onto others.

23. *THE OAK* (Lucian Pintilie, Romania, 1992)

As it would be difficult to exaggerate the catastrophic combination of brutality, deprivation, and official stupidity that constituted daily life under the dictatorship of Romania's grotesque Communist *ubu roi* Nicolae Ceauşescu, one has to wonder if Lucian Pintilie's *The Oak* isn't a bit understated—at least, in Romanian terms. By any other, this relentlessly bleak farce is a movie of imaginative hysteria that rattles with sustained fury. Blink, and you miss something outrageous.

Set in the final year of Ceauşescu's rule, *The Oak* begins in the land of allegory. Pintilie's handheld camera swooshes through an overgrown Bucharest housing project to find the inhabitants of one particularly filthy sty watching 8mm home movies of some Christmas past. The projected image—a little girl unmasking the *Securitate* man dressed as Santa and grabbing his gun so that she can pretend to shoot the jovial bigwigs at a power-elite holiday party—is flanked by all manner of domestic detritus (smashed model airplanes, overflowing ashtrays, stained volumes of Marx).

The child in the home movie has apparently grown into the fabulously unkempt Nela, electrifyingly played by Romanian stage actress Maia Morgenstern. A rangy, angular presence whose austere facade belies a seemingly limitless capacity for jagged, impulsive behavior, Morgenstern appears first as a gorgeous hag. Stooped and dissolute, she lurches around the apartment, smoking, sniffling, and fussing over her decrepit father—a veteran Communist and Securitate (State Security) colonel. The old man dies (spilling his milk), the projector topples. Childhood ends, and Nela, the literal offspring of the regime, leaves its fetid cloister.

Out in the world, Nela first attempts to donate her father's organs to science, only to be told that "it's not bodies we lack, it's refrigerators." (She settles for an official cremation, which she alone attends, storing the old man's ashes in a jar of Nescafé.) Her education continues apace when she's appointed to a teaching position in the provincial town of Copsa Mica. Her first train has to be evacuated when the bridge floods out. Dropped in the river and taunted by a rowdy crowd, she's transferred to another train just before a mob of besotted miners shove on board, punching passengers out of their way.

Welcome to People's Romania. Nela arrives at the grim factory nexus of Copsa Mica. ("If we respected European pollution standards, we'd have to evacuate the city," she's later told). There, insulated but marked by her shades and Walkman headset, she's spotted, grabbed, and gang-raped by a gaggle of grinning workers. After a fruitless struggle, a point-less police interrogation, and a ferociously doomed attempt to purchase a sausage in the local market, Nela is dumped in a hospital that doubles as a charnel house. The bed she's assigned has no mattress. Nela bounces down on the springs; the woman she displaces goes and sits on the floor.

In the hospital, Nela meets the trim and crazy Dr. Mitica, another maniacal trickster who grins with pain, eschews bribes, and is obsessed with saving the life of the Christlike patient whom the authorities wish to let die. Both constantly talking, Nela and Mitica take up with each other without any preliminaries. They're kindred spirits, a Dada couple in a dangerously absurd world. Compared to them, the people are a total rabble—Pintilie appears to be an eccentric sort of right-wing anarchist—and as a love story, *The Oak* suggests a comic nightmare version of *The Fountainhead*. Mitica attacks his superiors and gets himself arrested, but because he's the best surgeon in the hospital, they're compelled to retry his case—while he's asleep—and let him go.

The world runs on booze and drunken resentment; the narrative is a succession of little shocks. When Nela can't swallow her pills—the tap isn't even dribbling its usual brown sludge—she downs the contents of a handy vase. An argument in a moving car is unexpectedly punctuated when an irate pedestrian flings himself on the windshield. Pintilie rou-tinely places the camera inside a crematorium or rubs the viewer's nose in a spinning propeller. When Nela is detained for protesting Mitica's arrest, the first jet of water from the Securitate fire hose is directed at the audi-ence. This dramatic tumult is underscored by a backbeat of calculated mismatches, the time of day shifting drastically within a single scene. Nela and Mitica are out camping in a meadow when suddenly night falls, bombs drop, and paratroopers descend.

As breathless as the fiddle break in a Romanian *doina*, *The Oak* swirls around one time too many before ending, almost anticlimactically, with the greatest atrocity of all: The leitmotiv of damaged children peaks when a group of terrorists take a school bus hostage. But the carnage unleashed (apparently by Ceausescu's order) is curiously calming. By then, we're too jaded to care—which may be precisely Pintilie's point. The last image is the norm—a gun pointed at the audience.

24. *GARDEN OF THE SCORPIONS* (Oleg Kovalov, Russia, 1991)

Legend has it that Soviet montage was the fruit of experiments in editing, dictated by a postrevolutionary combination of material shortage and—particularly in the case of imported movies—ideological deficiency. Thus, reediting preexisting footage became a Soviet art form: Esther Shub assembled the first compilation documentary in 1926, the same year that newsreel images of American stars Douglas Fairbanks and Mary Pickford were appropriated to star in a Soviet comedy.

With *Garden of the Scorpions*, Soviet cinema comes full circle. The movie is a return to the Brave New World of the 1920s, even as it reinterprets the post-Stalinist 1950s for the post-Soviet 1990s. This self-identified "optical poem"—the first feature by Oleg Kovalov, a film critic from the former Leningrad—mixes and matches archival footage against the solemn, triumphalist themes of Shostakovich, Bartók, and Nino Rota, sifting through the rubble of official truth and reassembling the facts with a distinctively Russian sense of grandiosity and disorder.

Opening with a newsreel of a 1959 political rally (marching formations, ecstatic spectators, a parade that celebrates Soviet cinema with a float of the battleship *Potemkin*), *Garden of Scorpions* segues—or rather, disintegrates—into a documentary on the treatment of alcoholism. The hypnosis applied to one patient then serves to trigger episodes from the 1955 movie *The Case of Corporal Kotchetkov*, starring the very same actor. A cautionary analogue to Republic's *Red Menace*, commissioned by the Ministry of Defense and directed by Alexander Razumny (a filmmaker who was cranking out politically correct comedies in the early 1920s), *The Case of Corporal Kotchetkov* concerns a naive Soviet soldier seduced by a CIA-supported foreign spy.

Kovalov annotates the burgeoning of a chaste and patriotic romance between the innocent Kotchetkov and a deceptively wholesome Comrade Valya (who sells sundries from a kiosk located just beyond the military base): *The Case* is punctuated by clips from *Storm over Asia* (1928), from a study film on the classic Socialist Realist novel *How the Steel Was Tempered*, and from an inexplicable movie of toddlers striking poses on a turntable and kissing the Soviet flag. Any given montage sequence might be bracketed by shots of glowering "Corporal Kotchetkov" in hospital pajamas, as if to suggest that, like *The Cabinet of Dr. Caligari*, it's all in the mind of a mental patient. Describing his methodology for a German audience, Kovalov cited the so-called Kuleshov effect—the notion that in cinema, context is everything. An individual shot has no fixed meaning; its significance is a factor of the shots that precede and follow it.

Although Kovalov's rules seem inconsistent and his editing can be slack, *Garden of the Scorpions* sets up an intricate system of associations. Footage alternately coalesces into narrative and dissolves into a montage of discrete attractions. Valya and her genial grandmother stuff Corporal Kotchetkov with food; the girl then strums her guitar as the corporal sings patriotic folk songs, which blossom into a vision of official parades in Red Square. When, after a subsequent meal (or maybe the same one), the baffled corporal develops food poisoning, the movie bursts into a queasily colored hallucination of Western "decadence"—Times Square, *Jailhouse Rock*, Marilyn Monroe singing "Heat Wave"—and then schmoozing with Khrushchev on his 1959 visit to Hollywood.

Much of *Garden of the Scorpions* consists of comic vaudeville turns: It's a "Red" Sullivan Show. A big band celebrates those romantic Odessa nights. Athletes parade for the 1956 Spartakiade. Sergei Eisenstein clowns in the guise of a British bobby. Giulietta Masina flits by, dewy-eyed. A chorus of North Korean schoolchildren perform Russian folk songs. The most extensive performance belongs to the young Yves Montand, who appears on stage in the jaunty persona of a Citroen mechanic while wife Simone Signoret gazes adoringly from backstage. That Montand and Signoret were among the first Western European celebrities to visit Moscow after the 1956 invasion of Hungary is underscored by an abrupt cut to Budapest.[80]

Throughout, Kovalov interpolates bits of the natural world (Gila monsters, constellations, desert landscapes), as if to locate these disconnected shards of Soviet social reality in some organic context. Valya picks up a book; rather than of Marx and Engels, the interpolated illustrations are of dinosaurs, perhaps the same monsters whose bones we later see scientists excavate. In its intermittent sense of capricious, pseudofactual filmmaking, *Garden of the Scorpions* suggests Buñuel and Dalí's *L'Age d'or* (which initially posed as a documentary on scorpions) even more than it does our own 1950s compilation *Atomic Café* or even *WR*.

When Montand and Signoret's tour of the Soviet capital is intercut with the obvious miniatures representing Alexander Medvedkin's 1938 dream of the "new" Moscow, or when a boat filled with heedless jitterbuggers seems to cruise past a statue of Stalin, Kovalov effects a form of socialist surrealism. Meret Oppenheim's fur-lined teacup and Man Ray's cosmological eye are insinuated into the montage—the latter when Corporal Kotchetkov is picked up and interrogated as a traitor by a sleazy KGB operative, who informs him that Valya and her grandmother are a "nest of spies" but who subsequently turns out himself to be a double agent . . . maybe.

In the end, the nest of spies is arrested, and happiness runs rampant. Montand sings "Autumn Leaves" as tanks roll toward Budapest. Full mobilization brings storms, explosions, disasters, earthquakes. Crowds scan the skies. Animated planes fly over the never-built Palace of the Soviets. A proletarian and a peasant strike a heroic *pas de deux;* another crew of workers resist a tank. Khrushchev rides a train through New York; Brezhnev applauds. Who the hell were these guys? Once again, the decomposition of Soviet reality takes a chunk of our own with it.

CHAPTER 7

KV ANIV. DEL ASESINATO DE LOS ESPOSOS ROSENBERG

13 CUBA aereo 1978

My Nuclear

Family

So, were Julius and Ethel Rosenberg framed? Don't let's all answer at once, now. The question isn't so much theoretical as theological; it's ultimately an article of faith. Anyway, most of America resolved the issue at the trial in March 1951. Ask anyone on Main Street if the Rosenbergs were framed. "The who?" they'll say. "The Rosicrucians?" Or "Are you kidding? Of course those Commies stole the secret of the atom bomb. Why do you ask?"

In Europe and elsewhere, it's been a different story. Back in the 1950s, the Poles were producing plays—in Polish *and* Yiddish—about Julius and Ethel; the Hungarians were renaming streets after the *Roszenberg Házaspár;* the French were making mass demonstrations, complete with petitions signed by Picasso and Sartre. Well into the 1970s, Cuba issued a postage stamp to commemorate the twenty-fifth anniversary of the Rosenberg execution.

But in America, no one's thought too much about the Rosenbergs for quite a few years. That is, hardly anyone; for in America, thinking about the Rosenbergs was a question not just of religion but also of

---

This account of the October 1983 Town Hall debate between Walter and Miriam Schneir and Ronald Radosh and Joyce Milton was published in the January 31, 1984, issue of the *Village Voice* under the grandiose rubric "The Last Rosenberg Piece You'll Ever Have to Read." That wasn't true, of course. A dozen years later, with new material provided by both the CIA and several retired KGB operatives, the particulars of the case were still being debated. In 1990, I wrote another Rosenberg piece, imagining their trips to the New York World's Fair during the summer and fall of 1939. It was commissioned by *RAW* magazine—which ceased publication that year—and appears here for the first time.

neighborhood. And for the children of the Lower East Side, and their children and yea, unto their children's children, the memory of the Rosenbergs would burn like some perpetual *yahrtzeit* memorial candle above the tub in an Avenue B kitchen. Were the Rosenbergs framed? What, are you trying to tell me that they weren't?

In the last, desperate days of June 1953, the National Committee to Secure Justice in the Rosenberg Case opened its heart with an almost brutal honesty. "We Are Innocent!" their banners read. Not "they" but "we"—we who defend them, who identify with them. How many parents told their children, school kids like Michael and Robby Rosenberg, "Those people could have been us! Those boys—*they could be you!*"

That's not a nightmare you easily forget: Mommy and Daddy strapped in the electric chair because they voted for Henry Wallace or liked to hear Paul Robeson sing "Ballad for Americans." And so, one night on the eve of 1984, we gathered together at New York's Town Hall, where *The Nation* presented Walter and Miriam Schneir to defend once more the honor of the Rosenbergs in a debate with—playing for the *New Republic*—Ronald Radosh and Joyce Milton, hotshot authors of a new best-seller who used Freedom of Information Act access to FBI files to argue Julius's guilt.

The Schneirs seemed then to be in their fifties: He affected the sort of mustacheless beard worn by folk singers who favored hearty sea chanties, she exuded the brisk and smug enlightened professionalism of a high school guidance counselor. The first edition of their *Invitation to an Inquest* had appeared in 1966, and they had updated it periodically since then without budging an iota from their assumption of total Rosenberg innocence.[1]

Radosh and Milton were something else—a couple, to be sure, but not a real couple like Julius and Ethel or Walter and Miriam. Milton looked as though she might have been a toddler when the Rosenbergs got the chair. Radosh, by his own account, was a teenage Stalinoid in those days, and there was something weirdly familiar about him. With his thick glasses, smudgy mustache, and know-it-all attitude—good grief, he looked like Julius Rosenberg!

So it was a cold war family feud, institution against institution, true believer versus apostate. As for glamor: Brooklyn district attorney Elizabeth Holtzman was on hand to moderate, and the principals would reappear later with Ted Koppel on ABC's *Nightline*. Forty-third Street was filled with traffic. Young TV crews jostled aging West Side liberals. Rickety tables displaying the full range of sectarian literature monopolized the pavement in front of Town Hall—it was a reunion, like a SANE-sponsored peace march or a CORE-benefit hootenanny from twenty years before, except that now everyone was twenty years older (at least).

Yoo-hoo and kiss-kiss: We submerge ourselves and summon the ghosts. Irving Howe takes his seat in the orchestra, William Kunstler climbs up to the balcony (that's *The Nation*ville). I have the distinct sensation of being among my people, chosen or not, and Walter Schneir apparently agrees: "Friends, brothers and sisters," he portentously begins. But let's leave Walter for the moment and rehearse the Rosenberg story in its most elemental, horrifying form—the Gospel according to Walter and Miriam, one last time.

THE TRIAL OF JULIUS AND ETHEL R

> *It is wonderful in a way that two individuals did still count to so many people in a world as accustomed as ours to mass slaughter.*
>
> —Leslie Fiedler, "Afterthoughts on the Rosenbergs," *Encounter* (October 1953)

Someone must have denounced Julius Rosenberg, for without his having done anything wrong, he was arrested one fine June evening by the FBI.

The buzzer sounded just before the kids' bedtime. Julius opened the door, and a dozen men burst into the apartment. His wife, Ethel, was demanding to see a search warrant ("typical Communist remonstrance," the FBI report would comment) even as they snapped the cuffs on the thirty-two-year-old machine-shop owner and hustled him outside.[2]

"While Robby was asleep and I listened to *The Lone Ranger*," Michael, then seven, remembered, "the FBI came to our apartment to arrest our father." Bad guys were trying to frame the Lone Ranger by committing crimes with his trademark silver bullets. "Just as someone was exposing the fraud, an FBI man turned off the radio." Click—like that.[3]

A few agents remained to search the family's three-room, fifty-one-dollar-a-month, rent-controlled flat—a cramped elevator ride to the eleventh floor of Knickerbocker Village, east of Chinatown on Monroe Street. They found an old collection can labeled "Save a Republican Child, Volveremos, We Will Return! Joint Anti-Fascist Committee" and rattled it for silver bullets. The next time Julius or Ethel saw this ancient, prewar *pishke,* it had been transformed at the trial into Government Exhibit 27.

Yes, someone must have denounced Julius Rosenberg, and of course, someone did—namely, his twenty-eight-year-old brother-in-law and erstwhile business partner, David "Doovy" Greenglass. A former Young Communist, an ex-GI, and himself the father of two small children, Greenglass had already been visited twice that year by the FBI, once in connection with some stolen uranium and then again, six months later (alone at Rivington Street caring for the new baby, with wife Ruthie still hospitalized), in connection with the Secret of the Atom Bomb.

During this second interrogation, at something like two in the morning—infant squalling, kitchen a mess, whole cruddy apartment stale with cigarette smoke?—David Greenglass broke down and signed a confession. Five and a half years before, in January 1945, his brother-in-law, Julius, had given him an irregularly cut panel from a box of Jell-O. Six months after that, in Albuquerque, New Mexico, where David worked on an army base, a "friend" of Julius's showed up looking for information. Greenglass explained that he knew the guy was Julius's friend because the guy had the matching half of the Jell-O box panel. So Greenglass wrote out some classified information pertaining to the secret of the atom bomb. For this he admitted receiving five hundred dollars from Julius's friend, identified by the FBI as Soviet courier Harry Gold. (Gold had already confessed to receiving the money for this purpose from Anatoli A. Yakovkev, vice consul of the Soviet mission in New York.)

It was the crime of the century. When the FBI told Julius the charges against him, he laughed and called the story "fantastic," like something "my kids listen to on the radio."[4]

Of course—what didn't kids hear on the radio those days? After five years of uneasy peace, World War III had broken out in Asia. President Truman was calling up the reserves and asking Congress for $10 billion in armaments. Hearst columnist Westbrook Pegler advocated the death penalty for American Communists and their friends.[5]

Had world peace and American democracy ever seemed in greater jeopardy? On August 1, the U.S. Court of Appeals upheld the conviction of eleven officers of a legally constituted political party on charges of conspiring to teach and advocate the overthrow of the U.S. government. The next day it was announced that E. I. DuPont had received the contract to the produce the hydrogen bomb. Soon the newspapers were reporting a plan to equip New York City with bomb shelters at a cost of $450 million. Truman mobilized the marines on Monday, August 7. Thursday, he asked

Congress to grant him wide-ranging economic controls. Friday night, Julius heard over the prison radio that his Ethel had been arrested.

On August 11, twenty-five days into the unreality of their sundered life, Ethel Greenglass Rosenberg was summoned down to Foley Square to testify before a grand jury. As she left the courthouse to return home, she was taken into custody by FBI agents and charged, like her brother and husband, with a conspiracy to steal the secret of the atom bomb. Bail was set at $100,000. "I can still hear her on the telephone telling me she was under arrest," Michael would remember. "I have been told that my reaction was a heartrending scream which continued to give her nightmares for the rest of her life."[6]

Scarcely a day after splitting the Rosenberg family, the U.S. government began distributing detailed instructions for civilian defense in the advent of atomic war. "I try to think of the good, fine life we've led all these years and I am agonized with my longing to go on leading it," Ethel wrote Julius from the House of Detention.[7]

The conspiracy, meanwhile, was spreading. "Engineer Is Seized as Spy for Russian Ring," screamed the August 18 New York Times. "Deported by Mexico to Which He Is Believed to Have Gone to Get Passage to Soviet"—and, in smaller letters, "Fled Queens on June 21—Morton Sobell, Radar Expert Who Worked for Navy, Called a Friend of Rosenberg." In a parallel universe, Rosenberg doppelgängers Lona and Morris Cohen—he a veteran of the Abraham Lincoln Brigade, she a courier to the secret installations of New Mexico in August 1945—hurriedly left New York for Moscow.[8]

MacArthur invaded North Korea that autumn; the Chinese occupied Tibet. Over Truman's veto, Congress passed the Internal Security Act, which effectively transformed all American Communists into traitors. Puerto Rican nationalists attempted to assassinate the president, but he escaped to declare a state of national emergency that was still in effect several months later, when Julius, Ethel, and Morton Sobell went on trial.

On March 7, 1951—the same day that the House Un-American Activities Committee released a list of 624 subversive organizations—the state called its first witness. Max Elitcher, Morton Sobell's next-door neighbor—his friend since their days together at Stuyvesant, New York City's elite public high school—told an intricate, unverifiable tale implicating Sobell as a member of a Rosenberg spy ring. When cross-examined by the defense, however, the thirty-two-year-old engineer admitted that he had cooperated with the FBI because he faced a possible perjury rap for lying about a onetime political affiliation on a 1947 government loyalty oath. (During the trial, a thirty-two-year-old physicist named William Perl was arrested and charged with perjury for denying that he, like Elitcher, had known Morty and Julie at City College.)

Next, David Greenglass took the stand and repeated the Jell-O box story under oath. Elaborating on his brother-in-law's alleged espionage activities—and naming sister Ethel as the official spy ring typist—Greenglass (described in the press as a "smiling" witness) went so far as to maintain that, just before the arrests, Julius had offered him four thousand dollars to leave the country. Ruth Greenglass supported her husband's testimony but, under cross-examination, made it clear she felt that Julie actually owed them the money. Finally, pallid little Harry Gold—the mythomaniacal Philadelphia chemist who was a confessed and convicted Soviet courier—appeared to corroborate that he had paid David and Ruth Greenglass five hundred dollars for the secret of the atom bomb.

What was there to say? Julius could only deny all the fantastic activities that his in-laws and Max Elitcher had attributed to him. Yes, there had been a dispute over money. The business was doing badly, and David had been pressuring him for cash. David had even been making threats. Ethel agreed and delicately suggested that Ruth's nagging had probably driven her brother nuts (and even Ruthie had acknowledged Doovy's "tendency to hysteria.") Since nobody's testimony, however crazy, had linked Sobell to the secret of the atom bomb, he thought it best to keep quiet—particularly after witnessing the gusto with which the judge and prosecuting attorney interrogated Julius on the minutiae of his political beliefs and associations.

On March 28, 1951, the jury began its deliberations. On March 29—hours before Judy Holliday (who would later have to be cleared by the Senate Internal Security Committee) won an Oscar for her role in *Born Yesterday* (1950)—the Rosenbergs and Sobell were found guilty. Thirty-two years later in Town Hall, Walter Schneir is reminding everyone that the Rosenberg case came out of the most humongous investigation in FBI history. Did it represent American justice? "No! The conviction was unjust!" he suddenly shouts. (Smattering of applause, scattered cries of "Hear! Hear!") And *The Rosenberg File*, Schneir spits out contemptuously, this so-called definitive work by Ronald Radosh and Joyce Milton, is actually nothing less than the "second frame-up of Julius Rosenberg."

"You should have seen him at the School for Marxist Education," whispered the woman sitting next to me. "He held up the Radosh book and compared it to the Hitler Diaries!"

Hyperbole is crucial to the Rosenberg case. After deliberating over their crime for more than a week, Judge Irving R. Kaufman pronounced sentence. "I considered your crime worse than murder," he told the convicted couple.

> Your conduct in putting into the hands of the Russians the A-Bomb years before our best scientists predicted Russia would perfect the bomb has already caused, in my opinion, the Communist aggression in Korea, with the resultant casualties exceeding fifty thousand and who knows but that millions more of innocent people may pay the price of your treason.
>
> Indeed, by your betrayal you undoubtedly have altered the course of history to the disadvantage of our country. No one can say that we do not live in a constant state of tension. We have evidence of your treachery all around us every day—for the civilian defense activities throughout the nation are aimed at preparing us for an Atom Bomb Attack.[9]

Accordingly, Kaufman condemned the Rosenbergs to be fried in the electric chair until they were dead. If the evidence against Ethel was rather less than conclusive, there was one incontestable fact: She was the Bride of Rosenberg. (Morton Sobell could not be linked to the secret of the atom bomb; he received thirty years, with a recommendation against parole.) The only protests at the time came from the progressively enfeebled Yiddish press.[10]

But that was then. Back in the now of October 1983, Walter Schneir is just getting started. "Radish"—as he has named his opponent—has made "hundreds of errors," as well as several irregular citations. Some of the interviewed—including the Schneirs—are denying that they ever spoke to him at all. Others insist they have been wildly misquoted. Schneir produces what looks like a cheap (North?) Korean tape recorder. Brandishing it as though it were an accordion, he fumbles with the buttons and finally punches it on. Blast of static, and we hear his taped voice reading a passage from the book to some geezer. "Holy cow!" the geezer responds.

Eschewing the pulpit, Miriam takes up the argument. With preternatural calmness, she consults her notes and reminds us that it was Walter who, in 1957, broke the story about strontium 90 seeping into children's bones (children like me). "Our adversaries"—in contrast—"have revived the crude categories of cold war thinking," and this as we approach the year 1984. Miriam seems particularly anxious to clear the names of all the various City College of New York types—Joel Barr, William Perl, Al Sarant—whose names keep popping up in the Rosenberg's FBI file. (Only a few weeks before the debate, the *New York Times* reported that both Barr and Sarant had found their way to the Soviet Union.) These people, Miriam points out, are "suspects without crimes."

Suspects without crimes: It's an existential condition. And there's something about the Rosenberg case that you just can't get around. Julius and Ethel were Jews. So was Morton. So were David and Ruth and Max Elitcher (and Joel Barr and William Perl) and even Harry Gold. Of course, the defense attorneys were Jewish, but the prosecuting attorneys—Irving Saypol and the evil mastermind Roy Cohn—were also Jews. And the judge. Kaufman all but called Julius and Ethel the worst Jews who ever lived. They'd already been responsible for fifty thousand casualties "and who knows but that millions more . . ." In fact, the only place in the courtroom where you couldn't find a Jew was in the jury box. That made things a lot easier. Jury foreman Vincent Labonitte would remember feeling good that the trial was "a strictly Jewish show." "It was Jew against Jew," Labonitte recalled. "It wasn't the Christians hanging the Jews."[11]

So there was no one on the jury to explain how bad debts and family quarrels and City College in 1939 and the Lower East Side, just a few blocks from the courthouse, had all gotten mixed up with the secret of the atom bomb. "The great United States is proposing the savage destruction of a small, unoffending Jewish family," Ethel wailed from the death house. "A small, unoffending Jewish family whose guilt is seriously doubted throughout the length and breadth of the civilized world!" A Rosenberg Internationale! But was the whole world crying—or was it only People's Poland, the Left Bank, and Knickerbocker Village?—when, just before sundown on a *shabbes* in June (my sister's first birthday), the Rosenbergs went to their deaths.[12]

A few weeks later, Michael and Robert Rosenberg—ages ten and six—received an anonymous postcard. "Of course, you feel sorry for the loss of your parents," the note read. "But when you think of all the boys they killed in Korea, you should realize they deserved to die. Why don't you change your names and become Christians?"[13]

THE MOM-AND-POP FRONT

"Isaac—listen to me, for a Jewish pois'n dis is de greatest country vat ever vas, in de history of de voild!"

"Sure it is, Dad," said the contemptuous son, "as long as he plays the game their way."

—Philip Roth, *The Great American Novel* (1973)

A footnote in Michael and Robert's 1975 autobiography, *We Are Your Sons*, concludes that their parents "probably were members of the American Communist Party."[14]

If this footnote didn't exist, don't you think the Schneirs would be denying it still? The kids decided that, after all these years, maybe it was safe finally to say what Julius and Ethel had stubbornly refused to admit on the witness stand. Yes, they were Communists. But is it ever safe to confess one's communism under the regime of the bourgeoisie?

At Town Hall, the Schneirs have finished their opening remarks. It's time to hear testimony from that other couple—the in-laws, er, I mean, Ronald and Joyce. Ronald, we sense, is a seasoned pro at left-wing internecine vituperation. But Joyce doesn't seem to understand. She must be a neophyte. She's actually stung by Miriam's characterization of her book as "tawdry and ridiculous," "a mean-spirited historical hoax masquerading as scholarship." Joyce feels compelled to remind the Schneirs that *The Rosenberg File* is "no love letter to the government."

Joyce is obviously exasperated. Masquerading as scholarship, indeed! Look who's talking! That sanctimonious Miriam should only choke! Does the woman have no shame? Really! As, Joyce points out, even Morton Sobell has told the *New York Times* he would "quote, not take the position they"—Julius and Ethel Rosenberg—"were completely innocent." From the floor, up front, a staccato: "It's a lie!"

Here we go again. Because, after all, what does Joyce know anyhow? Was *she* at City College in 1936? Does she understand that, once upon a time, there were New York City neighborhoods where you could grow up poor and half-American and feel something like the revolution just around the corner? Does she know that? Does she care that, once upon a time, there were liberated zones in Williamsburg and Brownsville, in Red Hook and Harlem (which, like Brooklyn, kept sending a Communist to the city council), and up on Allerton Avenue in the Bronx? And what does she know from the Lower East Side, where Julius and Ethel came of age in the depths of the depression and Communists swam like fish through a rancid sea of misery? Yes, Communists—flaming red Communists—were as familiar to the area's quarter-million tenement-packed Jews as their *rebbes, gonifs,* and sewing-machine operators?

In the midst of chaos, the Communists embodied social cohesion— martial optimism. They were out there organizing youth clubs and co-ops, health plans and summer camps, strikes and dances. They were influential in the local Democratic machine; by 1937, they were supporting President Roosevelt. The Communists were Jews with ideas among Jews without money, offering a New Deal all their own, and they could conjure up the workers' paradise with a nostalgia so visceral that, if you were a child raised by a Communist family or in a Communist building or a Communist neighborhood, you might well believe that everyone in the Soviet Union was a Jew like you. And if you were a street kid like Doovy Greenglass, you, too, might have joined the Young Communist League, because you liked the handball there or a girl invited you to.

Ethel and Doovy grew up east of Pitt Street, off Delancey, a block from the live-chicken market beneath the grimy rattle of the Williamsburg Bridge. They lived in a coal-stove hovel behind their immigrant father's secondhand sewing-machine shop. Prostitutes frequented their building. A stable full of reeking pushcarts was located next door.

Skipping grades to finish high school (against the wishes of her illiterate mother), Ethel went to work at fifteen, organizing her shop by day, singing at the Loew's Delancey on amateur nights. She helped lead a strike at nineteen, and three years later, on the last night of 1936—after performing an aria from *Madame Butterfly* at a benefit in Lavanburg Homes (an ancient modern housing project, still tucked in the armpit of Houston Street and the East River Drive)—she met eighteen-and-a-half-year-old Julie Rosenberg. Soon they were inseparable, holding hands at anti-Hitler rallies and meetings to aid the Spanish Republic.

Julie's father—a sample maker from Russian Poland—had hoped that his studious son might become a rabbi. For a few years after his bar mitzvah, Julie studied Torah like a madman, sometimes four or five hours a day. Then, at fifteen, he discovered politics at a "Free Tom Mooney" demonstration on Delancey Street: his fate. Up at City College, Julius was part of the Young Communist League (YCL) crowd that swelled the dank cafeteria's Alcove Two. There were hundreds of Young Communists in those days. YCLers even commandeered the college newspaper to editorialize in favor of the Moscow Trials. True, the Tech that Julie attended was not a hotbed of radicalism like the School of Arts and Sciences across the street, but Rosenberg grasped the dogma and he was totally committed, an organizer for the American Students Union as well as an indomitable leafleter.

Julie's particular gang was called the Steinmetz Club. Named for a socialist engineer at General Electric, it was loosely affiliated with the YCL. Members included William Perl, Joel Barr, Morton Sobell, maybe Max Elitcher, and certainly someone reporting to the NYPD Red Squad. They were almost all guys from the Tech. Irving Howe, who showed up at the School of Arts and Sciences during Julie's junior year and who hung out in Alcove One with the ultras and the socialists, the Trots and the Lovestonites, dismissed the Stalinist engineering students as "hopeless careerists." And in a sense, he was right.[15]

In 1939, the year Julius Rosenberg received his engineer's degree from City College, the American Communist Party and YCL had a combined national membership of nearly one hundred thousand. The party was strong in New York and California, Chicago and Detroit; it was in tight with the United Electrical and Machine Workers, the International Longshoremen, the National Maritime Guild, the International Woodworkers, the Mine, Mill and Smelter Workers, the Fur and Leather Workers, the Transport Workers Union, the United Auto Workers, the American Federation of Teachers, District 65, and the American Labor Party.

America was in isolation, but the party was in the world, and the world, as Julie's father might have said, was falling apart like a badly made shirt. Here and in Europe, the options were apparent—it was socialism or barbarism. The Communists spoke out when Hitler occupied the Rhineland and annexed Austria. Jews were exiting Central Europe as best they could when, during the summer of 1938, England and France spurned the pleas of the Soviet Union and handed faraway Czechoslovakia to Hitler on a plate: Munich.

April 2, 1939, the Spanish Republic, likewise abandoned by the bourgeois democracies, capitulated to the Fascists. A thousand American Communists (how many from the Bronx?) had died in its defense.

MIDNIGHT IN THE CENTURY: A DREAM RECONSTRUCTION

Like some rattling cyclone, the New York IRT swoops you up and flies over the rooftops of Corona—twenty-four minutes from black-and-white Grand Central to the brand-new technicolor elevated station at Willets Point. Julius is sleepy. He was out late with his friends Marcus and Stella seeing *Confessions of a Nazi Spy*—a really courageous picture in which the anti-Fascist material struggle is vividly portrayed.

"The movie fails to expose the association between Nazism and international finance capital," Julius tells Ethel. "Still, it must receive our support." In his mind, he is composing a letter of congratulation to the Warner Brothers: "Last night I learned why crowds are cheering *Confessions of a Nazi Spy*. I never realized how much of a menace fascism was until I saw this picture. *Confessions of a Nazi Spy* may not be 'artistic' enough to satisfy Mr. Frank S. Nugent of *The New York Times* but it hits home to the millions of working people who are the ultimate defenders of democracy. P.S. *Juarez* is one of the grandest movies ever made."

Ethel is amused to see someone in the car reading last week's *Life*, the May 22 issue with World's Fair girl guide Barbara Wall on the cover—shoulders back, chin up, looking down her teensy-weensy nose with weirdly unfocused eyes. Miss Wall Street (as Ethel thinks of her) is a native New Yorker, twenty-one years old—the same age as Julius—who earns twenty-five dollars a week guiding the masses around the fair, and who got the job because she is presentable, healthy, courteous; has good diction; can act enthusiastic; and (Ethel understands) is not even remotely Jewish. Ethel knows all about Barbara Wall, because the same issue of *Life* reported the recent YCL convention in the stupidest possible terms—a photo spread titled "Earl Browder Scowls at Young Jitterbugs: Young Communists 'Get in Groove' at Party Rally."[16]

In fact, Comrade B.'s keynote address, "Reshaping the World of Today, Building the World of Tomorrow," had outlined precisely what had to be done to insure a progressive New Deal victory in 1940. Comrade F. called 1940 the most important election in U.S. history and pointed out that the Republicans were taking their cues from Hitler and Mussolini. Then, Comrade Carl R. made Madison Square Garden ring with a frenzy of enthusiasm when he announced that job security for youth was at the heart of the

YCL. Still, all *Life* could find to report on was the "Swing America" revue, once known as "Shirley Temple Is a Red."

Suddenly the train dips, and the passengers are on their feet. Mad surge of excitement as the shimmering Flash Gordon skyline materializes. The subway doors open, and the crowd spills out onto a flag-lined overpass leading directly to the fairgrounds. Julius and Ethel are stunned by the curvilinear, streamlined forms, the fluorescent lighting, the fountains, the ramps, the rippling streamers, the murals celebrating science and democracy. Are they really in Queens? America? On planet Earth?

No swastika flies at the fair. The air is clean. And, perhaps just beyond the dazzling whiteness of the monstrous Trylon and Perisphere, lies the rising sun of socialism. What was it that Lenin said? Socialism peers at us through the windows of capitalism. "The fair expresses the staunch American belief in progress—the possibility of making life better for the average man," Julius finally hazards.

"Which is just what irritates the 'smart people' who don't like democracy at close range," Ethel adds.

"Yet the fair is marred by the blemish of discrimination against the Negro," Julius is musing. "The officials of the World's Fair carry out the policy of the ruling class by employing Negroes as maids and porters."

"And why must the common people wait to enjoy these wonders of economic ease, these lovely homes and golden gardens?" Ethel wonders as they stroll past the Town of Tomorrow—housing project home of my childhood!

Julius smiles: "The fact that these inventions are in the hands of Wall Street monopoly, which not only keeps their prices up but which drains the people of the buying power with which to buy, dramatizes the great truth of our time—that society has long since reached the stage of industrial development when poverty, insecurity, and hunger could be banished from the face of the earth."

Julius and Ethel pick their way through the fields of outsize white statues, past the Fountain of the Atom, the Electrified Farm, the Lagoon of Nations. They cross over to the RCA building to admire Louis Ferstadt's mural. ("He draws Sir Hocus Pocus for the *Sunday Worker,*" Julius tells Ethel.)

Airplanes above, smell of hotdogs below. The Rosenbergs take a look at President Roosevelt on the tiny screen of the huge wooden Tele-Vision and then go into the AT&T building, where they line up to listen in on across-the-continent telephone conversations. "If the telephone monopolies would reduce their rates, we might have a telephone in our home, and so could millions of other Americans," Ethel remarks sweetly, and just loud enough for the people behind her to hear.

The highlight of the day is at hand. "Get a load of this." Julius thinks he hears the crowd and even the breeze murmuring as he and Ethel gaze up the huge shaft at the fearless figure thrusting skyward his bright red star of Communism—its ruby glow a beacon to all the world's nations. At last, Julius understands just why the reactionaries are so sore.

The heroic statue of the Soviet Citizen ("Teddy," the *Daily* calls him) rules this landscape, looming over the Court of States, just across the avenue from the proud replica of Philadelphia's Independence Hall. Coincidence? Hardly. "There is historic significance in this close tie between our country and the Soviet Union," Julius tells Ethel. She smiles. She is humming:

> *Hugs and kisses are the fashion*
> *But a steak must feed your passion*
> *You can't live on love. . . .*
> *You've got to keep that big bad wolf away from*
> *   your door*
> *Before he gets chummy.*
> *You've got to dig up three square meals a day*
> *'Cause you can't make love on an empty tummy.*

Oh, round, radiant Ethel in your cheap summer dress, there is historic significance between my thigh and your round tummy, between your country and our Soviet Union!

THE RADIANT FUTURE

> **W**hoever has lived for the future and has fallen for its beauty is a
> figure hewn in stone.
>
> —Julius Fučík (September 8, 1943)

Intimations of paradise: An elderly man proclaims it "the greatest thing I've ever seen." Children watch him smooth his calloused palm across the glittering wall. "He don't look like no 'red,'" says little Johnny Meegan of the Metropolitan Vocational School. "I am no 'red,'" the old man affirms, "I am a bluestone expert, twenty years in the business. I know my granite."

A short, fussy fellow overhears the bluestone expert and trots back to his family: "Genuine marble," he announces. They nod in mute assent, as if on cue. "Cost six million bucks," a strolling sailor informs his girl. Three teenagers pass by and raise clenched fists. Marble. Granite. Cement. The Iron Flood. The sun glints off Teddy's red star. So this is How the Steel Was Tempered, Julius thinks. Time, forward. The Soviet Pavilion here is twice as big as the pavilion at the 1937 Paris expo. "The most magnificent thing I ever saw in my life," says a solidly built man, well dressed and prosperous, looking straight at Julius.

Two proud red flags, two shining halls, two heroic steel statues, two great reliefs, ten mighty words carved in stone: "For the USSR, Socialism Is Something Already Achieved and Won." Inside, Julius and Ethel are welcomed by the mammoth group portrait of fifty Soviet notables, a gay crowd in Technicolor summer clothes, striding together out from the Gorky Park of Culture and Recreation. (Among them: S. M. Mikhoels, Alexei Tolstoy, Alexei Stakhanov, aviatrix Valentina Grizodubova, thirteen-year-old Pioneer Lesha Fadiev, and, clutching a bouquet against the bodice of her red dress, subway builder Tatiana Fedorovna.)

In the vaulted Main Hall are the huge paintings of Bloody Sunday, Lenin in Petrograd, and the Defense of Tsaritsyn, not to mention the thirty-foot-by-twenty-two-foot marble map of the entire Soviet Union, adorned with diamond letters and precious stones. (Moscow is a ruby star—but where is Birobidzhan?) "Imagine peering down at the whole immense country from the height of an unimaginable stratosphere," someone dreamily recites.

Set before yet another gigantic mural—Yuri Pimenov's ecstatic, festive, and joyous *Sports Parade*—is the marble-and-steel model of Palace of the Soviets, which, when completed in 1942, will be the world's tallest building. Photographs everywhere—so colorful and true—with movies shown in the pavilion ampitheater. Julius and Ethel hear a staccato burst of applause. Looking over, they see that the members of the Soviet government, including Comrade S. himself, have just flashed on the screen.

The murals depicting the system of free maternity centers, the photographs of smiling young doctors and laughing children, exude such health that Ethel wants to cry. Bursting with giddy warmth, she smiles at a man in overalls, one of the sturdy trade unionists clustered around the aluminum diorama of Magnitogorsk as it appeared, appears, and will appear after the First, Second, and Third Five-Year Plans. And Julius makes a beeline for a pretty Russian girl guide and learns plenty about the All-Union Agricultural Exposition, set to open in Moscow on August 1, 1939.

"The Exposition is a comprehensive review of the Splendid Victories already gained as well as a School of Socialist Agricultural Production and Stakhanov methods of work," Natasha tells Julius, who has rakishly introduced himself as an ordinary Indiana potato farmer. "The Exposition grounds stretch over an area of 840 acres. Altogether, over two hundred beautiful new buildings have been erected, and over one thousand painters and sculptors are even now decorating them with socialist art." She graces farmer Julius with a practiced smile.

Socialist art? Natasha continues: "As the comrade visitor approaches the main entrance to the grounds, the first thing to strike the eye is an excellently executed statue of a man and a woman—an industrial worker and a member of a collective farm."

Despite the uninflected quality of Natasha's phonetic English, Julius feels as if he's hearing the story of the Garden of Eden. *Rusland iz a ganeydn* (Russia is a paradise). He imagines—or rather, I do—Ethel and himself as the forward-striding worker-peasant couple. Ethel waves goodbye to the trade unionist, sees Julius nodding sagely at the girl guide, and wonders what's up. Meanwhile, Natasha drones on: "Passing through the arch and following Tractor Avenue, the visitor will see a colossal structure. This is the Grain Pavilion, which will display each and every type of crop cultivated in the USSR."

Ethel walks over. She squeezes Julius's arm. He is transfixed. "One of many paths that radiate from Mechanization Square, the Path of Honor runs past two panoramas reproducing in the most scrupulously realistic detail the miserable village life of prerevolutionary days. Alongside this Square is a separate section consisting of pavilions given to the food industry—Tea, Canned Goods, Meat, Beer, and even Ice Cream."

Nastasha casts her benign gaze on Ethel. "Of these, the Mechanization Pavilion—made of concrete, glass, and steel and standing astride the Tractor Avenue—is the most impressive and original. It is 480 feet long and 103 feet wide and is capable of accommodating ten thousand visitors daily." (Ethel nods at Natasha and tugs Julius's sleeve. "Just a minute, Eth," he hisses without looking at her.)

"All the pavilions are equipped with special sound projectors that will demonstrate motion pictures on popular science, such as *The Golden Fleece*, a film about a combine-harvester operator and deputy to the Supreme Soviet, Alexander Oskin. Last year, the work accomplished by Oskin was equivalent to the work of, let us see"—Natasha wrinkles her brow prettily—"1,637 people, 373 horses, twenty-five reaping machines, twenty-five threshing machines, and forty grain sorters."

Julius feels as if he could listen forever to this charming recitation, but even as the astonishing statistics trip from the girl guide's tongue, a heavy-set joker rudely inquires if there really is electricity in Moscow. "I can assure you there is plenty—and not only there." Natasha's merry laugh is like a cascade of silver bells.

The whole pavilion chuckles for joy as, arm in arm, Julius and Ethel discover a full-size replica of the Mayakovsky Square station. "Let's go home, Julie," Ethel giggles, but the tall, slim lad doesn't hear her. "Don't you wish you had a subway like this to ride to work in?" he's shouting.

It is thrilling to mingle. Julius hasn't felt this powerful since May Day. He's sure that even the hostile few must be deeply impressed by the dignity, grandeur and sheer power of the Great Land of Socialism. Everywhere, he observes expressions of incredulity—pleased incredulity—on the faces of visitors. Suddenly, without pressure, without previous thoughts or emotions, men and women begin to discuss a new life, a new society: Can this be true? Do the workers really own this? How do they do it? All around him, Julius overhears expressions of envy mixed with democratic utterances and spontaneous spurts of hatred for anything—everything!—that would threaten this gigantic realm of wonders. ("Is this what Trotsky and Bukharin would destroy?" someone cries. "You do right by destroying them first!")

This is the real world of tomorrow—rated first among foreign pavilions, according to a recent Gallup poll reported by a newspaper clipping in Julius's wallet. "This amazing demonstration is a greater glimpse of the future than any jaunt into the Perisphere," Julius remarks loudly. ("Can you imagine the day when Delancey Street will look like this?" Ethel says dreamily. "We'll call it 'Dzerzhinsky Street,'" her husband riffs.) Reluctantly, the couple leave. In the shop, they purchase one Teddy pin with red flag, a red packet of postcards, and a copy of *The Stakhanovite Movement Explained,* by A. Stakhanov: scientific evidence, pure and simple.

Outside, in red letters large and strong: "Labor in the USSR Is a Matter of Honor, a Matter of Glory, a Matter of Valor and Heroism." An excited man with a wire around his broken jaw fondles his brace and painfully speaks: "My friends, those are the words of Christ. That is a true Christian motto, representing the only real Christian government in the world. I defy anyone to deny it." No one dares answer him.

A large family eyeballs the statue of Comrade S. They are lower-middle-class, decent folks, typical American citizens, Julius thinks. "And they's supposed to be dumb," the father exclaims, masticating each word. "It only goes to show that maybe some other folks are the dumb ones." Just then, a retired U.S. naval officer makes it to the top of the Life Saver parachute jump and unfurls an American flag. Ha! He's still nineteen feet lower than Teddy's red star.

By the time the All-Union Agricultural Exposition opens, Julius Rosenberg and Ethel Greenglass Rosenberg are sharing a four-room Williamsburg walk-up with another married couple we'll call Stella and Marcus P. Their name for this dump is "Brooklyngrad."

It's August, and the narrow streets stink of garbage; so does the tunnel-like floor-through when you finally crack open the soot-encrusted windows for a view of the back house. Julius finds himself daydreaming about the Lagoon of Nations. Reading the *Daily*, he notes that the YCL is sponsoring a Jitterfish Jamboree at the Lido Pool up near City College on 140th and Seventh Avenue. "Wanna go?" he asks Ethel without much hope.

The YCL has a summer plan. Take your mind off the thermometer, get into the swim of league activities: (1) Build a real mass peace movement around resistance to fascism; (2) Prepare for the 1939 councilmanic elections; (3) Enroll new members. (Get to know your neighbors well, they'll want to join the YCL.) August 8, 1939: Paid informer Miss S. Liggetts files a report with the FBI that two tenents in her building—Ethel R. and Stella P.—have signed petitions nominating Peter C., Communist candidate for Brooklyn councilman.

That night, Julius dreams he is wandering through the Entertainment Zone of the 1942 Rome World's Fair. The sidewalks are crowded, the air is heavy. In the distance, a gigantic cash register is balefully revolving. Julius finds himself heading east on along a fascist Delancey Street—babies exhibited in glass vitrines, an Eskimo girl leading a two-headed cow, midgets riding on elephants. *Luftmensh* barkers grab his sleeve. Miss S. Liggetts is trying to follow him, surreptitiously writing in her stenographer's notebook.

Julius is looking for Ethel. He turns down Sheriff Street. Is this really her home? The tenement facade is decorated with the heads and bodies of outlandish ocean creatures. The hallway is disgustingly coated with greenish seaweed. Julius experiences a sense of hideous desecration. He recognizes the *Mona Lisa* and a famous painting of a beautiful, long-limbed angel standing naked on a giant scallop shell: "For us, socialism is something already achieved and won." Rain is falling, and as the bricks decompose, the melted mortar distends into a wig of weird plaster pincers—the ruling claws, Julius thinks, and smiles in his dream.

Now, Julius feels himself sucked between the legs of a fantastic female sea monster toward a gaping fish mouth that's actually some sort of box office. His mother-in-law, Tessie, is inside. Her leer would embarrass an Allen Street madam. She sells him a ticket for twenty-five cents. The dank hallway smells like the public swimming pool. It's actually a giant tank filled with jitterfish. One is milking a mummified cow. Another has keys on her torso like a human piano. A dozen more are acting like secretaries, making calls on floating telephones. The jitterfish spot Julius. They wink. When he tries to speak, they swim off laughing.

What is the meaning of the limp watches, the mannequins with bird-cage bodies? Such heedless destruction of humanist consciousness has surely paved the way for Hitler. Julius collapses onto a strangely shaped red couch. "You haf seat upon ze leeps of Hrrreta Harrrrbo," says the effete little man beside him. Julius thinks of the dead Spanish Republic. Is this a cadaver from the battlefield Jarama? Or the gigolo from an Astaire-Rogers musical? "I am Dolly," the man announces. "Do you not like my Lee-quid Lay-deez?"

Then they're back on Delancey Street. Just as Julius remembers he was to meet Ethel for a "Free Tom Mooney" rally at Madison Square Garden, Dolly hands him a paper:

> If you wish to recover the sacred source of your own mythology and your own inspiration, the time has come to reunite yourself within the historical bowels of your Philadelphia, to ring once more the symbolic bell of your imaginative independence, and, holding aloft in one hand Charles Steinmetz's lightning rod and in the other Neville Chamberlain's umbrella, to defy the storm of obscurantism that is threatening your country! Loose the Blinding Lightning of your Anger and the Avenging Thunder of your PARANOIAC INSPIRATION!

Gaaah! Julius wakes up in the dark with a hard-on. Ethel is sleeping beside him. She is warm and flushed. Her hair is plastered to her forehead. Her nightie is hiked up above her waist.

Like Julius, Stella is a movie fan. And unlike Ethel, who went to work at the New York Packing and Shipping Company at age sixteen, Stella is a college girl from a petit-bourgeois home. So there's much serious discussion of the cinema at Brooklyngrad.

When Stella and Marcus finally visit the World of Tomorrow and the Soviet Pavilion in the crazy days of late August, Stella is disappointed to find the scheduled screening of *Professor Mamlock* canceled. Who cares about that stupid Ribbentrop-Molotov Pact? For a month she's been hearing Julius's kitchen-table impression of the scene where the ridiculously stubborn German doctor argues with his son Rolf. (The moment when Rolf tells his father, "Don't insult my friends—these people are giving their lives to make humanity happy!" was, of course, too moving for Julius to spoof.)

Julius loves to show how old Mamlock loses his temper and kicks Rolf out. "I dunt vant any Commoonisht in mine how-s-s-s-s!!!" Julius bellows in a Sig Rumann accent while gesturing like a robot, then explains how—once Rolf has gone underground with the leather-jacketed Anni—brownshirt thugs invade the clinic and force the dazed Mamlock to parade through the streets of Berlin wearing a sign reading "Jude."

Stella has endured many such outbursts herself over the past two years, albeit without the satisfaction of seeing her father, also a doctor, marched down Flatbush Avenue as a humiliated Jude. Having ignored *Professor Mamlock* during its lengthy (Jewish) neighborhood run, she looked forward to catching it in the more-inspiring precincts of the Soviet Pavilion—only to be confronted with an unspeakable stinker about a combine-harvester operator who becomes a deputy to the Supreme Soviet. And that's why she dragged Marcus to Radio City to see *The Wizard of Oz*—another movie about a child who leaves home. Julius is contemptuous. Kid stuff! Judy Garland? His secret preference, as Dolly had intuited, is Greta Garbo.

It's International Youth Day, and the YCL is holding a torchlight parade around the Lower East Side up to Union Square. On the subway, Stella is still chattering on about this ridiculous children's film. "Really, Julius. It's an excellent movie. It's only unfortunate that the social angle is so comparatively nil."

Marcus catches Julius's humorously quizzical expression and, afraid his Stella is babbling like an idiot, quickly elaborates a progressive interpretation. (No less than Julius, he is a product of the Downtown Talmud Torah). The Scarecrow and Tin Woodsman represent a nascent peasant-worker alliance. The cyclone is highly evocative of the depression. What's more, given characters like the phony Wizard and the Wicked Witch (who in her "real life" incarnation owns the entire town), the filmmakers are very close to a supersatire of Hitler, Franco, and Mussolini. "Exactly," Stella sighs. Nonsense, Julius thinks. Still, by now, even he and Ethel have begun to call the Munichmen "munchkins."

The rally staging area is Norfolk and Delancey. At first, Ethel is delighted to see a huge throng blocking the intersection. Then she realizes that a handful of YCLers are surrounded by a jeering crowd, mocking them with Yiddish curses and *sieg heil* salutes. Pushing her way through, Ethel picks up a sign reading "Full Diplomatic and Economic Aid to the Polish People and Their Friends!" Handing Julius an "Embargo Japan and Germany!" placard, she spots her kid brother Doovy sullenly leaning on a "Defeat Fascist Aggression! Establish a Democratic Peace!" sign. "Julie, explain it to him," Ethel pleads, pushing her husband into Doovy's field of vision.

Only seventeen, Doovy is confused. Doesn't Julie think that the Soviet Union should be fighting the Nazis on the side of Britain and France? Patiently, Julius points out that the Polish government had forbidden the Red Army to cross its borders to fight the Nazi aggressor, and that the British and French governments supported this stand. Confidently, he quotes Comrade S.'s warning against pulling imperialist chestnuts out of the fire. But Doovy still doesn't get it. What gives? Is Comrade S. afraid of a fight?

"Look, Doovy, it's very simple," Julius starts again, shouting a bit to be heard over the din. "All along, the British angle has been to just let Germany go on—take Austria, Czechoslovakia, Hungary, Romania. Take the Ukraine, why not! Their whole plan has been to push Germany against the Soviet Union. The entire world knows what took place at Munich, and the exact same thing would have happened again. Germany would have gotten Poland without firing a shot. This way, Hitler has to fight to get Poland, and so will England and France have to defend her in their interests."

Doovy seems perplexed. Unconsciously, he begins flailing his "Defeat Fascist Aggression!" sign. Julius understands that words are not enough. He imagines that he and Doovy are standing outside the Soviet Pavilion. "Go inside and see for yourself," Julius says. In his mind's eye, Julius watches the boy waddle off to gaze with fascination at the models of the Dnieper Dam and the Palace of the Soviets. As Doovy emerges, visibly moved, Julius frames his triumphant query: "So. Do you think they should keep on building socialism? Or should they go to war to pull those imperialist chestnuts out of the fire?"

"Let them keep building," the new Doovy says fervently. Except that back on Delancey Street, the old Doovy is whining about something he saw in the papers. Julius raises his hand as if to cuff the beefy, broad-faced lad, then—just like his old Hebrew teacher—smacks his own forehead instead. "Forget about it! Doovy: All the lying editorials in the *Herald-Tribune,* the *Times,* and the Hearst press are designed to hide the Soviet peace role from the masses. The capitalist papers and dollar-dominated radio work overtime to poison America's mind. They should be reminded that during the Munich affair, the Soviet Union was the only nation that said the so-called peace was not a peace—but rather, giving Germany a stronger hand with which to aggress against other nations."

Doovy flinches. His shirt is flecked with Julius's spittle. Still, the onslaught continues: "With one stroke of the pen, Doovy, the Soviet Union has undermined all the work done so diligently by the Munchkin Axis. History roars—objectively!—with the force of this shattering blow to the Fascist war-making forces. Let the reactionary wolves howl, let the deserters run for cover!" To his pleasure, Julius discovers that an approving crowd has gathered around him. Ethel beams. Marcus and Stella are open-mouthed. The heart of the revolutionary masses beats double time as Julius invents whole new categories of invective, denouncing the stinking cesspool of hideous lies, the malicious slander of the distortionist press and their Trotskyite-Lovestonite stooges.

"Unbreakable unity! The Soviet-German nonaggression pact has burst upon the war-mongering, profit-seeking monopolies and imperialist dreamers with blinding effect! The Tory fantasy of destroying the Soviet Union has turned into the nightmare of a fading dead star in the black horizon of imperialism!" The cretin wind is at Julius's back. "Doovy," he smiles, suddenly expansive. "There is a light across the earth today, and that light stems from the Soviet Union. None of the rotten ruling cliques or poison-mouthed enemies of the working class can ever extinguish its brightness."

The Red Army has returned Vilnius to Lithuania—or rather, to the new Soviet Socialist Republic of Lithuania. Throughout the ancient city, joyful demonstrations hail their liberation. Julius is annoyed that the capitalist press has buried this important news—nor is he pleased that Ethel has talked him into accompanying Doovy to the fair, where admission has been reduced to fifty cents.

"This is why you must read the *Daily*," Julius tells his brother-in-law as they stand swaying on the packed El, noting the new anti-Soviet provocations in Finland. The crowd surges out at Willets Point, but Julius remains behind, then carefully leaves his newspaper on the seat—as neatly folded as a formal invitation. It's Columbus Day, and the fair is mobbed. Julius gives Doovy a quick tour, pointing out the sights. Doovy requires constant attention—with the affect of a zombie and the precision of a compass, the lad keeps veering off toward the Trylon and Perisphere. Cleverly, Julius seeks to amuse him. Barbara Wall Street herself could not have concocted a more diverting line of patter: "Look, Doovy! It used to be that no one sat on the grass. It wasn't 'polite,' not 'good manners.' Now, look at those families—working-class families—relaxing on the grass after viewing the exhibits."

Julius is almost trotting to the Soviet Pavilion. "Taxed to capacity!" he exclaims. "Statistics have shown a big jump in attendance almost immediately following the pact." Once inside, Julius is again, even more poignantly, overwhelmed by the hammer-and-sickle chandelier, the jeweled map, the huge paintings. He parks Doovy in the Hall of Socialist Economy and Labor. What he really wants to do is find Comrade Natasha, but the vivacious girl guide is nowhere to be seen.

Disappointed, Julius discovers that he's tailing a pair of elegantly turned-out young women. They're obviously college coeds. The small, dark-haired one in the blue sweater reminds him a bit of Sylvia Sidney in *One Third of a Nation*. Unfortunately, she seems to have taken a course in political science. "Oh, it's nothing but propaganda," she says of the colorful and joyous dioramas—designed by GOSETnik Isaac Rabinovich—that depict the resorts of Sochi, Kisolovodsk, and Borovoy, old palaces now turned over to the workers and collective farmers for their rest and recuperation.

To his horror, Julius realizes that the two girls are scoffing at everything. "Look at this!" one giggles as they pause in front of the two Soviet-made touring autos. "They even make cars!" The familiar way that she says "cars" twists Julius's gut. He steps in close. He can smell perfume. His heart is pounding. "Why, that's not a car," he says, "That's jist prop-a-ganda."

The girls turn around and look at him. "Really," the tall blonde sniffs. "Do you think the ordinary Russian worker can afford that car?" Julius smiles in disbelief. For a veteran of the CCNY alcove wars, this is really too easy. "Can the ordinary American worker afford it?" he replies and waits a beat. (If Julius's strong, salt-of-the-earth delivery is pure Henry Fonda, Doovy's ear-splitting guffaw is worthy of Goofy. Where did he come from, all of a sudden?) The tall girl turns quickly away, but her pretty friend just stares. "Fuck you," she says.

Julius blushes. He's dumbstruck. No, he thinks bitterly, your class never was and is not now interested in breaking down the barriers that stand between the wage-earning masses and . . . a free and abundant life. Fat, sweaty Doovy is meanwhile lasciviously rotating his hips and pointing toward his crotch. "Hey, suck this salami, Park Avenue!" Embarrassed, Julius sends his brother-in-law off to secure a place on line at the General Motors Futurama—pretending somehow that he is merely giving him directions. ("So where'd you find those two swell dames?" Doovy wants to know.)

Alone again, Julius wanders back toward the exhibit, fighting his way through a legion of swarming schoolchildren. On his way out, he checks the visitor's book:

Most beautiful exhibit at the fair! Jack and Sylvia

They're way ahead of us—World War Veteran

Magnificent—mere words cannot describe. Signed, the Smythe Family, Indianapolis

When I see this building I understand why the capitalist papers are ranting with rage. Lenin said Socialism is invinsable. Now we know, Mike K

My feelings of awe that workers could accomplish so much, Life-Long Union Member

More power to ya!!!

This building made me wide-eyed—truly the most beautiful exhibit at the Fair. Sid

It was grand. Thanks for giving us a peep at Tomorrow. —Mr & Mrs Lou Gottlieb, Brooklyn

What about the German agreement? An American Citizen

Julius picks up a pen and writes: "The answer is the downfall of fascism!" signing himself "A Better American Citizen." Then he switches hands and scrawls: "Oh boy, what progress! I wish I was there! David Greenglass."

Glowering Doovy has been on line for over an hour by the time Julius finally shows. (Relieved to be free of Doovy's company, Julius had strolled down to the General Electric Pavilion, admiring the Rockwell Kent mural and studying the shrieking crowds in cacaphonous Steinmetz Hall, where—with a deafening roar—the ten million volts of artificial lightning shoot out in sizzling thirty-foot arcs.) Together, the brothers-in-law wait another hour and twenty minutes in sour silence, inching up the ramp to the streamlined red-and-silver building. It's almost half past five before they step onto the moving platform and gratefully sink into the comfortable leather seats.

Each moving chair is equipped with its own little speaker. "Man has forged ahead since 1940," the solemn Voice of the Future informs them as they are smoothly propelled into the World of 1960.

"This is just like the conveyor belt assembly lines in the GM plants," Julius can't resist observing. Doovy ignores him. He's flying—entranced by the ecstatic lateral glide, the rapturous organ music, the deep authority of the recorded voice that explicates the enchanting bird's-eye vista of electrified dairy farms and modern university centers, futuristic fourteen-lane motorways and iridescent lucite amusement parks, thriving steel towns and gigantic dams, winking and blinking like the world's most elaborate model train set.

"There's one thing I like about this that's got nothing to do with GM's actual intention," Julius shouts over the sonorous voice. "This is an example of what the people of this country can do when they get the opportunity, once they are not hampered by monopolies like General Motors."

Just then the ride jerks to a stop, Julius and Doovy violently flung together as a new, more harshly amplified voice is heard: "Keep your seats, please, the tour will be resumed shortly."

Julius is delighted. Instantly, he's in Doovy's face. "The Soviet Pavilion is the real world of tomorrow—dramatic proof of the social progress of a nation living and thriving under a planned, scientific form of society— socialism—where the institution of private ownership of the means of production has been abolished, where exploitation of man by men has been uprooted forever, where a free community of peoples has been established and is moving confidently ahead with the construction of a life that grows happier every day."

("Keep your seats, please, the tour will be resumed shortly.")

"This, on the other hand, is a big-business fantasy designed to obtain the maximum efficiency from inhabitants. Did you notice, Doovy, how the cities were strictly divided into industrial installations, commercial centers, and residential areas? This is not a future civilization conceived and built for the peoples' benefit—but for the enhancement of maximum capitalist exploitation! But the Soviet Pavilion shows a socialist civilization created

by the people, for the people, and solely in the interests of the people."
Doovy prays that the ride will start up again.

("Keep your seats, please, the tour will be resuming shortly.")

"Doovy, I hope you noticed that of the thousands of words used to describe the wonderful capitalist future, not one was uttered regarding social conditions—not one word said about eliminating the evils of mass unemployment, for instance."

Julius is interrupted by a blast of static: "Due to mechanical conditions beyond our control, it will be necessary for those viewing the Futurama to leave their seats. The guards will escort you to the exits."

Along with six hundred other grumbling passengers, Julius and Doovy are taken across a catwalk and pushed through the emergency exit. Instead of emerging on the "1960" stage set, they find themselves deposited, blinking and dazzled, in a back alley filled with dumpsters.

"Hey, buddy—what happened?" Doovy demands of a figure in overalls. The mechanic explains that the moving-chair track had gone out of sync with the unloading platform. Doovy nods sagely and is mildly surprised to see Julius following the guard and demanding a souvenir pin.

"I have seen the future," Julius brandishes his trophy with a smirk. "And it doesn't work."

The fair is closed for the season. The Soviet Pavilion is being torn down. In its place, they'll erect a bandstand. It will be called the American Common.

Winter is approaching. Every day, the dogs of opportunism and pro-Fascism howl their false hearts out against the Soviet Union. Even Greta Garbo has joined the enemy camp. *Ninotchka,* her first film since *Camille,* has opened at Radio City at exactly the time when the Russian government alone is fighting for peace in the midst of imperial war. Such timing is hardly accidental. Julius picks a fight with Stella about *Mr. Smith Goes to Washington.* Stella loves the picture, calls it "a ringing indictment of political chicanery" and the best movie of 1939.

"Even better than *The Wizard of Oz?*" Julius sneers. This time, he doesn't attempt to conceal his contempt. "The atmosphere of exaggeration and unreality might be considered a virtue in *The Wizard of Oz,*" he tells her. "But not in a picture that purports to be about national politics."

Wounded, Stella compares *Mr. Smith* to *Juarez:* "This is not a fantasy,

Julius. In providing a lesson in democracy, it proves how truly great the screen can be."

But Julius is relentless. "Stella, why does Mr. Smith go to Washington? What exactly is his program? Can you tell me what his speeches are even about?"

"He's for honesty and . . . "

"Summer camps! I'm sorry, Stella, a genuine political conflict between those who are for democracy and those who are against it has to be something more than some hot air about fresh air."

Julius is pleased at having turned this phrase, but now Ethel intervenes. Life in Brooklyngrad is tough enough. "Julie, you know the movie isn't all bad. There's plenty of instruction that the man in the street hasn't had an opportunity to see before, and the exposure could even cause him to be a bit more inquisitive about government and politics."

What's this pact about? "Talk of democracy is cheap, Ethel," Julie shouts. "Talk of democracy in *Mr. Smith* comes a dime a dozen and is sickeningly meaningless." Without looking at Stella, he leaves the room.

On December 12, Julius sneaks off to a second-run movie house on East Fourteenth Street to investigate *Ninotchka* for himself. He doesn't exactly know why but he slouches in his seat as if afraid someone might recognize him. (Indeed, Miss S. Ligetts is surprised to see him there.) Luckily, Julius has missed the mortifying newsreel showing the bombing of Helsinki. Alone in the dark, he marvels at the scientific detachment with which super–girl guide Greta Garbo allows herself to be picked up by White Russian degenerate Melvyn Douglas and at the coolness with which she prepares to gives herself to him. Truly, the scientific certainties of Marxism-Leninism are a titan's shield!

Hope against hope: Julius finds himself waiting for Melvyn Douglas to realize that he is a social parasite. No use. Forget Finland, Julius feels like he's being pummeled. Not only does the movie exhibit a vicious reactionary and intellectually obscene viewpoint, but it includes every slander and lie that capitalism has ever used against the land of socialism—every stale, moss-covered anti-Soviet gag known to Louis B. Mayer. It is a malicious gesture devoted to ridiculing—and none too subtly—the 180 million Soviet citizens off the face of the earth.

Julius loses interest. He remembers the girl who cursed him at the fair. Suddenly, there is a shot of Greta Garbo marching as a Young Pioneer beneath the banner of Stalin in the May Day parade. She is so beautiful, so bereft, so . . . Communist. Julius begins to weep. He is still thinking of Greta Garbo when he walks, with defiant pride, across Union Square and joins the party.

A GREAT PATRIOTIC WAR

The road to hell is paved with good intentions.

—Karl Marx, *Capital: A Critique of Political Economy* (1867)

The least you can say for *The Rosenberg File* is that it doesn't present the Rs as passive victims. On the contrary: These are not innocent lambs but complex, highly motivated individuals. Julius appears as proud papa *and* courageous spy, Ethel as adoring mother, faithful wife, *and* ideological militant.

The Rosenberg File reads like a B movie—namely, *Walk East on Beacon*, in which the Communist spy network is made up of a florist, a cab driver, an undertaker, and a government clerk. ("The days of the dashing Mata Hari, Admiral Canaris, and Franz von Papen are gone forever," Columbia's 1951 press release explained. "The modern spy is the insignificant little man whom no one suspects. He receives no money, travels by bus, never frequents hotels, popular restaurants or bars. He is a dedicated Communist who never meets his superiors personally.")[17]

Maybe that's the problem. The scenario is insufficiently epic. The grubby details need to be embellished by Cecil B. DeMille. There should be scenes in the Kremlin as well as Knickerbocker Village, cutaways to the Warsaw ghetto along with Los Alamos, cameos by Tito and not just William Perl.

Of course, for a born-again anti-Communist such as Ronald Radosh, the Rosenberg story is nothing if not overdetermined. Once upon a time (June 1939), an ardent Young Communist married a onetime strike leader. But once upon a time (August 1939), a man named Stalin made a deal with a guy named Hitler. Nevertheless, once upon a time (allegedly December 12, 1939), Julius Rosenberg joined the Communist Party. Fade in during the bleak winter of 1939–40, six months after the accursed pact . . .

The Rosenbergs are managing on Ethel's salary (she's a secretary) while Julius hunts for work as a freelance tool designer. September 1940, he comes bounding up the stairs: "Honey, I'm home!" Julius has got a job with the U.S. Signal Corps. Joel Barr works there too. But political tensions are high, and after a few months, someone denounces him—calls his wife a Commie. Julius talks his way out of it and manages to keep his position. A close call, with heavy intimations that theirs may be a life of perverse Communist marginality. Then, four days after Julie and Ethel celebrate their second wedding anniversary, Hitler attacks Stalin.

Thank G-d! The Rosenbergs have moved back near the old neighborhood; they're living in a room at 107 Avenue A, just off Tompkins Square Park. Outside it's pure pandemonium. The Lower East Side has gone berserk. Two years worth of pent-up tensions explode. The Communists are running off leaflets, and people are grabbing them right out of the mimeograph machine. Everyone wants to know what the Communists are saying.

But everyone knows what they're saying. After all, the Communists have been primed to defend the socialist motherland for as long as they've been Communists. The Jews have been watching the Nazis beat on their cousins for nearly seven years. Behind the lines in Poland, the Germans are already operating death camps for German, Czech, and Polish Jews. After Hitler takes the Ukraine, civilian Jews are gassed en masse by mobile death squads. By late 1941, the Nazis are estimating they've exterminated as many Jews in Europe as there are still living on the Lower East Side.

Is it at this moment, as David Greenglass will later maintain, that Julius—the twenty-two-year-old civil service chairman of his union—makes a personal contribution to the war against Fascism by bringing home tube manuals from the Signal Corps and sending them to Russian comrades overseas? (The "Internationale" comes up tentatively on the soundtrack.) Or is it after December 7, 1941, when the Japanese bomb the American fleet at Pearl Harbor? Now the Communists can really go to war. America is mobilizing, and the Reds amaze their fellow conscripts by doing everything possible to get sent into action overseas.

Housewife-activist Ethel is working full time over on Avenue B as a volunteer secretary at the East Side Conference to Defend America and Crush Hitler. Julie gets a promotion. He buys Ethel an eighty-dollar fur coat. They move to a real home—a three-room flat on the eleventh floor of the Met Life Lower East Side housing project Knickerbocker Village. Their windows overlook the courtyard that the project's numerous party members refer to fondly as Red Square. Summer of 1942: Russian War Relief chapters in fifty-six American cities collect money and clothing for the Soviet people. The Nazis murder three hundred thousand Jews in Treblinka alone. Julius and Ethel conceive a child.

Branch 16B of the Communist Party Industrial Division—whose members the FBI will identify as Joel Barr, Alfred Sarant, Ethel Rosenberg, and Julius Rosenberg (chairman)—are meeting regularly at the new Rosenberg apartment. Pregnant Ethel is still working as a civil defense volunteer. And according to the deposition Ruth Greenglass will sign in 1950, hard-working Julie has decided to become active *outside* the party. Yes, as Max Elitcher tells the FBI, Julie dreams of doing something extraordinary for the Soviet Union but has yet to figure out how to make the connection. (The "William Tell Overture" begins to swell.)[18]

That winter, the Soviet victory at Stalingrad turns the war around. It's the lunatic acme of Russian prestige in the United States (blaring up-tempo Glenn Miller "Internationale"). The legendary March 29, 1943, issue of *Life* magazine comes spinning off the press—a masterpiece of Socialist Realism entirely devoted to our gallant Soviet ally. *Life* praises Marshal Stalin (portrayed on the cover by Margaret Bourke-White), calls Lenin "perhaps the greatest man of modern times," and extols the Russians as "one hell of a people. . . . To a remarkable degree, they look like Americans, dress like Americans, and think like Americans."[19]

It's *Invasion of the Body Snatchers* except nobody knows it. The same month, Michael Rosenberg is born. The young Jews of the Warsaw ghetto rise up in revolt that Passover, and David Greenglass gets his induction papers. (The war is depleting the YCL.) Close-up of David in boot camp, composing a message to his young wife one letter at a time. "Victory shall be ours," he scrawls and mops his brow. "The future is socialism's." And Ruthie rushes home all tearful and giddy from the May Day rally in Union Square to respond: "Perhaps the voices of 75,000 working men and women that were brought together today, perhaps their voices demanding an early invasion of Europe will be heard and then my dear we will be together to build—under socialism—our future."[20]

Summer of 1943: The "Internationale" segues into the Andrew Sisters singing "Don't Sit Under the Apple Tree (with Anyone Else but Me)." Teenage Ruthie's serving as president of her neighborhood Young Communist League. (Seven years later, she'll swear Ethel made her do it.) It's a heady moment. American Communists are actively recruited by the Office of Strategic Services (OSS) in Washington, D.C. (shot of cheerful Eugene Dennis being invited out to lunch). Communist martyr Julius Fučík is executed in Berlin, but here in the United States, the party is about to burst for joy.

Much discussion, as the year ends, of Comrade Browder's plan to dissolve the Communist Party now that no fundamental differences exist between the United States and the Soviet Union. In early 1944, even Branch 16B dissolves. There's a party at Café Society. Ethel has been having a terrible time with her colicky, demanding Michael. Nevertheless, she sings "One Fine Day" from *Madame Butterfly*. The FBI report neglects to mention whether she has a gardenia in her hair.

Meanwhile, out in America, Technician Fifth Class David Greenglass knows that something's happening, but he doesn't know what it is. "Please don't delay in sending me the Browder speech," he writes Ruthie in a panic. "Please send me that speech and whatever literature the New Committee of Political Education puts out. Darling, this is vital to my morale. Send all literature pertaining to the speech." Doovy doesn't want his Ruthie to miss the point. "Find out from Ethel what she and Julie think about it. Ask her to get the literature. Darling, I love you."[21]

In the terrible spring of 1944, Adolf Eichmann shows up in Budapest to supervise personally the hastily organized death-camp deportation of seven hundred thousand Hungarian Jews for gassing at Auschwitz. (Meanwhile, the American Communist Party has become the American Communist Association.) By summer, the Red Army has rolled the Nazis back to Poland, and gung-ho Julius is down in Washington. Max Elitcher will tell the court that he was working at the Navy Department when suddenly CCNY comrade Julius Rosenberg appeared out of nowhere and began invoking "the great role Russia was playing in the war and the great sacrifice she was making."[22]

Although Elitcher was sympathetic, he'd have liked to change the subject. Julius wouldn't shut up, telling him that "some persons"—namely, Elitcher's best friend, Morton Sobell—"were contributing to the Russian war effort by giving information concerning secret material and developments to the Russians, which they would not ordinarily receive." There was a pregnant pause, and then, "Julius asked me if I would contribute the same way."[23]

Even crazier, T/5 Greenglass finds himself assigned to a secret government installation in Oak Ridge, Tennessee. "Julie was in the house and he told me what you must be working on," Ruthie writes. "Sweets, I can't discuss it with you (and certainly no one else either) but when I see you I'll tell you what I think it is." Within days, Doovy is shipped to another top-secret army base—Los Alamos, New Mexico. That November, Ruthie goes to check it out.[24]

Poland is virtually liberated when next Greenglass and Rosenberg meet. At the trial, Greenglass will testify that throughout his furlough, Julie kept pumping him for information, getting him to make sketches. One night, he and Ruth have dinner down at the Rosenbergs, and Julie calls him into the kitchen. Doovy watches as Julie takes a scissors and slices the side panel off an empty box of Jell-O. Huh? Then he takes the panel and snips it, zigzag, in half. Tight close-up of Julie handing open-mouthed Doovy half the Jell-O box panel, superimposed over smug Doovy delivering his subsequent testimony. A phrase from the "Internationale" comes up, all ominous and discordant.

Shock cut: Julius is again denounced at work, only this time they fire him for lying about his membership in the now nonexistent Communist Party. The strain of motherhood has driven poor Ethel into a sort of nervous collapse. Julius's father, Harry, is so upset he refuses to see his headstrong boy or even speak to him for almost a year, and then only on his deathbed. (At the trial, Max Elitcher will testify that Julius was actually relieved to discover that the only thing the Signal Corps had on him was a photostat party card.) The war's still on, however, and Julius lands a better job with Emerson Radio, working on one of the contracts he used to inspect.

Life is complicated, but it's a time for cautious optimism. Julius buys Ethel a secondhand piano. The Red Army liberates Hungary. Stalin, Churchill, and Roosevelt meet at Yalta to map the postwar world. Ruthie has moved to Albuquerque, forty miles from Los Alamos. Doovy stays with her on weekends. A chill sets in that spring, after FDR dies. The House Un-American Activities Committee doesn't waste time opening hearings on Communist infiltration of the U.S. Armed Forces. The Red Army liberates Prague after May Day, and all of a sudden, Winston Churchill is calling for "Anglo-American armies" to police the world.

And now, the big set piece—Janet Leigh taking a shower in Tony Perkins's motel, Cary Grant finding himself on the flattest stretch of deepest Kansas. Sunday, June 3, 1945: Harry Gold gets off the train at Albuquerque, New Mexico, half an irregularly cut Jell-O box panel tucked in his pocket. The wacky bachelor *luftmensh,* who for sixteen years led his employer and coworkers to think he was married with twin children (one crippled by polio), makes his way through sleepy Sunday-morning streets, past the good folks on their way to church. He finds Ruthie's door and knocks—rat-a-tat-tat, like Beethoven's Fifth. Doovy—still in his underwear—opens up. Who the hell is this putz? he wonders. Then, the funny little guy flashes his piece of the Jell-O box, telling bleary Greenglass that he comes from "Uncle Joe" or "Julius R" or something.

Half a world away in the Moscow Kremlin, Joseph Stalin begins lick-ing his chops and rubbing his hands together like Ming the Merciless. Doovy is hypnotized. He sits down and, tucking his tongue in the corner of his mouth for concentration, spends the afternoon writing up notes on the high-explosive lens mold he's been working on at Los Alamos. This is the state secret—tangible and transcendent at the same time—the sacred mystery of power!

Gold goes for a walk, has a fantasy about a pastrami sandwich, con-cocts an imaginary second family living here in Albuqerque (Morris and Leona Cohen, maybe), comes back, collects the notes, and slips Greenglass an envelope with ten crisp fifties. Cut to the Kremlin: Stalin cackling like a fiend, smashing a tumbler of pepper vodka against the wall, dancing the hot kasatzki. (His purpose served, Earl Browder will be ousted from the leadership of the Communist Political Association, then purged from the newly reconstituted Communist Party.) The crime of the century? That August, the United States drops atomic bombs on two Japanese cities and ends the war.

Dissolve from maniac Stalin to newsreel clips of VJ day jitterbugging in Times Square, and segue into turgid vignettes of workers on strike. Thousands of demobilized soldiers are running around trying to figure out what to do. The camera picks out David and Ruth Greenglass trudging back to the Lower East Side (sad klezmer music mixed with Winston Churchill's "Iron Curtain" speech). Doovy, brother Bernard Greenglass, Julie, and another *zhlub* from Knickerbocker Village pool their pennies, opening a machine shop in the ancestral storefront of the moldering Greenglass tenement. The business moves first to East Third Street and then—under the name Pitt Machine Products—to East Houston Street, down the block from Julie's old Talmud Torah. Business is lousy.

In fact, the whole postwar world is turning out badly. Just before the 1946 congressional election, the U.S. Chamber of Commerce publishes a thirty-eight-page pamphlet, *Communist Infiltration in the United States: Its Nature and How to Combat It*. The Republicans distribute 683,000 copies. Returning vet Richard Nixon gets elected to the House of Repre-sentatives by maintaining that the New Deal is infested with Commies. Truman takes the hint: Proposing to stay in Europe to hold the line in Greece and Turkey, he orders the loyalty program that will snare Max Elitcher.

J. Edgar Hoover calls American Communists "masters of deceit." Will Ruth be telling the truth when she testifies in court that, around this time,

Julius claimed "he didn't care" whether Pitt Machine Products "was a success or not," because "he could always get ten or fifteen thousand dollars as a front for any business for his activities." These activities, David later informs the FBI, include the maintenance of two apartments—one in Greenwhich Village, the other on Avenue B—where Julius microfilms classified material on "thinking machines," "guided missiles," and "sky platforms." Ethel is once again pregnant.

A month after the second Rosenberg boy, Robert, is born in May 1947, the European situation is even more polarized. The Communists are purged from the French and Italian governments, while Czechoslovakia, the last of the coalitions, is refusing to accept the Marshall Plan. Flying saucers are strafing American jets, and American Communists are talking about the imminent arrival of American fascism. That fall, as HUAC opens its well-publicized investigation of subversion in Hollywood, the party prepares to go underground. Joel Barr loses his job and leaves the country.

If 1947 was bad, 1948 promises worse. It is suddenly apparent that the Tito regime is not a genuine popular democracy—not a heroic model of a whole people striding toward socialism—but the greatest betrayal in the history of the working class. The Yugoslav Communist Party has fallen into the hands of Trotskyites and nationalists. The United States, Britain, and France choose this moment to conclude a separate armistice with occupied Germany.

After the Victorious February in Czechoslovakia, the mood in Truman's Washington seems ominously bellicose. Out in Queens, only a few miles from the old fairgrounds, Morton Sobell is checking the price of air flights to Mexico, but according to Max Elitcher, Julius seems more confident than ever. As the party falls apart, his spy ring is expanding. Elitcher will report that Julius was bragging about a new Washington contact and a special briefcase he's got that, if it ever fell into the wrong hands, would fog any incriminating microfilm automatically! (Too bad he never thought to tell Elitcher to wear it on his head.) In June, Stalin finally makes his move—expelling Tito from the Cominform and blockading West Berlin.

Henry Wallace is running for president as the candidate of the new Progressive Party, campaigning to "End Jim Crow" and "Establish Full Friendship with Israel." It's about "Peace, Security, and Freedom—Wallace or War." That same summer, HUAC is investigating Alger Hiss, and the leadership of the American Communist Party is under indictment. "Could the Reds Seize Detroit?" wonders the August 3 issue of *Look* magazine. (Their multipage photo dramatization shows pistol-toting Communists spreading nocturnal "confusion throughout a terror-gripped city.")

In New York, which will give Wallace nearly half a million votes, members of the American Labor Party are losing their jobs in the municipal Department of Welfare. The cold war is on, and Julius goes into high gear. William Perl arrives from Cleveland, drops in on his old physics lab at Columbia, and allegedly checks out thirty-five classified test reports dealing with new helicopters and airplanes. (What was that fervent, doleful Progressive Party anthem Ethel was always humming? "Was at Franklin Roosevelt's side just a while before he died / He said: 'One world must come out of World War Two.' / Yankee, Russian, white or tan, Lord, a man is just a man. / We're all brothers and we're only passing through.")

According to FBI jailhouse informant Jerome Tartakow, Perl brings the material down to one of Rosenberg's apartments for a marathon microfilming session. Tartakow will claim Julius bragged that the job kept four men busy with two cameras for seventeen hours, "working against the clock so that Perl could return the documents before they would be missed."[25]

A few weeks later, Max Elitcher is tailed by the FBI as he drives up from Washington to New York. The scene is pure noir. Elitcher is almost hysterical. By the time the panicky engineer finds Sobell's redbrick semidetached house in the middle of Queens, his heart is pounding so fast that he might be Edmund O'Brien in *DOA*. At midnight, Elitcher will testify, he and Sobell drive from Queens into the city and deliver some sort of secret something or other to Knickerbocker Village. By the fall of 1948, the Communist Party leadership is on trial, Pitt Machine Products is failing, and—against all odds—Harry Truman defeats Henry Wallace.

(This is one long, long movie. The crowd at Town Hall is growing restless. Sol Stern, Radosh's first collaborator, squeezes into the spotlight. Guess what, Walter? He's got a tape recorder too. Stern plays garbled phone conversations with people who claim they were misquoted. Are there some who deny they were interviewed at all? Stern saves the best for last. Grinning, he depresses the button on his machine and out comes the unmistakable nasal voice of—Miriam Schneir. Yes, Miriam—prompted by Stern—prattling on and on about the Rosenbergs. The embarrassment is palpable. Did Walter know?)

Sometime in 1948, Bernard Greenglass drops out of Pitiful Machine

Products. Even Doovy—who now has a child of his own to support—is beginning to lose faith in Julie. Sure, the counterrevolution in Czechoslovakia fails, but the pep talks aren't working anymore. He's sick and tired of Julie's rap. According to Greenglass, Julie is claiming that "it doesn't matter if Stalin is sending his troops to be killed. What difference does it make as long as the victory is ours? Except"—dramatic pause, sound of the plug being pulled on the "Internationale"—"I won't be around for the final victory and neither will you."[26]

Cut the sound on Julius explaining "the objective necessity of history." Close-up of Doovy holding his head as *neither will you, will you, will you!* reverberates in the echo chamber of his brain.

(Whoa! Ronald Radosh is on his feet, gesticulating wildly and looking, he says, at the big picture. Like Schneir, he gravitates to the pulpit. Radosh is breathless. The words are tumbling out. He's not a simple-minded anti-Communist, he declares. He's even seen some kind of CIA report that fingers Julius as a spy—yes!—but he dismisses any connection between the American Communist Party and the KGB. The Schneirs are furiously taking notes.)

Back to the movie. There's a great blast of Charlie Chan music and an enormous cartoon map of China, across which Mao Zedong chases the comically scampering nationalists until they dive—kerplunk—into the ocean. Crash of cymbals; quick cut to Washington, D.C., and a frantic search in the State Department for the bureaucrats who lost China. In New York, a jury finds the American Communist Party leadership guilty of treason. Ethel begins therapy with a West End Avenue shrink.

Weird things are happening everywhere. In Budapest, the popular Communist leader László Rajk is arrested as a Fascist stool pigeon and Titoist agent. On July 25, 1949, the United States, Britain, Italy, West Germany, and France announce they've made a formal military alliance. Does this mean war? The American Communist Party destroys its membership list.

August 27, the town of Peekskill, New York, hosts the first open manifestation of American fascism as, inflamed by the local Chamber of Commerce and American Legion, a lynch mob runs amok and prevents Paul Robeson's annual concert to benefit the Harlem chapter of the Civil Rights Congress. At a defiant second concert, held in Peekskill the next Saturday, Robeson brings the crowd to its feet with his special version of the American anthem "Ol' Man River": "I must keep fightin' until I'm dyin'!" Then the buses back to New York run a gauntlet of stone-throwing hooligans—

the brave guards furnished by the Fur and Leather Workers Union are surrounded and attacked, while laughing state troopers look on.

The newspapers are full of nuclear ruminations. Then, a few days later, the Russians blow the equation to smithereens when they test their own atomic bomb. David Greenglass is beginning to freak. Ruthie is pregnant again. There's no more money in the machine shop, and—as he will recall after his conviction—crazy Julie is dropping hints that the Big Knock is coming. Doovy thinks that he hears Julius telling him to grab Ruthie, pack up the kid, and split the United States forever. . . .

Suddenly, everyone realizes that Radosh has launched into an irate denunciation of Joseph Stalin. What the—? Elizabeth Holtzman is startled. Radosh runs down the list of Stalin's crimes, winding up with "the monstrous, horrendous purge trial in Czechoslovakia."

"So, listen to Khrushchev," I hear some codger mutter.

My knowledgeable neighbor bursts into laughter. "I heard that when Radosh was a member of the Labor Youth League in Madison, he refused to even believe that the Secret Speech existed!"[27]

The diatribe is building to a climax. The American Communist Party, declares Radosh with beleaguered contempt, "was composed—not primarily of traitors—but of individuals who wasted their lives!"

Hissing fills the hall.

A ROSENBERG BY ANY OTHER NAME

It is an extremely painful thing to be ruled by laws that one does not know.

—Franz Kafka, "The Problem of Our Laws"

Is it really such a paradox that Stalinism was among the vehicles used by East European Jews to adapt themselves to America and the modern world?

Before the Great Depression, Jews accounted for a bare 15 percent of the American Communist Party rank and file. By the mid-1930s, the party was nearly half Jewish. Why? There was, of course, the party's stated goal of establishing a world without poverty, exploitation, and religious difference. There was the dovetailing of Communist internationalism and Jewish millennialism. Even the sentimental, fundamentally synthetic worldview of the Popular Front, with its militant egalitarianism and corny Americana, was tailor-made for the children of Jewish immigrants. The party's espousal of Pop Front culture allowed these children to transform the socialist ideals of their downtrodden parents into what was being called twentieth-century Americanism. Then, too, at least until the summer of 1939, there was the party's strong and implacable hatred of Adolf Hitler and Nazi Germany.

But what in this world can't happen to a Jew? As Julius Rosenberg awoke one morning from uneasy dreams, he found himself transformed in his prison bed into a gigantic, red-haired insect named Rudolf Slánský. The walls of Sing Sing had melted into air, and there he was, standing on a dais in the middle of the field. A military brass band was playing "Avanti popolo," and a distinguished-looking, if distinctly unwell, older man was placing an enormous medallion around his neck.

"*Dekuji*, Klem," Julius heard himself croak. "Thank you." The man called Klem seized one of Julius's numerous little legs and shook it with a palsied grasp. Julius glanced down his exterior skeleton to his new decoration and discovered that it was the Order of Klement Gottwald for the Building of Socialism. This was no dream. He was the first secretary of the Communist Party, an oversize cockroach, and all Czechoslovakia was celebrating his birthday.

"Honored Comrade," Klem was mumbling, "together with our whole party, I send you, on your fiftieth birthday, our heartiest congratulations and Bolshevik greetings. This occasion affords us the opportunity of looking back upon your life, which has been dedicated to our proletariat and the whole working population, and of paying honor to your greatest work toward the victory of socialism in our land. From your earliest youth, you entered boldly on the road of struggle. Inspired by the ideals of the Great October Revolution, you fought in the ranks against the treachery of the right-wing social-democratic wreckers, and ever since the founding of the Communist Party of Czechoslovakia, you have been its active warrior."

The creature they called the Slánský had devoted his entire adult life to the party. Son of a wealthy merchant—a Jew, some said, named Saltzman—he joined the Communists as a teenage militant. The Slánský could have enjoyed a safe career as a parliamentary politician, but he craved excitement and assumed dangerous tasks. In 1936, he even had to flee with his wife and son to Moscow. When war finally came, the Slánský insisted on parachuting behind German lines to fight the Nazis in Slovakia. He became a renowned partisan fighter. But it was after the war that he faced his greatest challenge. The Slánský had absolute faith in the Soviet Union he had fought to save. He submitted willingly to the authority of the

Comintern and, later, the Cominform. He became the chief interpreter of their policies for the Czechoslovak Communist Party. The February Revolution made the Slánský the most powerful cockroach in Czechoslovákia.

Unlike Gottwald, the Slánský had no experience in parliamentary politics. But he understood organization. It was the Slánský who accepted the difficult task of disciplining the bourgeoisie after their imperialist-inspired counterrevolutionary demonstrations of July and October 1948; the Slánský who fearlessly proposed the creation of forced-labor camps; the Slánský who amazed the Central Committee with his theoretical, ultra-Stalinist arguments to support the intensified class struggle. Let the reactionary wolves howl, let the deserters run for cover! By mid-1949, the Slánský was all but directing the State Security apparatus. He knew this was a direct contravention of the Czechoslovak Constitution, yet the times called for extraordinary measures.

The Slánský's responsibilities grew. He was kept informed of all security measures and approved every one of them. He received full reports on all prisoners who were interrogated. Soon he was being asked to judge suspects' guilt or innocence before their cases even came to trial. The more the Slánský discovered, the more suspicious he became. The entire party was in need of a purge. "It is necessary to examine every party member," he told the Central Committee. "Our party must pass through a process of purification."

Like a good Communist, the Slánský studied the international scene with keen interest. First, there had been the treachery of Tito and the loss of Yugoslavia. High in their own ranks, the Hungarians had uncovered a Titoist agent: László Rajk! The names of certain Slovak comrades had surfaced during the Hungarian investigation. Around the time that the FBI paid its first visit to the Greenglass hovel on Rivington Street, the Slánský made a public denunciation of a distinguished comrade for "bourgeois nationalism."

And then, State Security discovered the Czech Rajk. Actually, the traitor was a Slovak—a Slovakian Jew who called himself Otto Sling. Younger than the Slánský, the Sling was also a hero. When the Slánský and his family were fleeing to Moscow, the twenty-three-year-old Sling was fighting the Fascists in Spain. The Sling spent the war in England; later, he became the party boss of Brno. Like the Slánský, the Sling was an enthusiastic Stalinist—or so it seemed. State Security could accuse him of using creative legal procedures during the arrest, interrogation, and trials of various local party members. But the Slánský could hardly fault him there.

By autumn of 1951, however, someone had found a suspicious letter that the Sling had written ten years before, and he was arrested as a spy.

Gottwald's remarks were drawing to a close: "Dear Comrade . . . our whole party . . . our whole working people . . . salutes you . . . faithful son and warrior . . . filled with love for the working classes . . . and with loyalty to the Soviet Union and to great Stalin. . . . We wish you sound health . . . and many successes in your future work . . . *čest praci*!"

Julius fondled his award. Slingism had been the most depraved of deviations. No less than 169,000 party members had to be arrested. The Slánský had made himself cleanser of the nation, a force without pity. People thought this came naturally to a cockroach; yet inwardly, the Slánský suffered. His insect liver was giving him pain. Telegrams of congratulations from the leaders of fraternal parties were being read. Julius must have been woolgathering. Did he miss the one from Comrade Stalin? he wondered. That Stalin could have remembered the Slánský's birthday made all the suffering somehow worthwhile.

The summer of 1952 passed quickly. Julius grew used to his insect body, with its scores of legs and quirky liver. He even felt peaceful, as though his great contributions had at last been recognized. The party had announced plans to publish a two-volume selection of his articles and speeches under the title *Towards the Victory of Socialism*. His wife had remarked on his new tenderness, but he often found himself absently studying her face as if searching for some other blurry set of features.

Did anyone notice his lack of enthusiasm when he read in *Rude Pravo* that, in Poland, First Secretary Władisław Gomułka had been placed under arrest? At the next meeting of the Central Committee, Julius was relieved of his party secretaryship and made deputy prime minister. One day, as the leaves were falling, he capriciously canceled his appointments and went for a crawl by the banks of the Vltava. An old comrade approached him on the promenade but, instead of nodding hello, froze and began to scuttle grotesquely away. Julius overtook him. "Your work be honored! Are you afraid to congratulate me?" the deputy prime minister asked ironically.

"*Čest praci, čest praci.* They say you mean to defect," the man blurted out. What a fantastic notion! Julius hardly knew what to reply. Later, he made a note to have his friend investigated. But he soon forgot about it. The truth was, Julius was enjoying his semiretirement. The party had given him and his wife a comfortable villa. He was taking notes for an article, perhaps a book, on the contributions of the American socialist engineer Steinmetz. For the first time in many years, he was free to immerse himself in the study of science and technology. There was a dinner party at the prime minister's residence for the new Soviet ambassador. Various ministers and their wives attended, and Julius had captivated them with his detailed descriptions of sky platforms and thinking machines. ("But they'll never replace *you*, my dear," he joked to one young woman and roguishly brushed his orifice over her hand.)

It was an hour past midnight when the Slánskýs returned to their villa. Had there been a power outage? For some reason, the place was absolutely dark. Madame Slánska stumbled on the steps and twisted her ankle. Julius caught her and cursed his security men. In the age of sky platforms, you'd think they'd have thought of candles! Madame Slánska opened the front door and they entered, stepping from darkness into darkness. Then, every light in the house blazed on!

Madame Slánska screamed a typically Communist remonstrance as Julius was handcuffed. "What is the meaning of this?" he cried, though he already knew. As they dragged Julius out toward the car, he had a glimpse of his wife, pinned down by three security men. Everything was unreal, yet familiar. Jewish luck. Julius found himself once again in prison, strip-searched, bound in a straitjacket, and chained like a dog. He was beaten for hours, then interrogated until he lost consciousness. Of course, he refused to confess.

The next morning, the police gave in to his demands, and he was allowed to address a letter to the Central Committee. "I am aware of the fact that my arrest must have been due to serious—though to me unknown reasons," Julius wrote. "But as far as the suspicion against me, a suspicion that I committed some crimes against the party, is concerned, this must be due to some horrible mistake. Never in my life did I betray the party or damage it knowingly—never did I make pacts with the enemy." With his mashed feelers, every word—each character—was painful to form. "I am not an enemy," he concluded. "I am firmly convinced that the accusations against me will be proved false."

The fact was that all summer, even during his birthday celebration, people throughout Czechoslovakia had been denouncing Julius without even realizing it. Dragged before State Security, many comrades had mentioned a trivial association or simply the Slánský name, hoping that, through some mysterious alchemy, his uncorruptible innocence might rub off on them. Embarrassingly, State Security found themselves with a huge dossier. Not knowing what else to do, they persuaded the Sling, still awaiting trial, to denounce the Slánský.

Months passed. The beatings and interrogations continued. "The crimes I've been accused of are so great and of such a character that you can't even imagine them," Julius told his cell mate. When the interrogators heard that, they accused the former general secretary of being willing to drop an atomic bomb on Czechoslovakia if it served his imperialist masters. "Give me an atom bomb!" Julius screamed. North Korean military installations were being subjected to the heaviest air attacks anywhere since World War II. In Amerika, *See It Now* telecast a simulated atomic attack on New York; later that summer, air-conditioned movie theaters in ten large cities joined together to demonstrate the latest in atomic-war civil-defense procedures.

In his slow delirium, Julius hardly knew if he was dead or alive. Once, he succeeded in hanging himself with a window sash. The guards broke down the door. The doctor who revived him received a medal. At last, the trial began. The Sling, the Slánský, and a dozen others—most of them Jews or Slovaks (or both), all former high party officials—were produced in court. *Rude Pravo* called them a "rogues' gallery" of "Trotskyites," "Zionists," "bourgeois nationalists," "a repulsive gang of imperialist minions," "spies in dollar pay," "frenzied enemies of the Soviet Union," and "traitorous cosmopolitans." "All this together constitutes a creature by the name of Rudolf Slánský."

The trial was so skillfully rehearsed that when the prosecutor forgot a question, Eugen Loebl, the defendant on the stand, answered it anyway. Once-portly Sling had lost so much weight that, prisoners being forbidden belts, he was compelled to use one hand to hold up his pants. In the midst of his enthusiastic confession, the Sling gestured with both hands, and like a clown in the circus, his trousers collapsed into a puddle around his ankles. Although the judges, the prosecutors, the guards, the other defendants, and even the Sling burst out laughing, Julius barely paid attention.

He scarcely listened when Gusta Fučíkova, widow of the Communist martyr Julius Fučík, accused one of the defendants of handing over her husband to the Gestapo. Trembling with rage, she quoted her husband's final words: "Whoever has lived for the future and has fallen for its beauty is a figure hewn in stone. But he who, with the dust of the past, tries to build a dam against the Current of the Revolution, is no more than a puppet of rotten wood!" Only once did Julius hear something that tore a piece from his heart. The young son of another defendant—the same age as Michael?—stood up and denounced his father as "a creature who cannot be called a human being." Voice shaking with rage, the boy demanded "the heaviest penalty."

Rude Pravo agreed:

Three simple oak benches rock beneath the weight of the crimes these traitorous plotters have committed, and which they carry within themselves. But all this weight of treason, the accumulation of years of evil-doing, vampire treacheries, the vast clot of leeches, all this terrible weight has fallen from our people. It was hard to breathe beneath such a burden but the mercenaries of imperialism have not succeeded in suffocating us. Now, rid of them, we can work and sing with a quiet mind, and rock our children in our arms. Now it is the malefactors themselves who are smothering beneath the weight.

As the service, so the reward. To dogs a dog's death.[28]

A week after sentence was pronounced, Julius was taken out to be hanged. Numbly, he heard Otto Sling's last words: "I wish every success to the Communist Party, the Czechoslovak people, and the president of the republic. I have never been a spy." As they placed the noose around Julius's neck, he had a strange vision: Terrible angels, murderers in white gowns, were flying out from the Kremlin. When they got close, Julius could see their black bags and stethoscopes. They were doctors, he thought, Jewish doctors . . .

Julius was back in his cell. Gingerly he touched his neck. Not broken yet. Pen and pad were lying by his cot. He seized them and began writing a letter to Ethel: "The battle is raging fiercely now and the enemy has called on his reserves—the fabricators, the pen prostitutes . . ."

Speaking of which, there's an intermission at Town Hall. At least a third of the crowd leaves, and now it's dreary rebuttal time, endless citations of obscure FBI documents. ("There's a lot of a material that's still classified," my knowledgeable neighbor says.) But here's something interesting: Each side gets to call on a designated expert witness, a kind of friend in court. Defending the prosecution, James Weinstein, a former party member and editor of the socialist tabloid *In These Times,* makes a shocking announcement. "We"—Weinstein and his party friends—"would have willingly done the same thing if we were asked." There's an angry murmur. Some protocol has been broken; but why is Holtzman interrupting Weinstein? He's driven from the stage in confusion.

It's the Schneirs's turn now. What, did they open a cage? Out blusters Marshall Perlin—lawyer for the National Committee to Re-Open the Rosenberg Case—cross-examining Radosh. Comic anarchy: Perlin is bellowing, "Answer yes or no!" and Radosh is pointing and yelling, "Left-wing McCarthyism!" The audience seems beyond caring, and—hello?—why is Walter Schneir wandering out like some ancient mariner, heave-ho and sail away, heading for center stage? Is this "sleepwalkers of the world, awake"? Extraterrestrial point of order? Holtzman gives Walter her evilest evil eye, and he drifts back to his seat.

Or maybe it was a secret signal—because all of a sudden, there's Michael Meeropol (né Rosenberg) on his feet, making a point from the floor. "Our side believes that the FBI was building cases," he announces. "Your side"—he tells the Radish—"believes that the FBI was seeking after the Truth." As if objective truth could exist under the regime of the bourgeoisie! Meeropol is radiating innocence: He emits a faint glow, like an old-fashioned watch dial. Everyone has to applaud.

And then, following the Rosenbergs as always, it's Morton Sobell, hirsute and bearded yet somehow dapper in his red flannel shirt and brown corduroy jacket, making an obscure reference to an interview Milton gave on the left-wing listener-sponsored radio station WBAI. Milton is so pissed off, she's actually snotty to a man who served eighteen years in the slammer for refusing to talk. It's like a sitcom, *Morton and Milton*. Sobell claims to have been misquoted. "Well, Morton, now you know what it's like," says Milton ungraciously. "Morton Sobell knows they did it," my informant says. "He knows they did it and he thinks they were *right on!*"

That's it! That's the story! Sobell decides to spill the beans. For Whom Sobell Tolls! Who could possibly doubt him after all these years? But who could possibly make him talk for the record? Has he left a statement for history? I'm reminded of the old Lenny Bruce who-killed-Christ routine: "Awright, I'll clear the air once and for all and confess. Yes, we did it. I did it, my family. I found a note in my basement. It said: 'We killed Him,' signed Morty."

"Gotta make a phone call," I tell my neighbor and head for the lounge, squeezing past the three bored FBI guys stationed at the door.

By the time I get back, the audience is even more thinned out. People are lined up at the floor microphone or simply shouting comments from their seats. "Listen to this," my friend tells me. "Woody Allen was here and he *hated* Radosh." Oh yeah? How come? Her eyes are shining. She wrinkles her nose. "He wants Marshall Perlin to be in his next movie!" Meanwhile, a gaunt, middle-aged man—tall, with Coke-bottle glasses and a thick gray mustache—is holding forth at the microphone. The heaviness of his final consonants suggests first-generation English. His clothes are off the same rack at Morty Sobell's. He is transparent, like an angel.

"Who's that?" I wonder.

"Julie Rosenberg," my neighbor explains. "The Greenglass brother-in-law."

"What, do we get the whole family, the *ganze mishpokhe* here?" People, I notice, are listening to Rosenberg with growing interest.

"He's been reading the FBI files for years," she says. "Never thinks about anything else. For a long time he *was* the National Committee to Re-Open the Greenglass Case." Seated on the aisle is a little, round-faced woman in a voluminous pink poncho of Third World design. She's gazing up at Rosenberg with rapt attention. "His wife. David's sister," I'm told. "They brought up the Greenglass children." Of course.

Rosenberg seems to be leading up to something big. He keeps referring to Radosh's interpretation with infectiously pungent sarcasm. "A smoking gun?" Rosenberg cries, mimicking some ridiculous Radish assertion. "Here, my friends, is the smoking gun!"

Abruptly, Rosenberg doubles over, reaching between Ethel's knees into a Don't Buy Judy Bond Blouses shopping bag, and comes up hurling an armful of press releases. Most of them land in the next row, with a big wad lying in the aisle. There's a pause, then a mad scramble, shrieks, fainting. People are grabbing the papers out of each other's hands, someone seems to have collapsed with a heart attack. Oblivious to the pandemonium, Rosenberg is rocking from his shoulders back and forth.

"From the files of the FBI, HQ-NY 7,975, 7/16/50," he chants. "Quote. Dear Fuzzy, OK. Frame the Commie Jew Greenglass and if he don't talk, we fry him and that Commie Jew Bitch Ruth of his too. As ever, Edgar." Rosenberg is davening so hard, he's practically levitated. Ethel has burst into her rendition of "Ciriciribin."

May Day at midnight! What happened next, I don't have to tell you. There were car horns blaring on all over West Forty-third Street. A steel band was playing the "Internationale." We were flung back to 1950 and then somehow forward to 1984 and the Better World. Later, I heard that people had danced in Union Square until dawn.

When I awoke, it was nearly noon. Dressing quickly, I took the elevator downstairs, crossed the courtyard, and walked out onto Cherry Street. The sun was shining. Children ran and shouted in the playground. I jogged beneath the Manhattan Bridge, up Rutgers Street and through the LaGuardia Houses. Someone stepped from the shadows and grabbed my shoulder. It was just security checking IDs. I continued along Madison Street, zigzagged through the Ben Gold Towers, and emerged breathless, the Browder Bridge looming ahead. Beyond, the salmon-pink high-risers of Stalin Village marched strong and united, block after radiant block, all the way to Fourteenth Street and the offices of the *Village Voice*.

I had this article to finish, and the sentences were all jumbled in my head. A Spanish-English-Chinese placard on the corner announced a neighborhood celebration at the David and Ruth Greenglass Park of Culture and Recreation. Writing seemed too solitary an occupation. Experiencing the urge to mingle, I headed east toward the river. Hundreds had already gathered on the great lawn by the people's handball courts. Festive bunting hung from the lampposts. Uniformed park attendants were raising a colossal red star.

Watching them, I inadvertently stumbled into the midst of a square dance. "Yo," someone jovially advised. All around me was a vast formation of men and women, women and women, men and men, blacks and whites, Asians and Hispanics, in overalls and gingham dresses, executing an intricate do-si-do to "There Once Was a Union Maid." The proud voice of the people's artist Leadbelly issued from the flag-festooned public address system. I walked off a little ways and sat down by the river.

Happy babies crawled through the grass. Contented old comrades sat basking on the benches. Kibitzers from the kibbutz peered over the shoulders of pensive Class Struggle players. Here and there, small delegations of Foreign Friends threaded their way through the throng. There even seemed to be a group from Birobidzhan, chatting in Yiddish. The monorail glided into the station, discharging an animated group of Young Pioneers in red coonskin caps. Beeping twice for show, the train took off like a silver bullet. I could follow its gleaming trajectory as it followed the curve of the shoreline up past the United Nations complex, out over Roosevelt Island and then, in a brilliant pirouette, back toward Manhattan and the Marcantonio Town of Tomorrow. To think that the fare was only a nickel! I loved New York.

Sudden cheers. The battleship *Potemkin* was steaming upriver. Shouting and waving, the sailors on deck were tossing garlands of flowers on shore. They seemed to be singing, "I Dreamed I Saw Joe Hill Last Night," in phonetic English.

But then—the shining sun passed behind a dark cloud. There was a sudden chill. Queasy, I sat down quickly on the bench. Had some Trotskyite spiked last night's punch with LSD? Such things have been known to happen. Across the lawn, the great concrete slab of the people's handball court seemed to fissure. A mad profusion of orange lines and purple blotches covered its surface, graffiti spreading like time-lapse jungle rot. Something smashed into existence—it was a broken bottle of Muscatel. Rubbish was sprouting from the earth at my feet.

A wheezing old lady shuffled by, her walker scraping the concrete. Horrified, I watched the proud uniform of a park attendent decompose into a tattered "I Love New York" sweatshirt and putrid gray pants. With a spastic convulsion, the man tumbled backward and bashed his skull on the pavement. His shoes evaporated, his dirt-encrusted ankles were covered with oozing sores. A child darted by and deftly plucked a wad of greasy singles from his pocket.

White faces were winking out like lights after curfew. The public address system gave a strangled cry and fell silent. Over the menacing backbeat of faraway congas, I heard a distant scream. The light was feeble, sickly. The wind rattled the leaves and wantonly wrapped a yellowed newspaper around my knees. (Special to the *New York Times:* "Some Losers in Silicon Valley Said to Find Wealth in Spying.")

Walter Schneir's last words rang in my ears. "We know what reality is," he had said. "At least some of us do!" Shivering, I pulled anxiously at the sidelocks which now curled from my temples. What had I been thinking? It was Kol Nidre 1984, and the sun was nearly gone from the sky.

That night, I dreamed I interviewed Judge Irving R. Kaufman. We were in the Garden Cafeteria on East Broadway, and the plaster from the pushcart mural was flaking off the ceiling into our soup. "Harry Gold was a genius," the judge was telling me. "We had the suspects, he supplied the crime." A bag lady was ranting and calling us Communists. "My wife," the judge said wryly. "She's a social worker. Her name is . . . Rosenberg."

The judge leaned across the table and, sweeping some crumbs onto the floor, tugged at my sleeve. "The world was killing the Jews," he told me, enunciating each word individually. "Julius Rosenberg . . . feh!" Then we were walking by the Manhattan Bridge, as tawdry and ridiculous as the Las Vegas strip, and suddenly the wizened little judge grew younger and stronger and began shouting, "He backed the wrong horse. He made his bet and he had to pay! Understand? In this country, we pay our debts!"

Now we were in Foley Square, on the very spot where Ethel was arrested. "But to kill a man?" I asked. "We had to make an example," explained the judge, "an example for the whole world to see." He was bounding backward up the courthouse steps. "But even your wife?" I shouted after him. "I mean, even his wife?"

The judge was gone. Judgment Day dawned. Above the Municipal Building, I saw an angel limned against the sky and a hard rain about to fall. (How was it that my parents were teenagers again?) Then, I was looking for my kid sister, and we were running home to Knickerbocker Village, dashing across Worth Street, and at that moment, the sirens started wailing, and just ahead a great and scowling atomic bomb was suspended in the sky, poised to score a direct . . .

"h-i-t," I typed into the computer. Yes, I did finally make it to the office, flooded subways and all. That dream practically wrote itself; but the big questions are still hanging. So let's put it to the mainframe here.

Q: Were Julius and Ethel guilty?

A: AFFIRMATIVE. GUILTY OF WANTING THE BETTER WORLD.

Q: Does that make them innocent?

A: INNOCENT . . . MONSTERS.

Q: Does that mean they were traitors?

A: NEGATIVE. NEGATIVE. NEGATIVE. NEGATIVE. NEGATIVE. NEGATIVE. NEGATIVE. NEGATIVE. NEGATIVE. NEGATIVE. NEGATIVE. NEGATIVE. NEGATIVE. NEGA—

I had to pull the plug, the machine was just going nuts! But I think I understand. How could the Rosenbergs be traitors? Traitors! To whom? We're not just talking about the only Jewish couple in America to have their portraits done by Pablo Picasso, you know. The Rosenbergs never betrayed their beliefs, their friends. They kept the faith. They sacrificed everything—even their children. In a time when turning state's witness was touted as the greatest of civic virtues, the Rosenbergs went to their deaths without implicating a soul. We're not talking traitors—we're talking Stalinist saints![29]

Sure, the Rosenbergs were framed. How else was the state supposed to prove a conspiracy to steal its secrets? The evidence against Julius was slight, that against Ethel was nonexistent, and the charges were problematic, to say the least. (But then, governments have always reserved for themselves the right to declare arbitrarily who is a traitor.) "Always remember that we were innocent and could not wrong our conscience," they wrote in their last letter to Michael and Robby.[30]

However, the Rosenbergs were framed for an activity that all available circumstantial and psychological evidence suggests that they—or rather, Julius, supported as ever by Ethel—committed. Deny that, and you deny their martyrdom any meaning. (Whoever has lived for future. . . .) For some, the secret of Rosenberg guilt is more awesome than even the secret of the atom bomb. The same outrage blossoms whenever the subject is broached. Because the Rosenbergs are so pure that to talk about them at all is in some way to betray them.

Suspects without crimes, living dangerously in extreme situations: By day, they were a progressive petit-bourgeois Jewish couple; by night, fantastic world-historical figures, the Lone Ranger and Tonto of Knickerbocker Village. If the Rosenbergs had never existed, who of us would have dared to invent them?

NOTES

Introduction

1. Rem Koolhaus, "Field Trip," in *S,M,L,X-L* (New York: Monacelli Press, 1995), p. 222.
2. Cited in Martin Walker, *The Cold War: A History* (New York: Henry Holt, 1993), p. 157.
3. Cited in "Voices from Different Times, and Both Sides of the Wall," *New York Times,* 11/12/89, sec. 4, p. 2.
4. Stalinalle, for example, had been renamed Karl-Marx Allee on November 13, 1961.
5. These included concealed land mines, trip wires, alarms. The Death Strip was patrolled by Alsatian guard dogs and yet, like some perverse zoological garden, populated by white bunny rabbits. "Nail-studded boards randomly scattered at the foot of the inner wall can literally nail a jumper to the ground, spiking him on their five-inch prongs," wrote West German novelist Peter Schneider in his fictional account of such daredevil wall vaulters, while in the sewer beneath, the line between East and West Berlin was "secured by electrified fences, which grant free passage only to the excretions of both parts of the city" (*The Wall Jumper* [New York: Pantheon, 1983], p. 53).
6. Is *The Spy Who Came in from the Cold* not a despairingly left-wing film? Director Martin Ritt, a veteran of the Group Theater, was blacklisted in Hollywood between 1951 and 1957; he subsequently directed *The Front* (1976), as well as two militant paeans to labor, *The Molly McGuires* (1970) and *Norma Rae* (1979). The opposite story is *For Eyes Only* (the German title is in English), directed in 1963 by Janos Veiczi. Having obtained West German state secrets, an East German double agent must escape *back* across the Wall.

   Among other things, the "authorized National Border" divided the free world from the domain of our most reliable movie villains, the CommuNazi East Germans. Reviewing Robert Siodmak's *Escape from East Berlin,* which opened in New York on December 5, 1962, on a bill with *Swordsman of Sienna* and was based on the actual escape of twenty-eight East Germans who eleven months earlier had tunneled beneath the Wall, *Variety* (10/17/62) mused that "oddly enough, at times one tends to forget he is watching a depiction of a 1962 incident—it is almost as if the time is 1939 and the Nazis are in charge."

7. Cited in *Deutsches Historischesmuseum Magazin* (autumn 1991): 5.

8. Koolhaus, "Field Trip," p. 221.

9. Paul Goldberger, "Reimagining Berlin," *New York Times Magazine*, 2/5/95, p. 46.

10. Koolhaus "Field Trip," p. 222. In the summer of 1995, twenty-two years after he first made the proposal, Christo was finally permitted to wrap the Reichstag in sheets of aluminum-coated polypropylene, securing the bundle with five miles of blue rope.

11. Schneider, *Wall Jumper,* p. 12.

12. It is a sinister coincidence that the Night of the Broken Wall fell precisely on the fifty-first anniversary of *Kristallnacht*—the Night of the Broken Glass—and, now a national holiday, will thus supersede memory of the Nazi pogrom. This was, after all, Europe's Wailing Wall. A portion of it and the Death Strip might have been preserved, if only as the city's Holocaust memorial.

13. "After the Wall," *New Republic*, 12/4/89, p. 7.

14. See Randall Rothenberg, "A Soft Red Glow on Madison Avenue," *New York Times,* 12/2/89.

15. Cited in "Voices from Different Times," p. 2.

16. Jean-Luc Godard's *Germany Year Nine Zero* (1991), which had its origins in a French television request for a movie about "solitude," is another vivid essay on this transitional period. The imaginary landscape evaporates even as it is filmed. Just as the title suggests *Germany Year Zero,* Roberto Rossellini's 1947 neorealist drama of post–World War II Berlin, so the casting evokes Godard's 1965 *Alphaville,* the movie that portrayed then-contemporary Paris as the galactic capital of a comic-book future. Taking advantage of the new freedom to film in East Germany, Godard tracks *Alphaville*'s tough-guy hero Lemmy Caution (Eddie Constantine) through the decomposing German Democratic Republic of December 1990.

    To the degree that *Germany Year Nine Zero* has a plot, it follows Lemmy—a.k.a. "The Last Spy," installed as a mole in some East German backwater—as he makes his confused and gloomy way back west. A wealth of twentieth-century history is compressed into a single reference to the one-sentence intertitle from F. W. Murnau's 1922 *Nosferatu* that, for André Breton, famously contained the movie's entire poetic charge. "Once I crossed the frontier, the phantoms came out to meet me," Lemmy muses, approaching the site of the former Wall.

17. Georg C. Bertsch and Ernst Hedler, *SED* (Cologne: Taschen, 1990), p. 7. Five years after the Wall fell, a mysterious wave of German Democratic Republic nostalgia was reported spreading across eastern Germany. Nightclubs were decorated with portraits of Erich Honecker, among other former Communist leaders, and patrons who wore their Communist youth-group uniforms were admitted free. East Germany's most famous industrial product, the boxy, slow-moving, fuel-inefficient Trabant automobile— for which buyers once had to wait for a dozen years—had become a collector's item. See Stephen Kinzler, "In 'East Germany,' Bad Ol' Days Now Look Good," *New York Times,* 8/27/94, p. 2.

18. A kind of inadvertently Socialist Realist version of the surrealist favorite *Peter Ibbetson, The Promise* concerns a couple sundered by the Wall who continue to meet—not in their dreams, but during the course of various political thaws.

19. Stephen Kinzer, "Wanted: A Home for Two Watchtowers, w/History," *New York Times,* 12/29/93.

20. Peter Schneider, *The German Comedy: Scenes of Life after the Wall* (New York: Farrar, Straus & Giroux, 1991), p. 212. It was, Schneider wrote, "as though they were looking for, or maybe missing, something. . . . But perhaps this story is only a legend—like the Wall itself."

Chapter 1

1. Boris Groys, *The Total Art of Stalinism: Avant-Garde, Aesthetic Dictatorship, and Beyond* (Princeton: Princeton University Press, 1992), p. 6.

2. "Soviet Socialist Realist Paintings 1930s-1960s" (Oxford University Museum of Modern Art, 1992), "Agitation Zum Glück: Sowjetische Kunst der Stalinzeit" (Kassel Documente-Halle, 1993), "Stalin's Choice: Soviet Socialist Realism 1932-1956" (Institute for Contemporary Art, P.S. 1 Museum, New York, 1994), "Art and Power: Europe under the Dictators 1930-45" (Hayward Gallery, London, 1995), "Berlin-Moscau 1900-1950" (Berlinische Gallery, 1996).

3. David Elliott, "Engineers of the Human Soul," in *Soviet Socialist Realist Painting, 1930s-1960s*, ed. Matthew Cullerne Bown and David Elliott (Oxford: Museum of Modern Art, 1992), p. 6; Groys, *Total Art of Stalinism*, p. 17.

4. Igor Golomstock, "Problems in the Study of Stalinist Culture," in *The Culture of the Stalin Period*, ed. Hans Günther (New York: St. Martin's Press, 1990), pp. 118-19. In a sense, both men invert the party line, argued by Soviet critic Mikhail Lifshits in *The Crisis of Ugliness: From Cubism to Pop Art* (1968), that Nazism is a result of modernism (i.e., by destroying Renaissance perspective and hence humanist consciousness, the expressionists, the Bauhaus, and Picasso paved the way for Hitler). But while Golomstock identifies Socialist Realism with the art of Nazi Germany, Groys points out that Socialist Realism lacks the nostalgia and stylized antiquity of Nazi art. Socialist Realism is nostalgic (to the point of hysteria) about the present; it "judges the reality created in the Soviet Union to be the highest achievement of the entire course of human history." See Boris Groys, "The Birth of Socialist Realism from the Spirit of the Russian Avant-Garde," in Günther, ed., *Culture of the Stalin Period*, p. 123.

5. Vitaly Komar and Alexander Melamid, "What Is to Be Done?" *Artforum* (May 1992): 103.

6. Régine Robin, *Socialist Realism: An Impossible Aesthetic* (Stanford: Stanford University Press, 1992), p. 298.

7. "Introduction to the Soviet Pavilion, the World's Fair, 1939," in *The Aesthetic Arsenal: Socialist Realism under Stalin* (New York: The Institute for Contemporary Art, P.S. 1 Museum, 1993), p. 11.

8. Elliott, "Engineers of the Human Soul," p. 13.

9. Boris Kagarlitsky, *The Thinking Reed: Intellectuals and the Soviet State from 1917 to the Present* (London: Verso, 1988), p. 12;, cited in Helene Lewis, *The Politics of Surrealism* (New York: Paragon House, 1988), p. 126.

10. Cited in Matthew Cullerne Bown, *Art under Stalin* (Oxford: Phaidon Press, 1991), p. 17.

11. Maurice Nadeau, *The History of Surrealism* (Cambridge, Mass.: Belknap Press, 1989), p. 90.

12. Lewis, *Politics of Surrealism*, pp. 59, 121. Like Stalin, albeit less lethally, Breton periodically purged his followers. (Aragon, who quit the surrealists rather than break with the Communist Party, was Breton's Trotsky.) Even before Stalin found fascist wreckers, Salvador Dalí had been excommunicated by the surrealists for his "counterrevolutionary actions involving the glorification of Hitlerian fascism," in a show trial staged at Breton's apartment in early 1934. Five years later, Paul Eluard was expelled for allowing a Communist newspaper to print his poems.

13. André Breton, *What Is Surrealism? Selected Writings*, ed. Franklin Rosemont (New York: Monad Press, 1978), p. 155.

14. Robin, *Socialist Realism*, p. 74.

15. James H. Billington, *The Icon and the Axe: An Interpretive History of Russian Culture* (New York: Random House, 1970), p. 31; cited in Nina Tumarkin, *Lenin Lives! The Lenin Cult in Soviet Russia* (Cambridge, Mass.: Harvard University Press, 1983), p. 21.

16. Cited in Margaret Betz, "The Icon and Russian Modernism," *Artforum* 15 (summer 1977): 39.
17. György Szücs, "The Philosophy of Pictorial Sovereignty," in *Art and Society in the Age of Stalin,* ed. Péter György and Hedvig Turai (Budapest: Corvina, 1992), p. 49.
18. Joseph Bakshtein, "Notes on the Origin of Socialist Realist Iconography," in *Aesthetic Arsenal,* p. 57.
19. Gregory Battcock's *Super Realism: A Critical Anthology* (New York: Dutton, 1975) contains not a single reference to the Soviet photo-realism, which predates the American movement by some thirty years. "Photographs of things have become more real to Americans than the things themselves," Harold Rosenberg writes ("Reality Again," in *Super Realism,* p. 141), in effect describing another aspect of the Stalin era. It is worth noting that just as Soviet painters made use of photographs, so Soviet photographers have—often extravagantly—retouched their photos.
20. Robin, *Socialist Realism,* p. 74.
21. Ibid., p. 59; Peter Kenez, *Cinema and Soviet Society, 1917-53* (Cambridge: Cambridge University Press, 1992), p. 180; István Nemeskürty, *Word and Image: History of the Hungarian Cinema* (Budapest: Zrinyi Printing House, 1974), p. 162.
22. Cited in Mikhail N. Epstein, *After the Future: The Paradoxes of Postmodernism and Contemporary Russian Culture* (Amherst: University of Massachusetts Press, 1995), p. 191. Epstein suggests that the Russian affinity for simulation and facade derives from the nation's geographic location between two great belief systems. Where the West explains all illusions in terms of empirical reality, the East understands that the so-called material world is, in fact, illusory. "It is not surprising then, that the spectre wandering through Europe settled down and acquired reality in Russia," Epstein noted. "Throughout the course of Russian history, reality has been subjected to a gradual process of disappearance"—most recently, the collapse of Soviet reality (p. 194).
23. Cited in Victoria Bonnell, "The Peasant Woman in Stalinist Political Art of the 1930s," in *Aesthetic Arsenal,* p. 145.
24. Victor Serge, *Russia Twenty Years After* (Atlantic Highlands, N.J.: Humanities Press International, 1996), p. 195.
25. Ibid., pp. 218-19.
26. Heda Margolius Kovály, *Under a Cruel Star: A Life in Prague 1941-1968* (Cambridge: Plunkett Lake Press, 1986), p. 114; Eugen Loebl, *My Mind on Trial* (New York: Harcourt Brace Jovanovich, 1976), p. 186; Karel Kaplan, *Report on the Murder of the General Secretary* (Columbus: Ohio State University Press, 1990), p. 199. Kaplan, *Murder of the General Secretary,* pp. 207-8, 227-28; Loebl, *My Mind on Trial,* p. 186.
27. "Here is something heart-rending," Victor Serge writes in *Russian Twenty Years After:*

> Peasants of *kolkhozes* where the famine has just ended—the government having finally decided to leave them something to eat this year—write to the beloved Leader to thank him for such good living. As I read it, I see the dismal destitution in which the peasants live. I see a troop of emaciated Cossacks stop before a cinema, in an odour of rancid boots. They are delegates to a local conference. A new film is to be shown for them and it just happens to be *Peasants,* in which the members of a *kolkhoz* guzzle until they are gorged. And the screen shows this to members of *kolkhozes* who, themselves, fill up on food only on state occasions, three or four times a year. You also see a lovely young peasant girl, sleeping and dreaming of happiness: she is quietly crossing a park, pushing her baby carriage, and the gifted Leader, in his long military greatcoat, accompanies her at a vigorous pace. . . . O felicity! to have a child by him! (133)

Serge doesn't mention that, on waking from her animated dream, the ecstatic peasant girl begins kissing the husband who lies beside her.

28. Frank Lloyd Wright, "Architecture and Life in the USSR," *Design Trends* (October 1937): 61. As James H. Billington observed in *The Icon and the Axe,* "The mammoth mosaics in the Moscow subway, the unnecessary spires and fantastic frills of civic buildings, the leaden chandeliers and dark foyers of reception chambers—all send the historical imagination back to the somber world of Ivan the Terrible" (p. 536). By 1941, this analogy was quasi-official: Not only did Ivan's terror provide means to legitimize Stalin's, but the sixteenth-century czar's war against Livonia offered historical justification for Stalin's annexation of the Baltic states. Sergei Eisenstein's *Ivan the Terrible*—set almost entirely in the twisting corridors of a windowless cavern, a set that makes paranoia tangible—was paralleled by Valentin Kostylev's multipart historical novel of the same name and a 1922 biography reissued with quotations from Stalin.

29. Alexei Tarkhanov and Sergei Kavtaradze, *Architecture of the Stalin Era* (New York: Rizzoli, 1992), p. 117. The optimism that placed this completed monument to communism's "future triumph" (as Sergei Kirov called it) in the milky space behind the joyously forward-striding model workers of Aleksandr Deinekov's 1936 *Stakhanovites* had become a quotidian delusion by the time Efim Charski painted it into the hazy background of his 1952 canvas *J. V. Stalin and Ju. Tsedenbal on a Walk in the Kremlin.*

30. In 1958, Nikita Khrushchev had a huge open-air swimming pool constructed on the site.

31. "Afterword: A Talk with the Author,"in Milan Kundera, *The Book of Laughter and Forgetting* (New York: Penguin Books, 1981), p. 233.

32. Vladimir Paperny, "Moscow in the 1930s and the Emergence of a New City," in Günther, ed., *Culture of the Stalin Period,* p. 233.

33. The theme park has become an irresistible metaphor for the Soviet Union. Mikhail N. Epstein speculates that the reason Nikita Khrushchev was so insistent on touring Disneyland during his 1959 state visit to the United States was that "he wanted to learn whether Americans had succeeded in creating as perfect a simulation of reality as the Soviet model" (*After the Future,* p. 200). History might have been changed had the Soviet premier been permitted to study Disney's realm. The economist Peter Passell published a brief essay noting the similarities between the queues for Disneyland's attractions and those for consumer goods that characterized the no-longer extant Soviet Union: "Like the Disney Company, the Soviets were in the business of packaging fantasy. Needless to say, Mickey does it much better" ("Economic Scene," *New York Times,* 4/27/95, sec. D, p. 2). In late 1993, the *New York Times* reported that twenty-eight-year-old former East German tour guide Frank Georgi was planning a German Democratic Republic theme park on a tract of land twenty miles north of Berlin that had formerly been used to train East German army officers. Georgi envisioned the park as a repository for both East German artifacts (ranging from Trabants to gritty toilet paper) and attitudes. Clerks in the largely empty stores not only would be "surly and unhelpful" but, to add to the excitement, might actually be undercover police agents. The Disney theme parks also employ disguised security personnel, but Georgi's simulation of the German Democratic Republic would ensure that "guests who question the Communist system or criticize its leaders will be seized at some later point and thrown into jail" for sentences meted out in hours (*New York Times,* 11/9/93). Several years later, a similar, if unavoidably less authentic, theme park was announced for Fort Lauderdale, Florida. Other proposals include a Victims of Communism Memorial Museum—including a reconstructed Berlin Wall and re-created Soviet gulag—planned for the Old Tariffs Building in Washington, D.C., and the $100 million Stalin-era retropark planned for Kirov Park in St. Petersburg (*New York Times,* 12/23/95, p. 16).

34. Tarkhanov and Kavtaradze, *Architecture of the Stalin Era,* p. 182.

35. Heroes of aviation provided another avatar of the Soviet new man. "Stalin's falcons" were the first pilots to successfully stage a North Pole landing. By 1938, the Soviet Union held more than sixty world records, including those for distance, altitude, and speed.

36. Serge, *Russia Twenty Years After*, p. 127.
37. When the Hungarian painters of the early 1950s took up Socialist Realism, they carefully copied Soviet paintings, substituting for Stalin their singularly unlovely leader Mátyás Rákosi.
38. Golomstock, "Problems," pp. 115–16.
39. John Steinbeck, *A Russian Journal* (New York: Viking Press, 1948), pp. 50–51.
40. Serge, *Russia Twenty Years After*, p. 150.
41. Isaac Deutscher, "Marxism and Primitive Magic," in *The Stalinist Legacy*, ed. Tariq Ali (Harmondsworth, Middlesex: Penguin Books, 1984), p. 115.
42. Vitaly Komar compared *Prominent Muscovites*—which was exhibited in "Stalin's Choice" after P.S. 1 curators discovered it rolled up in the basement of the Tretiakov Gallery—to one of Jackson Pollock's contemporary canvases. "It has same visual aggressiveness," the artist told me. It was his dream, he added, that P.S. 1 would hold a "special day when all the paintings will be hung upside down—for people who like abstract art" ("Public School Exhibit Brings Stalin to Queens: Treasure Trove of Communist Kitsch," *Forward*, 1/28/94, p. 16).
43. Deutscher, "Marxism and Primitive Magic," p. 115.
44. Ilya Weisfeld, "Arts: *The Vow*," *International Literature* (1947): 66. Weisfeld explained that "it was first planned to produce *The Vow* in 1939. The events dealt with were taking place at the time Chiaureli filmed them, not as chapters of a newsreel but as epic episodes woven into the fabric of a narrative. In other words, *The Vow* is an epic of our day. It is the narrative of modern times by a contemporary, it is a successful attempt on the part of the artist to look at his own times with the eyes of a historian" (pp. 68–69).
45. André Bazin, "The Stalin Myth," *Movies and Methods II*, ed. Bill Nichols (Berkeley: University of California Press, 1985), p. 35.
46. Maya Turovskaya, "Notes on Women and Film," *Discourse* 17 (spring 1995): 20. Even the great Stalin was improved, by being made taller, as in Aleksandr Gerasimov's celebrated Stalin Prize–winner *Comrades Stalin and Voroshilov in the Kremlin after the Rain* (1938). Rather than star in newsreels, the diminutive, pockmarked leader preferred to be portrayed by carefully selected actors in extravagant docudramas. Unlike Hitler, as Peter Kenez has observed, Stalin was not a performer. He was the imaginary creator of an imaginary land. See Kenez, *Cinema and Soviet Society*, pp. 229–30.
47. Weisfeld, "Arts," p. 69.
48. "Fight Power with Spontaneity and Humour: An Interview with Dusan Makavejev," *Film Quarterly* (winter 1971–72): 7.
49. Twenty-odd years later, Makavejev's *Gorilla Bathes at Noon* (1994) proposed itself as the absurdist sequel to Chiaureli's pious World War II epic *Fall of Berlin* (1949): *The Fall of East Berlin*. Makavejev's protagonist, Major Victor Borisovich, is introduced in juxtaposition with the *Fall of Berlin*'s bombastic battle sequence where a triumphant Red Army storms the Reichstag—except Borisovich is squatting on an apartment rooftop. Subsequently, he's revealed to be the child of the lovers Alexei and Natasha, who are reunited in the presence of a suitably divine Stalin at *Fall of Berlin*'s ecstatic climax, and he is now the last Soviet soldier left in the no longer divided city.

   In addition to florid Sovcolor chunks from *Fall of Berlin* (some overdubbed with the soundtrack from the 1936 Nazi propaganda film *Triumph of the Will*), *Gorilla Bathes at Noon* incorporates footage documenting the decapitation and removal of Nikolai Tomsky's sixty-foot statue of Lenin, supposedly the world's largest, in the former East Berlin. "Ich bin ein Berliner," Victor Borisovich cries to the TV crew that attempts to interview him as he makes a perfunctory attempt at cleaning the paint-spattered statue. The end of *WR* is thus miraculously rhymed by the final shot in *Gorilla Bathes at Noon*, with the decapitated head of Tomsky's Lenin transported on a flatbed truck past a somber East Berlin housing tract. In most of Makavejev's films, sexual passion climaxes with death. Here, the ambiguous love object that dies is Soviet Communism itself. The abandoned Tomsky monument to Lenin has attracted, in addition to Makavejev and his crew, spontaneous offerings—flowers, ribbons, an invitation to public spitting, some Communist folk singers, and a gaggle of drunks and crackpots. There's also a sign reading "Hands Off History," an injunction that has more than once been hurled at Makavejev.

50. In a related strategy, Czech director Jaromil Jires had incorporated triumphalist newsreel footage from the early 1950s into his 1968 adaptation of Milan Kundera's *The Joke*, using this material to comment on as well as to establish the movie's setting.

51. Anders Åman, *Architecture and Ideology in Eastern Europe during the Stalin Era: An Aspect of Cold War History* (Cambridge, Mass.: MIT Press, 1992), p. 151.

52. Mészáros originally wanted to incorporate Soviet films of period. Compelled to substitute a Hungarian example of SR, she chose one that, in its climactic use of a Russian marching song, had provoked a class of high school students compelled to see it in 1952 to tear up the movie theater and assault its manager (J. Hoberman, "Budapest Tales," *Village Voice*, 11/6/84, p. 58). *Diary for My Children* includes the scene that presumably provoked the riot.

53. Kagarlitsky, *Thinking Reed,* p. 116.

54. Jan Kott, *The Theater of Essence* (Evanston, Ill.: Northwestern University Press, 1984), p. 93.

55. See J. Hoberman, *Gyula Gazdag: Lost Illusions/Found Metaphors* (Berkeley: Pacific Film Archive, 1987), p. 8. Similarly, one of Hungarian poet Miklós Haraszti's crimes was commemorating the centenary of Lenin's birth by organizing a public reading of Lenin's writings without providing politically expedient commentary.

56. Abram Tertz, *The Trial Begins and On Socialist Realism* (New York: Vintage Books, 1960), p. 199.

57. Claudia Jolles, "Erik Bulatov—Visions of Power, the Power of Vision," in *Eric Bulatov* (London: Parkett/ICA, 1989), p. 10.

58. Marc Field, "Komar and Melamid and the Luxury of Style," *Artforum* 16 (January 1978): 41.

59. Wang, born in 1956, was among the first Chinese artists to begin manipulating Mao's image in the late 1980s, when China developed its own equivalent of Sots Art as well as a minicraze for old Cultural Revolution anthems such as "The Sun Is Most Red and Chairman Mao Is Most Dear," which reappeared in disco arrangements. A 1989 *Portrait of Chairman Mao* by Shanghai artist Yu Youhan elaborates on Andy Warhol's well-known series of Maos, perhaps also referencing the student protesters who that year splattered the giant image of Mao in Tiananmen Square with paint: Yu not only represents the Chinese leader in (misapplied) lipstick and eyeliner but covers him with a garish panoply of floral patterns. The so-called Mao Craze survived the June 1989 massacre of students in Tiananmen Square. By 1992, the disco collection *Red Sun: Odes to Mao Zedong Sung to a New Beat* had sold fourteen million units (the next year brought "revolutionary" karaoke videos), and in Beijing, at least, the image of Mao emblazoned all manner of pins, pens, and T-shirts—the local equivalent of Garfield the Cat. For a detailed account, see Geremie R. Barmé, *Shades of Mao: The Posthumous Cult of the Great Leader* (Armonk, N.Y.: M. E. Sharpe, 1996).

60. Jamey Gambrell, "The Wonder of the Soviet World," *New York Review of Books,* 12/22/94, p. 35.

61. Stephen Kinzer, "Moscow Journal: Where Soviets Strutted, Capitalism Sets up Shop," *New York Times,* 11/8/94.

62. Harold Rosenberg, "The Old Age of Modernism," in *Art on the Edge* (Chicago: University of Chicago Press, 1983), p. 287.

63. Jack Burnham, "Introduction," in *Komar and Melamid: Two Soviet Dissident Artists,* ed. Melvyn B. Nathanson (Carbondale: Southern Illinois University Press, 1979), p. xxxix.

64. Other artists have been less adept. It is striking that in his 1980 *Man of Iron* and her 1986 *Diary for My Loves,* sequels to *Man of Marble* and *Diary for My Children,* respectively, Andrzej Wadja and Márta Mészáros produced works that, in their stern liquidation of ambiguity, resemble orthodox Socialist Realism. In *Man of Iron,* the actual Lech Walesa presides over the wedding of two fictional characters much as a Stalin impersonator brought together a pair of long-sundered lovers in the stupefyingly sublime climax of Chiaureli's *Fall of Berlin.*

65. Clement Greenberg, "Art and Kitsch," in *Art and Culture* (Boston: Beacon, 1961), p. 10.

66. "The Postcommunist Future," *Prague Post,* 2/11–17/92, p. 8.

67. Milan Kundera, "Interview with Alain Finkielkraut," in *Cross Currents: A Yearbook of Central European Culture* (Ann Arbor: University of Michigan Press, 1982), pp. 21–22.

Chapter 2

1. Miklós Haraszti, *The Velvet Prison* (New York: Basic Books, 1987), pp. 64–65.

2. Milan Simecka, *The Restoration of Order: The Normalization of Czechoslovakia* (London: Verso, 1984), p. 55.

3. *The Black Book of Polish Socialism,* ed. Jane Leftwich Curry (New York: Vintage, 1984), p. 151.

4. George Konrád, *The Loser* (New York: Harcourt Brace Jovanovich, 1982), p. 237.

5. Well, almost anyone: The opening of *Love Me Tender,* the routine western into which Elvis Presley had been hastily inserted, returned its production cost in something like two weeks.

6. The East European 1956 is the covert subject of Andrzej Wajda's 1958 *Ashes and Diamonds,* which cast the Polish James Dean, Zbigniew Cybulski, in pompadour and shades, as the embodiment of confused, romantic nationalism.

7. Cited in Charles Gati, *Hungary and the Soviet Bloc* (Durham: Duke University Press, 1986), p. 160.

8. William Shawcross, *Crime and Compromise: Janos Kadar and the Politics of Hungary since Revolution* (New York: Dutton, 1974), p. 105.

9. Former member of the Czech Communist Party's Central Committee Zdeněk Mlynář, in his account of the Soviet invasion, details Kádár's vain attempt to warn Dubček of Moscow's intentions. At the end of a secret meeting three days before the Soviet invasion, Mlynář writes that "Kádár asked [Dubček] almost desperately: 'Do you *really* not know the kind of people you're dealing with?'" (*Nightfrost in Prague: The End of Humane Socialism* [New York: Karz Publishers, 1980], p. 157}.

10. After seven lean years, Kádár was able to reimplement the NEM in 1979. A final irony: The NEM was recognized as a Communist vanguard by Mikhail Gorbachev, too late for Gorbachev to implement it himself. See Gati, *Hungary,* p. 175.

11. Cited in Antonin J. Liehm and Mira Liehm, *The Most Important Art: Eastern European Film after 1945* (Berkeley: University of California Press, 1977), p. 385.

12. Dziga Vertov's *The Man with a Movie Camera* (1929), by contrast, supremely expresses the utopian Communist vision of total surveillance. No aspect of society escapes the scrutiny cum celebration of the motion-picture apparatus.

13. Not only were Gypsies perfect subjects for the projection of Hapsburg nostalgia, but there was also—as I would discover—particular identification with this minority among the members of Hungary's heavily Jewish film intelligentsia.

14. Herbert Marcuse, *One-Dimensional Man: Studies in the Ideology of Advanced Industrial Society* (Boston: Beacon Press, 1966), p. 72. The rarely challenged Kádárist taboos

were largely concerned with the depiction of "counterrevolutionary" activity—namely, the articulation of whatever might offend the Soviet Union or Hungary's neighbors—and thus naturally included Marcuse's writings (which, like those of Leon Trotsky, were nonetheless available to members of the party elite).

15. Liehm and Liehm, *Most Important Art*, p. 391.

16. Louis Marcorelle, *Living Cinema: New Directions in Contemporary Film-Making* (New York: Praeger Publishers, 1973), p. 100. A professional survivor and a reliable political weather vane, Kovács not only made the first reformist film but was the first to sound the retreat. It was also he who authorized the 1975 purge of the BBS.

17. Judit Elek's 1967 *How Long Does a Man Matter?* focused on two workers (one just entering maturity, the other about to retire) to make a melancholy comment on working-class lives under the ostensive dictatorship of the proletariat. Like *Difficult People*, Elek's hour-long film was well received—winning the main prize for the short feature at the Oberhausen Film Festival.

18. *Sociology* is a term with a particularly Hungarian resonance, evoking not only such important native sociologists as Karl Mannheim and István Bibó but also the so-called literary sociology of the late 1930s, in which "village explorers" such as Gyula Illyés and József Darvas wrote firsthand reports of poverty and backward social conditions in rural Hungary. The tradition of sociologist as social critic was given further impetus during the NEM by András Hegedüs and George Konrád, among others. Indeed, an unofficial critique such as Miklós Haraszti's *A Worker in a Worker's State* (1972) was but a new form of literary sociology. Just as the village explorers were accused of *nemzetgyalázás* (slandering the nation) so, forty years later, Haraszti's account of conditions in a Budapest tractor factory resulted in his trial for "grave incitement."

19. While still a student in 1966, Haraszti versified in defense of Gypsies and, with Pór, established a campus Vietnam Solidarity Committee which, having caught the authorities by surprise, was forcibly merged with the Communist Youth Organization (KISZ), which necessarily toned down its anti-Soviet stance. Haraszti considers himself to have been more a cultural than a political radical. Among other things, he wrote protest songs for a folk-rock trio known as the Guerrillas, and expelled from the university in 1966, he managed to publish a collection of revolutionary songs, *Poets, Verses, Revolutions* (Miklós Haraszti, unpublished interview with the author, May 1997).

20. Ibid.

21. *Agitators* created a further provocation by including newsreel footage and making repeated mention of Leon Trotsky's name. The movie was banned as too "Guevarist," although Bódy, who played the Sinkó figure, would claim that Lukács saw and approved the film before his death.

22. Many of *Black Train's* passengers were Gypsies, and following in the tradition of Sára's 1962 short, Schiffer made gypsy life the subject of several subsequent documentaries, including his feature-length *Gyuri Csépló* (1977), a portrait of a young gypsy's ill-fated attempt to find work in Budapest.

23. Made with a nonprofessional, mainly teenage cast, *The Whistling Cobblestone* was the second feature, after *Agitators*, produced with the help of the BBS. The tone is blandly outrageous: A group of boys are sent to a KISZ summer work camp where, as the faulty public address system immediately tells them, "owing to technical reasons," there is no work. In the absence of any meaningful activity or honest explanation, the camp becomes a setting for spurious ceremonies, pointless contests, and empty excercises in "democracy."

24. György Báron, "The Failure of Paternalism: A Portrait of the Filmmaker Gyula Gazdag," *Mozgovilág* (1981).

25. J. Hoberman, "Shelf Life: Gyula Gazdag Interviewed," *Film Comment* (October 1987): 52.

26. Milos Forman and Jan Novak, *Turnaround: A Memoir* (New York: Villard Books, 1994), p. 134.
27. In fact, Kesadlová (who had already appeared in Prague's first large rock concert as part of a mod trio who sang "The Loco-Motion" in Czech) not only landed the job at the Semafor as a result of the movie but became the director's second wife.
28. Báron, "Failure of Paternalism."
29. Cited in Gati, *Hungary,* p. 161.
30. During the summer of 1971, the KISZ attempted to ban jeans and long hair from Buda Youth Park—despite presence of long-haired rock bands as entertainment.
31. Hungarian pop offered a way to critique Hungarian socialism. Portraying the band Pyramid in his never-telecast documentary *When I Was Born* (1978), Gazdag evoked both the Rákosi period and the events of 1956. His erstwhile BBS colleague György Szomjas (whose 1971 *Honeymoons*—on local girls who seek out tourists in hopes of landing a rich husband—was bracketed with *Selection* and *Black Train* as a key work of the "sociological" movement) took the exploration a bit further. *Bald-Dog Rock* (1981) appeared in the same year as Hungary's first filmed rock concert. The film's antiheroes, a shaggy bunch of decrepit hippies called the Colorado Band who have been playing together for a decade and have never managed to get a single radio gig, make a last stab at the big time. Recruiting a one-legged Gypsy bluesman and renaming themselves Bald Dog, they switch from pseudo-American pop to a more authentically Hungarian prole-rock, committed to wailing the "Köbánya Blues" (insolently named for Budapest's venerable workers' slum). In addition to featuring the Hobo Blues Band, *Bald-Dog Rock* provides a documentary look at scenes ranging from a rural hop where teens twist to a toneless official polka ensemble, to a pretentious official band performing amid a cloud of dry-ice vapors, to the rowdy crowds that Bald Dog attracts until, with loutish integrity, the band self-destructs. Although *Bald-Dog Rock* was the only Hungarian feature produced under Communism to explore the fecund world of the local rock scene, Szomjas pointed out that, in Kádárist Hungary, rock 'n' roll was the one cultural expression that could exist without state support, "because it is directly supported by the audience each night."
32. Hoberman, "Shelf Life," p. 54.
33. Báron, "Failure of Paternalism." When *The Resolution* was shown at the New York Museum of Modern Art in 1986, a Hungarian-speaking member of the audience re-marked that the party secretary and his peers seemed incapable of constructing a single grammatical sentence. Gazdag replied that actually, because of the camera, "they spoke a little bit better than usual."
34. Hoberman, "Shelf Life," p. 54.
35. The influence of Gazdag's example may be seen in several kindred documentaries pro-duced at BBS in the mid-1970s. Gábor Bódy's *Youth Organization Leaders* (1972) used a mix of interviews and "constructed situations" to mark the fifteenth anniversary of the Pioneer movement (that is, 1956). In *Admission* (1972), László Vitézy tracked the process by which an eighteen-year-old worker applied for admission to the Communist Party. István Dárday's feature-length *Taking an Oath* (1975) documented the organiza-tion of the KISZ induction ceremony.
36. J. Hoberman, "Peter Hutton: A Tale of Two Cities," *Artforum* 25 (October 1985): 94.
37. Hans-Magnus Enzensberger, "Constituents of a Theory of the Media," in *Raids and Reconstructions: Essays in Politics, Crime and Culture* (London: Pluto Press, 1976), p. 34.
38. Experience and the Future Discussion Group, *Poland Today: The State of the Republic* (Armonk, N.Y.: M. E. Sharpe, 1979), p. 25. "Any unexpected piece of news causes the entire social organism to react with alarm," Milan Simecka notes in *Restoration of Order.* "It immediately gives rise to wild speculation, and is received as sign of some

breakdown in the regime. This hypersensitivity is the product of years of practise in reading newspapers, listening to the radio and watching television. It often takes no more than the appearance of an unusual photograph, an unusual news presentation, or the absense of a cliché from its accustomed place, to unloose an avalanche of speculation" (p. 50).

39. Stan Brakhage, *Film Biographies* (Berkeley: Turtle Island, 1977), p. 16.
40. *Kieślowski on Kieślowski*, ed. Danusia Stok (London: Faber & Faber, 1993), p. 112.
41. Ibid., p. 81.
42. Larry Rohter, "East Bloc Film Makers Have Liberty to Say What They Truly Mean," *New York Times*, 4/30/90, sec. C, p. 16.

Chapter 3

1. Isaac Deutscher, *The Non-Jewish Jew and Other Essays* (New York: Hill & Wang, 1968), p. 25.
2. *Der Emes*, 11/7/25.
3. "Every anti-Semite smiles when hearing the word *Berdichev*," Vasily Grossman would write in a 1929 feuilleton on his birthplace. "A nest of speculators; a town where people live by trade and deceit," Berdichev is the antihomeland. See John Garrard and Carol Garrard, *The Bones of Berdichev* (New York: Free Press, 1996), p. 88.
4. Viktor Shklovsky, "*Jewish Luck*," in *Marc Chagall and the Jewish Theater* (New York: Guggenheim Museum, 1993), p. 158.
5. Isaac Babel, *1920 Diary*, ed. Carol J. Avins (New Haven: Yale University Press, 1995), p. 85.
6. Zvi Gitelman, *A Century of Ambivalence: The Jews of Russia and the Soviet Union, 1881 to the Present* (New York: Schocken/YIVO, 1988), pp. 123-24. The destruction of the shtetl was so overwhelming, Gitelman notes, that between 1918 and 1921, some three-quarters of the Russian Jewish population was without regular income (p. 122). Lenin cited in Enzo Traverso, *The Marxists and the Jewish Question: The History of a Debate 1843-1943* (Atlantic Highlands, N.J.: Humanities Press International, 1994), p. 132.
7. Shklovsky, "*Jewish Luck*," p. 158. During the summer of 1926, the young director Abram Room (once connected with a Yiddish theater in the Lithuanian city Jews called Vilna) made a twenty-minute documentary on the new Jewish settlements in the Yevpatoria District of the Crimea, from a script Shklovsky had written with the non-Jewish poet Vladimir Mayakovsky. Titled for the programmatic catchphrase of the era, even while self-consciously exhibiting a certain amount of "Jewish" humor, *Jews on the Land* opens with scenes of a war-devastated shtetl, then cuts to an elderly Jew wandering about an even more desolate wilderness searching, one imagines, for Jewish happiness. Soon, sod-brick settlements rise, and as irrigation ditches crisscross the once-barren plain, the now-productivized Jews are themselves transformed. Jewish irony becomes Communist kitsch: A newborn baby is named "Forget Your Sorrows." Tractor drivers and Young Pioneers take their pride of place, and the filmmakers emphasize that, among other livestock, these new Jewish "peasants" are raising pigs.
8. Isaac Babel, *Lyubka the Cossack and Other Stories* (New York: New American Library, 1963), p. 131.
9. See Gitelman, *Century of Ambivalence*, pp. 96-108; and Gershon Scholem, *The Messianic Idea in Judaism* (New York: Schocken, 1971).
10. "To grasp the extraordinary impact of the opening in Moscow of the Yiddish State Theatre, one has to remember that under the Tsars, Moscow, the Holy of Holies of Greek Orthodoxy, was practically out of bounds for Jews," Isaac Deutscher notes in his essay on Marc Chagall (in *Non-Jewish Jew*, p. 160). Benjamin Harshav notes that

GOSET's Yiddish name—Moskver Yidisher Melukhisher Teater—translates as the Moscow Jewish *Royal* Theater (in "Chagall: Postmodernism and Fictional Worlds in Painting," in *Marc Chagall and the Jewish Theater,* p. 40).

11. Cited in Nicoletta Misler, "The Future in Search of Its Past: Nation, Ethnos, Tradition and the Avant-Garde in Russian Jewish Art Criticism," in *Tradition and Revolution: The Jewish Renaissance in Russian Avant-Garde Art 1912-1928,* ed. Ruth Apter-Gabriel (Jerusalem: Israel Museum, 1986), p. 149. For Efros, this dual principle was exemplified by Marc Chagall, Natan Altman, and Robert Falk, all of whom reworked Jewish folk motifs in the light of European modernism. In this context, a generative event in Yiddish modernism was the 1911-14 expedition headed by the former social revolutionary S. Ansky for the Jewish Historic Ethnographic Society of Saint Petersburg. Armed with cameras and recording equipment, Ansky and his associates plumbed the tiny hamlets of Belorussia and the Ukraine, transcribing stories and legends; noting spells and remedies; collecting songs and proverbs; photographing old synagogues, historical places, and gravestones; purchasing ceremonial objects, jewelry, clothing, and all manner of antiquities. This material became the core of the Jewish Ethnographic Museum established in Petrograd in 1916. The fruits of Ansky's research included *The Dybbuk,* the poetic drama of possession and exorcism that he wrote in 1914 and which, after its premiere five years later, was to become the most important text of the modern Yiddish theater.

12. The theatrical collective HaBima (Hebrew for "the stage") was founded in 1917 by Nahum Zemach and David Vardi and, despite the Bolshevik antipathy toward Zionism, continued to perform in Hebrew through the mid-1920s. In 1920, then Commissar of Nationality Affairs Joseph Stalin overruled the Yevsektsia and resumed HaBima's yearly subsidy. The theater was put under the direction of Stanislavsky's protégé Yevgeny Vakhtangov. An Armenian with no knowledge of Hebrew, Vakhtangov staged *The Dybbuk* as pure theater—or nearly. To accentuate the play's class consciousness, the celebrated Beggar's Dance was given a heightened importance, with the bent, contorted creatures who attend the shtetl wedding representing the oppressed masses, siding with the wrong student against the bride's rich and sinful father.

13. Abram Efros, "The Artists of Granovskii's Theater," in *Marc Chagall and the Jewish Theater,* p. 156. A dozen years later, the ultramodern, ultra-archaic critic would be attacked as a "Russophobe" for his doomed attempt to forestall the Socialist Realist hegemony.

14. Louis Lozowick, "Moscow Theater. 1920s," *Russian History* 8 (1981): 143.

15. Having conveniently died two years before the October Revolution, Sholom Aleichem was the only Soviet Jewish culture hero who never fell from official grace. As the province of the poor and disenfranchised (not to mention a secular alternative to Hebrew), Yiddish literature was a priori politically correct. Sholom Aleichem's anti-authoritarian humor, identification with the Jewish masses, and gift for drawing characters as the product of social forces transcended his bourgeois origins and Zionist sympathies.

16. Efros, "Artists of Granovskii's Theater," p. 148. HaBima "radiated well-being," Efros wrote. "All the good fairies of aid and publicity surrounded it. It was supported by an amazing amalgam of Zionists, the Rabbinate, parts of the Communist party, and those liberal anti-Semites who considered the language of the Bible the only thing bearable about the Jews." On the evening of a HaBima premiere, he continued, "you could see the Moscow Chief Rabbi Mazeh next to Politburo member Kamenev [past member of the opposition Left, along with Trotsky and Zinoviev], nodding to each other in satisfaction" ("Artists of Granovskii's Theater," pp. 154, 155). The 1924 production *Three Jewish Raisins* was a trio of sketches satirizing rival Yiddish theaters. *Prince von Fliasko Drigo* mocked the Goldfaden melodramas of the itinerant Yiddish troupes, *Sarra Wants a Negro* burlesqued the "only in America" ethos of the New York Yiddish stage, while

A Night at a Hasidic Rebbe's parodied HaBima, incorporating Lev Pulver's Hasidic songs.

17. Efros, "Artists of Granovskii's Theater," p. 155. Describing the "Cubistic liveliness" of *200,000*, Berlin critic Alfred Kerr found GOSET's performers preternaturally expressive. The actors, he wrote, "talk not only with their hands but almost with their hair, their soles, their calves, and their toes. . . . The ghetto-figure and ghetto-manner appears in concentrated form—until it almost frightens the Western burgher" (not to mention the Western Jew). See Lois Adler, "Alexis Granovsky and the Jewish State Theatre of Moscow," *Drama Review* 24 (September 1980): 37; and Avram Kampf, "Art and Stage Design: The Jewish Theatres of Moscow in the Early Twenties," in Apter-Gabriel, ed., *Tradition and Revolution*, p. 140.

18. Walter Benjamin, "Moscow Diary," *October* 35 (winter 1985): 14. In contrast, novelist Joseph Roth considered the Moscow GOSET most Jewish when it attacked Jewish tradition: "Attacking the tradition is an old Jewish tradition. I was moved even when they mocked. They mocked, but they mocked in a Jewish way" (cited in Jacob Weitzner, *Sholem Aleichem in the Theater* [East Brunswick, N.J.: Fairleigh Dickinson University Press, 1995], p. 128).

19. Lozowick, "Moscow Theater," p. 143.

20. Melech Epstein, *Pages from a Colorful Life* (Miami Beach: I. Block, 1971), p. 95.

21. Babel, *1920 Diary*, pp. 35, 36.

22. In *Through Tears*, Sholom Aleichem's story "The Enchanted Tailor" is interwoven with tales of the orphaned cantor's son Motl Peyse to create an overall view of two imaginary towns, Zlodyevke and Kozodoyevka, whose names can be roughly translated as "thieves' den" and "goat's milk," respectively.

23. *Der Emes*, 3/15/28. Bested by Stalin at the Fourteenth Party Conference, Trotsky had been amazed to find that he and his supporters were subject, for the first time, to anti-Semitic innuendo. "Is it true?" he wrote Nikolai Bukharin in March 1926, shortly before *Benya Krik* went into production. "Is it possible that in *our party*, in Moscow, in WORKERS' CELLS, anti-Semitic agitation should be carried on with impunity?" See Deutscher, *Non-Jewish Jew*, p. 75.

24. M. Makotinsky, "Skvoz Slezy," *Kino* (Kiev) 39 (March 1928): 8-9.

25. Itzik Fefer, "Vegn Yidishn Film," *Kino* (Kiev) 39 (March 1928): 2.

26. Epstein, *Pages*, p. 95.

27. *His Excellency* is further schematized as a generational melodrama: "suffocating" under her father's rule, the rabbi's adopted daughter joins a clandestine band of youthful socialists. Here the battle lines are clearly drawn: Not only does the rabbi curse his child for her involvement with a "goy," he also excommunicates her Jewish comrades.

28. Since the early 1920s, the party had successfully channeled the Yevsektsia's anti-bourgeois antagonism, using the Jewish section to police the Jewish street. Later, the party would intimidate and ultimately eliminate these same activists by raising the specter of their Bundist past. Even as the beleaguered Yevsektsia made plans for its first conference since 1926, the party leadership met in January 1930 and "reorganized," dissolving all national sections.

29. Makotinsky, "Skvoz Slezy," p. 9.

30. Epstein, *Pages*, p. 97.

31. The couple are traveling with Nathan's black colleague Jim (Kador Ben-Salim, a Senegalese deserter from the French interventionist forces in Odessa, who had carved out a place for himself in Soviet movies). "You, also, are going home," Nathan declares.

32. Victor Serge, *Russia Twenty Years After* (Atlantic Highlands, N.J.: Humanities Press International, 1996), p. 175.

33. Katerina Clark points out that the industrial utopia envisioned during the First Five-Year Plan precisely embraced such automation: Might machine work not transform

human nature as its rational rhythms were impressed on undeveloped psyches? (*The Soviet Novel: History as Ritual* [Chicago: University of Chicago Press, 1981], p. 94).

34. Solomon Davidman, *Jewish Children in Biro-Bidjan: Stories* (New York, 1948).

35. Birobidzhan pamphlets, Klaw Library, Hebrew Union College, New York City.

36. B.-Z. Goldberg, "Russia's Daniel Boones: Jewish Pioneers Who Are Blazing a New Trail in Biro-Bidjan" (mimeographed text, 1934), cited in Zosa Szajkowski, *The Mirage of American Jewish Aid in Soviet Russia 1917-1939* (New York: Szajko Frydman, 1977), p. 163.

37. In March 1935, the Acme Theater, off Union Square in New York, opened a Yiddish-language "documentary featurette" on Birobidzhan. This hallucination was produced by Soyuzkino News and written and directed by M. Slunsky (later famous for his World War II documentaries), with a musical score by Lev Pulver.

38. Cited in Melech Epstein, *The Jew and Communism* (New York: Trade Union Sponsoring Committee, 1959), p. 313; Solomon Schwarz, *Jews in the Soviet Union* (Syracuse, N.Y.: Syracuse University Press, 1951), p. 181; *Nailebn* (October 1936): 36.

39. Boris Shumyatsky, "Perfecting Our Mastery," in *The Film Factory: Russian and Soviet Cinema in Documents, 1896-1939* (Cambridge, Mass.: Harvard University Press, 1988), p. 374.

40. Birobidzhan officially opened to foreign settlers in 1936; by end of the year, according to the Polish newspaper *Vilner Tog*, newcomers included Jews from Poland, Latvia, and Lithuania, as well as America and even Palestine.

41. Birobidzhan pamphlets, Klaw Library, Hebrew Union College.

42. *Seekers of Happiness* established the outer limits of an ersatz Soviet Jewish culture. But if only the most dogged true believers took seriously the movie's amalgam of Soviet ideals and ethnic Jewishness, the movie "rediscovered"as part of a 1959 jubilee held to mark the rehabilitation of Venyamin Zuskin, was nevertheless a popular revival in the relatively liberal Moscow of the early 1960s (as well as among the Russian Jewish immigrants who populated the Brighton Beach district of Brooklyn a decade later), where Zuskin's one-liners were treasured as a rare example of on-screen Jewish humor. In *Stalin against the Jews,* Arkady Vaksberg praises *Seekers of Happiness* as "a movie that lives in the memory of several generations of Soviet viewers and which influenced them in a way not intended by the Leader. . . . The hero, Pinya . . . hopes to find in Birobidzhan the happiness he naturally lacked in damned capitalist America. He wants to prospect for gold and become the equal of Rothschild himself—Rothschild being the pejorative symbol in Russia of the rich Jew. But instead of being an exposé, the film turned out to be touching and heartfelt" (p. 66).

43. Quoted in *Moscow Daily News,* 10/11/35, n.p.

44. By the late 1930s, Birobidzhan was deemed to be infiltrated, if not overrun, by spies, traitors, and Japanese agents. During the summer of 1937—soon after *Life* magazine ran his picture in their two-page spread on Birobidzhan—the chairman of the Birobidzhan soviet, Joseph Liberberg, was arrested and executed as a "nationalist Trotskyite and former member of the Labor Zionists." As his replacement, M. Koteles, did not know Yiddish, regional administration reverted to the use of the Russian language alone. Koteles, too, eventually was purged. See B.-Z. Goldberg, *The Jewish Problem in the Soviet Union* (New York: Crown, 1961), p. 199.

The June 1937 issue of *Nailebn* (New life), the monthly magazine of Birobidzhan published in both English and Yiddish, announced that work had begun on a second cinematic celebration of Birobidzhan, planned to open on the October Revolution's twentieth anniversary. The movie was never made, although the Moscow GOSET marked the occasion with its Birobidzhan-fest—a new play by Peretz Markish that, as Mikhoels wrote, would "reveal a new gallery of strong people." *Di Mishpokhe Ovadis*

(The family Ovadis) opened on November 7, 1937, and followed the same narrative as *Seekers of Happiness*. Mikhoels played a version of the honest Tsale Becker, while Zuskin again appeared as a *luftmensh*.

45. Babel, *1920 Diary*, p. 33.

46. Mikhoels's death ended the postwar resurgence of Soviet Jewish life. An additional ten thousand Jews had resettled in Birobidzhan between 1945 and 1948. The Moscow GOSET played to packed houses throughout 1946 and into 1948—until patrons noticed the black NKVD automobile parked outside the theater.

47. See Goldberg, *Jewish Problem*, pp. 97-114; Yehoshua Gilboa, *The Black Years of Soviet Jewry, 1939-1953* (Boston: Little, Brown & Co., 1971); Gitelman, *Century of Ambivalence*, pp. 230-42.

48. George Konrád, *The Loser* (New York: Harcourt Brace Jovanovich, 1982), p. 233.

49. In the first flush of perestroika, the newly reformed Filmmakers' Union created a "conflict commission" to investigate the problem of shelved movies. All were soon cleared, except for one. In November 1986, the conflict commission was informed by Goskino that it was "inexpedient to release *Commissar* into distribution in its present form." Not until Askoldov publically confronted the union leadership at the Moscow Film Festival seven months later was *Commissar* declassified.

50. Grossman was the coauthor, with Ilya Ehrenberg, of *The Black Book of Soviet Jewry*—a documentary account of the Nazi extermination of Russian Jews that was sponsored by the Jewish Anti-Fascist Committee—as well as author of the suppressed World War II novel *Life and Fate*. His cousin Nadya Grossman had been arrested in March 1933, as an associate of Victor Serge.

51. "I never saw Mikhoels, but I knew his widow," Askoldov told me. "She said that when Mikhoels woke up in the morning, he liked to dance. That's the origin of Bykov's 'sun dance'" (interview, February 1988).

52. Gedali tells the narrator that he wants "an International of good men," with "every soul registered and receiving a first-category ration card. Here, soul—eat, help yourself, get a kick out of life. It's you, Mr. Comrade, who doesn't know what people eat the International with." ("They eat it with gunpowder," Mr. Comrade replies, "and they season it with the best blood.") See Isaac Babel, "Gedali," in *Lyubka the Cossack*, p. 126.

53. Elena Stishova, "The Mythologization of Soviet Women: *The Commissar* and Other Cases," in *Red Women on the Silver Screen: Soviet Women and Cinema from the Beginning to the End of the Communist Era*, ed. Lynne Attwood (London: Pandora Press, 1993), p. 183.

54. Cited in Elena Stishova, "Passions over *Commissar*," *Wide Angle* 12 (1990): 63-64.

55. In fact, Askoldov—born in 1931 and neither a Jew nor of Jewish descent—maintained that *Commissar* embodied his own "hard experience of Russian society." The son of a revolutionary commissar twice sentenced to death (once for anticzarist agitation during World War I and again in 1920 by the invading Polish army), who survived both sentences only to be executed by Stalin in 1937, Askoldov benefited from the Khrushchev thaw, studying theater and managing to write a dissertation on Mikhail Bulgakov at a time when most of that writer's work, including *The Master and Margarita*, was still unavailable. See J. Hoberman, "Red Psalm," *Village Voice*, 6/21/88, p. 63.

56. See Gitelman, *Century of Ambivalence*, pp. 270-86.

57. Stishova, "Passions over *Commissar*," pp. 70-71.

58. Ibid., p. 71.

59. Ibid., pp. 72-73. The writer Konstantin Simonov—who, twenty-two years earlier, had denounced Trauberg and other "cosmopolitans" for attempting "to persuade the Soviet people to forget about their national traditions in art"—was one of *Commissar*'s few

defenders, telling the meeting that he did not "perceive any trace of anti-Semitism in the film. It has been made by a talented man. We ought to see this thing through the end. It's worth letting this thing continue."

60. Ibid., p. 73; J. Hoberman, "Ask Askoldov," *Village Voice*, 4/8/88, p. 61; Hoberman, "Red Psalm," p. 63; Anne Williamson, "Askoldov!" *Film Comment* (May–June 1988): 70.

61. Stishova, "Passions over *Commissar*," pp. 73, 71; Hoberman, "Red Psalm," p. 63.

62. Hoberman, "Ask Askoldov," p. 61.

Chapter 4

1. Slavoj Žižek, *For They Know Not What They Do: Enjoyment as a Political Factor* (London: Verso, 1991), p. 272; Peter Sedgwick, "Victor Serge and Socialism," *International Socialism* (1963): 23.

2. Victor Serge, *The Case of Comrade Tulayev* (London: Hamish Hamilton, 1951), p. 24; Victor Serge, *Birth of Our Power* (London: Writers & Readers, 1977), p. 100.

3. Claude Lévi-Strauss, *Triste Tropiques* (New York: Atheneum, 1970), p. 26.

4. Herbert R. Lottman, *The Left Bank: Writers, Artists, and Politics from the Popular Front to the Cold War* (Boston: Houghton Mifflin, 1982), p. 93.

5. Serge, *Comrade Tulayev*, p. 21.

6. Serge, *Birth of our Power*, p. 201.

7. George Orwell, "Arthur Koestler," in *Dickens, Dali & Others* (New York: Harcourt Brace Jovanovich, 1973), pp. 185–86.

8. Jean-Paul Sartre, "Situation of the Writer in 1947," in *What Is Literature?* (New York: Washington Square Press, 1966), p. 154.

9. Victor Serge, *Memoirs of a Revolutionary* (London: Writers & Readers, 1984), p. 14.

10. Ibid., p. 2.

11. Ibid., p. 1.

12. Ibid., pp. 7, 12.

13. Ibid., pp. 24, 19.

14. Ibid., p. 18.

15. Ibid., p. 19.

16. Ibid., p. 22. During the winter of 1916, Lenin and his cohorts Grigori Zinoviev and Karl Radek lived in Zurich; indeed, Lenin's house at 12 Spiegelgasse was diagonally across from the Cabaret Voltaire, where the Dadaists staged their first confrontational performances. After the revolution, Hugo Ball noted in his diary that Lenin "must have heard our music and tirades every evening. I do not know if he enjoyed them or profited from them. And when we were opening the gallery at Bahnhofstrasse, the Russians went off to Petersburg to launch the revolution. Is dadaism as sign and gesture the opposite of Bolshevism? Does it contrast the completely quixotic inexpedient, and incomprehensible side of the world with destruction and consummate calculation?" (*Flight Out of Time: A Dada Diary* [New York: Viking, 1974], p. 117). Years later, Hans Richter would recall "that the Swiss authorities were much more suspicious of the Dadaists who were after all capable of perpetrating some new enormity at any moment, than of these quiet, studious Russians . . . even though the latter were planning a world revolution" (*Dada: Art and Anti-Art* [New York: McGraw-Hill, 1967], p. 16).

Like almost everyone else, Serge would repress the influence of anarchism on modern culture. The 1890s, when the movement was at its bomb-chucking peak, marked the formative years of many modern artists—a number of whom, including most of the Fauves and the futurists, went through periods of anarchist involvement. Nietzsche, Stirner, Marx, Dostoyevsky, Tolstoy, Sorel, and Kropotkin were read by anarchists and artists alike. Each group, in its way, exalted individual freedom, railed against traditional restraints, and embraced impoverished marginal lifestyles. The futurists issued their first manifesto the same year that Victor Kibalchich became Le Rétif.

17. Cited in Richard Parry, *The Bonnot Gang* (London: Rebel Press, 1987), p. 90. Serge's youthful rhetoric strongly suggests Norman Mailer's defense of violence in his 1957 essay "The White Negro," even anticipating Mailer's notorious parenthetic assertion: "It can of course be suggested that it takes little courage for two strong eighteen-year-old hoodlums, let us say, to beat in the brains of a candy-store keeper, and indeed the act—even by the logic of the psychopath—is not likely to prove very therapeutic, for the victim is not an immediate equal. Still, courage of a sort is necessary, for one murders not only a weak fifty-year-old man but an institution as well, one violates private property, one enters a new relation with the police and introduces a dangerous element into one's life. The hoodlum is therefore daring the unknown, and so no matter how brutal the act, it is not altogether cowardly."

18. Serge, *Memoirs*, p. 34. The French May and the international success of *Bonnie and Clyde* provided a context for *La Bande a Bonnot: Les Anarchists,* directed by Philippe Fourastie from a script by J. P. Fabre, F. Beaurenaut, and Remi Forlani. Jacques Brel starred (although not as Bonnot); Michel Vitold played Serge. *Variety* (11/13/68) described *La Bande a Bonnot* as "a gangster film with a lot going for it . . . a political aura that reflects on today . . . well played and mounted with a period flair." (The latter touch included a sequence in a 1911 movie house.) "Pic does have a mythical quality in making the bandits sort of misguided anti-heroes," *Variety* noted, deeming the tone "basically anti-Establishment." At one point, Jean-Luc Godard was to have directed the movie.

19. Serge, *Memoirs*, p. 45.

20. Serge, *Men in Prison*, pp. 180–81.

21. Serge, *Memoirs*, p. 57.

22. Ibid., p. 58.

23. Serge, *Birth of Our Power*, p. 159.

24. Ibid., p. 162.

25. Serge, *Memoirs*, pp. 70–71.

26. Victor Serge, *From Lenin to Stalin* (New York: Monad Press, 1973), p. 10; Viktor Shklovsky, *Sentimental Journey: Memoirs, 1917-1922* (Ithaca, N.Y.: Cornell University Press, 1970), p. 174.

27. Serge, *Memoirs*, pp. 72–73, 76.

28. Ibid., pp. 76, 80–81.

29. Ibid., pp. 113–14.

30. Ibid., p. 72.

31. Victor Serge, *What Everyone Should Know about State Repression* (London: New Park Publications, 1979), p. 10.

32. Victor Serge, "Life and Culture in 1918," in *From Lenin to Stalin,* p. 123.

33. Serge, *Memoirs*, pp. 101, 141, 136, 137, 106, 139–40.

34. Ibid., pp. 123, 151. This was the Free Philosophic Society, led by the brilliant symbolist novelist Andrei Bely.

35. Ibid., p. 128.

36. Ibid., p. 160.

37. Serge's silence is striking, in that Stalin's responsibility for the failure of the German Revolution would become, for Trotskyists, an article of faith—as was the significance that the failed revolution had in clinching Stalin's victory in Russia. "It strengthened the development of the bureaucracy towards the nationalism to be proclaimed a year later in Stalin's monstrous theory," C. L. R. James wrote in his 1937 history *World Revolution, 1917-1936: The Rise and Fall of the Communist International* (Atlantic Highlands, N.J.: Humanities Press, 1993), p. 187. The chapter is titled "Stalin Kills the 1923 Revolution."

38. Serge, *Memoirs*, pp. 190, 186, 187.

39. Ibid., p. 193.

40. Ibid., p. 194. Illuminating a historical moment with the sudden light of a paparazzi's flashgun, Serge describes leaving a meeting in "some ramshackle apartment scarred by poverty." As he hit the street, Trotsky turned up his collar and lowered his hat, so as not to be recognized: "He looked like an old intellectual in the underground of long ago." Serge and Trotsky hailed a cab and began bargaining the fare, but the driver recognized Trotsky and refused to take their money. "Don't tell anyone this happened," Trotsky ironically advised Serge. "Everyone knows that cabmen belong to the petty-bourgeoisie, whose favour can only discredit us" (ibid., p. 220).

41. Ibid., pp. 216, 244.

42. Victor Serge, *Midnight in the Century* (London: Writers & Readers, 1982), p. 180.

43. Serge, *Memoirs*, p. 264.

44. Ibid., pp. 273-74.

45. Ibid., pp. 300, 307.

46. Lottman, *Left Bank*, p. 93.

47. Serge, *Memoirs*, p. 322.

48. Ibid., p. 328. Serge would soon be superceded as the object of Communist animus by the long-term fellow traveler André Gide, who published his critical exposé *Retour de l'U.S.S.R.* in November 1936.

49. *The Serge-Trotsky Papers*, ed. David Cotterill (London: Pluto Press, 1994), p. 86; Serge, *Comrade Tulayev*, p. 261.

50. See Cotterill, ed., *Serge-Trotsky Papers*, p. 168.

51. Serge, *Memoirs*, p. 340.

52. Victor Serge, "On the Eve," *Partisan Review* 9 (January–February 1942): 23.

53. An eighteen-year-old student in 1912, Breton was greatly impressed by the Bonnot Gang's social banditry and outlaw bravado. As late as 1920, when Breton and his cohorts graded historical figures on a scale from -25 to +20, Bonnot scored a respectable 10.36. (Charles Chaplin and Arthur Rimbaud topped the poll with 16.09 and 15.95, respectively.)

54. Mark Polizzotti, *Revolution of the Mind: The Life of André Breton* (New York: Farrar, Straus & Giroux, 1995), p. 494.

55. Serge, *Memoirs*, p. 368.

56. Victor Serge, "Thirty Years after the Russian Revolution," in *Russia Twenty Years After* (Atlantic Heights, N.J.: Humanities Press, 1996), pp. 325-26.

57. In February 1948, Malraux showed Serge's letter to *New York Times* correspondent C. L. Sulzberger, explaining that had Trotsky prevailed over Stalin, he—Malraux—would today be a Communist. Sulzberger understood Malraux's ploy as part of a third-force attempt to appeal to the Left while embracing the Marshall Plan ("Europe's Anti-Red Trend Inspiring Strange Tie-Ups: New Coalitions Courting Leftist Support to Bring Workers into Pale," *New York Times*, 2/14/48).

58. Serge, *Men in Prison*, pp. 65, 56, 34.

59. Serge, *Memoirs*, p. 263.

60. Cited in Richard Greeman, "Introduction," in Serge, *Men in Prison*, p. xxv.

61. Serge, *Birth of Our Power*, pp. 202-3, 190.

62. Victor Serge, *Conquered City* (London: Writers & Readers, 1978), p. 152.

63. Serge, *Midnight in the Century*, pp. 77, 53.

64. Ibid., p. 153.

65. Serge, *Birth of our Power*, p. 271.

66. Serge, *Conquered City*, pp. 2, 27, 39.

67. Irving Howe, *Politics and the Novel* (New York: Horizon Press, 1957), pp. 232-34.

68. Howe's original review of *The Case of Comrade Tulayev*, published in the Trotskyist

New International (January–February 1951), cautions radical readers to be on guard: "The material is so close to us, the point of view so congenial, the pathos so unbearable (the pathos in life, prior to our reading) that we are emotionally defenseless against the entire impact of the book" (p. 86).

69. Cited in Peter Sedgwick, "Introduction," in Serge, *Memoirs*, pp. xviii-xix.
70. Serge, *Comrade Tulayev*, p. 138.
71. Victor Serge, "The Future of Socialism V: The Socialist Imperative," *Partisan Review* (winter 1947): 511-12.
72. Harold Rosenberg, "Actor in History," in *Act and the Actor* (Chicago: University of Chicago Press, 1983), p. 161; Serge, *Conquered City*, p. 95.
73. Sartre and Serge were clearly antipodes. Serge's *Memoirs of a Revolutionary* notes the "most-discussed book" of 1939 (year of *Midnight in the Century*) was Sartre's "analysis in novel form of a case of neurosis, called *La Nausée*. An appropriate title" (p. 354).
74. Serge, *Comrade Tulayev*, p. 218.

Chapter 5

1. Tadeusz Konwicki, *A Minor Apocalypse* (New York: Farrar, Straus & Giroux, 1983), p. 7.
2. Milan Kundera and Philip Roth, "Afterword: A Talk with the Author," in Milan Kundera, *The Book of Laughter and Forgetting* (New York: Penguin Books, 1981), p. 230.
3. Ibid. In 1981, the Canada-based Czechoslovak Federal Council in Exile published information on alleged Soviet plans for the outright annexation of Czechoslovakia after 1984: "The trigger would be some artificially-created crisis which could be deemed by the Kremlin a threat to 'the security of Czechoslovak territory and of the socialist camp' from aggressive Western 'imperialists.'" See Frantisek August and David Rees, *Red Star over Prague* [London: Sherwood Press, 1984], pp. 157-58).
4. At least, some did. In an open letter published in *Commentary* (1984), Norman Podhoretz scolded Kundera for insufficient anti-Communism (and an implicit ingratitude toward the West):

> When I first thought of writing to you about this, I assumed that you would be appalled to learn how in America your work was falling into the hands of people who were using it for political purposes that you would certainly consider pernicious. But now *I* am appalled to learn that you have been cooperating with your own kidnappers. . . . You write a novel, *The Unbearable Lightness of Being,* containing a brief episode in which an anti-Communist Czech emigré in Paris is seen by one of the characters as no different in kind from the Communists back in Prague (both being equally dogmatic), and virtually every reviewer gleefully cites it by way of suggesting that in your eyes Communism and anti-Communism are equivalent evils.

How, one wonders, did Podhoretz miss the passage in which a Czech photographer's pictures of occupied Prague are rejected by a Swiss magazine in favor of a photo spread on a nude beach?
5. George Konrád, *The Loser* (New York: Harcourt Brace Jovanovich, 1982), p. 233.
6. Joseph Brodsky, "Introduction," in Danilo Kiš, *A Tomb for Boris Davidovich* (New York: Penguin Books, 1980), p. ix.
7. Or as George Konrád and Ivan Szelényi noted, "The Western visitor may even have [had] his envy aroused by the paradoxical distinction which the highest party, state, and police organs bestow by their close attention to every intellectual product of any consequence whatever and of course to its author as well, irrespective as to whether his

amorous or political vagaries are the object" (*The Intellectuals on the Road to Class Power: A Sociological Study of the Role of the Intelligentsia in Socialism* [New York: Harcourt Brace Jovanovich, 1979], pp. 81–82).

8. Irving Howe, "Books in Review: Serge's Novel," *New International* (January–February 1951): 86.

9. Philip Roth, "A Conversation in Prague," *New York Review of Books*, 4/12/90, p. 16.

10. I take Roth's own response to Writers from the Other Europe to be his 1985 novella *The Prague Orgy*, in which his alter ego, Zuckerman, travels to Czechoslovakia in search of a lost Yiddish manuscript. The literary intrigue is as extensive as the quest is futile. See Philip Roth, *Zuckerman Bound: A Trilogy and Epilogue* (New York: Farrar, Straus & Giroux, 1985), pp. 701–84.

    Zuckerman describes Prague as "the city I imagined during the war's worst years, when, as a Hebrew-student of little more than nine, I went out after supper with my blue-and-white collection can to solicit from the neighbors for the Jewish National Fund. This is the city I imagined the Jews would buy when they had accumulated enough money for a homeland. . . . What I privately pictured the Jews able to afford with the nickles and dimes I collected was a used city, a broken city, a city so worn and grim that nobody else would even put in a bid" (p. 760). Zuckerman romanticizes Prague as a sort of urban Birobidzhan. (Indeed, he is ultimately deported as a "Zionist agent.") At the same time, Prague is also an elaborate, thrill-packed theme park. "An honor to have entertained you here, sir," mocks the sleek government official who returns his passport at the Prague airport. "Now back to the little world around the corner" (p. 784).

11. Konrád and Szelényi, *Intellectuals*, p. 211.

12. Jan Kott, "Controlling the Writing on the Wall," *New York Review of Books*, 8/17/78, p. 17.

13. Milan Kundera, "Author's Preface," in *The Joke* (New York: Harper & Row, 1982), p. vii.

14. Kundera, *The Joke*, p. 26.

15. Ibid.

16. Ibid., pp. 240, 65.

17. George Konrád, "Letter from Budapest," *New York Review of Books*, 11/5/81, p. 49.

18. Géza Csáth, "The Surgeon," in *Opium and Other Stories* (New York: Penguin, 1983), pp. 74, 78.

19. Franz Kafka, *The Diaries of Franz Kafka 1910–1913* (New York: Schocken Books, 1965), p. 276.

20. The master's speculations on social anthropology, *Totem and Taboo* (with the sensationally Hapsburg subtitle *Some Points of Agreement between the Mental Lives of Savages and Neurotics*), were not published until 1913–14.

21. Neal Ascherson, "Introduction," in Ludvík Vaculík, *The Guinea Pigs* (New York: Penguin, 1975), p. xi.

22. Roth, "Conversation in Prague," p. 19; Brodsky, "Introduction," p. xv.

23. Roth, "Conversation in Prague," p. 19.

24. Having no small familiarity with this condition, the Hungarian Marxist philosopher George Lukács would disapprovingly describe Kafka's formula as "the terror generated by the world of imperialist capitalism (anticipatory of its later fascist progeny) where human beings are degraded to mere objects—this fear, originally a subjective experience, becomes an objective entity" ("Franz Kafka or Thomas Mann?" in *Realism in Our Time: Literature and the Class Struggle* [New York: Harper & Row, 1962], p. 52).

25. Sigmund Freud, *Civilization and Its Discontents*, trans. and ed. James Strachey (New York: W. W. Norton, 1962), p. 40.

26. Theodor W. Adorno, "Notes on Kafka," in *Prisms* (London: Neville Spearman, 1967), p. 251.
27. See Georges Bataille, *Literature and Evil* (New York: Urizen, 1981), pp. 127–43.
28. Franz Kafka, "Reflections on Sin, Suffering, Hope, and the True Way," in *The Blue Octavo Notebooks* (Cambridge: Exact Change, 1991), p. 91. Howard Fast, "The Metamorphosis," in *Franz Kafka: An Anthology of Marxist Criticism,* ed. Kenneth Hughes (Hanover, N.H.: University Press of New England, 1981), p. 12. Fast, too, was a dissident. Visiting Eastern Europe in 1948, John Gunther was "fascinated" by "the attention paid in Czechoslovakia, as in several of the other satellites," to Fast's "literary merits. . . . One would have thought that Fast was the only writer in the United States. We were seriously asked for how long a term he had been 'imprisoned,' and whether the fact that he was embroiled in legal difficulty over Communism meant that American publishers would be forbidden henceforth to issue any of his books!" (*Behind the Curtain* [New York: Harper, 1949], p. 229). In 1950, Fast served a stretch in the penitentiary for contempt of the House Un-American Activities Committee and consequently did have difficulty in publishing his novels. (He has long since been reincarnated as a best-selling author. Only in Amerika.)
29. Lukács, "Franz Kafka or Thomas Mann?" p. 92.
30. Cited in Antonin J. Liehm, "Franz Kafka in Eastern Europe," *Telos* 23 (summer 1975): 69.
31. Eugen Loebl, *My Mind on Trial* (New York: Harcourt Brace Jovanovich, 1976), pp. 45–46.
32. Philip Roth, "'I Always Wanted You to Admire My Fasting,' or Looking at Kafka," in *Reading Myself and Others* (New York: Bantam, 1977), pp. 233ff.; Harrison E. Salisbury, "Hungarian Authors End Strike; Czechs Follow Own Literary Line," *New York Times,* 10/12/57.
33. See Jaroslav Dresler, "Kafka and the Communists," *Survey* 36 (April–June 1961): 27; cited in Liehm, "Franz Kafka," pp. 54–55.
34. Paul Reimann, "Kafka and the Present," in Hughes, ed., *Franz Kafka,* p. 53; Edouard Goldstücker, "Franz Kafka in the Prague Perspective: 1963," in Hughes, ed., *Franz Kafka,* p. 60.
35. Goldstücker, "Franz Kafka," p. 69.
36. Ibid.; Ernst Fischer, "Kafka Conference," in Hughes, ed., *Franz Kafka,* p. 87.
37. Cited in Milan Kundera, "On Kafka and Chaos," *Vogue,* 1982, n.p.
38. Alexej Kusák, "Comments on the Marxist Interpretation of Franz Kafka," in Hughes, ed., *Franz Kafka,* p. 103; Jiři Hájek, "Kafka and the Socialist World," in Hughes, ed., *Franz Kafka,* p. 122.
39. Reimann, "Kafka and the Present," p. 59.
40. Franz Kafka, "An Old Manuscript," in *The Complete Stories* (New York: Schocken Books, 1983), pp. 415ff.
41. "The unrelenting pressure of the semi-nomadic military empires had the same significance for the peoples of Eastern Europe as did the danger of floods for the societies of China and Mesopotamia" (Konrád and Szelényi, *Intellectuals,* pp. 87–88).
42. Antonin J. Liehm, *The Politics of Culture* (New York: Grove Press, 1973), p. 283.
43. Liehm, "Franz Kafka," pp. 53, 72.
44. Ibid., p. 73.
45. So did writers. When, having recaptured the ministry of culture, the party's Stalinists attempted a new form of ideological precensorship, the June 1967 congress of the Czech Writers Union launched a counterattack—including speeches by Kundera and Vaculík. By October, Alexander Dubček and the Slovak Communists were demanding the separation of party and state. January 5, 1968, Dubček was elected general secretary. Prague

Spring was the only time a ruling party attempted to realize Lenin's promise that the dictatorship of the proletariat would last only as long as bourgeois opposition to the socialist construction.

46. Václav Havel, "On Kafka," *New York Review of Books*, 9/27/90, p. 19.

47. Cited in Liehm, "Franz Kafka," pp. 77-78. Roger Garaudy and Ernst Fischer, the leading Western Communists at Liblice, publically denounced the Soviet Union in the invasion's aftermath.

48. Ibid., p. 79.

49. Ibid., p. 80.

50. By 1970, Alexander Dubček was an inspector in the Slovakian trolley works and Kundera reduced to publishing abroad. (*The Farewell Party*—the last novel he wrote in Czechoslovakia—uses an infertility clinic as a sort of Blandings Castle backdrop for a weekend of erotic intrigue, which, typically, ends in murder and exile.) In 1975, Kundera moved to Paris. Two Other European contemporaries—George Konrád and Danilo Kiš— were also in town. By the end of the decade, both Konrád and Kiš had returned home. But as predicted in his novel, Kundera's joke never ends. He achieved Western literary stardom with *The Book of Laughter and Forgetting* in 1979 and was stripped of Czech citizenship the same year.

51. Ivan Klíma, "An Upheaval for Czech Readers," *New York Review of Books*, 10/20/94, p. 64.

52. Tadeusz Konwicki, *The Polish Complex* (New York: Farrar, Straus & Giroux, 1982), p. 100. Indeed, in considering the region, one has to wonder whether Communism constructed the Other European reality or whether this reality—as Lenin himself feared—had, in fact, made Communism what it became.

53. Géza Csáth, "Musicians," in *Opium*, p. 136.

54. Kafka, "Reflections on Sin," p. 88.

Chapter 6

1. See Jan Barna, *Eisenstein: The Growth of a Cinematic Genius* (Boston: Little, Brown, 1973), pp. 121-26.

2. The events of Great October were several times reenacted as revolutionary theater. The last great mass spectacle was *The Storming of the Winter Palace*, performed on November 6, 1920, on Uritsky Square, with some seven thousand performers (including a five-hundred-member orchestra) mainly mobilized from Red Army and Navy drama groups. The piece was staged like a battle—the director issuing instructions via field phones, light signals, and motorcycle couriers. In anticipation of Eisenstein's movie, some of the performers had been actual participants in the October Revolution. The warship *Aurora* was anchored on the exact spot on the Neva.

3. Barna, *Eisenstein*, p. 122.

4. Victor Serge, *Memoirs of a Revolutionary* (London: Writers & Readers, 1984), p. 225.

5. Ian Christie and Richard Taylor, eds., *The Film Factory: Russian and Soviet Cinema in Documents 1896-1939* (Cambridge, Mass.: Harvard University Press, 1988), p. 219.

6. Proletkult is short for the Proletarian Cultural and Educational Organization. The year 1924 also brought *Voyage of the Red Star Detachment to the Land of Marvels*, wherein a group of Young Pioneers time-travel to 1957 to find the whole earth united by an international Communist revolution.

7. Ian Christie, "Down to Earth: *Aelita* Relocated," in *Inside the Film Factory: New Approaches to Russian and Soviet Cinema*, ed. Richard Taylor and Ian Christie (London: Routledge, 1991), p. 82.

8. It was reported that "Miss Rand spoke an estimated three thousand words before any members of the Committee could insert a word in edgewise or otherwise. In her view,

Louis B. Mayer was not much better than an agent of a foreign government inasmuch as the film he produced showed the Russians smiling, which Miss Rand said, 'is one of the stock propaganda tricks of the Communists—to show these people smiling.'" Questioned about this, she elaborated: If Russians smile, "it is privately and accidentally. . . . They don't smile in approval of their system." A member of the Motion Picture Alliance for the Preservation of American Ideals, Rand subsequently wrote a *Screen Guide for Americans*—a series of dos and don'ts that the Alliance published and distributed. See Gordon Kahn, *Hollywood on Trial: The Story of the Ten Who Were Indicted* (New York: Bonie & Gaer, 1948), pp. 32–33.

9. *The Unconquered*, Rand's theatrical adaptation of *We the Living*, opened on Broadway during the 1939–40 season, six months after the Hitler-Stalin Pact. Perhaps because producer George Abbott was best known for staging comedies, *The Unconquered* (which ran only seven performances) was unfavorably compared to Ernst Lubitsch's *Ninotchka*, released a few months earlier: "Its attempts to satirize the dogmatism and efficiency of the Communist bureaucrats—which, as *Ninotchka* proved, are marvelous targets for satire—are heavy-handed and ineffectual," Richard Watts Jr. wrote in the *New York Herald-Tribune*, 2/14/40.

10. Edward R. Tannenbaum, *The Fascist Experience: Italian Society and Culture, 1922–1945* (New York: Basic Books, 1972), p. 235. Jerry Tallmer, "Found: The Long-Lost *Living,*" *New York Post,* 11/24/88.

11. *My Friend Ivan Lapshin* was German's third feature. His first, the gritty *Trial on the Road* (1971), also based on a story by Yuri German, was shelved for fifteen years—accused, like Alexander Askoldov's *Commissar,* of "deheroicizing" Soviet history, in this case the partisan war against the Nazis.

12. Considered a talented conformist, the elder German had his own problems after 1949, when he published a story whose hero had a "Jewish-sounding" last name. See Gleb Struve, *Russian Literature under Lenin and Stalin 1917-1953* (Norman: University of Oklahoma Press, 1971), pp. 343–44.

13. Cited in Julian Graffy, "Unshelving Stalin: After the Period of Stagnation," in *Stalinism and Soviet Cinema,* ed. Richard Taylor and Derek Spring (London: Routledge, 1993), p. 227.

14. Alexei German, interview with the author, 3/25/87.

15. Victor Serge, *Russia Twenty Years After* (Atlantic Highlands, N.J.: Humanities Press, 1996), pp. 199–200.

16. J. Hoberman, "The Last Days of Pompeii," *Village Voice,* 3/31/87, p. 57.

17. German precipitated a latent quality in his father's work: "In *Lapshin* as written by my father, I felt a Chekhovian intonation. That is why he moved the location from Leningrad to a small town: the smaller the town, the smaller the boss, the sadder and more accurate—this was our feeling—the story would be" (cited in Taylor and Spring, eds., *Stalinism and Soviet Cinema,* p. 265).

18. *Burnt by the Sun*'s production coincided exactly with the power struggle between Boris Yeltsin and Mikhalkov's then friend Vice President Aleksander Rutskoi, leading to Yeltsin's abolition of the Duma, Rutskoi's abortive countercoup, a state of emergency, and an election in which nationalist buffoon Vladimir Zhirinovsky won a plurality. In 1995, Mikhalkov played a benign cosmonaut in a TV commercial for Prime Minister Viktor Chernomyrdin's "Our Home Is Russia" Party and successfully ran for the Duma on the party's slate. (Other celebrities employed by Our Home Is Russia were supermodel Claudia Schiffer and the American rap star M. C. Hammer.) Yeltsin, meanwhile, capped his TV campaign by arranging an election-eve broadcast of *Burnt by the Sun* over Russia's largest network.

19. Richard Dyer, "Entertainment and Utopia," in *Genre: The Musical,* ed. Rick Altman (London: Routledge & Kegan Paul, 1981), p. 177.

20. Ibid.
21. Ross Terrill, *The White-Boned Demon* (New York: William Morrow, 1984), p. 250.
22. According to Juri Jelegin, "By the middle Thirties Soviet Russia was in the throes of a mania. Gray-haired professors and members of the kolkhoz, generals and workers were taking dancing lessons. Voroshilov and Molotov were diligently studying the intricacies of the tango and the rhumba" (*Taming of the Arts* [New York: E. P. Dutton, 1951], p. 257).
23. This transformation was topped only by Alexandrov's lone postwar musical, *Spring* (1947), in which Orlova appeared as dancing astrophysicist. Hollywood's equivalents are the eponymous heroines of *Ninotchka* (1939) and MGM's ham-fisted clone *Comrade X* (1940), in which Hedy Lamarr appears as an even more healthily libidinous and sexually experienced Communist than Greta Garbo's Ninotchka.
24. Twenty years later, Tanya's cavorting would be echoed in East Germany's *New Year's Punch* (1960), wherein a limber comrade uses a factory railing as a balance bar, and in Romania's *I Don't Want to Marry* (1961), which features a mass mambo performed on a mirrored stage by a cadre of comely dancers in factory overalls.

    The 1996 German documentary *East Side Story*, a sardonic *That's Entertainment!* assembled by Dana Ranga and Andrew Horn, culls production numbers from tunefests set in the now-Ruritanian realms of the Soviet Union, Czechoslovakia, and East Germany. Although the precedent for these GDR confections would appear to be the Soviet *Carnival Nights* (1956)—Eldar Shengalaya's MagiColor remake of *Volga Volga*—the East German genre developed largely because, unlike other bastions of socialism, the GDR was compelled to compete with a linguistically compatible Western culture industry.
25. Retitled *Tanya, The Shining Path* opened in New York in March 1942, less than three months after the United States had allied itself with the Soviet Union in the war against Nazi Germany. "Russky glorification of the proletariat rates as first class morale hypo in any language," *Variety* (3/4/42) allowed.
26. Jelegin, *Taming of the Arts,* p. 264. Turovskaya appears in *East Side Story.*
27. Sergei Eisenstein, "About Ivan Pyriev," in *S. M. Eisenstein: Writings, 1934-1947,* ed. Richard Taylor (London: British Film Institute, 1996), pp. 292-93. During the early 1950s, with the "classic" Soviet musicals in constant revival, the Pyriev model spread throughout Eastern Europe. (Perhaps beyond: In MGM's 1950 *Summer Stock,* Judy Garland sings an ode to her tractor.) Typical is the 1951 Czechoslovak production *Road to Happiness*—the title tells all. Jiřina Svorcova, a party militant offscreen as well as on, returns—singing—to her home village. Having studied agriculture, her greatest hope is to be a *tractoristka:* "You can hear the vibration of the engine from afar," she trills.
28. Donald Morrison, ed., *Mikhail S. Gorbachev: An Intimate Biography* (New York: Time/New American Library, 1988), pp. 67-68; Alessandra Stanley, "Russians Begin to Gild the Communist Past," *New York Times,* 12/30/95, p. 1. In her memoir *Under a Cruel Star: A Life in Prague 1941-1968* (Cambridge, Mass.: Plunkett Lake Press, 1986), Heda Margolius Kovály recalls the enthusiasm with which Jiři Stano, the editor-in-chief of the scientific publishing house at which she worked (albeit "a young man of rather dim intellect and minimal industry"), greeted the movie:

    At the time [1951] there was a film being shown in Prague which Comrade Stano liked to discuss, with deep emotion, calling it the pinnacle of Socialist Realism and a masterful reflection of Soviet life. It was called *Cossacks from Kuban* and it featured buxom young women and handsome young men turning hay and harvesting wheat to the accompaniment of a four-part chorus of socialist work songs. Perfect harmony reigned in this classless paradise and one of our editors, in what was obviously a fit of temporary insanity, remarked that the film had struck her as just another grade-B operetta. The remark rendered the collective speechless. The editor was asked to conduct a self-critique at the next meeting and, with the help of all the comrades, to correct her erroneous views. She was asked to continue correcting them for some ten more meetings and, had it not been for the complete exhaustion of everyone concerned, she would still have been doing penance in 1968. (p. 98)

29. Put in production a few months after Japanese attack on Pearl Harbor, *Casablanca* is set days, perhaps hours, even moments, before. "If it's December 1941 in Casablanca, what time is it in New York?" wonders Humphrey Bogart's Rick. "I bet they're asleep in New York. I bet they're asleep all over America." Rick is clearly a premature anti-Fascist, if not an out-and-out lapsed Communist. Made with twenty-twenty hindsight, the movie is replete with references to his "isolationism" and "foreign policy" and ends with the romantic sacrifice he makes to rejoin the anti-Fascist fight.

Despite later denials, Curtiz (né Mihály Kertész) was involved in the nationalized film industry—first in the world—created during Hungary's brief Council Republic. Indeed, Curtiz directed Hungary's first agitprop film, *My Brother Comes* (1919), an illustration of Antal Farkas's popular poem that ended with a title imploring the world's workers to unite.

30. According to the memoir subsequently published by the Davies's chauffeur Charles Ciliberti, Mrs. Davies returned from her visit to the Molotov dacha gossiping with her secretary about the Western toiletries in the commissar's bathroom (*Backstairs Mission to Moscow* [New York: Booktab Press, 1946], p. 45).

31. *New York Times, 5/9/43.*

32. Stephen J. Whitfield, *The Culture of the Cold War* (Baltimore: Johns Hopkins University Press, 1991), p. 144. Interviewed by Griffin Fariello for his oral history *Red Scare: Memories of the American Inquisition* (New York: W. W. Norton, 1995), Koch recalled that "not too many years ago, the *New Yorker* film critic, Pauline Kael, was here for lunch. And to my amazement, she said, 'Aren't you embarrassed now, that you once wrote *Mission to Moscow*?' I said, 'Look. It's the thing I value most in my life—that I was able to stand for something that needed to be said.' And she shut up and didn't say anything more!" (p. 276).

Mission to Moscow was followed, in late 1943, by two more pro-Soviet super-productions, depicting the effect of the German invasion on ordinary Russians. MGM's *Song of Russia,* which featured Robert Taylor as an American conductor who falls in love with and marries a Russian pianist—not to mention a *kolkhoz* harvest number worthy of Ivan Pyriev—was actually written by two then Communists, Paul Jarrico and Richard Collins. The independent Goldwyn production *North Star,* directed by Lewis Milestone from Lillian Hellman's script, with music by Aaron Copland and Ira Gershwin, was *Life*'s Film of the Year. Other Hollywood movies made in support of America's new Russian ally include Columbia's teenage partisan quickie *Boy from Stalingrad* (1943); United Artists's *Three Russian Girls* (1944), which remade the Soviet film *The Girl from Leningrad;* RKO's *Days of Glory* (June 1944), in which a ballerina becomes a partisan; and Columbia's *Counter-Attack* (1945), adapted from a Soviet play by future Hollywood Ten-nik John Howard Lawson.

33. Did Romm believe in this? In 1945 the director had been instructed to contact Michael Chekhov in the United States and persuade the émigré actor to return to the Soviet Union. In the new climate (even while *The Russian Question* was in production), Romm's assignment was cited as a politically suspect instance of "groveling before the West." Ivan Bolshakov, the Soviet film minister, was preparing to submit Romm's case to a court of honor. Romm, however, forestalled his trial by implicating V. I. Pudovkin, one of the prospective judges, who had, in fact, recruited Romm to write to Chekhov. Pudovkin then persuaded Bolshakov to drop the matter. See Peter Kenez, *Cinema and Soviet Society, 1917-1953* (Cambridge: Cambridge University Press, 1992), p. 224.

34. Cited in Kenez, *Cinema and Soviet Society*. Romm's follow-up *Secret Mission*, released in 1950, showed American generals plotting with Hitler in an attempt to keep Germany fighting on the eastern front.

35. According to *Time* (5/24/48), the contretemps had its genesis at a Madison Square Garden rally for Wallace: "When the revival meeting was over, about a thousand right-thinkers—Wallaceites, Communists, fellow travelers and troubled innocents—clumped determinedly two blocks east to the huge Roxy theater. They lugged picket signs and clutched bundles of leaflets, which had been prepared in advance. They were out to boo the opening of *The Iron Curtain*." There they met the Catholic War Veterans. "For the next half-hour the Roxy's sidewalk was busier than Union Square on an old-time May Day." Picketed in New York for two weeks, *The Iron Curtain* was subsequently attacked by *Pravda* and *Izvestia*; protested in Stockholm, Havana, Paris; and banned in Siam and the Netherlands.

36. Jack Smith, "Taboo of Jingola," in *Wait for Me at the Bottom of the Pool: The Writings of Jack Smith*, ed. J. Hoberman and Edward Leffingwell (New York: High Risk Books, 1997), p. 103.

37. Beginning in 1939, the populist National Peasant Party had established a number of "people's colleges" that enabled hundreds of working-class and peasant students—including András Hegedüs, among other Communist leaders, to complete high school and university studies. After World War II, the 160 student hostels of the National Federation of People's Colleges were administered jointly by the National Peasant and Communist parties as part of the Communists' "national frontist" policy, and with the intention of training a new elite. Although both László Rajk and Jószef Révai were advocates of the people's colleges, the schools were too autonomous for Rákosi. That their origins were Hungarian populist rather than Soviet Communist recapitulated an ongoing struggle in Hungarian—as well as Communist—politics. After Rajk's fall in 1949, the people's colleges were disbanded and forcibly merged into the Federation of Working Youth (DISZ).

38. Milan Kundera, *The Book of Laughter and Forgetting* (New York: Penguin Books, 1981), p. 63. "I too once danced in a ring," Kundera writes:

> It was in the spring of 1948. The Communists had just taken power in my country, the Socialist and Christian Democrat ministers had fled abroad, and I took other Communist students by the hand, I put my arms around their shoulders, and we took two steps in place, one step forward, lifted first one leg and then the other, and we did it just about every month, there being always something to celebrate, an anniversary here, a special event there, old wrongs were righted, new wrongs perpetrated, factories were nationalized, thousands of people went to jail, medical care became free of charge, small shopkeepers lost their shops, aged workers took their first vacations ever in confiscated country houses, and we smiled the smile of happiness. Then one day I said something I would better have left unsaid. I was expelled from the Party and had to leave the circle.
>
> That is when I became aware of the magic qualities of the circle. Leave a row and you can always go back to it. The row is an open formation. But once a circle closes, there is no return. It is no accident that the planets move in a circle and when a stone breaks loose from one of them it is drawn inexorably away by centrifugal force. Like a meteorite broken loose from a planet, I too fell from the circle and have been falling ever since. (pp. 65–66)

39. Cited in János Kenedi, "The Critics Confrontation," *New Hungarian Quarterly* (summer 1969): 209.

40. Eric Bourne, "*Confrontation* Film," *Christian Science Monitor*, 5/9/69.

41. Harold Rosenberg, "The Heroes of Marxist Science," in *The Tradition of the New* (Chicago: University of Chicago Press, 1982), pp. 178–79.

42. Ibid., p. 187.

43. Totally adhering to the strategy of the Popular Front from 1945 through 1948, the Hungarian Communist Party never mentioned the "dictatorship of the proletariat." Party spokespersons, especially Mátyás Rákosi, did not neglect to criticize those overly "sectarian" comrades who were nostalgic for the Council Republic.

44. Michael Gallagher, "*Angi Vera*: A Conversation with Pal Gabor," *Cineaste* (spring 1980): 33.

45. George Konrád and Ivan Szelényi, *The Intellectuals on the Road to Class Power: A Sociological Study of the Role of the Intelligentsia in Socialism* (New York: Harcourt Brace Jovanovich, 1979), pp. 171ff. For Rosenberg, the Communist is a special sort of intellectual: "The Communist belongs to an elite of the knowing. Thus he is an intellectual. But since all truth has been automatically bestowed upon him by his adherence to the Party, he is an intellectual who need not think" ("Heroes," p. 184).

46. Gallagher, "*Angi Vera*," p. 33; Rosenberg, "Heroes," pp. 186–87.

47. Bacsó's earliest credit is the script for the 1953 Socialist Realist extravaganza *Young at Heart*. In any case, *The Witness* hardly harmed his career. In his survey "Hungary: The Magyar on the Bridge," David Paul maintains that "Bacsó's movies draw big crowds in Hungary, but few of them travel well; the Bacsó brand of comedy does not translate easily across cultural barriers" (in *Post New Wave Cinema in the Soviet Union and Eastern Europe* [Bloomington: Indiana University Press, 1989], p. 196).

48. Gábor Péter, purged in May 1954, would wind up as librarian in a fashion design institute. In George Konrád's *The Loser* (New York: Harcourt Brace Jovanovich, 1982), Gábor appears as G., "a nimble-fingered but not overly bright Jewish tailor" of "unassuming appearance": "[G.] had a lackluster mind, a predisposition to stomach trouble and no malice, but he was an expert conspirator. He weathered the underground years without once getting arrested, though he carefully interrogated his comrades who had been imprisoned. The techniques used by the police interested him the way chess and fishing might interest another man" (p. 171).

49. I first saw *The Witness* during the summer of 1979 while researching the Hungarian movie industry in Budapest. After a ban of ten years, the movie had recently opened without prior notice at a rundown theater, played there unadvertised for a few days, and then disappeared. Although the Hungarofilm official whom I initially asked about the movie studiously pretended not to know what I was talking about, a local filmmaker tipped me off to *The Witness*'s reappearance: "Suddenly, it is playing again. This is typical of how things are done here—open but not publicized, out of circulation but not banned." The movie theater, small and surrounded by scaffolding, was packed; the audience reaction seemed enthusiastic.

50. The script is drawn from Hrabal's first book, an autobiographical account of his experience as a state-employed "recycler" of industrial scrap. The manuscript was first submitted in 1958, printed and banned in 1959, then republished in 1965 as *I Am Selling the House I Don't Want to Live in Any More*.

51. Not even a month after the invasion, Menzel was permitted to attend the 1968 New York Film Festival, which included his *Capricious Summer*—as well as Jan Němec's *Report on the Party and the Guests* (1966) and Milos Forman's *The Fireman's Ball* (1967), two movies that were initially banned, then released, and would never again be publicly shown in Czechoslovakia. Interviewed by the *New York Times*, Menzel explained that so far, the Czechoslovak film industry was continuing to operate without censorship. "No one in Czechoslovakia wants the return of capitalism," he added. His compatriots wanted to return neither "to the time before the war when we were governed by a few

rich" nor to the period of the 1950s "when we were governed by a few, not very intelligent bureaucrats" (Harry Gilroy, "Menzel Says Czech Film Is Still Free," *New York Times*, 9/18/68).

52. Sharp-eyed viewers may note a sudden shift in visual quality in this sequence and one other. The scene deteriorates when, having been pressed into service, the cook asks what happened to the disappeared dairy farmer (the only Marxist idealist among the male prisoners) and is consequently apprehended as he rushes to his wedding bower. A scene in which Angel and another comrade wash a nubile young girl in the name of socialist hygiene is similarly deteriorated. According to Menzel, after *Larks* was banned in its entirety, these scenes were cut from the negative, and when the movie was finally released, they had to be replaced from a lone existing positive print. He told a panel that I moderated at the 1990 Jerusalem Film Festival that he prefers to believe the footage was destroyed by a friend (his guardian angel, perhaps) for the best of motives, "to protect me from myself."

53. Vera is played by Signe Hasso—herself a sort of refugee, having relocated to Hollywood during World War II, where she appeared in thirteen movies, including *Johnny Angel* (1945), *The House on 92nd Street* (1945), and *To the Ends of the Earth* (1947).

54. In a similar spirit, the actual American Communist Steve Nelson is shown committing an imaginary murder in *I Was a Communist for the FBI*, the 1951 movie that—based on the ghostwritten memoirs of undercover agent and expert witness Matt Cvetic—has been called Warner Brothers's "apology" for *Mission to Moscow*, and which received an Oscar nomination as the year's best feature-length documentary.

55. Throughout the autumn of 1951, rumors circulated throughout Munich that the former Czech Communist Party secretary Rudolph Slánský was poised to defect. According to Stewart Steven's *Operation Splinter Factor* (Philadelphia: Lippincott, 1974), "a peculiar piece of theater was reenacted for a week at the American airfield. Prominent Czech emigres were taken there every night to await 'an important arrival.' They were not told, as they stood with senior American officers at the end of the runway night after night who the 'important arrival' was to be. But they all guessed: Rudolf Slánský" (p. 196). Slánský was arrested when he returned home from an official reception on the night of November 23, 1951.

56. Antonin J. Liehm, *Closely Watched Films: The Czechoslovak Experience* (White Plains, N.Y.: International Arts and Science Press, 1974), pp. 401-2.

57. This hardly seems as strange now as it once might have. *Red Planet Mars* maintained some kind of relevance at least twenty years after it was made. Attempting to rent the movie (available for ten dollars from Budget Films) for a film program during the summer of 1972, I learned that it was unavailable—having been heavily booked by the navy as shipboard entertainment.

58. The 1954 W. Lee Wilder cheapster *Killers from Space* (1954) also features Peter Graves as a nuclear scientist—in this case, "taken over" by aliens from the planet Astron Delta. Like the real-life J. Robert Oppenheimer, the "alienated" scientist is subject to official suspicion and surveillance. His wife is questioned by the authorities—"Has he made any new friends lately, you know, people not in the usual group?"—and he is actually caught, at one point, by a vigilant FBI, man leaving a message for his controllers under a rock in an otherwise deserted canyon.

59. *Silver Dust* was screened for an elite audience of American filmmakers as an example of cold war stereotyping during the so-called Entertainment Summit organized in Hollywood by the postperestroika Soviet Cinematographers' Union. See Aljean Harmetz, "US and Soviet Film Makers Debate Stereotypes," *New York Times*, 3/22/87.

60. *Life* pointed out that one of the "riot" pictures was actually a prizewinning *Life* photo of a woman straining for a glimpse of candidate Eisenhower at a 1952 Republican rally.

61. Ede Pfeiffer, *Child of Communism: My Education behind the Iron Curtain* (New York:

Thomas Crowell, 1958), p. 128. In 1986, a House of Representatives subcommittee chaired by Representative Edward Markey of Massachusetts issued a report, "American Nuclear Guinea Pigs," detailing thirty-one experiments, starting in 1945, that used American citizens as "nuclear calibration devices for experimenters run amok." The subjects, some of whom were injected with plutonium, were typically drawn from hospital, nursing home, and prison populations. At the end of 1993, Secretary of Energy Hazel O'Leary disclosed that, over a period of forty-five years, the United States had detonated over two hundred unannounced nuclear explosions—some for the express purpose of studying the effect of fallout on the unsuspecting population—and had conducted radiation experiments on some six hundred human subjects.

62. Glen M. Johnson, "We'd Fight . . . We Had To": *The Body Snatchers* as Novel and Film," *Journal of Popular Culture* (summer 1979): 5–14.

63. Seymour Stern, "*Invasion of the Body Snatchers:* An Interpretive Program Note," *Classic Images,* no. 67 (n.d.): 10–11.

64. Noel Carroll, "You're Next," *Soho Weekly News,* 12/21/78, p. 32.

65. An instant staple of low-budget sci-fi, the *Body Snatcher* premise informed two great 1960s cheapsters, *Creation of the Humanoids* (1962) and *Night of the Living Dead* (1969); was given a feminist twist in the mid-1970s with *The Stepford Wives* and Valie Export's avant-garde *Invisible Adversaries* (1976); and was finally celebrated for itself with Philip Kaufman's 1978 remake. While the original opened on a double bill with *The Atomic Man* (a British pickup) and was deemed too disreputable to warrant a *New York Times* review, Kaufman's version was released for Christmas and hailed by Pauline Kael in the *New Yorker* (12/25/78) as "the American movie of the year—a new classic."

66. In a February 1995 interview, Yevtushenko told me that, although he initially idolized Castro as a symbol of struggle against an authoritarian regime, his doubts regarding the Cuban leader went back as far as the June 1961 controversy around the banned, Havana-by-night documentary *P.M.* Yevtushenko says that he attended a private screening of the movie with Fidel and his brother Raul and the next day was invited to the special meeting since known as Castro's "Words to the Intellectuals." Here, the Cuban leader amazed Yevtushenko by denying he'd ever seen *P.M.* and invoking instead the negative opinion of an unidentified comrade: "I saw then another face of Fidel." (Yevtushenko's perhaps self-serving account is supported by the testimony of former Fidelista Carlos Franqui in his memoir *Family Portrait with Fidel* [1984].)

67. Elie Abel, *The Missile Crisis* (Philadelphia: J. B. Lippincott, 1966), p. 144.

68. Roy Medvedev, *Khrushchev: A Biography* (Garden City, N.Y.: Doubleday, 1983), p. 220.

69. Twenty years later, ICIAC produced an answer of sorts: Manuel Octavio Gómez's 1983 *Patakin* was the first Cuban movie musical. Taking its title from an African word for "fable" and its choreography from the Hollywood (or East German?) musicals of the late 1950s, *Patakin* transposed two figures out of Yoruba mythology to contemporary Cuba. Shangó, the thunder god, is an irresistible lumpen layabout, while his nemesis, Ogún, is a staid model worker who drives the tractor on a collective farm.

At once campy and gung ho, naive and cynical, *Patakin* manages to have most things both ways. A production number on the collective farm—"Work's a treasure, let's all sing"—parodies Hollywood and Soviet models, showing off Cuban technology as well as the compañeras' bare midriffs. The film pokes mild fun at bureaucracy and favoritism, proposing a critique of the machismo familiar in the Cuban movies of the 1980s. "All men want to be Shangó," Ogún's lady friend Caridad tells him. "Not even you want to be Ogún." Ogún defeats Shangó in a climactic boxing match, but the latter's appeal is never denied. The finale, during which a mob of Tropicana showgirls storm the ring with balloons and confetti, has even Caridad scold Ogún for kayoing the "fun guy."

70. *One, Two, Three* combines elements of two earlier Billy Wilder scripts, both set in Paris and filmed in 1939: *Midnight*, in which a penniless showgirl masquerades as a Hungarian countess and a Hungarian count works as a cab driver, and especially the highly successful *Ninotchka*, in which an exiled White Russian enlists the power of Western consumer culture to thaw Greta Garbo's Communist militant. According to Wilder, the initial inspiration for *One, Two, Three* was the September 1960 UN session for which Nikita Khrushchev, Fidel Castro, and a host of other world leaders descended on New York. His original idea was to star the Marx Brothers as a trio of jewel thieves who are mistaken for the Latvian delegation to the United Nations and provided with an unwelcome police escort to the General Assembly, allowing them to wreak havoc.

71. "*One, Two, Three:* Timetable Test," *New York Times*, 12/17/61.

72. Bernard F. Dick, *Billy Wilder* (New York: Da Capo Press, 1996), p. 70.

73. Kevin Lally, *Wilder Times* (New York: Henry Holt, 1996), p. 326.

74. The greatest of the Elvis impersonators is Hungary's László Komar. To hear his "Egy Éjszaka" (One night) is to have the yearning of 1956 defamiliarized and telescoped into one eerie blend of rushed Hungarian polysyllables and mumbled phonetic English.

75. It is at this point that the scarcely unaware Agnes assumes a particular function of the Kádárist order by dictating the appropriate letter for Marika to write her husband: Their activities consist of work, worrying about and waiting for news from him, and watching TV. (The perfect instrument of social control, the television beams an unending succession of parades, soccer matches, and math classes into the apartment. By the end of the movie, it is just a clock.)

76. The preperestroika Cold War II of the 1980s was marked by the return of several Hollywood genres from the early 1950s—extraterrestrial invasion, nuclear warning, and foreign-adventure films came lurching back to life like Boris Karloff in *The Bride of Frankenstein*. In this sense, *Red Dawn*'s major precedent was *Invasion U.S.A.* (1953), a cautionary vision set in a Radio City gin mill, made in one week for $127,000 by Albert Zugsmith: Five average American barflies are punished for their petulant beefing about high taxes and the machinations of the military-industrial complex when a mysterious stranger hypnotically sloshes his brandy glass to induce a threadbare mass hallucination of Commie paratroopers machine-gunning panic-stricken congresspeople under the Capitol rotunda, brave New York cab drivers dying in defense of Wall Street, and Bela Lugosi-like aliens establishing a "People's Republic of America."

77. Milius, a self-described "zen fascist," has all the earmarks of a professional bad boy. ("I just love the Bomb," he told one reporter. "It's sort of a religious totem to me—like the plague in the Middle Ages or the Mongols." J. Hoberman, "Getting Offensive: John Milius Sees Black and White," *Village Voice*, 8/21/84, p. 54.) Although *Red Dawn* was among the movies screened at the March 1987 U.S.-Soviet "Entertainment Summit," Milius was not invited or perhaps chose not to attend.

78. Reviewing *Red Dawn* in *The Nation* (9/15/84), Andrew Kopkind called it "the most convincing story about popular resistance to imperial oppression since the inimitable *Battle of Algiers*." *Red Dawn*, which grossed a respectable $40 million in the United States, subsequently became a cult classic for the survivalist Right. The *New York Times*'s front-page analysis of "[Timothy] McVeigh's mind" (12/31/95) coyly led with the Oklahoma City bomber's obsession with *Red Dawn*: "He rented movies, playing one about a Colorado football team over and over."

79. Bart, who had acquired Kevin Reynold's screenplay, says that *Red Dawn*'s original concept resembled William Golding's *Lord of the Flies* in focusing on the situation of children who cope with the absence of parents by brutalizing one another. Even Milius, who, according to Bart, took part of his payment for rewriting Reynold's script and directing the picture as "an exotic new weapon of his choosing"—was taken aback by Haig's alterations: "Wandering into my office one day, [Milius] confided his concern

that he was being railroaded into what he described as 'a flag-waving, jingoistic movie'" (Peter Bart, "Doing It McVeigh's Way," *Variety,* 6/16–22/97, p. 2).

80. "One could hear people humming well-known songs together with the North Korean girls' chorus and sometimes even singing 'C'est si bon' with Yves Montand," Svetana Boym wrote of a U.S. screening of *Garden of the Scorpions* attended by many ex-Soviet citizens. "The film reveals how [such] nostalgic emotion can be manipulated. According to the director, the film presents 'superidealization and superparody at once.'" Just as the actor who plays Corporal Kotchetkov is cured of alcoholism through hypnosis, so the movie "offers us another kind of hypnotic session that both evokes and helps to attenuate the symptoms of a nostalgic ailment" ("Post-Soviet Cinematic Nostalgia: From 'Elite Cinema' to Soap Opera," *Discourse* [spring 1995]: 81).

Chapter 7

1. The Schneirs ultimately modified their position to allow that Julius Rosenberg did engage in minor "nonatomic" espionage activities—this in the light of the so-called Venona tapes, Soviet intelligence messages decoded during World War II but released by the National Security Agency only fifty years later, that clearly refer to Julius under the code name Liberal. See their "Cryptic Answers," *The Nation,* 8/14–21/95, pp. 152–53.

2. Ronald Radosh and Joyce Milton, *The Rosenberg File: A Search for the Truth* (New York: Holt, Rinehart & Winston, 1983), p. 97

3. Robert Meeropol and Michael Meeropol, *We Are Your Sons: The Legacy of Ethel and Julius Rosenberg* (Boston: Houghton Mifflin, 1975), p. 5.

4. Ibid.

5. James Aronson, *The Press and the Cold War* (Indianapolis: Bobbs-Merrill, 1970), p. 107.

6. Meeropol and Meeropol, *We Are Your Sons,* p. 14.

7. Ibid., p. 15.

8. The retired Soviet spymaster Pavel Sudoplatov tells the story of the Cohens in his memoir *Special Tasks* (Boston: Little, Brown, 1994), pp. 190–92. Sudoplatov calls the Rosenbergs "minor couriers" (p. 177) recruited by the KGB in 1938 (p. 213), "a naive couple overeager to cooperate with us . . . The fact that the Rosenbergs were arrested promptly after Greenglass confessed indicates that the FBI was not seriously determined to discover the extent of the Rosenberg spy ring. The FBI appeared to be acting just like the NKVD, following political orders rather than handling the case professionally" (p. 216). See also Ronald Radosh and Eric Breindel, "Bombshell," *New Republic,* 6/10/93, pp. 10–12.

9. Cited in Walter Schneir and Miriam Schneir, *Invitation to an Inquest* (New York: Pantheon, 1983), p. 170.

10. See Deborah Dash Moore, "Reconsidering the Rosenbergs: Symbol and Substance in Second Generation American Jewish Consciousness," *Journal of American Ethnic History* (fall 1988): 21–37.

11. Radosh and Milton, *Rosenberg File,* p. 288. Deborah Dash Moore points out that "the Rosenberg case hastened and legitimized the purge of the Jewish left from the organized Jewish community" ("Reconsidering the Rosenbergs," p. 26).

12. Meeropol and Meeropol, *We Are Your Sons,* p. 207. On the night of June 19, 1953, according to Arthur Miller, the audience for the original Broadway production of his Salem witchcraft drama *The Crucible* "stood up and remained silent for a couple of minutes, with heads bowed," after the third-act execution of the play's innocent protagonist John Proctor. "The Rosenbergs were at that moment being electrocuted in Sing Sing. Some of the cast had no idea what was happening as they faced rows of bowed and silent people, and were informed in whispers by their fellows. The play then became

an act of resistance for them" (*Timebends: A Life* [New York: Penguin Books, 1995], p. 347).

13. Meeropol and Meeropol, *We Are Your Sons*, p. 221.
14. Ibid., p. 326n.
15. Irving Howe, *A Margin of Hope* (New York: Harcourt Brace Jovanovich, 1982), p. 66.
16. *Life* (5/22/39) took considerable pleasure in describing this "sociological swing." "Communist cats punished each other with the energy of class unconscious collegians. Marxist interpretation of dance tableau below: the woman symbolizes capitalist society, supported by the worker who in turn is crushed in the scissors-grip of greed" (p. 24).
17. "DeRochemont Announces New Film," *Walk East on Beacon* (1951) clippings file, Performing Arts Research Collection, New York Public Library.
18. In March 1997, retired KGB colonel Alexander Feklisov identified himself as Julius Rosenberg's Soviet contact, meeting with him frequently between 1943 and 1946: "He didn't understand anything about the atomic bomb, and he couldn't help us. And still they killed him. It was a contract murder" (cited in Alessandra Stanley, "KGB Agent Plays Down Atomic Role of Rosenbergs," *New York Times*, 3/16/97).
19. "The Peoples of the USSR" and "The Father of Modern Russia," *Life*, 3/29/43, pp. 23, 29.
20. Radosh and Milton, *Rosenberg File*, p. 59.
21. Ibid., p. 63.
22. Ibid., p. 132
23. Ibid.
24. Ibid., p. 65.
25. Ibid., pp. 298-99.
26. Ibid., p. 73.
27. In a letter to the *Village Voice* (3/6/84), Radosh wrote, "At the time of Khrushchev's speech I was indeed a young Communist attending the University of Wisconsin. But I had committed the heresy of reading Isaac Deutscher on Stalin, and was more than prepared for the Chairman's revelations."
28. Cited in Josefa Slánská, *Report on My Husband* (New York: Atheneum, 1969), pp. 31-33.
29. The Rosenbergs were executed midway through our short twentieth century. Did the great Stalin, dead for three months, welcome their scorched and tormented spirits to the workers' paradise in the sky? Memoirs taped by Nikita Khrushchev in the late 1960s, but released only in September 1990, recall that Stalin "mentioned the Rosenbergs with warmth." See "Words of Thanks," *Time*, 10/1/90, p. 75. Although the former Soviet premier assumed Stalin was grateful for the help the Rosenbergs—"neither agents nor spies [but rather] people sympathetic to our ideas [who] acted on their progressive views"—provided in accelerating production of the Soviet atomic bomb, it seems likely that Stalin appreciated more the diversion the Rosenberg case provided from the Slánský trial and Soviet anticosmopolitan campaign.
30. Meeropol and Meeropol, *We Are Your Sons*, p. 216.

INDEX